The Letters of Paul

A New Interpretation for Modern Times

Sylvia Moss

BOOKS

Winchester, UK
New York, USA

Copyright © 2005 O Books
Deershot Lodge, Park Lane, Ropley, Hants, SO24 OBE, UK.
Tel: +44 (0) 1962 773768 Fax: +44 (0) 1962 773769
E-mail: office@johnhunt-publishing.com
www.O-books.net

U.S.A. and Canada
Books available from:
NBN,
15200 NBN Way
Blue Ridge Summit, PA 17214, U.S.A.
Email: custserv@nbnbooks.com
Tel: 1 800 462 6420
Fax: 1 800 338 4550

Text: © 1989 Sylvia Moss

This reissue is of a title originally published in the U.S.A. as
The Letters of Paul: A New Spiritual World View published by
Triad Publishers, Oregon, U.S.A.
Library of Congress Catalog Card Number: 89-51921

Design: Text set in Minion by Jim Weaver Design, Basingstoke, UK
Cover design: Krave Ltd

ISBN 1 903816 94 7

All rights reserved. Except for brief quotations in critical articles
or reviews, no part of this book may be reproduced in any manner
without prior written permission from the publishers.

The rights of Sylvia Moss as author have been asserted in
accordance with the Copyright, Designs and Patents Act 1988.

A CIP catalogue record for this book is available from the British
Library.

Printed by Maple-Vail Manufacturing Group, USA

TABLE OF CONTENTS

PREFACE v

AN OPEN LETTER TO MODERN TIMES 1

INTRODUCTION 3

INTRODUCTION TO ROMANS 9

ROMANS 11

INTRODUCTION TO FIRST THESSALONIANS 89

FIRST THESSALONIANS 91

INTRODUCTION TO SECOND THESSALONIANS 105

SECOND THESSALONIANS 105

INTRODUCTION TO GALATIANS 113

GALATIANS 114

INTRODUCTION TO FIRST CORINTHIANS 135

FIRST CORINTHIANS 137

INTRODUCTION TO SECOND CORINTHIANS 209

SECOND CORINTHIANS 211

INTRODUCTION TO PHILIPPIANS 248

PHILIPPIANS 250

INTRODUCTION TO COLOSSIANS 263

COLOSSIANS 264

INTRODUCTION TO EPHESIANS 277

EPHESIANS 279

INTRODUCTION TO FIRST TIMOTHY	297
FIRST TIMOTHY	299
SECOND TIMOTHY	317
POSTSCRIPT	318
APPENDICIES	319
Appendix A – Issues of Sexuality	319
Appendix B – The Body of Christ	322
Appendix C – Judgement and Karma	323
Appendix D – Vicarious Atonement	324
Appendix E – The Judas Principle	325
GLOSSARY	328
BIBLIOGRAPHY	330

PREFACE

If one asks the Higher Realms what world service one is ready for, assuming one has already committed to be of service, the answer may come as a surprise. In the summer of 1988, through my friend Sylvia Schechter, I asked the question and Hilarion came through with a most unexpected project after 2,000 years, the revising of the Letters of Paul by the one who was incarnate as Paul. Not feeling particularly worthy of such an awesome endeavor, I stated my wonderment: "Why me?" The answer quickly came back: "I do not waste time making my choices!" Because both Sylvia and myself are dedicated to world service, we undertook this task for Hilarion.

Hilarion, within the esoteric frame of reference, is an elder of the Council of the Illumined working to lift humanity to higher levels by a direct outpouring of love and teachings. These elders, though many but operating as one, are those beings who by some travail of soul, by vast experience and sacrifice, have advanced to a degree of evolution far beyond most human beings. They are, in a sense, the Higher Self of humanity and watch over, protect and guide its unfoldment.

The book was produced in the following way: first, looking at the King James Version of the letter at hand (The King James Version being used at Hilarion's request), Sylvia served as amanuensis for Hilarion's dictation of the revised letter. Then I took this text and looked for those questions that were raised by the new text or have been raised about Paul's writings in the past. Many of the questions of the past were answered in the introduction or commentary – or in the text itself. The questions were then asked and answered in a recorded discourse with Hilarion following each appropriate chapter of the letter under consideration.

Hilarion has his own unique style of dictating or "writing". We have tried to protect this style because it is very reminiscent of Paul's style with many parenthetical phrases and "oh by the way" thoughts. The style is neither that of Sylvia nor myself and can be seen in other books by Hilarion.

We have tried to make it easy for the reader to both compare the new text with the King James and to place the Discourses close to the appropriate text; the King James is on the left hand column with Hilarions revision on the right. Within the text are numbers referring to the questions asked about that particular passage. The questions and answers (all the answers are Hilarion's) for each chapter immediately follow that particular chapter and are titled Discourse. At the end, in the appendices, are contributions by Hilarion on several subject areas that needed further expansion. The temptation was strong to add much more to the appendices but that material needs to be in further works.

We would encourage the reader to examine the content of the revision carefully and let it speak to the heart without concern as to the nature of the source. The passages soar as we are inspired to a higher consciousness that comprehends the Oneness of all. Christ is the head of the "whole" body, not just the Church. As the text speaks to your heart, know that the spirit of Paul, along with countless others, is with you and is aiding all of humanity towards an evolutionary "breakthrough".

Finally, I would like to honor Donald Keys for "fine tuning" the manuscript and offering loving support and to Lawrence Schechter who cheered us on. To my wife Ronda I wish to give special thanks as she "wrestled" with Hilarion and as she gave superb editing support when it was needed most.   L.D.

Hilarion's Team

Sylvia Moss Schechter, Co-founder of the Alcyone Light Center and Baconian Foundation, was the channel through whom Hilarion dictated and discussed his thoughts.

Lewis E. Durham, MTh. EdD., United Methodist Clergyman, asked the questions in the Discourses, organized the material a gave general oversight to the project.

Shari Kalb, diligently and expertly transcribed, typed and entered into the computer the considerable material.

AN OPEN LETTER TO MODERN TIMES

An open "letter" to modern times from the one who was Saul of Tarsus – later known as Paul, the apostle of God . . .

Greetings:

Almost two thousand years ago, I chose to incarnate into a Jewish tradition within a family that lived in the area of the Middle East where much dissent raged. Indeed, this particular pocket of the Eastern Mediterranean is one in which dissent seems to have been more tradition than otherwise, throughout the long ages of man. The events which surround the life of the one Saul of Tarsus, and the subsequent "conversion" into a messenger of God's word, have been the subject of deep controversy down the centuries ever since.

There are two basic problems which beset humanity in its evolutionary endeavors; the one is the interpretation of the law on the physical and political level; the other is the interpretation of the Divine Laws, the Universal Law, that is. Each of the world's major religions has asserted that theirs was the "real truth in accord with the 'correct' interpretation of those Laws". In fact, thus far in the recorded history of humankind, none of the major religions has correctly translated the Divine Laws into a harmonious understanding that can be carried into daily life. This has been left to small pockets of what one might term "Mystery Schools", which have carried the thread of truth across the ages of man.

The Eastern religions have asserted their particular teachings and, to a large extent, have been successful for the way the Eastern mind works. The peoples of the Orient have certainly a very different attitude toward all forms of life than do the peoples of the West. Western thought has largely been hampered by the erroneous suppositions of that which has called itself after the name of Christ. The Musulman was a ready ear for the word of Mohamet, as a means to offset the socio-political differences between the Arabic nations and the Semetic-Hebraic. In fact, all have segments of Universal Truth, none have all of that truth. All extant religious thought must, in rightness of its own measure, be respected.

The measure of that religion which has been given the name Christian is that of a religion of transition. The churches which have been established in the past two thousand years, since the life and teaching of Jesus, have served a deep need in the hearts of many and cannot be discounted entirely even though much that has been taught has been of considerable error.

First of all, the one whom we call Jesus, was born a man, of fleshly parents. He was prepared as a Great Initiate during his early life, and when the time came for him to begin his ministry, Jesus (whose Hebraic name is rightly Jeshua Ben Joseph, Jesus being the Roman version) gladly gave over the body which he had so lovingly prepared for the earthly entry of the Christ.

That same Christ does not have any church, nor does he adhere to any religion. His teaching is universality, and is offered likewise to Jew, to Muslim, to Buddhist and all others alike. One does not have to be a "christian" as the church of that name sees it, in order to become part of the great Body that is in Christ.

The interpretation of the messages of Christ in Jesus, and indeed those teachings which I as Paul gave to the followers after His Way, have been sorely misrepresented and misunderstood down the long passage of the centuries since those days.

It were an easier pill to swallow if we take what has been accepted over the centuries and modify, rather than to sweepingly throw it all out and say, "I did not say any of that, or what I did say was subject to gross misinterpretation," etc. One might, if one so chose, begin again. But then if one did that, they would not be the letters of Paul to the Romans or the Corinthians. So, I feel it better to take what has been generally regarded as my work, erroneously or otherwise, and to put it into modern idiom with some modifications that are the truths rather than the errors being perpetuated.

It is now my earnest hope that in the writing of the real message, those errors may be (for those willing to receive) rectified. I choose to use the words of the first major translation into English – contained in the King James edition. My reason for this is that subsequently down the centuries, there have been many newer translations containing words which did not exist at the time of Medieval Britain. I therefore feel that with each new translation, including newly coined phrases and words inserted in an effort to "keep pace with expanding English vocabulary", there has merely been a deeper rift from the original words that Paul meant.

One must realize that the words were first recorded in Greek, and then in the Latin Vulgate. Eventually they were (attempted) to be translated into existent English, and finally we have the modern versions in the expanded English of today.

If we stay with the early text of the King James, even though to modern minds obscure, we do at least deal with a version which is the least adulterated by successive minds in their efforts to get at what Paul meant. It was not the task of the translator to get at what Paul meant; it was their task to translate as simply and truthfully from the original as was within the ability of the translator. However, many of the clerics to whom fell the task were unable to resist the temptation of putting on whatever inference suited their personally inculcated belief system of the moment.

We therefore take chapter by chapter, translating into the idiom of the present day. Words which are at this time substituted reflect the thoughts behind them which this time are my own, moving back into the time when the messages were sent, and into the thought which then lay behind the sending.

In the discourses which will follow we will take each of those areas of thought and we will discuss thoroughly what lay back of it at the time. If necessary, we will also look at what lies back of the same thoughts for modern times.

And so to it. And may the Blessings of God the Father, God the Son, and God the Holy Spirit which is the Divine Mother of the Universe, keep our hearts and minds in Their Love and Wisdom while we work.

Hilarion

INTRODUCTION

First of all, we should come to a clear understanding that the Bible is a collection of documented happenings, between each of which are tremendous gaps – lapses in time which leave the researcher with the task of trying to piece together in his/her imagination exactly what that time lapse may have been. Such gaps abound in the recorded story of the life of Jesus. What recorded documentation is available but briefly sketches the birth of Jeshua ben Joseph and the surrounding circumstances. There is no record of His life in early childhood, up to the time of His approaching bar mitzvah – during which time He is recorded as speaking with the elders in the temple. He then disappears from the record until the time of His Ministry at the age of 33, until His trial some three years later. There is little in the record which would accurately establish the passage of time, even at this point. After the event of the trial and execution, there is even less upon which to pin a time scale in the lives of the Disciples, now termed "Apostles" (for reasons which we shall discuss at a later point). Both Acts and Romans are extremely sketchy in regard to statements of time. One must also remember that all that is written comes down from the spoken word, passed on long after the actual circumstances of the event in question.

Neither Luke nor Mark were present at the time of Jesus, and the one Saul of Tarsus was not at the time very conscious of Him. When Saul's name first begins to appear around 30 AD., he was yet a young man in his mid-twenties. Since recorded history is even uncertain as to the actual period in which Jesus did live, we will assume for the sake of creating less confusion, that the records as currently extant, surround what is commonly accepted. Any disputation as to the date of birth of Jesus is for another time and subject, and not at the moment, of relevance to the text in hand.

Saul of Tarsus was the son of a relatively wealthy family. His father, though Jewish, was also a Roman citizen who had a position in local government and was a tent maker by trade. Though a native of Tarsus, Saul was very conversant with the aristocratic Greek language, as well as certain colloquial dialects learned from his mother. The young Saul was a scholar and eventually studied for a time at the great school in Alexandria, followed by further studies of Hebraic law in Jerusalem. He was therefore extremely proficient and knowledgeable both in secular and sacred law. It has been recorded that Saul was a tent-maker. It was common in that time for young men to learn a trade as well as being a scholar. The making of tents was such a trade that appealed to Saul, though it was not his main occupation.

After returning to Tarsus, Saul for a time worked in the office of the local governor of Celicia, where he eventually obtained a post as official prosecutor. Usually he examined those who were reported or accused of crimes of state (political or treasonable) rather than domestic. It was in this capacity that he travelled regularly to Antioch and occasionally to Caesarea and to Jerusalem.

Although some time passed since the event of Jeshua ben Joseph, there is still a great deal of restlessness among the peoples of Judaea and Ituraea. Some still await the coming of a promised "Messiah" while others firmly believe that He whom they crucified was that One. The followers of Jeshua have called together those who faithfully believe, but much of their work is carried out in secret. The Essenes dare no longer practice their faith openly, and indeed many have left the area to live in the deserts of Arabia. Some have moved to the School at Persepolis, and some have gone even as far as Egypt. The major insurrectionist faction, the Zealots, still work underground in the area mostly around Jerusalem, though some have been known as far afield as Antioch. Pockets of the new followers of the One they are calling the Christ have been uncovered as far away as Damascus.

Saul is eventually transferred to Jerusalem where he continues his studies with Dr. Gamaliel. While there, he questioned and reported on one Steven. The document bearing Saul's signature became Steven's death warrant. The Hebraic Law was such that the one signing the warrant must also witness the execution by stoning. A young Greek doctor, visiting from Rome, witnessed the execution also, and it was a long time before Lucanus, later known as St. Luke, forgot or forgave Saul for this cruel act, though they did eventually become very close friends.

Young and somewhat fanatical of purpose, Saul was fired with zeal and enthusiasm for the strict observance of the law, as he then saw it. In his zeal, he desired to uncover and punish anyone who could be seen as guilty of insurrection. This included any "cult" which had been proclaimed illegal. One such in the city of Damascus had come to his attention, and he pleaded with Gamaliel and the Elders to allow him to go to Damascus to uncover this cult, and bring the offenders to justice.

That which occurred on the road to Damascus is stated very briefly in the biblical account. Let us therefore give a more detailed and explicit rendition at this point. We are well aware in the present day, that soul chooses that which it shall learn in any lifetime. Soul is the one who chooses the way also, in which lessons will be learned. No matter how advanced upon the path of the soul's purpose such a one may be at the time of entry into the mortal plane, that one does pass again through a recapitulation as it were, of earthly experience, up to the point in time when soul knows that it is "ready to get on with the major purpose of that lifetime's existence". Immediately prior to this revelation, it is quite the norm for such a one to experience disquiet within the Being. This is quite often manifest in anger, frustration against the pressures of life, and is often countered by the personality in question becoming even more fanatical of purpose. Until, that is, the light dawns upon that personality, that this is not the true purpose of soul. Saul the young man was no exception to this program. His zeal was simply an expression of his inner turmoil.

Upon the road to Damascus there came upon him a soul-awakening experience which was not altogether unexpected. For some time, the Higher Self had tried to gain access to the awakening mind of Saul. Finally, it required the forceful encounter with the Christ in all of His Majesty to complete that awakening in Saul. In a blinding flash, the Truth dawned upon him. Saul and the Christ were not divided, but One. The law which he had studied for most of his life so assiduously, was not something to set Saul apart from the work of Jeshua, the Nazar-Essene, but something that bound him as a brother to continue to elucidate. In that moment of revelation, Saul realized that his life's work would be dedicated to the real truth, the meaning of the Law of God, as taught by Jeshua, the embodiment of the living Christ.

What a task! As one in a blind stupor, Saul continued on his way to Damascus, and there, instead of proceeding with his letters to the synagogues, he instead went to the home of a man named Judas* to whom he had been directed by the Christ. He had also been required to fast and pray until further notice. During that time of deep introspection and private meditation he saw no one. After three days of fasting and meditation, Saul was visited by Ananias. Judas and Ananias together spoke of many things concerning the truth of the ministry of Jeshua, the Living Christ. After they had sojourned together for a few more days, Saul had a further deep revelation. It was as though his life until that moment had been totally "blind" to reality.

Reality now opened up before him as quite the opposite of his erstwhile beliefs, and his soul began to take over. During meditation he began to converse quite easily with what he understood as his Higher Self and occasionally, that wonderful presence that he encountered on the way to Damascus, filled him with light supernal.

Eventually, Ananias and Judas were convinced that Saul had received the gift of inner sight, and they offered him baptism into the Body of Christ so that he might also be filled with the Holy Spirit as had been promised to all.** Some of the original Disciples of Jeshua were at that time in Damascus, and it was with great joy that they attended the baptism of Saul, renaming him at his re-birth, Paul – the Brother of Christ.

Before going any further, there are a few general comments that I would make at this point concerning the life and ministry of Jesus the Christ which have been under considerable dispute down the centuries of written history. I find it difficult to imagine why, because if one looks only at the course of record, one must clearly see that there are discrepancies which do not make sense. These have been glossed over by successive authoritarian sectors of the Christian church. They have never been answered in a satisfactory way.

In that small area of the Middle East, which was part of the Roman occupation, were several groups of insurgents. There was a great deal of excitement caused by one group because there lived and worked among them one who began to speak with authority concerning the law, the Universal Law, not just the law of the land – all the written laws of the Jewish

---

* This is the same Judas that was erroneously believed to have betrayed Jesus and then hung himself. See the Appendix on the Judas Force.

** This took place in the year of our Lord 33 AD. when Paul was at the age of 28 years (about 4 years after the crucifixion of Jesus).

faith, but things which had to do with Universal Law were spoken of by him in a manner of supreme authority. We know what followed as a result. But how long do you suppose it would take after that event for the message to be conveyed to outlying countries? How long do you suppose it would have taken for a small group of people – Peter, John, Philip and the others? It is written that many of those immediate band of disciples went to distant countries; Philip to Scythia, Peter eventually to Northern France, James – brother of Jesus – to Spain. How long do you think it took for them to gone to those places at that time? Certainly, many, many months.

How long, therefore, would you suppose that it would take for the message to become widespread? Do you suppose, for instance, that the messengers would even be readily heard, excepting in such areas as Celtic Britain where the Christian druids were already very strong, and excepting in areas where the great mystery schools of the world already existed? And do you suppose that their authority was taken into the eventual creation of the Catholic church? Not at all.

The beginnings of it were widespread. Christianity was stronger indeed in Byzantium than in Rome. There was, in fact, a considerable time lapse before Rome began to pay any real attention to the message. When, eventually, the message was allowed to become, shall I say, visible rather than secret, it was for wholly political reasons. If one, therefore, examines all of that historical fact, one has to begin to look again at the significant lapse in time between the life of Jesus and the beginnings of the authoritarian statements of the emergent church of Rome. When we look carefully we will begin to have a better grasp of what lay behind many of the recorded teachings which were set down with all apparent authority.

Called as an Apostle

In what sense should I call myself an Apostle, rather than a Disciple? In what sense should anyone call himself an Apostle? First of all, those who had received instruction in the true faith, the Wisdom of the Ages, set their feet firmly upon the Path of the Initiate into those Universal Wisdoms. During His Ministry, Our Lord taught further mysteries to his close band of followers who were already initiates of certain degree. Of those initiates, his closest circle were Joseph of Arimathea, His father Joseph and, of course, Mary, His mother. Since Jeshua's family were all of the Essene persuasion, there were many other members of the Essene Brotherhood also in Jeshua's close circle.

During His youth, whilst Jeshua travelled to many of the great centers of initiation in Persia, India, Tibet, Greece, Britain and Egypt, certain others who would eventually be "chosen" were undertaking their own training period. These were the people whom Jeshua eventually called forth with the information that "the time was come". At the moment when He became aware that this time was drawing to a close, toward the final act, He took aside certain of His more advanced Initiate/Disciples, namely Mary the Magdalene, John the Beloved, Peter, Brother James, and He gave them further instruction into the Higher Mysteries. It was indeed into the hands of these few, and Mary and John in particular, that Jeshua the Embodiment of Christ, now placed the Apostolic succession.

What is an apostate, other than one who has totally eschewed all worldly parties, sects, governments, in order to follow the One Pure Light. To serve the Great Brotherhood of Christ, and to be filled with the Power of the Holy Spirit, is the only true apostasy – and only such a one, who has attained to a high degree of personal, sacrificial initiation, is truly an Apostle of God.

How did Paul, that same Saul of earlier years, become such a one? After the first awakening to the truth, Paul set out as assiduously to learn the full extent of the message of Christ as he had previously studied the Hebraic Law. During the years that followed, he spent a great deal of time with Ananias and Judas, sometimes with Peter and Philip; and eventually he travelled to Samos to visit with John. His studies placed his feet upon the path of higher initiation, and eventually Paul visited many of the great centers where the deeper mysteries were revealed to the initiated. The major reason for much of his travel was to visit such schools and to add to his understanding. Paul spent a great deal of time in Arabia and Persia (especially Persepolis) and he also visited the Greek schools in Crete, Samos, Macedonia, Olympus and Corinth.

During those years in which we who were the Disciples of Jeshua, the Christ, studied to increase our own learning, we also travelled into the areas where small groups of believers lived. It was our intent to assist those groups, to encourage them in their faith, and to help them to grow in strength and number. Often, as we travelled, we would bear letters to such groups, or verbal messages. Equally so, when it was known by myself that others were to visit certain groups, I entrusted mostly verbal messages with the Brothers and Sisters who travelled. Rarely at first were the messages set down in writing. Only much later did it become essential for the written word. The reason for this, as is usual with emergent groups, was that it came to our attention that misunderstandings and even corruption of the true message of Our Lord began to infiltrate.

In speaking of my own intent, I wrote to set the record straight, in order that misunderstanding not be perpetuated. I also wrote of my feelings and thoughts, and elicited response in like manner from my friends who were also striving to walk the Path of Truth. At no time upon the Path to Truth does one assume to have all the answers, except if one be the Living Christ Himself. And even He went through all of the trials and the errors that beset the rest of us. It is the mercy of the Supreme Godhead, that the Great Ones are not unseen and intangible deities, but our ever loving elders who have trodden the Earthly path before us, and are therefore fully acquainted with sorrows and grief trials and temptations. From this vantage point, they are then able to assist every aspect of human frailty.

Hilarion as Paul

To those who wish to know, Hilarion is the name by which I am known upon that plane which we call the fifth. It is the level of being of those whom we shall call elders of the human race who have themselves passed through the many rounds of incarnation during which times they too have known all of the struggles and vicissitudes of life upon the earth plane until, by their own efforts, they have, as it were, passed through the course and have received their diploma, shall we say. It is similar to perhaps receiving one's diploma of mastery in a modern university and after one has received that recognition of having passed a specific degree, one is then presumably able to teach the knowledge gained to others. It is our desire to be of assistance to those members of humanity who have not yet passed through that school of life until they too are residents of that fifth plane. Humanity is upon the fourth plane. And so, my brothers and sisters who are part of that fifth plane remain ever close to be of whatever help and assistance we may render. In that I rejoice that I am able to so assist.

Each one of my brothers and sisters upon this plane have many lifetimes of record and some of those more familiar lives to fellow humans are given in order that one might have a degree of recognition; one of my own earlier lives being that of Saul of Tarsus, otherwise known as Paul. In the same way that my brother whom we know upon this plane as Kuthumi, was Francis of Assisi and also Pythagoras, and so on. My own work upon the fifth plane is that of organizing those things which concern humanity which are part of the intuitive development, part of the work of what is known as the fifth ray of scientific exactitude. All of the research upon scientific levels eventually comes from the organization of the intuitive. I think that explains who I am to some extent.

INTRODUCTION TO THE LETTER OF PAUL TO THE ROMANS

Who were the Romans and to whom was I, then incarnate as Paul, addressing my letter? As history has written correctly, which is unusual, there was in those times a considerable commerce between Rome and those outlying provinces which were governed by the Roman empire. The commerce was conducted between the Roman legions for the benefit of their own personal needs and the home country, basically. The supplies that went to the outlying countries were quite often given in trade for produce that came from the country in question. And, of course, as with all other trading situations attendant upon commerce, there were the artisans and what would now be called the professionals: the writers, the lawyers, the accountants, etc.

Quite naturally, among the travellers to and fro, there was discussion concerning the affairs of the countries which were occupied. Certain events which had taken place in that country occupied by Rome, which was a little kingdom of Herod, had come under a certain amount of excited speculation because of the activities of certain anti-Roman sects, one of which reported to have in its ranks a person who had been eventually crucified under somewhat astonishing circumstances. One has to bear in mind that history has been extremely erroneous concerning the emergence of the Christian faith. It was not until some considerable time after the event that the teachings of Jesus were, in fact, in any way or by any one body or people, accepted.

Those who had been the immediate followers of Jesus met with considerable resistance outside of their own circle. Some, in fact, were severely persecuted for their adherence to the message that had been attributed to Jesus.

As you well know, I was, in the beginning, one of the chief persecutors. It was not until my conversion that I accepted not only what He had said, but the truths that lay behind His words. Even though, in a sense my own conversion was, in that lifetime, instantaneous, like all others, when one catches a glimpse of the profound light, one does not immediately change one's whole existence prior to that time. There are plateaus and there are valleys. I went through the valley of the shadow for a long time after that incident which is so famous. And after I had begun to sort things out in my own mind, I then commenced to work with others for whom this somewhat startling occurrence had also made its mark. We began to exchange our thoughts and our intelligences in much the same way as one does in this modern age. Whatever would occur to such as myself would be written down and transferred to others who were of like mind, also taking tentative steps along the path. The exchanges became more enlightened, shall I say, as we ourselves became more certain of our subject. Although I personally ceased to be a persecutor of those who followed the teachings of Jesus, the persecutions themselves did not cease. Others took up where I left off and I myself was counted among the ranks of the persecuted from that point on. Many there were who had to leave their homeland and seek refuge in other lands.

There were also soldiers who had been stationed in the area of Jesus' ministry who had perhaps seen, or heard rumor, and who had spoken with others who had seen and who naturally then, on return to Rome, would speak of these matters to the curious with a certain amount of personally invented authority. And it was in this way that brethren of the faith began to gather together, much as one does today in what we call the New Age, where people gather together to have meditation or to do whatever it is they wish to do that helps them to be strong or to further that which they desire to learn. Those little groups would meet together to discuss their feelings and thoughts, to perhaps hear the message of one who had just returned from that land, and eventually to read the letters they had received from the brothers who were now considered to be the elders of this new thought.

In the course of time I became, in the eyes of those outlying groups, their figurehead, the authority, and down the years, the Great Apostle. I tell you, at the time when those letters were written, I was as much an authority as are you here and now in the knowledge of what is to come for the Aquarian Age. That is, no more and no less than any other of the recipients of Christ. I set down my letters to those people who were my equals and my brothers and sisters in Christ. My thoughts, in exchange for theirs. If we have that fact quite clear in the beginning we can proceed.

THE LETTER OF PAUL TO THE ROMANS

1 *Paul, a servant of Jesus Christ, called to be an apostle, separated unto the gospel of God,*

2 (Which he had promised afore by his prophets in the holy scriptures),

3 Concerning his Son Jesus Christ our Lord which was made of the seed of David according to the flesh;

4 And declared to be the Son of God with power, according to the spirit of holiness, by the resurrection from the dead:

5 By whom we have received grace and apostleship, for obedience to the faith among all nations, for his name:

6 Among whom are ye also the called of Jesus Christ:

7 To all that be in Rome, beloved of God, called to be saints: Grace to you and peace from God our Father and the Lord Jesus Christ.

8 First, I thank my God through Jesus Christ for you all, that your faith is spoken of throughout the whole world.

9 For God is my witness, whom I serve with my spirit in the gospel of his Son, that without ceasing I make mention of you always in my prayers;

10 Making request, if by any means now at length I might have a prosperous journey by the will of God to come unto you.

11 For I long to see you, that I may impart unto you some spiritual gift to the end ye may be established;

12 That is, that I may be comforted together with you by the mutual faith both of you and me.

13 Now I would not have you ignorant, brethren, that oftentimes I purposed to come unto you (but was let hitherto), that I might have some fruit among you also, even as among other Gentiles.

1 (1-2) This letter comes from Paul, called to be an apostle and servant of that same Christ who was embodied in the life of our Lord, Jesus. He who was a special Messenger in the service of the Universal Office of the Christ, appointed to speak the truth concerning the Universal Laws. This had long been promised in the words of earlier prophets, and as written in the holy scriptures.

(3-7) The messages of Jesus were the Gospels of God. Jesus himself was a descendant of the House of David by human genealogy.[1] He was patently marked by the Christ as Son of God, to be endowed with the Power of that Spirit of Holiness, which enabled Him to rise again from the dead. He is our Lord, from whom we hold our commission as messengers, to advance the consciousness and faith of all nations. You at Rome are also called upon to align with Christ. To you all then, who are beloved of God, and called to be Christ's people grace and peace from God and from our Lord Christ.

(8-17) I must tell you how much I thank God for you all, since the news of your faith has become known everywhere. For as God is my witness, whom I serve with all of my heart in the Gospel of His Son, I assure you that you are always in my prayers. I also pray that I might soon come to visit you, for I long to see you, so that I might impart to you certain spiritual gifts, so that you may become fully established.

Romans 1

14 I am debtor both to the Greeks and to the Barbarians; both to the wise, and to the unwise.

15 So, as much as in me is, I am ready to preach the gospel to you that are at Rome also.

16 For I am not ashamed of the gospel of Christ: for it is the power of God unto salvation to everyone that believeth; to the Jew first, and also to the Greek

17 For therein is the righteousness of God revealed from faith to faith: as it is written, The just shall live by faith.

18 For the wrath of God is revealed from heaven against all ungodliness and unrighteousness of men, who hold the truth in unrighteousness.

19 Because that which may be known of God is manifest in them; for God hath shewed it unto them.

20 For the invisible things of him from the creation of the world are clearly seen, being understood by the things that are made, even his eternal power and Godhead; so that they are without excuse:

21 Because that, when they knew God, they glorified Him not as God, neither were thankful; but became vain in their imaginations, and their foolish heart was darkened.

22 Professing themselves to be wise, they became fools,

23 And changed the glory of the uncorruptible God into an image made like to corruptible man, and to birds, and four-footed beasts, and creeping things.

24 Wherefore God also gave them up to uncleanness through the lusts of their own hearts, to dishonour their own bodies between themselves:

Also, so that we may enrich each other by our mutual faith. I have long wished to come to be with you, but have been prevented by other matters. I would like to see the same results with you in Rome as I have seen among other people, for I have a Universal obligation to make plain the message of the Gospel of Christ. I see that Gospel as the very Power of God working for the upliftment of all. I see in it, the Divine Plan for the enlightenment of human consciousness – a process begun by the individual within themselves, and continued by their acts of Faith. Even as the Scriptures of Old say: The just shall live by their faith.

(18-23) In the course of human evolution, many messengers have there been, who have disclosed the concern which God and His angels have for those who render the truth void by their wickedness. Many there have been down the ages, who have spoken of the Universal Truth – the invisible attributes of divinity, and the eternal power revealed in all things created. There is no excuse for wrong doing and ill behavior of a humanity that refuses to acknowledge its errors. Instead of giving praise and thanks to Divinity for blessings and gifts freely bestowed, humanity prefers fatuous argument. By professing themselves so wise, they become as fools. They change God's glory into the corrupt image of human standards.

(24-32) Humanity has many times turned aside from Universal Law and Truth, and has preferred falsehood; paying homage to the animal self rather than to the Higher Self and the Creator; who is alone worthy of homage – Amen.[2] In the exercise

Romans 1

25 Who changed the truth of God into a lie, and worshipped and served the creature more than the Creator, who is blessed for ever. Amen.

26 For this cause God gave them up into vile affections: for even their women did change the natural use into that which is against nature:

27 And likewise also the men, leaving the natural use of the woman, burned in their lust one toward another, men with men working that which is unseemly, and receiving in themselves that recompense of their error which was meet.

28 And even as they did not like to retain God in their knowledge, God gave them over to a reprobate mind, to do those things which are not convenient;

29 Being filled with all unrighteousness, fornication, wickedness, covetousness, maliciousness; full of envy, murder, debate, deceit, malignity; whisperers,

30 Backbiters, haters of God, despiteful, proud; boasters, inventors of evil t°hings, disobedient to parents,

31 Without understanding covenant-breakers, without natural affection, implacable, unmerciful:

32 Who knowing the judgement of God, that they which commit such things are worthy of death, not only do the same, but have pleasure in them that do them.

of free will, humanity has given itself to passions which have defiled the body. Women have exchanged the normal practices of sex, for intercourse with things abnormal and unnatural.[3] Men have been swept into lustful passions with each other. Such deviation does of course harm the psyche, and the person pays the consequences karmically.[4] In becoming separated from the Higher Self, humanity sinks into the abyss of degeneration. Being filled with all manner of wrongdoing, immorality, covetousness, malice, envy, backbiting, gossip, boasting, disobedience to parents, humanity fell to God-hating. They lost all sense of natural affection and had no use for justice or mercy. Despite the teachings down the ages, of the Universal Wisdoms and the Law, namely, that such actions place at risk even the soul – they not only continue these practices, but approve of them in others.

DISCOURSE CHAPTER ONE

1.   Q: I notice, for instance, in the beginning of 1:3-4 that you re-worded it in a way that eliminated the chance of there being any support for what the scholars call the "adoptionist theory": that somehow, Jesus was adopted in his young years. For me it is not a crucial issue, but for some scholars it has been.

    A: Let us, first of all, address the "adoptionist theories". Jesus was not adopted. It is as simple as that. Jesus was the son of Mary and Joseph was his father. It is as simple as that. I think that answers the question. Jesus, the man, that is. Let us make a differentiation at this point, because in the birth process Jesus was a man as are all men and women.

2.   Q: In 1:24-32, what was going on at that time that caused such a focusing on sexual issues? In modern times we might focus on the problems of destroying the planet or corporate greed, nuclear threat, those kinds of things. In that particular time Paul seemed to be very concerned about sexual issues.

    A: Yes indeed. In the cyclical evolution of humanity, we seem to go through periods when humanity at large is no longer seeking after things of the spirit. In the involutionary spiral, rather, the masses are devoted to the seeking after materialistic acquisition and the gratification of the lusts of the flesh. One will recall those statements in the Old Testament of the Bible that this had occurred on a number of occasions, and the elders who oversee the evolution of humanity had issued many warnings to get back on course.

    Rome was becoming exceedingly degenerate at that time. The court of Herod was no less so and as always, when the course is of such involutionary nature, the Great Ones choose to come down among us yet again to set matters back on course. The evolutionary path is one of gradual attainment toward co-creatorship, seeking after the Divine within each individual and coming eventually to the knowledge that we are part of a whole, not single individuals whose sole purpose is self-gratification.

    It was the purpose of the Nazar-Essenes and other such groups to create small centers where the true teachings might be imparted to those desirous to learn. Within these schools the message has ever been for humanity to rise above the lower animal instincts and come to the point of illumination. There has been, therefore, a great deal of discourse around the subject of materialistic acquisition, a great deal of error recorded concerning my own words in particular about sexuality and it would be good to clear those issues. There is a very great difference between the use of all God-given talents and all that the human has been given for his growth and the prostitution of those talents. Let me say clearly, here and now, that I am not advocating celibacy. That is a total error. If we truly believe

Discourse Chapter One continued:

that God created humankind in his or her own image, we must ask ourselves why were we given sex difference? When humanity took upon itself the denser, grosser, physical vehicle, the sexes were divided into male and female. Neither one is greater than the other. They are equal. Be very sure of that. Any religious school which states that the female is any less than the male, in any way, is coming from an error in concept. Male and female created He them in His own image.

The great creator spirits created that which has the potential to be perfect. The Divine Spirit resides within a physical vehicle that has the potential to be perfect for it was designed after perfection and in that perfection the human was given sexuality that humanity might dwell together as male and female in order to procreate the human species and in order to live together as families, to learn together, to develop relationships together and in order to progress together back to that divinity which is inherent in all.

What, however, has happened in progressive civilizations, or I should say perhaps, not progressive civilizations, but in repeated civilizations down through the history of humanity? There has come a time in what the east would call the Kali Yuga, a seeking after animalistic behavior, when human sexuality no longer dwells within the boundaries of the divine intentions, but seeks such distractions as prostitution and, in some cases, homosexuality.

Q: I think part of the problem here is that the homosexual community looks upon the Pauline letters as one of the reasons that they have been persecuted for centuries. They wonder why they were singled out. Many would say that they are world servers. I also wonder how it fits into the whole karmic idea, the fact that souls can come and work out their karma at different times and maybe they are here at one time as homosexuals and not at other times.

A: The persecution of the homosexual arose directly out of the misinterpretation of the church of Rome regarding the subject of celibacy. In pronouncing that it was necessary for the male priests to be celibate, and in making a great issue out of celibacy, while it was noteworthy that most of the high ranking officials and the Pope himself was never celibate, one creates a great danger. It is not within human nature or God-given to be celibate. And if for any reason, the natural and perfectly correct instincts of humankind are suppressed, then that suppression will result in a state of imbalance.

Imbalance, when carried to extreme, can become self destructive and it can lead to distractions from the evolutionary path of a kind which are not desirous. During the long history of the Catholic church imposed celibacy has created surreptitious homosexuality on a very, very large scale. It was, I would venture

Discourse Chapter One continued:

to suggest, out of a need to vindicate the situation of the priesthood that, even down to modern legislature, homosexual persecution has been continued, more particularly, in the middle ages against the male population and arising directly out of the priesthood. In the middle ages the female was not given to homosexuality in the same way because there was too much cloistering of the female and too much fear. In modern times only has the female been allowed freedom to the extent that she would choose homosexuality over heterosexuality. This of course is not the case in ancient Rome or Greece. Lesbians were quite prolific in Greece. Have we answered that do you think?

Q: Only in part. I can imagine the question "what does Hilarion think now"?

A: We should really, I think, address the whole situation of homosexuality. It does, indeed, have a great deal of karmic responsibility, and in a considerable number of cases creates a retardation on the course of evolution. There are, of course, exceptions to that statement. But for the general purpose of humanity, the male and the female were intended to grow together in sexual intimacy, not promiscuous intimacy. In the case where that kind of sexual intimacy occurs between two of the same outward physical sex, that is two men or two women, it is because they have a disproportionate attitude toward their animus or anima, the psyche, which is invariably of karmic origin and which those in question have come together in order to work out. But it were better if, instead of working out on the physical level their karmic task, the individuals in question would move toward the raising of the spiritual pursuits into those higher levels, into their higher chakras, to turn the sexual energy into a different form. But each soul proceeds at a pace which is in accord with that being and it is not for others to pass judgement upon the method or the speed. We need, at this point in time, above all, to move away from outworn religious concepts and to move into the new dispensation in the spirit of love and compassion for all of creation. Does this answer?

Q: Yes, I think that goes a long way. This will be like a breath of fresh air to the world.

3. Q: You use the phrase in 1:26-27 "women have exchanged the normal practices of sex for intercourse with things abnormal and unnatural". Many women, as well as men, engage in various forms of self-stimulation and consider it perfectly normal and natural. They might see this phrase and wonder what you mean by it.

A: Let us not speak of titillation by whatever means. We are referring directly to illicit intercourse and no other. Whatever mechanical devices the females

Discourse Chapter One continued:

and males wish to use is something entirely of their own choice and is of no consequence to anyone else. I was speaking then and would speak again today in this modern age of illicit sexual relationship with that which is forbidden by law, Universal Law, namely, intercourse with animals and such.

4. Q: At the time you wrote the letters there was no term for homosexual (1:27) like the term exists now. People were not labelled homosexuals. People are labelled homosexual now and are condemned as a class of people. What is your response at this point?

A: Indeed, this is correctly as you have stated. However, the underlying issue is not in doubt. The underlying issue is that it is not the normal course for males to have sexual relationships and it is not the normal course for females to have such relationships. As I stated earlier, the intention in the creative sense is for the coming together of the male and the female in a state of marital harmony in order to create the family life together for learning together in relationship and for the creation within the individual of a sense of balance. As was stated earlier, the subject of sexual celibacy is totally in error: male and female were created as separate sexes at a specific point in the evolutionary pattern of the species. Prior to that, before coming into the more gross flesh, the sexes were not separated. They were of a more androgynous nature. Thus, if we are speaking of the point in time at which there was separation, it is within the desire body of each being to reunite with that from which it was separated and in the majority of cases, this means a seeking after a satisfactory relationship with a member of the opposite sex. Not all, there are some allowable exceptions to this but in the main, to seek after a harmonious and lasting relationship with a member of the opposite sex and to create family life together for the benefit of bringing in other souls onto the earthly plane through the human mother – this is the intention; and it were ever to be encouraged that sex other than for that specific reason should be eventually raised above the level of animal pursuit to the level of creative spiritual endeavor.

ROMANS 2

2 Therefore thou art inexcusable, O man, whosoever thou art that judgest: for wherein thou judgest another, thou condemnest thyself; for thou that judgest doest the same things.

2 But we are sure that the judgement of God is according to truth against them which commit such things.

3 And thinkest thou this, O man, that judgest them which do such things, and doest the same, that thou shalt escape the judgement of God?

4 Or despisest thou the riches of his goodness and forbearance and longsuffering; not knowing that the goodness of God leadeth thee to repentance?

5 But after thy hardness and impenitent heart treasurest up unto thyself wrath against the day of wrath and revelation of the righteous judgement of God;

6 Who will render to every man according to his deeds:

7 To them who by patient continuance in well doing seek for glory and honour and immortality, eternal life:

8 But unto them that are contentious, and do not obey the truth, but obey unrighteousness, indignation and wrath,

9 Tribulation and anguish, upon every soul of man that doeth evil, of the Jew first, and also of the Gentile;

10 But glory, honour, and peace, to every man that worketh good, to the Jew first, and also the Gentile:

11 For there is no respect of persons with God.

12 For as many as have sinned without law shall also perish without law: and as many as have sinned in the law shall be judged by the law;

2 (1-3) Yet let me say, lest you be inclined to judge – that no one is in a position to judge others. At whatever point one is inclined to condemn another, one automatically condemns self, since we are all mirror reflections and have committed the same offenses. The laws of cause and effect are totally impartial, and no one can consider themselves beyond those laws.

(4-11) The Higher Self of each being is that one's own judge. Be not beguiled into thinking that patience, mercy and generosity are signs of weakness. Repayment by kindness in response to evil doing, is the only way to effect repentance. The obstinate, who refuse to repent, are simply storing up further karma for themselves.[1] That very law of cause and effect renders back to every one according to their works. There are no exceptions. By patiently improving one's consciousness, through seeking after goodness, harmlessness and virtue, we build up an honorable karmic record. By refusal to obey the natural laws, we degenerate toward an endless round of death and rebirth.[2] Only the path of goodness brings honor, peace, and ultimate glory. The lords of karma again I say, are strictly impartial. No one receives preferential treatment.

(12-16) It is not familiarity with the Universal Law[3] which justifies unfoldment – it is the obedience to those laws. Those who are not yet sufficiently evolved to be aware of the Universal Laws, live their lives without reference to them and will leave this life accordingly. Those who begin to prove their knowledge of the laws by the very light of their own nature,

Romans 2

13 (For not the hearers of the law are just before God, but the doers of the law shall be justified.
14 For when the Gentiles, which have not the law, do by nature the things contained in the law, these, having not the law, are a law unto themselves:
15 Which shew the work of the law written in their hearts, their conscience also bearing witness, and their thoughts the meanwhile accusing or else excusing one another);
16 In the day when God shall judge the secrets of men by Jesus Christ according to my gospel.
17 Behold, thou art called a Jew, and restest in the law, and makest thy boast of God.
18 And knowest his will, and approvest the things that are more excellent, being instructed out of the law;
19 And art confident that thou thyself art a guide of the blind, a light of them which are in darkness,
20 An instructor of the foolish, a teacher of babes, which hast the form of knowledge and of the truth in the law.
21 Thou therefore which teachest another, teachest thou not thyself? Thou that preachest a man should not steal, doest thou not steal?
22 Thou that sayest a man should not commit adultery, does thou not commit adultery? Thou that abhorrest idols, does thou commit sacrilege?
23 Thou that makest thy boast of the law, through breaking the law dishonourest thou God?
24 For the name of God is blasphemed among the Gentiles through you, as it is written.

demonstrate the effect of those laws operating in their hearts. Their own very consciousness endorses the existence of such laws, and these guide their actions. Their actions will be accountable to the laws of cause and effect, even as plainly stated in the Gospels.

(17-29) To all of you, my readers, who bear the name Jew, I would say: take your stand on the laws.[4] Be proud of them. Those who know God's Divine Plan and are able, through the knowledge of the laws, to appreciate moral values, I say make sure that you obey them. Before you profess to guide the blind, and be a light to those in darkness, are you confident that you yourselves walk fully in the light? You may profess to instruct those with no spiritual wisdom, those who are like babes, for you have a certain grasp of the basis of true knowledge. This is undoubtedly an advantage. When you teach others, are you not teaching at the same time yourself? If you ask that others not steal, then make doubly sure you do not steal anything. If you demand that others not commit adultery, then make very sure that you do not, even in thought. When you abhor idols, make sure you are not yourselves sacrilegious. How honest are you toward the property of the temples of other faiths? Everyone knows well how proud you are of the law, but the dishonor to God is proportionate to the knowledge in the hearts of others, that they see you breaking the law. The very name of the God

Romans 2

25 For circumcision verily profiteth, if thou keep the law: but if thou be a breaker of the law, thy circumcision is made uncircumcision.

26 Therefore if the uncircumcision keep the righteousness of the law, shall not his uncircumcision be counted for circumcision?

27 And shall not uncircumcision which is by nature, if it fulfil the law, judge thee, who by the letter and circumcision dost transgress the law?

28 For he is not a Jew, which is one outwardly; neither is that circumcision which is outward in the flesh:

29 But he is a Jew which is one inwardly; and circumcision is that of the heart, in the spirit, and not in the letter; whose praise is not of men, but of God.

of the Jew is being cursed among the members of other faiths, because of your very behavior. Circumcision is only meaningful where the law is upheld, and those who are not of the Jewish faith are equal to the circumcised, when they uphold the law. Are you still not aware that the meaning of "Jew" is not an outward matter, but is a deep spiritual attainment? An initiation?[5,6]

DISCOURSE CHAPTER TWO

1. Q: You started using the word karma and karmic (2:9-12). As you know, it is not in the original letters. Most Christians will wonder why you are using those terms.

   A: So much of that which has been taught down the ages by that church which called itself after the Christ falls short of the true message. I deliberately introduced the word "karma" because it immediately replaces what was deliberately missed out so long ago. When it became the choice of a very small group of people to decide what would go into the written word and what would be omitted, part of their decision was to pronounce upon the whole concept of reincarnation. If one does not reincarnate, of course one cannot use the word karma because there would be no such thing. Therefore, very early in the modern treatment I wish to make it clear that the law of cause and effect in relationship to human involvement in karmic debt is fact. Reincarnation is fact, whether or not the Catholic Church likes it.

   Q: Can you talk a little more about karma. This question is coming from a telephone conversation I had with my sister who responded in a way that most Americans would because of their lack of knowledge of what little they have

Discourse Chapter Two continued:

heard of karma, coming from the east. She said "Oh you mean when you go back as insects or animals"? I said no, I do not believe that is what Hilarion is talking about.

A: Most certainly it is not. There have been many strange beliefs down the ages, not least of which that the soul is contained within the "beans." Again, the law of cause and effect is the term I much prefer to use; one has used the term karma simply because it is a well known expression in this day and age coming from the east; but the law of cause and effect is that which we prefer. In one sense it is extremely simple. To every single thing there is a cause and to every single thought there is an effect. It is as simple as the fact that when I have completed my in-breath, I shall breathe out. If I did not do so, I would expire, would I not? When one recognizes that the very thoughts which we entertain have already set in motion the form which lies behind those thoughts, then we can also acknowledge that all of those patterns create a field which bears energy and the energy will come back to the sender. It is totally unavoidable. It is part of the very law of that first cause which was the creative impulse – the great out-breath which even itself shall cease and return to the creator as the in-breath. Do you see what I am saying?

Q: I guess if one sees that in terms of being in the image or being created in the likeness of God, that in-breath and out-breath, that you are part of that divine spirit. I am trying to think if this would answer the person coming with an incomplete knowledge of eastern philosophy. Does that say that soul might choose to come down in some other form than human? I do not know that they would see the clarity of that.

A: It is not within the natural law that one so choose. There is a great deal of misconception concerning this subject. Once beings have evolved to the state of humankind, they do not return as insects or animals or plants. Each species remains within its own kind after that stage of evolution has been completed. The only way that it would be possible for a being to take so retrograde a step would be for that being to have totally denied all of the assistance of its kind and to be so intrinsically evil as to incur loss of soul. And yet, divine compassion is such that such a fall is still able to be slowly, very very slowly, re-evolved, yet not upon the same sphere of consciousness. It would be upon another planet whose evolutionary pattern is within the limitations so described. I think that clears.

2. Q: You left out the phrase that was used of "the Jew first and then the gentiles" (2:9-10 and 1:16). This was used in the letters of old, do you wish to say something regarding this?

Discourse Chapter Two continued:

A: Do you wish me to pinpoint a very specific answer or do you wish me to properly answer the situation: You see, one has to remember – in the current exercise what we endeavor to do is correct much of the misunderstanding around the written work which has been called The Letters of Paul. It is not my particular desire at this moment to get into lengthy esoteric discourse. Were I to do so, the whole thing would have to be totally rewritten at this point. So much of what is contained in the New Testament is erroneous. The words of Jesus have been wrongly recorded. My words have been wrongly interpreted. Much of what was attributed to my words was not written by me in the first place and so on.

It is our endeavor at this present time to try to correct what has been written, not to discourse too much about the real law and the real truth. This is a whole other work. I will, however, say something to the effect that the statement was deliberately omitted because this has been, indeed, one of the major difficulties down through the ages, "first Jew and then gentile", the whole issue of the fact that our Lord the Christ chose to come into a Jewish family. I too happen to be Jewish by birth; the whole question of whether or not the Jews were the chosen race; the whole question of whether or not one should give the message to the gentiles is so vast and so vexed that it bears treating as a whole subject. I would, therefore, prefer to leave that issue other than saying yes, I did deliberately leave it off for a very good reason. I would prefer to leave that issue until a little later when the whole subject of Jew versus gentile is dealt with at length.

3. Q: You use the word "law" in several different ways (2:12-16). Sometimes it seems to be referring to Jewish law, sometimes to Universal Law and sometimes to maybe secular law.

A: Exactly so. The art, I think, is for us to be together satisfied that the particular branch of the law is very clear in each individual place.

Q: In 2:12-16 you also state, "it is not familiarity with Universal Law which justifies unfoldment, it is obedience to those laws". I think it is clear you are referring to Universal Law.

A: There is a point I would like to make here. One has to remember that the one, Paul, was trained as a lawyer and speaks from the point of view of one who recognizes the law from many levels. He is of Jewish family and as a male has had much to do with the Torah. He has studied the law from the point of view of the secular and he is now working with the Universal Law as he has been made aware by the Universal Christ. Therefore, the word "law" in Paul's vocabulary was paramount, shall we say. One who is an architect tends to view most things through the eyes of an architect. One who is a doctor views through the eyes of

Discourse Chapter Two continued:

the medical practice. One who is a lawyer tends to see everything in terms of how it fits the law, be it the law of the land, be it the law of a particular religion, or be it that which he now haltingly understands as Universal Law.

4. Q: In 2:17-23, which starts out "To all of you my readers who bear the name Jew, I would say take your stand on the laws", it seems that you are shifting to a different definition of law and I want to clarify that. Is the law you are referring to there the law of the Old Testament, the Torah, and is that different from the Universal Law that you talk about in the paragraph before?

   A: No, it is not. That statement could be regarded as a trap. Perhaps it should be clarified. All created form moves within the boundaries of certain specific laws which we do not need to get into in detail at this point in time. Those laws could be referred to as universal guidelines. They are, in fact, rules of nature herself; principles to which all of nature conforms. It has ever been the task of the adepts who are universally aware of the laws of creation, the Universal Laws, to endeavor to make those better known upon the many planes of existence. The great illuminati of the ages have held as their primary purpose the teaching of those laws. Planet earth, for some reason, has been particularly laggardly, especially in the evolution of the human, that is, in its adherence to those principles.

   One must always remember that the point in time when the being arrives at such a level of understanding, one becomes a part of those principles and therefore, laws as such are no longer necessary for they are automatically observed by the knower. For those who are not yet upon such a level of understanding, there have to be translations into guidelines which will assist humanity in its acquisition of deeper knowledge. Such were the laws written by Hammurabi in Babylonian times and so on. Therefore, that which one refers to as "the law", when it is set at the level of human standards, becomes a code of ethics. When I admonished those who called themselves Jew to remember the law, I was pointing out that the true Jew is one who knows within his very being the nature of the Universal Law and therefore abides within that law. One has to remember what I have said regarding the true calling of the name "Jew", and not the connotation popularly assumed.

5. Q: At the end of chapter two you add a new word, the word " initiation". Would you comment on that word?

   A: Yes, indeed. There is one other point which I should like to make here and that is this: one has to remember that the letters we speak of were written in the vernacular of the Greek of that day. Not even in the classical Greek; it would have been to no purpose whatsoever for Paul to write to a group of widely differing

Discourse Chapter Two continued:

and mostly uneducated people in the tongue which was used among the scholarly. The vernacular of the Greek of that day was scant in its vocabulary. Some of the words which I have now used in translation did not even exist in the vernacular of the Greek.

It would be like someone (I can say this through my channel because of her background in this life) who is a scholar of pure English trying to translate a letter written by a Roman in common Yorkshire, which is not even English but a remnant of the anglo-saxon. Therefore, for someone to arrive in the middle ages with a set of texts written in the vernacular of the Greek at the time when those letters were written, approximately 20 years after the event of the crucifixion, there had to be many words introduced by the translators. If one should also then recall that English at the time of the translator was very, very scant, one has to accept that down the ages many words have been introduced which were not in the original text. There were many such words in the vernacular Greek that have been put in by the translators into first Latin and then by the translators into medieval English, and finally the modern translations into modern English have introduced words that did not exist previously.

So this whole argument about words surrounding the translation of what Paul either wrote or did not write really creates unnecessary stumbling blocks. It is not so much a question of did Paul use that word or did he not, because in many cases he did not; such words did not exist. Having now put that very general picture before you we will go back to the word you spoke of, initiation.

Again, there was much which one denied in the translations of the middle ages because so much was regarded as pagan. Anything which rang of pagan mystery schools was to be avoided almost to the point of anathema. And of course, initiation would be in that category for very obvious reasons. However, I feel it is important to make the statement in which that word was contextually used.

Q: The passage preceding it says "Are you still not aware that the meaning of Jew is not an outward merit, but is a deep spiritual attainment, an initiation" (2:29).

A: Indeed, indeed. You see, this is a very, very difficult subject for not so much the Christian but the Jew of this day. It would be very difficult for the modern Jew to accept that a Jew is not one who is born of a Jewish mother. This is indeed a status, an Israelite is a status. It is not an accident of birth. That which is of the remnant of a people who existed upon this earthly plane in a much earlier round goes back in time much further than we need to worry about here; a seed race, a root race, the remnant of which is the Jew.

Discourse Chapter Two continued:

The knowledge of the universal wisdoms was passed down through the priest initiates, the king priests, the closest of which at the time prior to the Exodus of the bible, was actually contained in the country of Egypt. The pharaoh, the king priest, of pre-dynastic Egypt that is, upheld the wisdoms of the ages which were passed down within the mind of the Egyptian pharaoh. The great mystery schools of Egypt along with the whole temple body of Egypt taught these great wisdoms and when one had passed from the lesser rites all the way through those initiations into the mysteries and eventually passed through the portals of the final initiation, then and only then was one an Israelite, one who walked with the light of God. Here indeed is an initiate and in truth, only those few who have passed through that degree of knowing should call themselves Israelite. It is not a country, it is a very high status, one which received universal recognition. Moses was such an adept. He endeavored to pass on the traditions to the priesthood and we are relatively aware of what happened.

6. Q: You make the comment in the last section of chapter two that the Jews have dishonored the law; I do not know if you are referring to something regarding the temples, but the very name of the God of the Jews is being cursed. Did you have in mind specific events that were occurring at that time?

A: Indeed. It was the very thing which the Lord Jesus also condemned; the use of the temple for total misrepresentation, misinterpretation of the true laws, "Thou Shalt Not Kill" being one. And yet, those who called themselves holy continued to make sacrifice, the sale of such items, the bringing into one's sacred area those things which have to do with commerce, and sacrilegious commerce at that. Jesus made it very plain that blood sacrifice was totally incorrect. It is the sacrifice of one's own lesser personality which is being called for. This will never be achieved by the sacrifice of animals and the shedding of blood in the area of the temple in order to purchase a foothold upon the path. The whole concept of blood sacrifice was conceived in error and perpetuated in a manner which is totally foreign to the pursuit of higher paths of spirit.

ROMANS 3

3 What advantage then hath the Jew? or profit is there of circumcision?

2 Much every way: chiefly, because that unto them were committed the oracles of God.

3 For what if some did not believe? Shall their unbelief make the faith of God without effect?

4 God forbid: yea, let God be true, but every man a liar; as it is written, That thou mightest be justified in thy sayings, and mightest overcome when thou art judged.

5 But if our unrighteousness commend the righteousness of God what shall we say? Is God unrighteous who taketh vengeance? (I speak as a man.)

6 God forbid: For then how shall God judge the world?

7 For if the truth of God hath more abounded through my lie unto his glory; why yet am I also judged as a sinner?

8 And not rather, (as we be slanderously reported, and as some affirm that we say), Let us do evil, that good may come? Whose damnation is just.

9 What then? Are we better than they? No, in no wise: for we have before proved both Jews and Gentiles, that they are all under sin,

10 As it is written, There is none righteous, no, not one:

11 There is none that understandeth, there is none that seeketh after God.

12 They are all gone out of the way, they are together become unprofitable; there is none that doeth good, no, not one.

13 Their throat is an open sepulchre; their tongues they have used deceit; the poison of asps is under their lips:

14 Whose mouth is full of cursing and bitterness:

3 (1-9) The most intimate sign of belonging to God, which is called circumcision, is only meaningful if you keep the laws. There is much advantage in every way to being a Jew, chief among these being that to the Jew was committed God's message. What matter if some did not believe these messages. Did that make the Word itself of no meaning? We may accept that the Word of God is truth, even if every member of humanity is proved a liar. If by our own wrongdoing, we prove God to be good, then shall we say His Word is untrue when it is said that we reap punishment? God forbid – for then, how shall God's Truth be measured? If God's Truth be more abundant because I deny it, then how would I be denounced? Similarly we might argue, why not perpetrate evil in order that God's Truth may be even more conspicuous? (There are some who have slanderously reported my suggesting this, but such an argument is due total condemnation). By no means are those who profess the Jewish faith any better than others. All of humanity falls into the same sin of disregard to the law.[1]

The Scriptures say:

(10-18) There is none righteous, not one. There is none that understands, There is none that seeketh after God. They have all turned aside, they are together become unprofitable. There is throat is an open sepulchre; With their tongues they have used deceit; The poison of asps is under their lips; Whose mouth is full of cursing and bitterness.

Romans 3

15 *Their feet are swift to shed blood:*
16 *Destruction and misery are in their ways:*
17 *And the way of peace have they not known:*
18 *There is no fear of God before their eyes.*
19 *Now we know that what things soever the law saith, it saith to them who are under the law: that every mouth may be stopped, and all the world may become guilty before God.*
20 *Therefore by the deeds of the law there shall no flesh be justified in his sight: for by the law is the knowledge of sin.*
21 *But now the righteousness of God without the law is manifested, being witnessed by the law and the prophets;*
22 *Even the righteousness of God which is by faith of Jesus Christ unto all and upon all them that believe: for there is no difference:*
23 *For all have sinned, and come short of the glory of God;*
24 *Being justified freely by His grace through the redemption that is in Christ Jesus:*
25 *Whom God hath set forth to be a propitiation through faith in His blood, to declare His righteousness for the remission of sins that are past, through the forbearance of God;*
26 *To declare, I say, at this time His righteousness: that He might be just, and the justifier of him which believeth in Jesus.*
27 *Where is boasting then? It is excluded. By what law? of works? Nay: but by the law of faith.*
28 *Therefore we conclude that a man is justified by their ways; And the ways of Peace they have not known. There is no fear of God before their eyes.*

none that doeth good, no not one. Their Their feet are swift to shed blood; Destruction and misery are in their ways; And the ways of Peace they have not known. There is no fear of God before their eyes.

(19-20) Now we know well, the message of the law, to those who live under it. Every excuse may die on the lips of those making them, and no living being may think himself beyond the law of cause and effect.[2] No living being can justify himself before God with a record of perfect performance of His laws. The very straightness of those laws shows us how crooked we really are.

(21-31) But we may take heart, for through Jesus the Christ there is a new message of hope. Though the law is amply attested by the prophets of old, all may now be acquitted of falling short (and everyone falls short of the true beauty of the Divine Plan) through the redemptive act of Jesus the Christ.[3] He is the means of propitiation, which was accomplished by the shedding of His blood,[4] to be received and made effective in ourselves by faith. There is then no more boasting of good works – simply that we have total faith. This propitiation is for all of humanity, and does not in any way render the laws void. On the contrary, it upholds the law and puts it in perspective.

Romans 3

29 Is he the God of the Jews only? Is he not also of the Gentiles? Yes, of the Gentiles also:

30 Seeing it is one God, which shall justify the circumcision by faith, and uncircumcision through faith

31 Do we then make void the law through faith? God forbid: yea, we establish the law.

DISCOURSE CHAPTER THREE

1   Q: In 3:1-11, you changed the phrase "under the power of sin" to "a disregard of the law". Do you wish to comment on the shift in the use of the word sin?

A: I had a tendency to make that shift. Having used a phrase with that word "sin" in it, it felt to me rather necessary to begin to establish what, in fact, is regarded as sin. Again, in universal terms, there is no such thing. In human terms this word has been used rather frequently, more by the Catholic church than any other, to represent a fall. What we need to establish is who is falling and by whose standards and what is the eventual outcome.

It has been the misfortune for humanity down the ages to suffer the torment of fear; fear of recourse if one were to err and fall into sin by some indignant God. I have noted with interest throughout the many translations of my work that the name sin has been an attempt to establish that "Paul unrelentingly was striving after perfection and anything which fell short of his view of the perfection of God was inevitably sinful". Let us set the record straight. The demonstration given to humanity by the Lord Jesus, overlighted as He was by the Christ, was that it is indeed possible for all of God's creation to become perfected and to move back into a state of divinity equal to that which He Himself achieved. It is the decision of each and every soul as to the timing, as to the method, of that achievement. Where each individual soul lies along the path to that achievement, is between that one and whatever he feels as God. It is not for anything outside of that being to pass judgement upon.

How can we therefore say that someone else is a sinner? The very way in which we judged we too are judged. Sin, the teaching of sin, is a means of coercion through fear. And yet, we are not islands, we are not upon the earthly plane in order to work upon ourselves to the exclusion of others. We need also to be

Discourse Chapter Three continued:

aware of how our actions affect all of the people around us and we need to be also aware that when we have attained a certain measure in our own understanding, when we arrive at a certain level in our own understanding, we then reach the point when we recognize the need to assist our younger brothers and sisters toward that same understanding. We do not assist by condemnation but only by love and compassion in the knowledge that we too have walked the same path. What then is sin?

2. Q: In 3:11-20, "How we know well the message of the law and those who live under it, every excuse may die on the lips of those making them and no living being may think himself beyond the law of cause and effect". My question again, is the law of cause and effect the same as the law of divine purpose?

   A: The law of karma might easily be equated with divine purpose. Since divine purpose is intended that each soul shall, by its own effort attain, and attainment is achieved by the inexorable working of the law of cause and effect, yes, one might say it is the same as divine purpose in that sense.

3. Q: At the beginning of 3:21 and 3:31 it says " but we may take heart for through Jesus the Christ there is a new message of hope. Though the law is amply attested by the prophets of old, all may now be acquitted of falling short". Again, are we talking about universal divine law or is this something else?

   A: Yes, we are talking particularly about the fact that the prophets of old who were equally in authority concerning Divine Law, and who equally not only attested to that law, but made great effort to set humanity upon the right path, have been, down the ages, misconstrued and misinterpreted variously until yet again the greatest of them all needs must return to say it again. We are dealing here with a set of circumstances which have been created by the will of those who set themselves in authority at specific points in history. Let us take for example, Ezekiel. It was deliberated at considerable lengths by the gathering of the rabbinical Elders whether or not that which is termed the Book of Ezekiel even be admitted into the writings, into the record. After considerable argumentation upon that subject, a version supposedly being the word of Ezekiel, was allowed; and yet, that version is so far from the reality of what was said by Ezekiel for the record, that it is not a record, it is simply a statement of the wishes of those rabbinical Elders. This has been the case in so many instances that there is not a great deal of veracity surrounding the words of the prophets of old. Those prophets, indeed, came with a mightiness of truth. Their message is not available any longer. All that is available is that which the mind of recent history has allowed. And now we are going through the same thing again with the words of our Lord Jesus and with my own words.

Discourse Chapter Three continued:

4. Q: How did the "blood of Christ" affect us and can you add some more to that?

    A: Yes, indeed. It is the purpose of the seemingly endless rounds of incarnation to move toward the ultimate return to First Cause. I use the term First Cause as being that of the Godhead. In those many lives with the many lessons that we have encompassed, we gradually move away from the need to satisfy the lusts of the flesh. We gradually move toward the light. Eventually along that path we recognize that we are no longer satisfying the individual self and we begin to work in a group for the benefit of the greater good and for the easement of the suffering of the rest of humanity.

    At a point in time in one's path of initiation when one recognizes that one has arrived at the need to serve, one is then accepted by an Elder of the race and one commences the life of service. Then begins a further series of lives in which soul undertakes the path of service in its many forms and so progress is made through the various schools of initiation until the point when it is no longer necessary to come back to this earthly plane unless one so chooses. The Christ and those members of the Galactic Council whom humanity, or some members of humanity call the Hierarchy, are those who have elected to stay upon this earthly plane along with their chosen helpers until all of humanity has passed through to a certain level of awareness.

    It can be said of each member of that team that theirs is a role which is sacrificial. Each has gone through a life or lives which has been the ultimate sacrifice of the self as a demonstration to the rest of humanity of what it really takes if one indeed has set aside all in order to bring this beautiful planet and all who dwell upon her into that state of divinity. That which the adept Jesus chose to do in that life was the ultimate demonstration to all who would follow thereafter of total sacrifice. It was an enactment of something that has been carried out several times before, Jesus was not the first: the giving of that sacred blood back to the earth and the taking upon Himself the suffering vicariously for all of humanity. By that act, at the beginning of the Piscean age, He again made certain for the rest of human life, the ability to move beyond the animal nature into the realm of pure spirit. In this sense, indeed, His blood was shed for our atonement, at-one-ment.

ROMANS 4

4 What shall we say then that Abraham our father, as pertaining to the flesh, hath found?

2 For if Abraham were justified by works, he hath whereof to glory; but not before God.

3 For what saith the scripture? Abraham believed God, and it was counted unto him for righteousness.

4 Now to him that worketh is the reward not reckoned of grace, but of debt.

5 But to him that worketh not, but believeth on him that justifieth the ungodly, his faith is counted for righteousness

6 Even as David also describeth the blessedness of the man, unto whom God imputeth righteousness without works,

7 Saying, Blessed are they whose iniquities are forgiven, and whose sins are covered.

8 Blessed is the man to whom the lord will not impute sin.

9 Cometh this blessedness then upon the circumcision only, or upon the uncircumcision also? For we say that faith was reckoned to Abraham for righteousness.

10 How was it then reckoned? when he was in circumcision, or in uncircumcision? Not in circumcision, but in uncircumcision.

11 And he received the sign of circumcision, a seal of the righteousness of the faith which he had yet being uncircumcised: that he might be the father of all them that believe, though they be not circumcised; that righteousness might be imputed unto them also:

12 And the father of circumcision to them who are not of the circumcision only, but who also walk in the steps of that faith of our father Abraham, which he had, being yet uncircumcised.

4 (1-8) Let us for a moment consider the position from the standpoint of our ancestor, Abraham. Abraham might well be proud of what he achieved on human terms, but not before God. The scriptures have said that "Abraham believed God, and it was counted unto him for righteousness". The worker receives his pay, not as a gift, but because his employer owes a debt.

If we have faith in Him who gives all gifts, then our faith is considered as righteousness. That is the gift of God, irrespective of our achievements. In the words of David: "Blessed are they whose iniquities are forgiven and whose sins are covered. Blessed is the man to whom the Lord will not impute sin."

(9-25) An important question arises as to whether this happy state is only for the circumcised. At the time that Abraham was recognized for his faith, he was not circumcised. It was afterwards that the sign of circumcision was given to him, as a symbol – to set the seal upon him. Abraham is in this way counted as the "Spiritual Father" of all those who since that time, have reached the same level of initiation. The ancient promise made to Abraham and his descendants that they would eventually possess the world, was given not through achievement within the law, but through true faith. For when all is said and done, if one strictly kept the law, but did not have faith, then the whole point of that promise would be lost. We have already stated that the law itself makes no promises, it merely works inexorably. If there were no Universal or Natural Laws, then of course there would neither be any question of breaking them. It is

Romans 4

13 For the promise, that he should be the heir of the world, was not to Abraham, or to his seed, through the law, but through the righteousness of

14 For if they which are of the law be heirs, faith is made void, and the promise made of none effect:

15 Because the law worketh wrath: for where no law is, there is no transgression.

16 Therefore it is of faith, that it might be by grace; to the end the promise might be sure to all the seed; not to that only which is of the law, but to that also which is of the faith of Abraham; who is the father of us all.

17 (As it is written, I have made thee a father of many nations), before him whom he believed, even God, who quickeneth the dead, and calleth those things which be not as they were.

18 Who against hope believe in hope, that he might become the father of many nations; according to that which was spoken. So shall thy seed be.

19 And being not weak in faith, he considered not his own body now dead, when he was about an hundred years old, neither yet the deadness of Sara's womb:

20 He staggered not at the promise of God through unbelief, but was strong in faith, giving glory to God;

21 And being fully persuaded that, what he had promised, he was able also to perform.

22 And therefore it was inputed to him for righteousness.

23 Now it was not written for his sake alone, that it was imputed to him;

24 But for us also, to whom it shall be imputed, if we believe on him that raised up Jesus our Lord from the dead;

25 Who was delivered for our offenses, and was raised again for our justification.

therefore a matter of faith, that through Grace God gives His blessing to all who can becalled the "Children of Abraham", that is to those who have lived in faith according to the law, but particularly to all of those who have lived a life of deep service, as did Abraham. To which-ever group any one of us might belong, it could still be said that Abraham is in a very real sense, our "Spiritual Father". The scriptures say: I have made thee a Father of many nations … before the Spirit who is able to give new life to the dead, and who gives name to all things. At that point in time, Abraham was already around the age of one hundred, yet he had no off-spring. He did not know whether this was his own impotence, or his wife's apparent barrenness. Yet when these words were spoken to him, Abraham was not daunted, and he kept his trust most strongly. Eventually Sara begot a child. This was not all recorded simply for Abraham's credit, but in order to express a Divine Principle.[1]

COMMENTARY CHAPTER 4

Further elucidation anent Abram – Abraham:

It was the Lord Christ who appeared to one Abram on the plain of Mamre. He it was, who called Himself the Mighty One, whom Abram should henceforth follow – Follow in the ways of perfection which I shall show you.

He it was who later called upon Abram to make the supreme sacrifice that all are called upon to make at a specific point along the way of the initiate. All are asked, eventually to give up everything upon the material plane. Home, goods, family, and even their very life itself in service to the Christ (even as that Supreme Being later demonstrated Himself, through the cooperation of Jesus). Abram was challenged: would you make sacrifice to God, of that very Son whom God gave to you, Isaac, who means Abiding Spiritual Joys? Would you sacrifice that joy by giving up the personification of it? Abram's response was that he would, yes, go even this far if God required it of him.

At this point, the angel of the Lord, again Christ Himself, stayed the hand of Abram, and said that he had passed the final test. From this point forth, Abrah-am, would be the High Initiate whose precedent would be the model and example for all generations to come. In this sense, Abraham was the first man (and therefore progenitor) of the 5th root race to be so recognized. Abraham was at this point given ability to directly refer to the akashic records, and to study with the Great Ones in the higher realms. Thus he was prepared and gratified to become the *leader* or a "Spiritual Father" of the race thereafter.

DISCOURSE CHAPTER FOUR

1 Q: In 4:24-25 there is a very traditional statement about the death and resurrection of Jesus in the King James and revised versions that you have left out and inserted " in order to express a Divine Principle". Why did you leave out the death and resurrection and put in Divine Principle?

A: This, if fully stated, will be the most shattering of all for the establishment to accept. The fact that the one Jesus had achieved such a degree of mastery, was upon the initiatory path so far advanced, that he was able to demonstrate the Divine Principle of the fourth level of initiation: that of total crucifixion of self, the lesser self, and to fully give of the body and the blood and the being of that self for humanity, that from this point outward we all have as example that supreme act. Did in fact Jesus die upon the cross or did he who is the Supreme Master place himself into a state of suspension from which, three days later, he was able to resurrect and continue with his fleshly life until the moment in time when he chose, as that adept, to leave this mortal plane in a method of his own choosing, even as all such high adepts may do? The statement of his death and resurrection has been taken literally down the ages and the attitude of the death by crucifixion has been the symbol of a church which called itself after the name of Christ rather than the glorious message of the resurrection into eternal life which, through his example, becomes the attainable destiny of us all. Will they, I wonder, accept that the word "death" meant death to the baser physical instinct in order to give life to that which is immortal? Let us so hope.

ROMANS 5

5 Therefore being justified by faith, we have peace with God through our Lord Jesus Christ:

2 By whom also we have access by faith into this grace wherein we stand, and rejoice in hope of the glory of God.

3 And not only so, but we glory in tribulations also: knowing that tribulation worketh patience;

4 And patience, experience; and experience, hope:

5 And hope maketh not ashamed; because the love of God is shed abroad in our hearts by the Holy Ghost which is given unto us.

6 For when we were yet without strength, in due time Christ died for the ungodly.

7 For scarcely for a righteous man will one die: yet peradventure for a good man some would even dare to die.

8 But God commendeth his love toward us, in that, while we were yet sinners, Christ died for us.

9 Much more then, being now justified by his blood, we shall be saved from wrath through him.

10 For if when we were enemies, we were reconciled to God by the death of his Son, much more, being reconciled, we shall be saved by his life.

11 And not only so but we also joy in God through our Lord Jesus Christ, by whom we have now received the atonement.

12 Wherefore, as by one man sin entered into the world, and death by sin; and so death passed upon all men, for that all have sinned:

13 (For until the law sin was in the world: but sin is not imputed when there is no law.

14 Nevertheless death reigned from Adam to Moses, even over them that had not sinned after the similitude of Adam's transgression, who is the figure of him that was to come.

5 (1-11) Therefore, because our faith justifies our being, we find that we have peace between ourselves and God through the inner Christ, by which we all have access to grace. We may all rejoice in this hope of grace and God's glory. This is achieved through trials and tribulations, out of which come patience and hope. When we have hope, we are not ashamed of our trials, because we recognize that it is through the Divine spark of God's love in our hearts that we receive the blessing of the Holy Ghost. This principle was totally demonstrated by the Christ. It was not for those that had already attained, that the demonstration was made, but for those still without the strength of such certainty. Such was the love of God, that while we were in that darkness, Christ made an ultimate sacrifice for us all. Since His blood was shed, we can all now know that we may attain the Christ consciousness, within our own being. Such was the atonement in which we rejoice.[1]

(12-21) All of us have ignored the law of nature in our material pursuits, and for that cause, all have come to experience degeneration and death. Ignorance or disobedience to the natural laws has been termed 'sin'. There is no 'sin' in the natural world; sin was only imputed when man ignored those laws. Death reigned from Adam to Moses, for once the laws have been broken, all become part of that transgression.[2] Jesus the Christ came to remind us of the natural laws with the gift of His promise, that we can redeem ourselves through adherence to His principles. However much we have strayed from the

Romans 5

15 But not as the offence, so also is the free gift. For if through the offence of one many be dead, much more the grace of God, and the gift by grace, which is by one man, Jesus Christ, hath abounded unto many.

16 And not as it was by one that sinned, so is the gift: for the judgement was by one to condemnation, but the free gift is of many offences unto justification.

17 For if by one man's offence death reigned by one; much more they which receive abundance of grace and of the gift of righteousness shall reign in life by one, Jesus Christ).

18 Therefore as by the offence of one judgement came upon all men to condemnation; even so by the righteousness of one the free gift came upon all men unto justification of life.

19 For as by one man's disobedience many were made sinners, so by the obedience of one shall many be made righteous.

20 Moreover the law entered, that the offence might abound. But where sin abounded, grace did much more abound;

21 That as sin hath reigned unto death, even so might grace reign through righteousness unto eternal life by Jesus Christ our Lord.

natural laws, we may be assured that when we turn from our ignorance, and accept the gifts which God gave to us through Christ, we shall be once again on the path to eternal life.

DISCOURSE CHAPTER FIVE

1   Q: In 5:10-11 of the Revised Standard Version it states "since therefore we are now justified by his blood which more shall we be saved by Him from the wrath of God, where while we were enemies we were reconciled to God by the death of His Son, much more now that we are reconciled shall we be saved by His life". In 5:11 " but only so, we also rejoice in God through our Lord Jesus Christ, through whom we have now received our reconciliation". You do not use the term "reconciliation".

A: My earlier statement, I think, covers this also but let me elucidate a little further. You see, there is no such thing as reconciliation. Because there is no such thing as judgement. We are not reconciled to a God of judgement, to a jealous God, to a God of anger and wrath. This was the erroneous God of which I spoke a few moments ago. The God of the Old Testament of the Hebrew world was not part of the Godhead. We will not get into that at the moment. But there is, in effect, no need for the word reconciliation because nothing is being reconciled. Our Lord, through the mission of Jesus, demonstrated to all of us what is required in order to attain the highest level of our own divinity. We are all a part of that divinity. We are given free will to choose the time, the method and how long we wish to spend in that pursuit along the path to illumination. The only being who creates any kind of judgement upon our actions is self. There is no condemnation, for we all recognize the love of God through Christ in Jesus. If there is no condemnation of our actions, then there is equally no requirement for reconciliation outside of ourselves.

2   Q: In 5:14 in the King James and RSV there is a statement that Adam caused all the sin and we are all buried in sin with Adam and that one man, Jesus, has brought us all to grace – the doctrine of the 'Original Sin'. You left that out. Do you have anything to add regarding that?

A: Again, a total historic misconception concerning Adam. The misconception is surrounding the assumption that Adam was a single human male, whereas the Adamic race was a race which surrounded what is called "the fall". The fall is simply the coming into the more gross, fleshly, animal body from which period onward it became necessary to remember the path back to the Divine. It is not involving that which has been called sin. It is simply a statement surrounding the evolutionary pattern of humankind in general. I think we need not go further than that, because, as you say, it was very well covered in my last statement. (It does not harm to be repetitive because only by repeating similar statements in different circumstances will it become really acceptable.)

ROMANS 6

6 *What shall we say then? Shall we continue in sin, that grace may abound?*

2 God forbid. How shall we, that are dead to sin, live any longer therein?

3 Know ye not, that so many of us as were baptized into Jesus Christ were baptized into his death?

4 Therefore we are buried with Him by baptism into death: that like as Christ was raised up from the dead by the glory of the Father, even so we also should walk in newness of life.

5 For as we have been planted together in the likeness of his death, we shall be also in the likeness of his resurrection:

6 Knowing this, that our old man is crucified with Him, that the body of sin might be destroyed, that henceforth we should not serve sin.

7 For he that is dead is freed from sin.

8 Now if we be dead with Christ, we believe that we shall also live with Him:

9 Knowing that Christ being raised from the dead dieth no more; death hath no more dominion over Him.

10 For in that He died, He died unto sin once: but in that He liveth, He liveth unto God.

11 Likewise reckon ye also yourselves to be dead indeed unto sin, but alive unto God through Jesus Christ our Lord.

12 Let not sin therefore reign in your mortal body, that ye should obey it in the lusts thereof.

13 Neither yield ye your members as instruments of unrighteousness unto sin: but yield yourselves unto God, as those that are alive from the dead, and your members as instruments of righteousness unto God.

14 For sin shall not have dominion over you: for ye are not under the law, but under grace.

6 (1-6) What, therefore, shall we do now? Shall we continue to sin, so that grace may keep on saving us? God forbid. We must acknowledge that when we were baptized in the name of Christ, we made a choice. That choice is to accept His atonement and walk in newness of life through the glory of God. We can no longer live in our old ways.[1]

(7-23) In a sense, we were all crucified with Christ, and we therefore were all resurrected with Him. If we truly accept this, we can no longer carry on ignoring the truth. The message that Christ taught was that death has no dominion over us. It is said that the "wages of sin is death, but the gift of God is eternal life through Christ, our Lord". What this means is that all that we do, all of our actions, are accountable to the laws of cause and effect. Once we expiate that karmic responsibility and arrive at a time when we acknowledge the laws and live by them – we may also arrive at that point when we no longer fear death. We then acknowledge that the transition we call death is merely passage into another realm of existence which goes on into eternity.[2,3]

Romans 6

15 What then? Shall we sin, because we are not under the law, but under grace? God forbid.

16 Know ye not, that to whom ye yield yourselves servants to obey, His servants ye are to whom ye obey; whether of sin unto death, or of obedience unto righteousness?

17 But God be thanked, that ye were the servants of sin, but ye have obeyed from the heart that form of doctrine which was delivered you.

18 Being then made free from sin, ye became the servants of righteousness.

19 I speak after the manner of men because of the infirmity of your flesh; for as ye have yielded your members servants to uncleanness and to iniquity unto iniquity; even so now yield your members servants to righteousness unto holiness.

20 For when ye were the servants of sin, ye were free from righteousness.

21 What fruit had ye then in those things whereof ye are now ashamed? For the end of those things is death.

22 But now being made free from sin, and become servants to God, ye have your fruit unto holiness, and the end everlasting life.

23 For the wages of sin is death; but the gift of God is eternal life through Jesus Christ our Lord.

DISCOURSE CHAPTER SIX

1. Q: In the beginning of 6:1-6, the King James and RSV states that "we are buried within by baptism and death and we shall certainly be united within in a resurrection like His". Is there something you would like to say regarding the death and resurrection here?

    A: I think more is warranted here because the underlying concept there is one which has been entertained down the various centuries in the church of Rome, at any rate, which would imply that all who die remain buried and dead until such time as there will be a clarion call from the angel forces which will summon all of those dead to resurrect into some glorious heavenly state somewhere from whence they shall be counted as either the sheep or the goats. Let us dispense with that error in concept at this point as being nonsense. As you say, I think it is then fully covered.

2. Q: In 6:7-23 you have really reduced the use of sin, especially the idea of sin having dominion or reigning over us in our mortal bodies to make us obey their passions, in other words, that sin was coming from the outside. You left that out. Do you wish to comment on that?

    A: Yes, in the sense of your own words, lest it be interpreted that whatever we call sin is coming from the outside. There are numerous temptations which fall upon the path of a seeker after truth. Nonetheless, whether or not we succumb to those temptations, comes entirely from within ourselves. There is nothing outside of that self which is cause.

3. Q: In 6:19-23 you have said something about developing a different concept of death vis a vis the crucifixion. If the karmic laws were already in place, then what did the death of Christ save us from?

    A: This is a good question. What in fact happened at the time of that particular demonstration was the saving of endless rounds of karmic debts. Yes, to a great extent, the laws of cause and effect were in place, but the demonstration entered into by the Christ through the office of Jesus was a covenant made which expiated a tremendous amount of human karma at that point in time. Had he not elected to do this, humanity may have become bogged down in the morass of their own endless pendulum of karmic responsibility out of which it might have been impossible to extricate. It is as it were a purchase that our Lord Christ made on behalf of humanity in order to save those endless rounds and in order to set those of humanity willing to accept, upon a path which might far more easily be sustained.

Discourse Chapter Six continued:

Q: It seems like mankind has been very busy building up another heavy load of karma, how does that purchase made 2,000 years ago affect modern man?

A: Indeed, a very good question. There are numerous channels through which the law of cause and effect may be enacted or activated. Primarily there is what one might call a group karma. Attendant upon this earthly plane there are situations which are, in effect, pre-arranged within a specific group of individuals who, down through many lives, have worked together. Part of the operation upon this earthly plane is seeking out those who are part of one's group and working upon the furtherance of that group action. In this sense, there is an inevitable group karma which each member of that body of the whole assists in processing. There is also racial karma – the whole race at large, be they the people who call themselves at this time Celtic or those who call themselves Semitic or those who are known as Teutonic and so forth.

From the point in time where history became written, there is a build up of what might be termed racial karma. The problems that are inherent within a specific race are those which the whole of that race are working to alleviate. Then there is the individual karmic pattern set by each being. While it might be supposed that each individual personality is working at that one's own level and thus, within the boundaries of the law of cause and effect, creating and expiating karma, it must also be remembered that each of those individuals is also interweaving with his or her group and the karma that collectively that group incurs, and again in turn, the group is interweaving with what might be various racial karmic patterns. It is not very often that a group is a member collectively of one race. Usually groups are members of several races and therefore, there is the interweaving of the racial pattern of those many races.

One can, therefore, see that if the subject of karma were to be left entirely to the workings of the individual and the way in which that individual interacts with the group, and then the way the group interacts with the races, the prolongation of karmic responsibility could be non-ending. Humanity has not yet made sufficient progress in its evolution to fully register the fact that we are not separate little islands of individuality; we are all interconnected. That which affects the individual also affects the group, also affects the race and eventually affects the whole of civilization in a continuum that goes on down through the whole history of the human race, and to some extent, even before that.

Discourse Chapter Six continued:

Therefore, there are those great ones who have come to this earthly plane at intervals throughout those ages who have taken upon themselves the responsibility of the whole race. And through the purchase of their own atonement, they have set the balance. The last one to do that was the one whom we call Jesus the Christ. Because of the evolutionary process and the amount of time still available to that evolutionary process, it was necessary for an even greater act of atonement to be made within the law of cause and effect than had been the case in earlier civilizations. And so, by his supreme act, and by the overlighting of the Universal Christ, that Supreme Master gave of His own being and that of the hosts who stood behind Him upon the higher planes in order to purchase His own atonement and that of humankind. That action, having been set in motion at that point in written history, is in motion for all time.

From that point forward, because of that supreme example, each individual working upon his own balance, and each group recognizing its group responsibility, is now able – if it so chooses – to work from the level of karmic responsibility which allows all that has passed to be set in balance and, as it were, to work from here forward with a clear record. There are many souls coming into this earthly plane at this time who, therefore, do not hold any karmic responsibility from the past and who work on what might be termed "instant balancing" as they go along in this present life. There is still a vast racial responsibility and it is the work of each group within those areas to become so aware of those responsibilities that the racial karma also might be set in balance.

All of this was made possible by a group of souls who have repeatedly come to this earthly plane and, by vicarious atonement, have taken on the suffering of the whole of humanity, often quietly, often without recognition, until the time when certain members of that group came together at a period in written history in that land in the eastern Mediterranean where such an act of group steadfastness allowed Jesus the man to become the embodiment of the Universal Christ.

In these times which we are now facing which have been called the Aquarian Age, the whole of humanity shall become aware of group responsibility in which the solidarity of purpose shall be equally visible as that which created the ability of Jesus the Christ to do what he had to do. One could write a book around each of the questions. Perhaps one day all of those books shall have been written and in that day, humanity shall no longer have the need of them.

ROMANS 7

7 *Know ye not, brethren, (for I speak to them that know the law), how that the law hath dominion over a man as long as he liveth?*

2 For the woman which hath an husband is bound by the law to her husband so long as she liveth; but if the husband be dead, she is loosed from the law of her husband.

3 So then if, while her husband liveth, she be married to another man, she shall be called an adulteress; but if her husband be dead, she is free from that law; so that she is no adulteress, though she be married to another man.

4 Wherefore, my brethren, ye also are become dead to the law by the body of Christ; that ye should be married to another, even to him who is raised from the dead, that we should bring forth fruit unto God.

5 For when we were in the flesh, the motions of sins, which were by the law, did work in our members to bring forth fruit unto death.

6 But now we are delivered from the law, that being dead wherein we were held; that we should serve in newness of spirit, and not in the oldness of the letter.

7 What shall we say then? Is the law sin?: God forbid. Nay, I had not known sin, but by the law; for I had not known lust, except the law had said, Thou shalt not covet.

8 But sin, taking occasion by the commandment, wrought in me all manner of concupiscence. For without the law sin was dead.

9 For I was alive without the law once: but when the commandment came, sin revived, and I died.

10 And the commandment which was ordained to life, I found to be unto death.

11 For sin, taking occasion by the commandment, deceived me, and by it slew me.

7 (1-6) You know very well, my brothers (for I speak to those that know the law) that the law exercises authority over a man for as long as he lives. For instance, a married woman is bound by the law to be faithful to her husband as long as he lives. When he dies, she is released from that tie. In this country, what that means is that while that husband is still alive, were she to marry another man after divorce, she would still be considered adulterous.[1] Only if the first husband is dead would this not be so. I say to you that our Lord Christ came to release us from such laws. His very message is a new law. From now on, we are all "married" to the new law – the true laws of God, that we bring forth the fruits of His truth. In the old laws, it is as though we were dead . . . (for the old interpretations of those laws have held us in bondage). Now our spirits may be refreshed to serve in newness of spirit.

(7-20) Does this mean that the law itself is sinful? God forbid we should interpret it that way. No, but our old interpretations of the natural laws have created sinners out of us all. When we were created, we were in ignorance of such interpretations, and thus we were not considered sinners. It is the interpretations that have been put on natural laws that have made sinners out of us all.[2] The very laws which were given to us that we might have life, thus became the laws that brought to us death. The laws themselves were holy and just, but such was the interpretation put upon them, that they turned that which was good into bad, and that which is bad, into good.

43

Romans 7

12 Wherefore the law is holy, and the commandment holy, and just, and good.

13 Was then that which is good made death unto me? God forbid. But sin, that it might appear sin, working death in me by that which is good; that sin by the commandment might become exceeding sinful.

14 For we know that the law is spiritual: but I am carnal, sold under sin.

15 For that which I do I allow not: for what I would, that do I not; but what I hate, that do I.

16 If then I do that which I would not, I consent unto the law that it is good.

17 Now then it is no more I that do it, but sin that dwelleth in me (that is, in my flesh), dwelleth no good thing; for to will is present with me; but how to perform that which is good I find not.

18 For I know that nothing good dwells within me, that is, in my flesh. I can will what is right, but I cannot do it.

19 For the good that I would I do not: but the evil which I would not, that I do.

20 Now if I do that I would not, it is no more I that do it, but sin that dwelleth in me.

21 I find then a law, that, when I would do good, evil is present with me.

22 For I delight in the law of God after the inward man:

23 But I see another law in my members, warring against the law of my mind, and bringing me into captivity to the law of sin which is in my members.

24 O wretched man that I am! Who shall deliver me from the body of this death?

25 I thank God through Jesus Christ our Lord. So then with the mind I myself serve the law of God; but with the flesh the law of sin.

(21-25) I say, delight in the true law – the law of God, which the inner self knows. Our higher self is well aware of the true law, and it is that which Jesus the Christ spoke plainly. We now have the choice: to follow the true laws of God, or to continue to follow the pursuits of the lesser self which lead us into error.

DISCOURSE CHAPTER SEVEN

1. Q: In 7:1-6 referring to the analogy of the married woman who was bound by the law to be faithful to her husband, you use the phrase "in this country what that means is..." The detectives would like to know what country are you talking about?

    A: This country was, directly speaking, of the precincts of Jerusalem at that time. You see, this was the only country at that time in which those laws were so rigorous. They certainly were not so in Greece or in Rome.

    Q: In regard to this analogy, you evidently were aware as Paul was of the possibility of some kind of misinterpretation. If the new law releases one from the old laws, such as the marriage laws, is it possible that one might take this analogy to mean that beyond the law one is free from ethical conduct or is there a new ethic?

    A: Outside of this earthly plane there are no written laws per se, and indeed, within this earthly plane there are none. The only people who need written laws are those who have not yet arrived at a state of higher consciousness. For those whom written laws are no longer necessary there is not that within their consciousness that would even consider a pattern of behavior which makes written laws necessary. It is the work of the individual to create that within the self that goes beyond the law of humankind in order to become part of the universal ethic. Do you recall the words of Jesus when challenged regarding the commandments? There is in truth only one law, "Thou shalt love the Lord thy God with all thy heart, with all thy mind and all of thy self and thou shalt love thy neighbor even as self'. There are no other laws to one who is capable of so doing.

2. Q: In 7:7-15 in the King James version Paul is reported to have linked the law with sin, or that the law introduced and caused sin. You shift that and use a new kind of concept that it was the interpretation of the law that is the problem. For modern day people, they need to know something more about what you mean by interpretation of the law. Do you have something specific in mind, are you speaking in terms of Torah?

    A: The true laws that I was thinking about when I said this the true Universal Laws are not the same as those laws which were written for humanity as expressed from the time of Moses and that have been interpreted by the Torah. The true Universal Laws indeed go back to the time of the creation of all that is. And out of that creation came the laws. At a point in time those of humankind, and in particular, those races who occupied the Middle East of the Earth, around the eastern Mediterranean that is, had so far moved away from those divine laws that it became necessary to rewrite that which would remind humanity of the laws of natural order. The laws of natural order in their statement were not understood. Therefore, it became necessary to write a code of ethics which humanity might more readily accept and understand.

Discourse Chapter Seven continued:

And so, in many places around the earth, there were given such codes as standards by which humanity might live in relationship one to another. There are several interpretations of the laws of natural order that were left to the mediumship, I might call it, of the elders of those people at that point in history. There is considerable deviation from the original understanding of the laws of natural order that were brought down to this earthly plane and the subsequent writing of codes of ethics which were undertaken directly upon this plane; and it is that interpretation to which I refer when I say that it is the law itself, in some instances, written by those elders which has given rise to that which then has been called "sin" down to the ages.

Q: You have left out of your version your famous personal statement (7:15-25) that most people saw as autobiographical where you describe your own struggle with sin and that you cannot do what you want to do, and you do that which you do not want to do. Would you like to say something about that?

A: I would hardly re-interpret, omitting the use of the expression "sin" and then continue to retain my supposed reference to my own sin. Somewhere near the beginning of our discourses I recall making the statement "at the time of my own awakening and the entrance into that glorious light, and the recognition of my own relationship with the Universal Christ, my whole being was brought back on course and I became aware of the true purpose of that life into which I had currently been born". But as I remarked then, enlightenment is not a sudden occurrence which then takes the recipient permanently into the higher planes. There are in all lives the peaks and the valleys. I, who had been born Saul, went through a considerable period in the valley and spent many years in search of truth; and even after arriving at that point of truth in my life, to the time when I felt confident to spread the message to others, I was still not foolish enough to imagine that I had yet attained a state of perfection and oft referred to the very fact of my imperfection. Looking upon those with whom I interacted as being brothers and sisters along the path, and being happy to share with them insights which I had gained and to humbly ask for their insights which might be of help to myself and other people. In much the same way that humanity is doing in this modem day, there were many times when I despaired of myself. There were many times when I did not consider myself equipped to do that which, in a spurt of enthusiasm, I had undertaken; but each time I was given the strength through the Christ and by the example of our Lord Jesus and I was again filled with joy and light and the fervent desire to spread that which I became increasingly aware and certain of to others. I think that is perhaps the more correct interpretation of what was written.

ROMANS 8

8 There is therefore now no condemnation to them which are in Christ Jesus, who walk not after the flesh, but after the Spirit.

2 For the law of the Spirit of life in Christ Jesus hath made me free from the law of sin and death.

3 For what the law could not do, in that it was weak through the flesh, God sending his own Son in the likeness of sinful flesh, and for sin, condemned sin in the flesh:

4 That the righteousness of the law might be fulfilled in us, who walk not after the flesh, but after the Spirit.

5 For they that are after the flesh do mind the things of the flesh; but they that are after the Spirit the things of the Spirit.

6 For to be carnally minded is death; but to be spiritually minded is life and peace.

7 Because the carnal mind is enmity against God: for it is not subject to the law of God, neither indeed can be.

8 So then they that are in the flesh cannot please God.

9 But ye are not in the flesh, but in the Spirit, if so be that the Spirit of God dwell in you. Now if any man have not the Spirit of Christ he is none of his.

10 And if Christ be in you, the body is dead because of sin; but the Spirit is life because of righteousness.

11 But if the Spirit of Him that raised up Jesus from the dead dwell in you, He that raised up Christ from the dead shall also quicken your mortal bodies by His Spirit that dwelleth in you.

12 Therefore, brethren, we are debtors, not to the flesh, to live after the flesh.

13 For if ye live after the flesh, ye shall die: but if ye through the Spirit do mortify the deeds of the body, ye shall live.

14 For as many as are led by the Spirit of God, they are the sons of God.

8 (1-13) There is now therefore no condemnation for anyone who believes and follows the truth which Jesus the Christ taught. All we who do this, follow not after the lesser self, but after the Spirit. It is the very truth of the law which the Christ in Jesus made manifest, that frees us all from the ways of the flesh, and eventual death. The law of itself could not do this, because it had been reduced to the terms of the lesser self.[1] God sent His own Son to re-interpret the law, that its rightness might be once again seen and followed. When we interpret the universal laws through the Spirit, which is the higher self, then we can no longer interpret those same laws through the eyes of the lesser self. Unto all those who live by the higher laws, there is the promise of Life and Peace.

(14-25) The lesser self is at enmity with the higher laws of God. If, therefore, one follows only after the needs of the flesh, one cannot attain the things of the higher self or spiritual man. When once we recognize that the Divine dwells in each of us, then we are of Spirit. This was the very message of Christ, in whom we all now believe. When we begin to walk the path of Divinity, and accept the Inner Christ, then we cease to attach so much importance to things of the flesh. The very Spirit that raised up Christ Jesus from the dead, dwells in each one of you. All those who accept this fact are equally Sons of God, and we may all call upon the name of God, even as did He.[2] The Divine in each of us bears witness to the very fact that we are all equal, and joint heirs to the realms of Spirit. Even as He suffered and was glorified,

16 The Spirit itself beareth witness with our spirit, that we are the children of God:

17 And if children, then heirs; heirs of God, and joint-heirs with Christ; if so be that we suffer with Him, that we may be also glorified together.

18 For I reckon that the sufferings of this present time are not worthy to be compared with the glory which shall be revealed in us.

19 For the earnest expectation of the creature waiteth for the manifestation of the sons of God.

20 For the creature was made subject to vanity, not willingly, but by reason of him who hath subjected the same in hope.

21 Because the creature itself also shall be delivered from the bondage of corruption into the glorious liberty of the children of God.

22 For we know that the whole creation groaneth and travaileth in pain together until now.

23 And not only they, but ourselves also, which have the first fruits of the Spirit, even we ourselves, groan within ourselves, waiting for the adoption, to wit, the redemption of our body.

24 For we are saved by hope: but hope that is seen is not hope; for what a man seeth, why doth he yet hope for?

25 But if we hope for that we see not, then do we with patience wait for it.

26 Likewise the Spirit also helpeth our infirmities: for we know not what we should pray for as we ought: but the Spirit itself maketh intercession for us with groanings which cannot be uttered.

27 And He that searcheth the hearts knoweth what is the mind of the Spirit, because He maketh intercession for the saints according to the will of God.

so may we be glorified. Any suffering that we undertake on Earth is worthwhile for our progress toward Divinity. Although much that we undertake upon Earth is learned through suffering and travail, we shall set this as naught when we attain the perfection that Christ promised is possible for each of us.[3]

(26-30) We are encouraged by this truth in the just hope that we may each attain to His glory, through our continued efforts. Therefore let us all work diligently and with patience upon that path. The spirit of each one of us makes intercession in those higher realms, and we know that all things work together towards a common good. Those who follow the heart, and who love one another and follow God may consider themselves as true followers of Divine Purpose. We are all predestined to follow in the footsteps of the Son of God who is the Christ.

(31-39) What then might we say in consideration of all this? We need no longer fear, for when God is with us, nothing can be against us. Does not that same God who gave His own Son also give us all things freely?

Romans 8

28 And we know that all things work together for good to them that love God, to them who are called according to His purpose.

29 For whom He did foreknow, He also did predestinate to be conformed to the image of His Son, that He might be the first born among many brethren.

30 Moreover whom He did predestinate, them He also called; and whom He called, them He also justified: and whom He justified, them He also glonfied.

31 What shall we then say to these things? If God be for us, who can be against us?

32 He that spared not His own Son, but delivered Him up for us all, how shall He not with Him also freely give us all things?

33 Who shall lay anything to the charge of God's elect? It is God that justifieth.

34 Who is he that condemneth? It is Christ that died, yea rather, that is risen again, who is even at the right hand of God, who also maketh intercession for us.

35 Who shall separate us from the love of Christ? Shall tribulation, or distress, or persecution, or famine, or nakedness, or peril, or sword?

36 As it is written, For thy sake we are killed all the day long, we are accounted as sheep for the slaughter.

37 Nay, in all these things we are more than conquerors through Him that loved us.

38 For I am persuaded, that neither death, nor life, nor angels, nor principalities, nor powers, nor things present, nor things to come,

39 Nor height, nor depth, nor any other creature, shall be able to separate us from the love of God, which is in Christ Jesus our Lord.

Only God, or the Divine in each of us can justify our actions. Who then can condemn us? Who shall separate us from the love of Christ? Shall we be daunted by any kind of tribulation, distress, persecution, famine, nakedness, or peril of any kind – even the sword? It is written that we must "die" to the lesser self daily, even as sheep for the slaughter. Yet in all of these things we are more than conquerors through Him that loved us. Through Him, I am persuaded that neither death, nor life, nor angels, nor principalities, nor powers, either present or to come, not height or depth, not any other being can separate us from the love of God which was demonstrated by the Christ in Jesus our Lord.

DISCOURSE CHAPTER EIGHT

1. Q: In Romans 8:1-13 there are a number of issues. First of all it might be good to have some definitions. There is a need to define what you mean by "lesser self", "the body", "the flesh", and what is their relationship?

   A: Yes indeed. We do, in fact, use the more metaphysical terminology because this was the teaching to which I refer. During the time of His ministry Jesus did indeed make these matters very clear to those people with whom he spoke and we as His messengers continued with that same, particularly John, to whom was entrusted the cloak of authority after Jesus left the earthly plane. We have endeavored to make it plain to humanity that we are not our body. When I have used the term "flesh" I speak of that coat of flesh which covers this skeletal frame and which altogether makes up the physical dimension of the being.

   What was meant by the words of Jesus and my own words is that we were reminding people that the outer physical form is that which contains the divine spirit. We reminded people, indeed, that there are other levels, finer dimensions, than that which is recognized merely upon the level of physical form. The work which we who elect to teach must needs undertake, is to first of all help the human being to understand that he is not his fleshly body. That is only the vehicle which helps the being to operate. One has to think in terms of body, mind and spirit. One has to recognize that the body is indeed a temple wherein Spirit dwells and that the mind is the vehicle which is, one might say, the bridge between the two; the connecting point between that which is of the physical and mortal plane and that which is of the higher and finer realms of Spirit and all that lies between.

   When I use the term "lesser self", I am reminding people that it is dangerous from the point of view of evolution to the higher realms to allow the being to exercise his thought too often upon the level of the gross physical. It was an invitation to humanity to allow the mind to aspire to things of a higher direction. Through the vehicle of the mind and the pattern of thought, one moves forward in one's aspiration to those matters eternal. Does this answer the question?

   Q: It gets us started. I think we need to go a little further. Is the "lesser self" the same as the body or something different?

Discourse Chapter Eight continued:

A: It is and it is not. The "lesser self" is the vehicle of human thought. The body is only a body as long as it is occupied by the finer vehicle, the finer substance. When the finer substances depart, the body disintegrates and therefore, the use of the word "body" is assuming that that body is fully tenanted by the finer vehicles, the finer essences.

Q: I am still not real clear on what the "lesser self" is. One of the major issues down through the ages and it has come out in New Age thought and in the humanistic movement is the fact that for centuries, particularly in the Catholic church, the flesh was seen as evil. Only the Spirit is good and there was a dichotomy that said all natural functions, sex, etc. were really evil and the Spirit was good. For instance, you say "the lesser self is at enmity with the higher laws of God; if therefore one follows only after the needs of the flesh, one cannot attain the things of the higher self or spiritual man". It seems this is in danger of perpetuating this dichotomy that separates body, mind and spirit.

A: I see what you are saying, very well. It all comes down to motive. Let us be very clear that there is nothing evil within the body itself and the exercise of those bodily functions which are a part of nature, all are part of a divine creation and are not in any way of themselves evil. What has been evil in man is that which he has chosen to do with those bodily functions and those things which have been perpetrated against one's fellow human beings. It is not the body itself or the bodily function that have created this, it is the exercising of the human mind. This, you see, is what I meant when I said the mind acts as the link between the lower nature, otherwise lesser self, and the higher. The sex act has nothing in it which is to be considered evil. It is a part of that God-given creation of the human form for a specific purpose which, in its highest form, is able to carry the two people who come together into the highest realms of beauty. This is true of all of the natural created world. It is only what the lesser mind of humanity has done with these things that has created it as evil. Therefore, it is the work of the soul, of the higher self, to continually overlight the being in the endeavor to lift the motivation out of the level of self-gratification to the point when every act of that one is carried out for the higher purpose and the greater good, not only of that soul but for all. When one's motives are wholly of the truth and pure, then all that one does is also pure and part of God. That is possible to attain while still in the fleshly vehicle as was clearly stated by Jesus and has been equally clearly stated by all of the great teachers who have come to this earthly plane.

Discourse Chapter Eight continued:

Q: I gather that the lesser self is very much connected to the higher self; the motivation, intent, emotions and all those things that make up the spirit of a human being. But again, it is the level at which it is aimed; it is a matter of whether it is coming from a higher consciousness or from a base intent and motivation. The lesser self is not the flesh or the body in essence.

A: In a sense it can be said that the lesser self is the tempter; that which the church has erroneously called Satan. It is part of creation which allows the being to fully discover its own self. The one who created all recognized the darkness and the light. The darkness is equally of God. We must all recognize our own darkness as well as that which is light as being a part of our own divinity. For it is only by the continual testing and that which is learned from that testing that the one goes forward in the several attainments to which we all aspire. Darkness and the darker side of self is no more separate from God than is the light. The lesser self is not separate from the higher. It is there that we may grow

Q: Previously you made the statement that Christ had purchased the accumulated karma. Last time I asked the question "Is that an ongoing purchase"? and you said "Yes, it continues to be available". Is the acceptance of the saving act of Christ through faith a kind of shortcut to the law of cause and effect? By having our karma purchased, can we bypass the need for reincarnation to work on our karmic debts?

A: Oh no. We shall not get away with that one. We all who enter the earthly plane do so in the full knowledge of our karmic debt. In a sense, the need to reincarnate and the law of cause and effect are synonymous because when one is upon the earthly plane in a specific incarnation, one carries within the lesser vehicle, the lesser self, that which is called the astral.

Let us recap on the subject of lesser self for a moment. The physical plane personality is comprised of the fleshly body (the gross body) and the etheric vehicle together with the astral or emotional body. Upon the higher planes the three bodies which are the Buddhic, the Atmic and the Monadic, or the higher ego self, respond to the same stimuli, the will, and, to a certain extent, emotions, excepting that the emotions on the higher level are not negative. Then we have, as was described before, the mind vehicle which is a bridge between the higher and the lower planes.

When a soul elects to enter again into the fleshly plane, it does so in order to learn certain lessons; and upon arrival into the mortal plane that which is stamped upon the astral body which is called emotional reaction, forms continually an impression upon the etheric counterpart. If one were to be able to see the etheric

Discourse Chapter Eight continued:

counterpart of the physical body at any given time, one might be very disturbed when one sees the effect that negative thinking has upon that etheric counterpart. And so it is a constant operation of the human condition that the higher self endeavors to assist the lower self to remove negative thinking.

At whatever point in time the soul elects to leave the physical plane and withdraw from that vehicle, whatever is accumulated by the etheric counterpart transfers into the higher realms in its exact appearance at that point in time. It is then the work of soul upon the higher planes to restore whatever is out of balance within that being. That is often quite an arduous task upon the astral planes. Each individual soul still, and all, has to do this; there is nothing which has made that particular exercise unnecessary, nor ever will be I doubt.

What was meant when it was said that the Christ through Jesus had purchased on behalf of humanity much of the blackness of the karmic debt, was that He, like the other great ones before him, had taken upon His own vehicle much of that debt in order to make it possible on a level of frequency for the rest of humankind to proceed at a faster pace. In other words, in a sense, it was helping humanity to increase its pace but not to completely take away the need for the individual to work at his (or her) own karma.

Let us use an analogy: If one has a child and that child has, because of his own stupidity, gotten himself into such a mess that it is quite impossible to get out of it without the help of a loving parent, that parent will come to the aid of the child and say "here you are now, let us set things straight. We will pay your debts but we cannot live the rest of your life for you, you have that to do for yourself. Please bear in mind that we have set you straight this time and from now on be an adult, live your own life and take the consequences". The child might continue from that point to remember and live accordingly. And there will be many times when he will fall and will have to right himself. This, in a sense, is what our Lord did for humanity. Does this clear the issue?

2. Q: Yes, it does. In 8:14-25, it is stated "The very spirit that raised up Jesus Christ from the dead dwells in each one of you. All those who accept this fact are equally sons of God". Is it necessary to accept the Christ event or story? What about those people who are not of that tradition, the Buddhists, the Hindus or others, do they have to accept the Christ event or story in order to be sons of God, or is there another way for them?

A: Oh no, indeed, they do not have to accept the Christ event, namely the crucifixion of Jesus. But they do indeed accept the Christ. The Universal Christ is part of the creation of all things. If a soul has chosen in this life to be a follower after

Discourse Chapter Eight continued:

the Buddha or any other, that is simply a path which they have chosen because there are certain aspects within that field that in this life they wish to pursue. However, it is no more possible for any soul to attain to a level which approaches the path toward divinity and yet deny the Christ than it is for a human body to have no heart and still live. Whether or not any one individual life follows after a different pursuit, the acknowledgement of the universality of the Christ is as the grass; soul cannot live without it. It is part of the essence of being.

Q: We still have in this world of ours religious wars; we are having them right now between Christians and Muslims, between Hindus and Buddhists, between Muslims and Jews, Catholics and Protestants. They are killing each other because of their various exclusive claims. It is hard to say to someone, even though it is very true, that everyone must acknowledge or accept the universal Christ. A person who at this time is a Muslim or a Buddhist or Hindu may find that difficult to acknowledge. It is tearing our world up in some places.

A: You see these are not the planes of the entities. These are the planes of those establishments which have arisen. The more enlightened of the eastern religions acknowledge Jesus as a prophet. Mohammed certainly acknowledged Jesus as a fellow prophet. The Koran acknowledges the fact. It is the succession of establishments which have called themselves after the name of those prophets that have created the problem, not the prophets themselves. In fact, each and every one of those prophets have not required that establishments be created in their name at all. There has been particularly in the church which has called itself after the name of Christ a very erroneous and malignant concept concerning their aspect of the truth. It is not the nature of the true Godhead or of the Universal Christ to create that which separates. Indeed, absolutely the reverse is the truth. There is no separation from the love of God through Christ no matter what particular path the soul purports to follow in any one lifetime. Those wars, conflicts which have been perpetuated down the ages and now are still continuing are a source of deep, deep sadness in the very heart of those who came to teach the opposite of that which is happening. This is part of man's inhumanity to man. It is not a part of the teaching of those in whose name these things are perpetuated.

3. Q: In 8:19-20 in the King James and RSV version, Paul talked about creation. You left out the part referring to the struggle that creation was having. One of the biblical scholars* says that Paul did not seem interested in nature, as different from Jesus who referred to nature constantly. Paul seldom used illustrations from nature. How does Paul feel about nature and the natural order?

Discourse Chapter Eight continued:

A: Since that is a question that has been raised, I suppose it is one that needs to be answered. Liken it to the seven colors in the visible spectrum. Each of those colors has a particular quality of expression. Interestingly enough, the ray of expression which is my own particular aspect is one which is far more closely connected with the things of nature than are most of the others. It is often the case, that to which we are most connected is that which we least express vociferously. It is so much a part of our own being that we tend not to refer to it. But, this is speaking of the one whom I Am and not particularly Paul.

Jesus was dealing with a group of people in that time and place who were in the main simple folk; and, as with young children, the way to get across the message which one wishes to convey is to put it into symbology that they will best understand. The Master therefore chose frequently to express the great universal truths through the medium of the natural environment which the people of his day could well understand. I might have thought that was well known or well understood. Since the man Paul was not walking with those same groups of people but rather, was moving out into wider spheres, it was no longer necessary to perhaps put the words into parables, but rather to say in his own words what it was he wished to convey. The method used by Jesus is an age old method of hiding the great universal wisdoms in simple form that people might readily appreciate and therefore better understand. Many of the great universal wisdoms indeed in this modem age may be found in fairy stories, mythology, even in nursery rhymes that are spoken to children. This is a method understood by the great ones throughout the ages of humanity and the Master was using this method yet again. (It is very important and good that we do this because any question raised by the questioner is obviously one that is on the minds of the many.)

---

* Knox, John: Exegesis, The Epistle to the Romans: *The Interpreter's Bible*, P. 520, Volume IX, Abingdon Cokesbury Press, Nashville, 1954.

ROMANS 9

9 *I say the truth in Christ, I lie not, my conscience also bearing me witness in the Holy Ghost,*

2 That I have great heaviness and continual sorrow in my heart

3 For I could wish that myself were accursed from Christ for my brethren, my kinsmen according to the flesh;

4 Who are Israelites; to whom pertaineth the adoption, and the glory, and the covenants, and the giving of the law, and the service of God, and the promises;

5 Whose are the fathers, and of whom as concerning the flesh Christ came, who is over all, God blessed for ever, A-Men.

6 Not as much through the word of God hath taken none effect. For they are not all Israel, which are of Israel:

7 Neither, because they are the seed of Abraham, are they all children: but, in Isaac shall they seed be called.

8 That is, they which are the children of the flesh, these are not the children of God: but the children of the promise are counted for the seed.

9 For this is the word of promise, At this time will I come, and Sara shall have a son.

10 And not only this; but when Rebecca also had conceived by one, even by our father Isaac;

11 (For the children being not yet born, neither having done any good or evil, that the purpose of God according to election might stand, not of works, but of him that calleth;)

12 It was said unto her, The elder shall serve the younger.

13 As it is written, Jacob have I loved, but Esau have I hated.

14 What shall we say then? Is there unrighteousness with God? God forbid.

9 (1-5) As that very Christ is my witness, I tell you the truth. The power of the Holy Spirit is with me. I tell you though, there is something which causes me deep concern. It is my own fellow Israelites and blood kindred. No matter what it might cause me, I shall have to tell the truth concerning certain matters, or even I am not following the law according to the true message of Christ, the Son of God. This is the truth: Who are the Israelites to whom were given the laws, the covenants and the opportunity to serve God and to receive the Promise?

(6-13) Not all who call themselves "Isra-elites" have the right to do so. Who are the Fathers of Israel whom Christ came to call back to the truth? Just because one might call oneself the "Seed of Abraham" in no way means that this makes one a true Is-ra-el-ite. They might all, from Isaac onward, be considered of that lineage in the flesh, but this certainly does not make them of the true lineage of the initiated.

(14-17) Remember that Abraham had two sons. One was by Sara, the other by Hagar, the Egyptian, who was the elder son. At that time, the pharaoh of Egypt was the king-priest who was the possessor of the universal truths. Through that line was the message of initiation available to all people. Those who followed the path of truth through the many lives of the initiate, were given the right to call themselves Is-ra-el-ite – the Holy Temple of the Living Light.

Romans 9

15 For He saith to Moses, I will have mercy on whom I will have mercy and I will have compassion on whom I will have compassion.

16 So then it is not of him that willeth, nor of him that runeth, but of God that sheweth mercy.

17 For the scripture saith unto Pharaoh, Even for this same purpose have I raised thee up, that I might shew My power in thee, and that My name might be declared throughout all the earth.

18 Therefore hath He mercy on whom He will have mercy, and whom He will He hardeneth.

19 Thou wilt say then unto me, Why doth He yet find fault? For who hath resisted His will?

20 Nay but, O man, who art thou that repliest against God? Shall the thing formed say to him that formed it, Why has thou made me thus?

21 Hath not the potter power over the clay, of the same lump to make one vessel unto honour, and another unto dishonour?

22 What if God, willing to shew His wrath, and to make His power known, endured with much long-suffering the vessels of wrath fitted to destruction:

23 And that He might make known the riches of His glory on the vessels of mercy, which He had afore prepared unto glory.

24 Even us, whom He hath called, not of the Jews only, but also of the Gentiles?

25 As He saith also in 0-see, I will call them My people, which were not My people; and her beloved, which was not beloved.

26 And it shall come to pass, that in the place where it was said unto them, Ye are not My people; there shall they be called the children of the living god.

(18-26) Justice and mercy shall be given to all who truly follow the path toward Divinity. It is not the birthright of any one race or people. The Divine Laws do not set Jew above gentile, for all are equal within the pursuit of divinity.[1]

(27-29) We who are Jews came from a much earlier race and time, yet the Creator has made it plain that those who were then called "His People" are not His only people. All are the children of the Living God. All of the prophets of old make the same commentary – to the effect that there is a remnant, a seed of that ancient race still extant on Earth. They are the true Is-ra-el-ites, the followers after righteousness, the seekers of the inner truths of initiation. They come from all races and are in no way confined to those who call themselves either Jew or Gentile.

Romans 9

27 Esaias also crieth concerning Israel, Though the number of the children of Israel be as the sand of the sea, a remnant shall be saved:

28 For He will finish the work, and cut it short in righteousness: because a short work will the Lord make upon the earth.

29 And as Esaias said before, Except the Lord of Sabaoth had left us a seed, we had been as Sodoma, and been made like unto Gomorrah.

30 What shall we say then? That the Gentiles, which followed not after righteousness, have attained to righteousness, even the righteousness which is of faith.

31 But Israel, which followed after the law of righteousness, hath not attained to the law of righteousness.

32 Wherefore? Because they sought it not by faith, but as it were by the works of the law. For they stumbled at that stumbling stone;

33 As it is written, Behold, I lay in Sion a stumbling stone and rock of offence: and whosoever believeth on Him shall not be ashamed.

(30-33) Those who call themselves Israelites have not followed universal law any more than those who call themselves by any other name. True Israelites of any nation are those who follow the Divine Laws. We have stumbled over this particular stumbling block, and now have clarity and truth through the message of Christ. Whoever believes that message need not be ashamed.[2]

DISCOURSE CHAPTER NINE

1. Q: It appears to me that you are changing the concept of God that is portrayed as Paul's concept in the King James version (9:22 and 9:28). For instance, in Chapter 9 you have left out references to God's wrath and judgement. Are you developing a concept of God that does not have as much wrath or judgement?

    A: There is no such entity as a wrathful, jealous God. In truth, the Supreme Godhead whose name cannot be spoken, the First Cause, Source of all things seen and not seen, created and not created, has created all that is as an ongoing process through which we all move, in which we all learn, no matter on what level we might be in existence. When one moves beyond the level of this earthly plane, there are no such negative emotions as anger or jealousy. For even those who have passed into the fifth kingdom, negative emotions are a thing that belong to the confinements of the earthly plane. They are not part of divinity in any way. That God to which the Old Testament refers is not, beloved ones, is not the Supreme Godhead. The one whom the Old Testament bible refers to as Jehovah is not the Supreme First Cause. That will rock the boat a little, will it not?

    Q: There appears to be a contradiction. You stated previously that the darkness is equally of God. "Darkness and the darker side of self is no more separate from God than is the light" (refer to page 48 paragraph #2). Then a little later you made the statement that "negative emotions are not part of divinity in any way". I wonder how those two statements fit together.

    A: Negative emotions are not part of divinity. So far as we are aware of the attributes of divinity, that source of all creation does not have emotions. Although part of what we might call first cause, darkness and light – as two distinct attributes, are separated in the form of energies; one might also consider the magnetic as opposed to the electric; the masculine as opposed to the feminine. These are polarities. And it is within the process of human evolution to begin to recognize that all is part of self and that self is part of all other within creation. That which we term evil is the opposing force, the opposite polarity which enables the evolving being to seek out the truth. It is indeed a truth that without the one opposite we cannot discern and define the other polarity. In other words, if one did not experience hatred, one could not discern what is love. If one did not experience cold, one could not define what is heat. The difference upon the earthly plane of interaction is that humanity reacts to each of these experiences. On the higher planes there is no reaction. What reactionary excesses create are problems within the astral emotional vehicle. And it is within that emotional vehicle, which is part of the incarnatory form, that we have our human difficulties. That emotional body is not part of the higher nature and therefore, cannot be considered to be a part of the Godhead.

Discourse Chapter Nine continued:

Q: Does that imply that the lower self is not part of the Godhead, that only the higher self is part of the Godhead?

A: No, it does not. It means that this is the learning process which is experienced upon the material level and when one eventually proceeds beyond the need for those exercises, one moves into the higher planes. Perhaps one should explain at this point there is a notion in the minds of many individuals which supposes that when one leaves this fleshly form, one moves into higher realms where all is peace, harmony and light. This is not the case. When the being leaves the fleshly vehicle, that one does so in the state of consciousness at the point of departure. That state of consciousness does not suddenly change when one arrives, as it were, at the other side. It remains exactly the same. However, because of the greater clarity which that one has of observation and because of the ability of the helping hands who are there present, it is possible for such a one to make assessment more easily and to look at those things which are outstanding and to bring those things into a more balanced state. This is work which is much more easily accomplished when not confined within the fleshly form. But there is a difference; it is a total misconception to imagine that when one leaves this gross flesh, one is immediately catapulted into an area where the consciousness is much higher. This is an ever ongoing process, no matter which realm one might occupy. I think that answers your question.

May I say, my dear friend, that questioning is something that we will never dispense with.

Q: You've made the statement that we cannot deal with Divine Law or Universal Law, or Natural Law in this document. Last time you made a reference that there was a place people could go to in order to find out what the universal law is. Could you be specific about that?

A: There are many treatises extant. That of brother Djwhal Khul is perhaps one of the most complete. Those who wish need only study his work. I myself have written several treatises which I called the *Teachings of the Temple;* one might study that. I see no reason whatsoever to repeat myself in this particular exercise. Those teachings are available for anyone who wishes to obtain them. And of course, there is the *Book of Dzyan* and there is the translation of the *Keys of Enoch.* If anyone wishes to make a study of the Universal Laws as they apply to this earthly plane, they need go no further than to study those works (See Bibliography in Appendix).

2. Q: Can you give some historical background to chapters 9, 10 and 11? There is some question among biblical scholars as to why they were included in the

Discourse Chapter Nine continued:

letter to the Romans. These chapters deal with the Jewish question. These three chapters are different than the other chapters in Romans. They have a benediction at the end. Was this a sermon that Paul had given that he included or was there discussion of this issue in the Roman church. It didn't seem like it fit with the rest of the letter and the Biblical scholars were wondering why it was there?

A: The three chapters to which you refer I think speak about the Jewish question and the country, do they not?

Q: Yes. And it says "will they openly be saved"? It deals with the fact that Jesus was sent to the Jews and they rejected him and then went to the Gentiles, but God's plan is still working...

A: It is really speaking of the whole dissent of the Israelite nation. The question, first of all, about these three chapters; why were they so apparently separate? I was writing at the time a general discourse to that small group of people in Rome concerning my own feelings about the message of Jesus and its significance and ramifications; and then it occurred to me that this might create a situation there in Rome because there were not only those present who were gentiles but also those who were of the Jewish persuasion and yes, indeed, those chapters as we now call them, were the subject of a separate discourse which was enclosed in the dispatches.

There is a very, very delicate issue in this whole subject of Israel. I suppose this is as good a time as any to address what that delicate issue really is. Really, it concerns the whole subject around Moses and the Exodus, and of the belief dear to their hearts even in this modern time, that they were given a promised land which should be maintained at all costs throughout history. It is sad, sad indeed, to see what that has done down through the ages.

Let us first begin historically and take a look at those countries which bordered the eastern end in that part of the world which we call Asia Minor.

And let us imagine certain war-like tribes, each one governed by a tribal chieftain who, along with many other pockets around the world, sought for more land, more hospitable land, places in which to grow their crops, settle their people, raise their animals. It has ever been the way to infiltrate into those lands which were felt to be more hospitable and, if necessary, to conquer them by war, bloodshed. Those war-like Semitic tribes spawned a course across those lands of the mideast even down into the delta lands of what was Egypt. In the course of history the story of their conquest of the Delta is very, very different than that which has been believed by the people of Israel since that time.

Discourse Chapter Nine continued:

They fought and wrested that land which became known as Israel from the peoples who were aboriginal to the country, took it by force, maintained it by force, and are continuing to do so to this day against all of the laws of the creator. There is no such country as Israel, my friends and the people who occupy it do not have an ancient right to it. Within all nations there are those who have attained levels of initiation who are the seed of the real truth, who maintain the knowledge of the higher wisdoms and who, throughout the evolutionary pattern of humanity, have held fast to those wisdoms. In that part of the world those who were of the faith which was called Jew were such because they indeed were the seed of the truth of the creator, brought in from a much earlier race who had been upon the earth plane long aeons prior to the beginning of written history in approximately 3000 B.C.

One of those seeds who carried the truth and the wisdom was Abraham. Those who have been recorded biblically as the prophets and the great priests are the seeds and they have attracted to themselves small pockets, usually of twelve, for that is part of the law. The groups again would meet in order to maintain the true knowledge, the wisdoms of the ages. And those who had passed to a specific degree of initiation at which he or she could be classified as the illumined one, was then an Israelite, a member of the body of the illumined. Those who fought and wrested the very soil of the delta lands of Egypt away from the natural inhabitants, the Egyptians, and who held the Egyptians in slavery for many, many decades, eventually paid a price. The Egyptian pharaoh who had maintained his throne in the regions of Thebes eventually overthrew the usurpers and the tables were turned. Those who called themselves children of Israel were, in turn, enslaved.

Eventually in history came the one Moses and we have the record of his Exodus from Egypt with those semitic people. Again, within the greater body there was the small nucleus, the seed, which was the bearer of the ancient wisdoms. It was the work of Moses the initiate and his brother Aaron and his sister Miriam to bring forth those wisdoms and return them out of the land of Egypt into a more clement country where the people might again settle in peace and learn again the true laws which they had long forgotten.

We are well acquainted with what has happened since that time. Jesus came into this earthly plane along with His group of twelve in order to set humanity back on course, in order to set the record straight, and to remind the people of His day of the truth and the nature of the law. Among the people into whom He chose to be born He was not heard by most. Therefore, it became necessary to take those words of truth, the reminder of the true laws out to other nations, other lands where there were pockets of the initiated, the mystery schools such

Discourse Chapter Nine continued:

as the Celtic druids; such as that at Persepolis; such as that in Greece and Eleusis etc., to remind the world of the truth and to set the course back toward the real Godhead, the true light. And here we are 2,000 years later and humanity is still disregarding the truth.

It takes a long time to discourse on the reason why it was necessary to write a separate part of the whole letter. It was greatly needed at that point in time to set the record straight to those elements in Rome who were of the Jewish tradition as separate from those who were not in order that they would be aware of the truth and deal accordingly.

ROMANS 10

10 Brethren, my heart's desire and prayer to God for Israel is, that they might be saved.

2 For I bear them record that they have a zeal of God, but not according to knowledge.

3 For they being ignorant of God's right-eousness, and going about to establish their own righteousness have not submitted themselves unto the righteousness of God.

4 For Christ is the end of the law for righteousness to every one that believeth.

5 For Moses describeth the right-eousness which is of the law, That the man which doeth those things shall live by them.

6 But the righteousness which is of faith speaketh on this wise, Say not in thine heart, Who shall ascend into heaven? (That is, to bring Christ down from above):

7 Or, Who shall descend into the deep? (That is, to bring up Christ again from the dead).

8 But what saith it? The word is nigh thee, even in thy mouth, and in thy heart: that is, the word of faith, which we preach;

9 That if thou shalt confess with thy mouth the Lord Jesus, and shalt believe in thine heart that God hath raised him from the dead, thou shalt be saved.

10 For with the heart man believeth unto righteousness; and with the mouth confession is made unto salvation.

11 For the scripture saith, Whosoever believeth on Him shall not be ashamed.

12 For there is no difference between the Jew and the Greek: for the same Lord over all is rich unto all that call upon him.

13 For whosoever shall call upon the name of the Lord shall be saved.

14 How then shall they call on him in whom they have not believed? And how shall they believe in Him of whom they have not heard? And how shall they hear without a preacher?

10 (1-4) Brothers, my heart's desire and my prayer to God is that Israel might be saved. They certainly are zealous of God, but that zeal is not based on true knowledge. Being ignorant of the true laws, and setting about the establishment of their own laws, they cut themselves off from knowledge of the truth. The message that Christ gave us is the law, as everyone who believes His word shall discover. It is the same truth that was given by Moses. Those who accept these true laws shall live by them.

(5-13) The righteousness of the true law says this: Do not ask who shall go to heaven or bring Christ down from some realm above, nor should you question who shall descend into the lower realms and whether Christ shall again ascend from there. What the law says is that each one has the true word, faith, in their own heart and may speak it through their own mouth. If we accept the message and the demonstration of the Divine Laws as demonstrated through Christ in Jesus, then we also accept that within each of us is the potential to become even as He, which is life eternal.

In this there is no difference between Jew and Greek, for the same Lord is available equally to all, and His message is the means by which all may follow His example.

(14-21) You might ask, what of those who did not see Him or hear Him? How can one call on One in whom they never believed? And how can they ever believe unless someone proclaim Him? Who will in fact go to proclaim without being sent? The old scriptures say "How beautiful are the feet of them that

Romans 10

15 And how shall they preach, except they be sent? As it is written, How beautiful are the feet of them that preach the gospel of peace, and bring glad tidings of good things.

16 But they have not all obeyed the gospel. For Esaias saith, Lord, who hath believed our report?

17 So then faith cometh by hearing and hearing by the word of God.

18 But I say, Have they not heard? Yes verily, their sound went into all the earth, and their words unto the ends of the world.

19 But I say, Did not Israel know? first Moses saith, I will provoke you to jealousy by them that are no people, and by a foolish nation I will anger you.

20 But Esaias is very bold, and saith, I was fond of them that sought me not; I was made manifest unto them that asked not after me.

21 But to Israel he saith, All day long I have stretched forth my hands unto a disobedient and gainsaying people.

preach the gospel of peace and bring glad tidings of good things"! Even Esaias (Isaiah) says "Lord, who has believed our report"? Faith comes only by hearing the Word of God. I say have they not, in fact, heard? I say indeed, the Word has gone forth to the very ends of the Earth and everyone has heard it. Israel has known very well, through first Moses, who said: "I will provoke you to jealousy by that which is no nation and with a nation void of understanding will I anger you …" Isaiah was even more daring when he said "I was fond of them that sought me not. I was made manifest by them that asked not after me … " Then, speaking of Israel, he said "All day long I stretched out my hands to those people who were disobedient and gainsaying."[1]

DISCOURSE CHAPTER TEN

1.   Q: Are you familiar with the Interpreter's Bible that I am using as a reference?

A: I don't think so.

Q: It is an 18 volume work done on the Bible put out by a committee. It is mainline Protestant. One of the people who wrote this* refers to Paul's "propensity of quoting the Old Testament" and his comment is "such a way of interpreting scripture may be, according to our modern standards, faulty to the point of being absurd, but it conforms to typical rabbinical exegesis in Paul's time". Do you want to comment on that?

A: Yes indeed, this is a very good question and one which does require attention. You see, the whole point behind the ministry of Jesus was as I have already stated to attempt to set the record straight. It is one thing to speak in parables to the simple folk in the villages of His day and quite another to go into the temple and address the rabbinical elders as their equal. If you recall, there were numerous occasions where He did that. In order to let it be seen that He was equal to them in his knowledge of the law, it was necessary to speak in terms of that which is written as the law by the Torah. When I myself spoke, it was in the same context because of course, at the time of writing the letters of Paul, there was no such thing as an Old Testament and New Testament. There were simply records of the words of the prophets of old from which the Torah had been composed – a composition of the words of the prophets and a composition of the written laws from those times. There was nothing else from which to draw that one might address in their terms. It would be the same in this modern day if I was to go forth and speak and say to people "read the words of my brother DK". Unless people were aware of what I meant, this is a foolish statement. Therefore, one has to address the hearer on the level of that which they know. And so far as the rabbinical elders were concerned at that time, all that most of them knew was the Kabbalah and the Torah and their various interpretations.

---

* Ibid: Page 563

ROMANS 11

11 *I say then, hath God cast away His people? God forbid. For I also am an Israelite, of the seed of Abraham, of the tribe of Benjamin.*

2 God hath not cast away His people which He foreknew. Wot ye not what the scripture saith of Elias? How he maketh intercession to God against Israel saying

3 Lord, they have killed thy prophets, and digged down thine altars, and I am left alone, and they seek my life.

4 But what saith the answer of God unto him? I have reserved to myself seven thousand men, who have not bowed the knee to the image of Baal.

5 Even so then at this present time also there is a remnant according to the election of grace.

6 And if by grace, then it is no more of works: otherwise grace is no more grace. But if it be of works, then is it no more grace: otherwise work is no more work.

7 What then? Israel hath not obtained that which he seeketh for; but the election hath obtained it, and the rest were blinded.

8 (According as it is written, God hath given them the spirit of slumber, eyes that they should not see, and ears that they should not hear;) unto this day.

9 And David said, "Let their table be made a snare, and a trap, and a stumbling block and a recompense unto them":

10 Let their eyes be darkened, that they may not see, and bow down their back alway.

11 I say then, Have they stumbled that they should fall? God forbid: but rather through their fall salvation is come unto the Gentiles, for to provoke them to jealousy.

11 (1-6) I say then, has God cast away His people? I would say "God forbid – for I too am an Israelite of the line of Abraham and of the tribe of Benjamin". God has not cast away the very people who were foredestined by Him. Do you not remember what the scripture said of Elias (Elijah) how he pleaded with God on behalf of Israel? He said "Lord, they have killed Thy prophets and dragged down Thine altars and I am left alone and they seek my life". How did God answer him? "I have left for myself seven thousand men who have not bowed the knee to the image of Baal". In just the same way, there is at this present time a minority who are elected, by grace, and if they are so chosen by grace, then this has nothing to do with their good works, otherwise what would be the point of grace.

(7-10) So what is our conclusion? That Israel did not obtain that which it sought? Only a chosen few got there and the rest were blind? According to the scriptures it is said "God hath given them the spirit of sleep, eyes that would not see and ears that would not hear, unto this day." David, said "Let their table be a snare and a trap and a stumbling block and a recompense unto them. Let their eyes be darkened that they may not see, and let their backs always be bowed."

67

Romans 11

12 Now if the fall of them be the riches of the world, and the diminishing of them the riches of the Gentiles; how much more their fullness?

13 For I speak to you Gentiles, inasmuch as I am the apostle of the Gentiles, I magnify mine office:

14 If by any means I may provoke to emulation from them which are my flesh, and might save some of them.

15 For if the casting away of them be the reconciling of the world, what shall the receiving of them be, but life from the dead?

16 For if the first fruit be holy, the lump is also holy; and if the root be holy, so are the branches.

17 And if some of the branches be broken off and thou, being a wild olive tree were graffed in among them, and with them partakest of the root and fatness of the olive tree;

18 Boast not against the branches. But if thou boast, thou bearest not the root, but the root thee.

19 Thou wilt say then, The branches were broken off that I might be graffed in.

20 Well; because of unbelief they were broken off and thou standest by faith. Be not high minded, but fear:

21 For if God spared not the natural branches, take heed lest He also spare not thee.

22 Behold therefore the goodness and severity of God: on them which fell severity; but toward thee, goodness, if thou continue in His goodness: otherwise thou also shall be cut off.

23 And they also, if they abide not still in unbelief shall be graffed in: for God is able to graff them in again.

(11-12) In response to this, I ask, "Have they stumbled, that they fall?" and I answer, "No, rather it was through their apparent fall that the means of salvation has been made plain to all people, even those we call the Gentiles." It is mostly through the pursuit of the material planes rather than the affairs of the Spirit that has caused humanity to fall. If I say this to the Gentiles equally as I say it to my own flesh and blood, then am I not equally an apostle of Christ, and minister to that office, equally for all?

(13-24) If the first fruit of the tree is holy, then we might assume that the branches too, and the tree itself, is holy. If some of the branches of that tree were to be broken off, and in their place some branches of the wild olive were grafted, so that they eventually would become the same as the whole tree, then why would we want to feel superior to the grafts? Remember, it is not the branches that support the tree, it is the roots that support the branches. Perhaps one might say that the branches were broken off so that the others could be grafted in.[1] I do not believe it is quite like that. I believe that lack of faith caused them to be broken, and those who have faith still remain. But we must be careful, because if God did not spare the natural branches of the tree, we should not assume that He will spare us. We must all look to our actions and continue to seek goodness, otherwise we too may be cut off. Using that same analogy, God is able to graft us all back into our natural family tree.

Romans 11

24 For if thou were cut out of the olive tree which is wild by nature, and wert graffed contrary to nature into a good olive tree: how much more shall these, which be the natural branches, be graffed into their own olive tree?

25 For I would not, brethren, that ye should be ignorant of this mystery lest ye should be wise in your own conceits; that blindness in part is happened to Israel until the fullness of the Gentiles be come in.

26 And so all Israel shall be saved: as it is written. There shall come out of Sion the Deliverer, and shall turn away ungodliness from Jacob:

27 For this is my covenant unto them, when I shall take away their sins.

28 As concerning the gospel they are enemies for your sakes: but as touching the election, they are beloved for the fathers' sakes.

29 For the gifts and calling of God are without repentance.

30 For as ye in times past have not believed God, yet have now obtained mercy through their unbelief:

31 Even so have these also now not believed, that through your mercy they also may obtain mercy.

32 For God hath concluded them all in unbelief that He night have mercy upon all.

33 O the depth of the riches both of the wisdom and knowledge of God! How unsearchable are His judgments, and His ways past finding out!

34 For who hath known the mind of the Lord? Or who hath been His counselor?

35 Or who hath first given to Him, and it shall be recompensed unto Him again?

36 For of Him, and through Him, and to Him, are all things: to Whom be glory for ever. Amen:

(25-32) Do not be in ignorance of this mystery. Do not be wise in your own conceit. It is partly this kind of blindness that has been the problem for Israel, and shall be so until the full number of those whom we call Gentiles is also reckoned. All of Israel will be saved, as the scriptures say: "There shall come out of Sion the Deliverer, and shall turn away ungodliness from Jacob. For this is My covenant unto them, when I shall take away their sins". So far as the gospels are concerned, they appear to be "enemies" of God's elect yet they are beloved for the Father's sake. Gifts and covenants of God are not subject to be rescinded. You know this yourselves, for even while in the past you did not believe, yet you still obtained His mercy during your unbelief.[2]

(33-36) How deep are the riches of God and how inscrutable His ways. Which of us has known the mind of God, or has been His counselor? Which of us has first given gifts to God before He gave them to us? Therefore of Him and through Him are all things, to Whom be glory forever.

DISCOURSE CHAPTER ELEVEN

1. Q: In 11:17-22 you use the illustration concerning the olive tree where the branches were cut off and grafted on were the branches of a wild olive; I think it is in reference to the Judaic roots and tree and the grafting on of the gentiles. You used the phrase "otherwise we too may be cut off" and my question is who would do the cutting?

   A: In this sense my reference is equal to saying in the same way that we judge, so too we are judged. In the cutting off of those whom we do not consider equal, we again incur the law of cause and effect and we build up for ourselves the very strong possibility that in another life we will be the ones who are not considered equal and therefore cut off. This is what I mean.

2. Q: The biblical scholar, John Knox* tries to express for Paul a problem that Paul had. He states, "Paul has done his best and when he writes these final sentences (of chapter 11) he is probably thinking of the entire argument to explain the meaning of the revelation of God in Christ, but he recognizes doubtless more acutely than any modern critical reader how full of gaps and/or inassimilable incompatible elements his argument has been. This is true not because he has not done well with what he has tried, but because the thing he has tried can never be done well, although we can never cease trying to do it, for who has known the mind of the Lord? God's being is the ground of our life. He is the source, the sustainer and end of all that exists. From Him, to Him and through Him are all things. How can we hope to comprehend Him who holds us and all things in His hand"? In other words, be is saying that there are gaps and things that are not understandable in Paul's writings but he did his best because what he was dealing with is in some ways incomprehensible.

   A: As a commentary upon my work that is very noteworthy. I myself could not express it any better. No matter in passing as the I that I Am in this moment, no matter what plane of existence one is working upon, That Which Is is so far beyond our imagining, how may we indeed interpret? We may only assume from the light of our own clarity and continue to ask at all times that the clearer light may be shown to us. Even as we attain that greater light, the source from which it comes also moves on ahead of us. We see fragments face to face and so much more is still seen through a mirror darkly, even though I am now become a man; a good point on which to end. Peace be with you.

---

* Ibid: Page 578

ROMANS 12

12 *I beseech you therefore, brethren, by the mercies of God, that ye present your bodies a living sacrifice, holy, acceptable unto God, which is your reasonable service.*

2 And be not conformed to this world, but be ye transformed by the renewing of your mind, that ye may prove what is that good, and acceptable, and perfect, will of God.

3 For I say, through the grace given unto me, to every man that is among you, not to think of himself more highly than he ought to think; but to think soberly, according as God hath dealt to every man the measure of faith.

4 For as we have many members in one body, and all members have not the same office:

5 So we, being many, are one body in Christ, and every one members one of another.

6 Having then gifts differing according to the grace that is given to us, whether prophecy, let us prophesy according to the proportion of faith;

7 Or ministry, let us wait on our ministering; or he that teacheth, on teaching;

8 Or he that exhorteth, on exhortation: he that giveth, let him do it with simplicity; he that ruleth, with diligence; he that sheweth mercy, with cheerfulness.

9 Let love be without dissimulations. Abhor that which is evil; cleave to that which is good.

10 Be kindly affectioned to one another with brotherly love; in honour preferring on another;

11 Not slothful in business; fervent in spirit: serving the Lord;

12 Rejoicing in hope; patient in tribulation; continuing instant in prayer;

13 Distributing to the necessity of saints; given to hospitality.

12 (1-2) Brothers, one thing I ask most strongly, and this is that you take more care of your bodies, as the Holy Temple wherein the soul dwells. This is your reasonable service to God. Do not conform so much to the things of this world, but rather be transformed by the renewal of your thinking, so that you may discover the living proof for yourselves of what is acceptable and perfect according to God.

(3-8) I have personally been given the grace to be able to tell you these things, every one of you. Let no one among you think of themselves more highly than others, but be careful to remember that God deals with each one according to his belief.[1] The human body has many parts, many organs, and each has its own function. So too we are each members of one Body, the body of Christ, and therefore we are each a part of the other, We all have different gifts, in accord with our individual talents. If our gift is that of prophecy, then let us prophesy according to that gift and the amount of faith we have in it. If we have the gift to minister, then let us minister, if it is to teach, then let us teach. Let those who wish to give, give freely, those that rule, do so wisely, and let those who wish to administer to the sick do so with good cheer.

(9-13) Abhor that which is evil and cling to that which is good, let there be no pretence at love. Deal kindly with one another, be honorable. Do not let laziness spoil your daily work and when you serve the Lord, do so with zeal. Be patient in all tribulation and rejoice always in hope. Let your prayers be constant. Give freely of your hospitality, and remember generously all those in need.

Romans 12

14 Bless them which persecute you: bless, and curse not, weep with them that weep.

15 Rejoice with them that do rejoice, and
16 Be of the same mind one toward another. Mind not high things, but condescend to men of low estate. Be now wise in your own conceits.

17 Recompense to no man evil for evil. Provide things honest in the sight of all men.

18 If it be possible, as much as lieth in you, live peaceably with all men.

19 Dearly beloved, avenge not yourselves, but rather give place unto wrath: for it is written, Vengeance is mine; I will repay, saith the Lord.

20 Therefore if thine enemy hunger, feed him; if he thirst, give him drink for in so doing thou shalt heap coals of fire on his head.

21 Be not overcome of evil, but overcome evil with good.

(13-21) If anyone should persecute you, then you must bless, rather than curse them. Rejoice with those who rejoice, and weep with them that weep. Consider everyone as equals, and do not allow your egos to put you higher than others. Do not give back evil for evil, but always be honest and upright in the eyes of others. As much as it is within your nature to do so, be at peace with all. Dear ones, do not seek vengeance, it is far better that you cool your anger, for the Lord has said that He will deal with injustice.[2] If your enemy is hungry, feed him, if thirsty, give him drink – for in doing so, you will make him ashamed. You are then not overreacting to evil, but rather, overcoming it with goodness.

DISCOURSE CHAPTER TWELVE

1. Q: You make a statement in 12:3 "Do not judge each other but let it be between God and the person because God will deal with each one according to their faith". Is this another way of saying the law of cause and effect or is this something different?

    A: The word "faith" I think there is an erroneous choice of wording. It is not in accordance with the true meaning of faith. What I was stating there is that we must not be the judge of another, no matter what the circumstance. Judgement of the actions of any being is a matter between that being and his own faith in that sense – his own concept of what is God. That which we look upon as the God-head, the Supreme Knower of all things, is the ultimate judge of what we all do and that ultimate source judges not, but leaves it to the discretion of each individualized soul to know what it is that they have created; and they themselves will expiate that effect in their own timing. Therefore, we do not, at any time, profess to judge another. Is that adequate? Perhaps we should substitute faith with the word belief. Faith has a different connotation than the word belief.

2. Q: In 12:19, you stated that "God is not a God of wrath, vengeance, etc." You state that "the Lord has said that He will deal with injustice." How does He deal with injustice? For many people that is a crucial question right now. How does God deal with what is happening to the planet?

    A: In the same way that everything else is dealt with; by the law of cause and effect. The karmic lords note all things including injustice. Whether that injustice be individual from one to another, or whether it be racial from one country to another, it is fully recorded by the Lords of Karma and that karma which is incurred shall be expiated in the same way. If it is a racial affair then the race will work out the karma. If it is an individual or a family affair, that family and the individuals who are part of that family will work out their karma. This is one of the laws which cannot be changed. In accordance with that which you do, so shall you receive. It is inevitable. Therefore, if any form of injustice is created between one party and another, one may rest assured that restitution shall occur sooner or later, sometimes when it is least expected and not always in the same lifetime. And of course, in the case of racial karma, it is quite often not in the same lifetime.

ROMANS 13

13 Let every soul be subject unto the higher powers. For there is no power but of God: the powers that be are ordained of God.

2 Whosoever therefore resisteth the power, resisteth the ordinance of God: and they that resist shall receive to themselves damnation.

3 For rulers are not a terror to good works, but to the evil. Wilt thou then not be afraid of the power? Do that which is good, and thou shalt have praise of the same:

4 For he is the minister of God to thee for good. But if thou do that which is evil be afraid; for he beareth not the sword in vain: for he is the minister of God, a revenger to execute wrath upon him that doeth evil.

5 Wherefore ye must needs be subject not only for wrath, but also for conscience sake.

6 For this cause pay ye tribute also: for they are God's ministers, attending continually upon this very thing.

7 Render therefore to all their dues: tribute to whom tribute is due; custom to whom custom; fear to whom fear; honour to whom honour.

8 Owe no man any thing, but to love one another: for he that loveth another hath fulfilled the law.

9 For this, Thou shalt not commit adultery, Thou shalt not kill Thou shalt not steal, Thou shalt not bear false witness, Thou shalt not covet; and if there be any other commandment, it is briefly comprehended in this saying, namely, Thou shalt love thy neighbour as thyself

10 Love worketh no ill to his neighbour: therefore love is the fulfilling of the law.

13 (1-6) All of our souls are subject to our higher selves and that higher power is God given.[1] Anyone who refuses to accept this refuses to accept the Divine Law, and creates for himself unnecessary suffering. Those who are in control do not turn against things that are good, but things that are bad. Should we then be fearful of our own higher power? Understand and do that which is good and the benefit shall be apparent to you. Your higher self is that which speaks of Godliness within you, but if you choose not to hear that counsel, then you had better be wary, for you incur the karmic responsibility that you alone will be required to expiate, even sometimes like a sword in its severity. The higher self and God's angels are ever at watch; the Lords of Karma let nothing go unnoticed. Therefore give to everyone their just due and honor the customs of all people.

(7-10) Although there are higher laws, the laws of God, and although we have our higher selves which are aware of the higher laws of God, this does not exonerate anyone who is in the physical form from adherence to the laws of the country in which the individual may find him or herself. I do not say is born, but may find him or herself, because it is quite immaterial whether one resides in the country of his birth. One should obey the laws of the country in which he or she is residing. In the same sense as when our Lord said "Render unto Caesar that which is Caesar's and render unto God that which is God's", I too urge you not to break the laws of the land in which you live. It is rightful that you pay your due taxes and that you pay attention to just laws, for many of the laws

Romans 13

11 And that, knowing the time, that now it is high time to awake out of sleep: for now is our salvation nearer than when we believed.

12 The night is far spent, the day is at hand: let us therefore cast off the works of darkness, and let us put on the armour of light.

13 Let us walk honestly as in the day; not in rioting and drunkenness, not in chambering and wantonness, not in strife and envying.

14 But put ye on the Lord Jesus Christ, and make not provision for the flesh, to fulfill the lusts thereof.

are written in order to keep a peaceful state of existence where possible. Do not be indebted to anyone, simply love one another. Those who love others fulfill the law. In order to comply with that law, you must not commit adultery, kill, steal, bear false witness against another. You should not covet someone else's possessions. In short, there is really no other command than that you love your neighbor as you love yourself. True love does not do another person harm, therefore love is the fulfillment of the law.

(11-14) It is time to wake up – there is less time than we think. The night is almost over, and the day is coming soon. We therefore need to stop doing those things that are of the darkness, and put on the full armor of the light. Let us walk honestly in the light of day. We cannot spend our time in rioting, drunkenness, and in following after sexual excesses.[2] We must not spend our time in envy and strife. We must cease making so much effort in satisfying the needs of the flesh, and rather expend our energies from now on in pursuits of the Spirit – even as we were shown by our Lord, Jesus the Christ.

DISCOURSE CHAPTER THIRTEEN

1. Q: In the beginning of chapter thirteen you talk about the soul and the higher self. What is the difference between higher self and soul?

   A: That which is usually referred to as soul is in fact a collective term for the three vital bodies of the higher self. As we have stated previously, the total self is in fact a seven faceted being. That which is generally regarded as the higher self operates on the level of will, wisdom, love and active intelligence and essentially the three facets of the lower self work with the same impulses, with the mind as it were the bridge between the two. Therefore, when we speak of higher self, as has been explained earlier, we speak of the three bodies, the Buddhic, the Atmic and the Monadic. Essentially all are part of the immortal soul. They are the finer bodies; and so when we speak of soul or what some call the causal body, we in fact speak of the three finer essences of being.

   Q: So higher self and soul are basically synonymous terms, they are interchangeable?

   A: Some people refer to soul as being the Monad per se, exclusively, whereas higher self is the being which has all three vehicles. Loosely one can regard both as being the higher self I suppose. But ultimately the soul is the Monad, the causal body; that which exists when all else has gone back into the One as of course all do eventually.

2. Q: In 13:13 your original comment was on walking honestly in the light of day, we cannot spend our time in rioting, drunkenness and in following after sexual pleasures. That sounds like an anti-sexual statement.

   A: No it is not, it is simply admonishing that one does not follow after lustful sex which is promiscuous. I think I have adequately stated that the sexual act is a natural God-given function. It is when it is carried to extreme and used wrongly that I can quarrel with it.

   Q: Would you want to enter those words, lustful and promiscuous sexual pleasures.

   A: Yes, I think so. Sexual excesses are really what we refer to in this case.

ROMANS 14

14 *Him that is weak in the faith receive ye, but not to doubtful disputations.*

2 For one believeth that he may eat all things: another, who is weak, eateth herbs.

3 Let not him that eateth despise him that eateth not; and let not him which eateth not judge him that eateth: for God hath received him:

4 Who art thou that judgest another man's servant? To his own master he standeth or falleth. Yea, he shall be holden up: for God is able to make him stand.

5 One man esteemeth one day above another: another esteemeth every day alike. Let every man be fully persuaded in his own mind.

6 He that regardeth the day, regardeth it unto the Lord; and he that regardeth not the day, to the Lord he doth not regard it: He that eateth, eateth to the Lord, for he giveth God thank; and he that eateth not, to the Lord he eateth not, and giveth God thanks.

7 For none of us liveth to himself and no man dieth to himself.

8 For whether we live, we live unto the Lord; and whether we die, we die unto the Lord: whether we live therefore, or die, we are the Lord's.

9 For to this end Christ both died, and rose, and revived, that He might be Lord both of the dead and living.

10 But why dost thou judge thy brother: Or why dost thou set at nought thy brother? For we shall all stand before the judgement seat of Christ.

11 For it is written As I live, saith the Lord, every knee shall bow to me and every tongue shall confess to God.

12 So then every one of us shall give account of himself to God.

14 (1-4) Don't enter into needless discourse about these things, but accept that people all have their own ways. Some believe that it is alright to eat whatever they wish, while others feel that in order to be more spiritual they eat herbs. There is no point in either feeling that theirs is the right way, for who are we to judge. Judgement is between each person and God. Only God knows where we each are in our progress.

(5-9) Again, some think one day is more holy than another; others think that all days are equal. This is something that each considers for himself. If we remember that every day is holy to the Lord, then if we count any day as not holy, we disrespect the Lord. When we eat, we give thanks for the gift given by God; if we do not eat, we still give thanks to God. No one either lives or dies of his own cause alone. Whether we live or die, we are still part of God. It was in order to demonstrate this very fact that Christ died and then rose again.

(10-13) Why do you judge or belittle each other? We all stand, equally, before the judgement seat of Christ.[1] It has been written that the Lord said every knee shall bow to Him, and every tongue will confess God. So then, let it be clear that we are each responsible to God alone, and cease to judge one another. Hear this, rather. Do not cause another person to fall by actions which you have set up.[2]

13 Let us not therefore judge one another any more: but judge this rather, that no man put a stumbling block or an occasion to fall in his brother's way.

14 I know, and am persuaded by the Lord Jesus, that there is nothing unclean of itself: but to him that esteemeth anything to be unclean, to him it is unclean.

15 But if thy brother be grieved with thy meat, now walkest thou not charitably. Destroy not him with thy meat, for whom Christ died.

16 Let not then your good be evil spoken of:

17 For the kingdom of God is not meat and drink; but righteousness, and peace, and joy in the Holy Ghost.

18 For he that in these things serveth Christ is acceptable to God, and approved of men.

19 Let us therefore follow after the things which make for peace, and things wherewith one may edify another.

20 For meat destroy not the work of God. All things indeed are pure; but it is evil for that man who eateth with offence.

21 It is good neither to eat flesh, nor to drink wine, nor anything whereby thy brother stumbleth, or is offended, or is made weak

22 Hast thou faith? Have it to thyself before God. Happy is he that condemneth not himself in that thing which he alloweth.

23 And he that doubteth is damned if he eat, because he eateth not of faith: for whatsoever is not of faith is sin.

(13-23) I am totally convinced by the words of the Lord Jesus, that there is nothing that is unclean, of itself. Things can only be impure if we want to consider them so. If anyone is displeased with the things that we do, we must cease to do them out of love. Do not upset another person, who is also a part of Christ. Remember that true spirituality has nothing to do with what we eat or drink, but is a matter of faith, peace and joy in Divine power. If we diligently follow these precepts, we serve Christ, we are acceptable before God, and men. Let us therefore seek those things which preserve peace, and the upliftment of each other.

DISCOURSE CHAPTER FOURTEEN

1. Q: In 14:10 you use the phrase "before the judgement seat of Christ". Is this the same as law of cause and effect or the judgement seat of God?

    A: That which is referred to in this manner in no way contradicts what has already been said about karma. I think here a little clarity is required in the sense that the Lord Christ is the Supreme Head of the archangelic realms. Since that is so, He stands in authority over all of the streams which affect humanity including karma. The Lords of Karma and the Lords of Destiny are all under His guidance. In this sense that particular expression may be explained.

2. Q: In 14:13 you use the sentence "Do not cause another person to fall by actions which you have set up". I was wondering about the phrase "set up".

    A: What is meant here is that it is quite often possible to take a course of action oneself knowing that by so doing one will inevitably lead another into a harmful situation. My statement in effect is that it were better to avoid taking any kind of action if in so doing one knows that this is harmful to another, or will cause that other person to do something which is harmful to himself. One might in this case be thought as having been "set up" to use current phraseology.

ROMANS 15

15 We then that are strong ought to bear the infirmities of the weak and not to please ourselves.

2 Let every one of us please his neighbour for his good to edification.

3 For even Christ pleased not Himself; but, as it is written, The reproaches of them that reproached thee fell on me.

4 For whatsoever things were written aforetime were written for our learning, that we through patience and comfort of the scriptures might have hope.

5 Now the God of patience and consolation grant you to be likeminded one toward another according to Christ Jesus;

6 That ye may with one mind and one mouth glorify God, even the Father of our Lord Jesus Christ.

7 Wherefore receive ye one another, as Christ also received us to the glory of God.

8 Now I say that Jesus Christ was a minister of the circumcision for the truth of God; to confirm the promises made unto the fathers:

9 And that the Gentiles might glorify God for His mercy; as it is written, For this cause I will confess to thee among the Gentiles; and sing unto thy name.

10 And again He saith, Rejoice, ye Gentiles, with his people.

11 And again; Praise the Lord, all ye Gentiles; and laud him, all ye people.

12 And again, Esaias saith, There shall be a root of Jesse and he that shall rise to reign over the Gentiles; in him shall the Gentiles trust.

13 Now the God of hope fill you with all joy and peace in believing, that ye may abound in hope, through the power of the Holy Ghost.

15 (1-6) Those of us who are stronger should help others who are weak. Let us each help others toward the higher life. Christ did not come simply to please himself, but to assist us all. If another is worthy of reproach, then so am I. All of the old writings have been left for our learning, so that through diligently seeking, we may have enlightenment. Let us hope that we may exercise the same patience and encouragement to each other, as God allows to us, through the example of Christ Jesus so that we may be of one mind and voice in giving God the praise; that same God whom Jesus the Christ called Father. Let us think of each other in exactly that same way.

(9-13) Christ chose to be born into the Jewish line in order to fulfill the prophesies made to the Patriarchs, but not for that alone. He also was teacher to the Gentiles, so that they too would be aware of the Divine Laws. In His own words, He asked that Jew and Gentile alike praise the One God and accept the truth. Isaiah said "There shall be a root of Jesse and He that shall rise to rule the Gentiles. In Him shall the Gentiles trust". May that same God of Hope fill you with all joy and peace in your belief, so that hope may abound through the power of the Holy Spirit.

Romans 15

14 And I myself also am persuaded of you, my brethren, that ye also are full of goodness, filled with all knowledge, able also to admonish one another.

15 Nevertheless, brethren, I have written the more boldly unto you in some sort, as putting you in mind, because of the grace that is given to me of God.

16 That I should be the minister of Jesus Christ to the Gentiles, ministering the gospel of God, that the offering up of the Gentiles might be acceptable, being sanctified by the Holy Ghost.

17 I have therefore whereof I may glory through Jesus Christ in those things which pertain to God.

18 For I will not dare to speak of any of those things which Christ hath not wrought by me, to make the Gentiles obedient, by word and deed.

19 Through mighty signs and wonders, by the power of the Spirit of God; so that from Jerusalem, and round about unto Illyricum, I have fully preached the gospel of Christ.

20 Yea, so have I strived to preach the gospel, not where Christ was named, lest I should build upon another man's foundation:

21 But as it is written, To whom he was not spoken of, they shall see: and they that have not heard shall understand.

22 For which cause also I have been much hindered from coming to you.

23 But now having no more place in these parts, and having a great desire these many years to come unto you;

24 Whensoever I take my journey into Spain, I will come to you: for I trust to see you in my journey, and to be brought on my way thitherward by you, if first I be somewhat filled with your company.

25 But now I go unto Jerusalem to minister unto the saints.

(14-21) I myself am convinced that you are filled with sufficient knowledge and goodness that you may be of help to one another. Nevertheless, I have been outspoken in what I have said to you because of the power and grace that God has given me. I have been entrusted with the ministry of the Word of God through Christ, to pass on to the Gentiles, so that their lives might also be sanctified by that same power. All that I know has been given to me through Christ, otherwise I would not have the ability to speak of these things. He has performed miracles before me by the power of the Spirit of God, so that all the way from Jerusalem as far as Illyricum I have ably preached the message of Christ. I have tried as far as possible to go to those areas where the name of Christ would have otherwise been unknown, and in this way, I have avoided building upon someone else's foundations.

(22-29) This has, however, been the main thing that has prevented my visiting you. Now though, since much of my work in these areas is complete, I should be able to come to you when it becomes possible for me to go to Spain. I trust, after I have seen you, you will then be able to speed me on my journey there. At the present time, however, I must return to Jerusalem, to assist Christ's people there. The people of Macedonia and Achaea have been kind enough to make a contribution to help the poor in Jerusalem. This is very pleasing for it shows that when those people recognize their spiritual connection, they also wish to help in worldly matters of need.[1] As soon, therefore, as I have taken this help to them, I shall set off for Spain. I am assured

26 For it hath pleased them of Macedonia and Achaia to make a certain contribution for the poor saints which are at Jerusalem.

27 It hath pleased them verily; and their debtors they are. For if the Gentiles have been made partakers of their spiritual things, their duty is also to minister unto them in carnal things.

28 When therefore, I have performed this, and have sealed to them this fruit, I will come by you into Spain.

29 And I am sure that, when I come unto you, I shall come in the fullness of the blessing of the gospel of Christ.

30 Now I beseech you, brethren, for the Lord Jesus Christ's sake, and for the love of the Spirit, that ye strive together with me in your prayers to God for me;

31 That I may be delivered from them that do not believe in Judea; and that my service which I have for Jerusalem may be accepted of the saints;

32 That I may come unto you with joy by the will of God, and may with you be refreshed.

33 Now the God of peace be with you all. Amen.

that when I arrive in your midst we shall all receive great blessings in Christ.

(30-33) Meantime, please brothers, for the sake of our Lord Christ, lend me your help by your prayers, so that I shall be kept safe from my opponents in Judea, and also in order that the things I bear to Jerusalem for their aid, shall be acceptable.[2] I look forward with joy to my visit with you and, God willing, shall be refreshed there. Now may the God of peace be with you. Amen.

DISCOURSE CHAPTER FIFTEEN

1. Q: What was the significance of the collection that you were making for the people in Jerusalem?

    A: The fact that for many decades those who preferred to follow the teachings of our Lord were unable to live in normal circumstances. Most lived in abject poverty as a result of their chosen path. On the other hand, many of the people in Rome and those in Greece and Thessaly were by comparison fairly well to do and I made it my business and that of my helpers to offer the opportunity to assist brothers and sisters who were still in Jerusalem so that it would be possible to procure for them those things that were needed to help the sick particularly and to help the children and the aged. After all, if those bands of people who elected to follow the teachings were unable to do so in a very concrete manner and show their love even to those who they had not seen, then what purpose was there. I felt it important that one not only preach The Word, but live by it. Therefore, each time I set forth I endeavored to return to the faithful in Jerusalem or to send word and help by messengers.

    Q: The biblical detectives were trying to figure out if you collected for a few years and made one trip or whether this was frequent.

    A: No, no, this was something I did all the time.

2. Q: In 15:30-31 you mention that you wanted the prayers of the people in Rome to help protect you against those who might do you harm in Judea. Do you wish to say who it was that you needed protection from?

    A: Mostly the Romans by this time. You will remember of course that I started out being their instrument. And now, suddenly here I am Christ's instrument. This always creates conflict. There were, among the governors throughout Judea, those who regarded me as a turncoat. My position was at best uneasy and often quite dangerous. My point therefore was to ask for the assistance of my brothers and sisters in the light that a positive field of light would at all times be around me which it is not always possible for the person to maintain for themselves alone. In such dangerous situations, it is of great benefit to have the thought forms of others assisting. This is why group prayers, group meditation is always important; where two or three or more are gathered together, the positive thought form that is created is infinitely more strong than ever any individual may attain.

    Q: Why did you go to Rome and was it as a prisoner from Jerusalem?

    A: Oh, I went to Rome under my own steam of course. Eventually I was taken to Rome as a prisoner but I had visited there of my own volition on earlier

Discourse Chapter Fifteen continued:

occasions, quite naturally. One always had to be careful travelling in Rome and in Judea, either one. It was highly dangerous for reasons that I have just stated. But where there is work to do it must be done. One does not regard danger to one's person about that path which one has chosen.

Q: That raises another question, did you get to Spain?

A: No, I did not.

Q: Most scholars feel you didn't.

A: Yes, indeed.

ROMANS 16

16 *I commend unto you Phoebe our sister, which is a servant of the church which is at Cenchrea:*

2 That ye receive her in the Lord, as becometh saints, and that ye assist her in whatsoever business she hath need of you: for she hath been a succourer of many, and of myself also.

3 Greet Priscilla and Aquila my helpers in Christ Jesu:

4 Who have for my life laid down their own necks: unto whom not only I give thanks, but also all the churches of the Gentiles.

5 Likewise greet the church that is in their house. Salute my well beloved Epaenetus, who is the firstfruits of Achaia unto Christ.

6 Greet Mary, who bestowed much labour on us.

7 Salute Andronicus and Junia, my kinsmen, and my fellow prisoners, who are of note among the apostles, who also were in Christ before me.

8 Greet Amplias my beloved in the Lord.

9 Salute Urbane, our helper in Christ, and Stachys my beloved.

10 Salute Apelles approved in Christ. Salute them which are of Aristobulus' household.

11 Salute Herodion my kinsman. Greet them that be of the household of Narcissus, which are in the Lord.

12 Salute Tryphena and Tryphosa, who labour in the Lord. Salute the beloved Persis, which laboured much in the Lord.

13 Salute Rufus chosen in the Lord, and his mother and mine.

14 Salute Asyncritus, Phlegon, Hermas, Patrobas, Hermes, and the brethren which are with them.

16 (1-2) I commend to you our sister Phoebe. She is a member of the Church at Cenchrea. Since she brings to you my letter, I would ask that you receive her properly and assist her in any way that she needs help.

(3-16) I would ask also that you give my greetings to Priscilla and Aquila, my helpers in Christ.[1] They have laid down their very lives to help me, and I give not only personal thanks to them, but also to the churches that they are part of. Salute Epaenetus whom I love well, and who was the first of the Achaeans to be converted to Christ. Please also give my love to Mary who gave so much help too, and Andronicus and Junia my own kinspeople. They were prisoners with me and well known among the servers of Christ. In fact they were part of the body of Christ before I was. Give my greetings to my well loved Amplias, and to Urbane and Stachys, also Apelles. I send greetings to the household of Aristobullus, and that of Narcissus, and to my kinsman Herodion. Greetings to Tryphena and Tryphosa and to Persis who work hard for the Lord. Especial greetings to Rufus, such a great Christian, and his mother who has been mother to me also. Greetings to Asyncritus, Phlegon, Hermas, Patrobas, Hermes and their brothers, Philologus, Julia, Nereus and his sister, Olympas and all the workers who are with them. Give each other a holy kiss. The churches of Christ all salute you.

Romans 16

15 Salute Philologus, and Julia, Nereus, and his sister, and Olympas, and all the saints which are with them.

16 Salute one another with an holy kiss. The churches of Christ salute you.

17 Now I beseech you, brethren, mark them which cause divisions and offenses contrary to the doctrine which ye have learned; and avoid them.

18 For they that are such serve not our Lord Jesus Christ, but their own belly; and by good words and fair speeches deceive the hearts of the simple.

19 For your obedience is come abroad unto all men. I am glad therefore on your behalf but yet I would have you wise unto that which is good, and simple concerning evil.

20 And the God of peace shall bruise Satan under your feet shortly. The grace of our Lord Jesus Christ be with you. Amen.

21 Timotheus my workfellow, and Lucius, and Jason, and Sosipater, my kinsmen, salute you.

22 I Tertius, who wrote this epistle, salute you in the Lord.

23 Gaius mine host, and of the whole church, saluteth you. Erastus the chamberlain of the city saluteth you, and Quartus a brother.

24 The grace of our Lord Jesus Christ be with you all. Amen.

25 Now to him that is of power to establish you according to my gospel, and the preaching of Jesus Christ, according to the revelation of the mystery, which was kept secret since the world began.

26 But now is made manifest, and by the scriptures of the prophets, according to the commandment of the everlasting God, made known to all nations for the obedience of faith:

27 To God only wise, be glory through Jesus Christ for Ever. Amen.

(17-20) One final warning: Take especial note of people who cause offence and divisiveness. These things are contrary to the teachings you have learned and need to be avoided. Such people do not serve Christ, but their own lesser nature. They often deceive by fair words. Your steadfastness has become well known abroad, I am happy to say, and I would prefer that you stay on course. Let God deal with the others, and may His Grace be with you.[2]

(21-23) Timothy my companion and Lucius and Jason and Sosipater my kinsmen send their greetings. (I Tertius who have written down this letter for Paulinus, send also my own greetings). Gaius our host, and all of the Church here, send their greetings to you as does Erastus the City treasurer, and Quartus one of the brothers.

(24-27) I now commend you all to the Grace of our Lord Jesus Christ. He it is who has the power to sustain you. That which is now being revealed is part of a teaching which has been held secret since the beginnings of the world. Those Ancient Wisdoms shall no longer be a mystery as in the days of the prophets, but shall become known to anyone in any nation, who wishes to be obedient to them. For this I praise God, to Whom is all honor and glory, through Jesus the Christ, for ever. Amen.

Written from Corinth late in the year of Our Lord 56 AD.

DISCOURSE CHAPTER SIXTEEN

1. Q: There is considerable discussion about chapter 16 as to whether it was part of the original or whether it was added on at a later time. This is the chapter with all the names in it.

    A: I made the notes while still in Ephesus and the final touches were put on to it in Corinth and therefrom dispatched. The salutations were all added in Corinth to the notes already made. It is a question of having made notes, now what will I say to this group and what will I say about that subject, and one makes frequent notes. Eventually one has it all together and then puts it into a cohesive form to send; and having done that, one then adds the final touch. In that sense those were strictly additions.

    Q: Our biblical detectives have trouble with the reference to Priscilla and Aquila because they were supposedly in Ephesus and not in Rome. Were they in both places or are they different people?

    A: No they are not different people. It is simply that they were at the time in Rome. They too travelled around you know. Priscilla incidentally is the one who actually wrote to the Hebrews while on her travels. A very dear friend.

2. Q: There is a paragraph in 16:17-20 which is different and that is the "warning chapter" where you warn them against people who cause offence and divisiveness. Was it added as an afterthought?

    A: It was; "oh, and by the way."

    Q: One of the biblical scholars said that is what Paul probably did. He probably had a scribe he was dictating to and said oh, just add this.

    A: Exactly so.

    Q: Was there a specific target for that "by the way"?

    A: Oh there was indeed. Yes. You see Rome above all, well perhaps Rome and Judea in a sense had the same problem. We have the intercourse between the political aspects coming from Rome, remembering that the country and in particular, the capital, Jerusalem, had been held in close scrutiny by Rome for some considerable time by the time I wrote my letter. One had to be careful not only of what one said but to whom one said it.

Discourse Chapter Sixteen continued:

There were elements in Rome, young Jews coming from Jerusalem whom one might have expected could be trusted. It was however, later discovered that many of them were not trustworthy. The same could always be said throughout Judea. People whom one might expect to be trustworthy, were doubtful. Often those whom one might have doubted turned out to be totally strong. Since I travelled frequently it would mean a different camp. I felt it wise to admonish people to be on guard. And so it came in a sense of an "oh, by the way, be careful".

Q: Part of the question here is that there had been discussion as to whether this section was added later and maybe referred to the Gnostics. Then the other scholars say that was after Paul's time and the Gnostics hadn't really raised their heads yet.

A: I am not quite sure I am following you. You are saying that some say that this came as an afterthought of my own whereas others are saying that this is an afterthought added by translators.

Q: Probably the translators.

A: No, it was my own afterthought.

I feel very pleased with the way we are working together. And so, dear ones, the blessings of God the Father, God the Son and God the Holy Ghost, the Divine Mother, be with us and remain with us now and always. And may the love of God which is in Christ be in our hearts this day and evermore. Peace be with you.

THE INTRODUCTION TO THE FIRST LETTER OF PAUL TO THE THESSALONIANS

I should like now to commence the work of the other letters in a more strict chronological order.

The letter (so called) to the Romans, was given first because it appears first in the Bible for a good reason. This has been acknowledged down the centuries not so much as a true letter, but rather more of a discourse on my thoughts and feelings. It therefore became the dial upon which most Paulian theology was recorded (erroneously or otherwise). Best therefore, that this be the barometer once again of the tone which the new discourses will set.

We will now turn to Thessalonians, which was the first of my actual letters (in the stricter sense of that title). We will remember that this letter was written in the year of Our Lord 50 AD., some 17 years after the event which has been described as the "Conversion of Saul". During those years there is very little of record concerning my evolution up to the point of writing the notorious letters. Let me therefore state that this was not, of course, the very first time I had set myself down to write to the many groups around Asia Minor and Eastern Europe which had sprung up during those years of the ministry of my Brother Apostles and myself.

This first letter to the Thessalonians contains one of the most important theological discussions in the whole Bible and we should look more deeply at the meaning. It is not possible to translate that deeper meaning within the context of the actual translated work from the King James' version into modern and more truthful idiom. I will therefore deal with the chapters in question now, fully, bearing in mind that humanity has made much progress in its understanding since the days in which those words were (attempted) to be translated.

I speak to the message in chapters 4 and 5 which talks about the words of God regarding those who are "dead", and the matter of "staying awake to the Second Coming..."

This message was very deep and was put within the context of the larger letter, for those who at that time were sufficiently advanced on the initiatory path, to fully understand what I was getting at. I am speaking of the very essence of the message of Christ in referring to the consciousness of humanity which, I stated, must at all times seek fervently to become one body with Christ. That is, to bring the individualized body of light into the same vibrational frequency as that of the Universal Christ. We shall, all of us, one day become part of His Garment of Light. This is a much higher relevance than the translation of the old texts, for it speaks to the evolutionary path of humanity and has nothing whatever to do with the "dead" rising at the last "trump" to be judged.

Whether one still adheres to the old Hebrew Zohar in the belief of the coming of a Messiah, or whether one is a Christian who believes in the second "Coming of Christ", or whether one is an esotericist and thinks in terms of the descent of the Fifth Kingdom, it is all the same. The important truth is that there shall be a descent of the Lord of Light. When this event happens, the most righteous will be "caught up" to receive blessings, and as co-regents in His Kingdom, the "Body of Christ", they will assist in the final anointing of His Saints on Earth.

What is meant by the words "The Lord Himself shall descend from Heaven with a shout, with the voice of the Archangel and the Trump of God, and the dead in Christ shall rise first; then we that are alive shall be caught up together . . ."? Namely: In these last times, the Earth shall undergo great changes in order to release the negativity of emotions which have entrapped her own Body of Light. In the releasing of matter, there shall be seen within the surrounding auric field (skies) of Earth a great "message", a clarion call signalling all who are clear enough to understand. We shall be called to participate in a Higher Intelligence, which will be the New Order of Evolution.

You must understand that these things work in cycles. There are great periods of evolution and involution marked in the precessional passage of the Zodiac. Within the physical form of Earth and all who live upon her, there is an etheric counterpart, a "Light Body" which continually replicates not only the physical personality but also builds upon the light body as it passes into other dimensions. The knowledge of all that has ever been present in the many rounds of incarnation is contained in the cellular memory. Eventually man passes beyond the programming of the RNA/DNA molecules within the physical form and passes into a Being of Light. The physical body is therefore the least important. When the Essential Being is released from the entrapment within the flesh, the Body of Light takes over. The Light body is composed of units of light which pulsate to an ever increasing frequency or vibratory rhythm. It is the work of these units of light (memory banks) within the individualized being to constantly monitor the frequency, until each aligns with the quickening pulse, not only of the planet on which that one finds itself, but also to be aligned with the incoming frequencies of the overlighting impulse. That quickening impulse shall return to Earth during the passage through the influence of Aquarius.

THE FIRST LETTER OF PAUL TO THE THESSALONIANS

1 Paul, and Silvanus and Timotheus, unto the church of the Thessalonians which is in God the Father and in the Lord Jesus Christ: Grace be unto you, and peace, from God our Father and the Lord Jesus Christ.

2 We give thanks to God always for you all, making mention of you in our prayers;

3 Remembering without ceasing your work of faith, and labour of love, and patience of hope in our Lord Jesus Christ, in the sight of God and our Father;

4 Knowing brethren beloved, your election of God.

5 For our gospel came not unto you in word only, but also in power, and in the Holy Ghost, and in much assurance; as ye know what manner of men we were among you for your sake.

6 And ye became the followers of us, and of the Lord, having received the word in much affliction, with joy of the Holy Ghost:

7 So that ye were examples to all that believe in Macedonia and Achaia.

8 For from you sounded out the word of the Lord not only in Macedonia and Achaia, but also in every place your faith to Godward is spread abroad; so that we need not to speak any thing.

9 For they themselves shew of us what manner of entering in we had unto you, and how ye turned to God from idols to serve the living and true God;

10 And to wait for His Son from heaven, whom He raised from the dead, even Jesus, which delivered us from the wrath to come.

1 (1) Paul, Silvanus (he who was the chief amanuensis of our Brother, Peter, latterly) and Timothy have pleasure to send our greetings to the Brethren in Thessaly. May the Grace of God the Father, and the Blessing of Christ who was in Jeshua[1] be with you.

(2-7) We continually give thanks for you and we remember you in our prayers. We are encouraged by the unceasing work of faith that you perform, by your labors of love and by your patient hope. We are well aware that you are part of the Brotherhood of the Elect, for our good news was given to you not only in words, but was apparent in the power of the Holy Spirit that came upon you. You fully realized when we formulated your community, what manner of teachings we gave to you. It was a great joy to us that you became followers of the truth as taught by Jeshua the Christ.

(8-10) We support you as excellent examples to all of the other believers throughout Macedonia and Achaia. In fact so well has your message been heard and understood throughout those areas, that it seems unnecessary for us to further address these matters. From all this, it is self evident how you understood what we said. You have set aside idolatry for the One True Faith. You now serve the Living God, and you shall remain faithful unto the Day when we all shall see the Living Christ, and be delivered from the Wrath to come.[2]

DISCOURSE CHAPTER ONE

A. We are going to address the subject of Thessalonians, aren't we. Before you start asking questions of me, I would like to ask a general question. It is noted that the subject of Romans has been one of perhaps more controversy than all the other letters. This is one of the main reasons why I chose to take the subject of Romans first, not merely that it appears first in the sequence of the collection which is called the New Testament. This, in my current thinking, is rather strange because the letters to the Thessalonians, in fact, contain a subject far more controversial and I wonder what is your comment thereto.

Q: I think the reason Romans may have gotten more attention is the fact that it is the (as you yourself stated) more systematic presentation of all of Paul's thought. That may be the main reason. As far as I am aware, particularly First and Second Corinthians, all of them got a good deal of attention; Romans just had more to bite into.

A: Possibly more obvious statements to bite into. The references in Thessalonians which I might have thought more controversial because they deal with the whole subject of death and rebirth, are not stated so in the translated letter. I feel that perhaps the more esoteric message has been completely overlooked down the years. Yes? Good then, shall we proceed?

1. Q: You have started using the name Jeshua instead of Jesus.

   A: Jeshua was the Hebrew name. Jesus was the name that was given by the Romans. Therefore, when writing to the Romans, I used the name which they most remembered. When writing to other areas in which the Romanized version is not so familiar, I mostly used the Hebrew name which is Jeshua.

2. Q: In regards to First Thessalonians, Paul, in the versions we have, makes reference in all his letters to the "parousia" the immanent coming of Christ. (1:10 and 4:18). Did Paul believe that the second coming was immanent? If not, what was encouraging this belief among the early Christians? I realize that you deal with your own views in the introduction to Second Thessalonians.

   A: Yes indeed. There is a great deal of mistaken concept between what is regarded as the imminent coming of Christ and the actuality. The high wisdoms indicate that the coming of Christ shall be in the heart of each individual being. It is not strictly referring to a descent of a physical person.

Discourse Chapter One continued:

Although it is at this point in time, namely the year 1989, a little closer to the point when those who are now known more widely as the Spiritual Hierarchy may quite well indeed return on the physical plane level in order to pave the way for the eventual return in the physical person of the Christ, but it is a Christ office, not the return of one Jesus of Nazareth, that which we speak. That Christ office is no longer held by the same Jesus of Nazareth. It is now held at the moment, by one whom we know as Maitraya. That is the office of the Universal Christ.

The office of World Teacher which is the one that was fulfilled by Jeshua ben Joseph is now held jointly between our Lord of the second ray Kuthumi and Jesus. And so from the higher spiritual or esoteric standpoint, we are not now talking about the same thing that people were talking about back in those days. The early churches believed quite ardently in a physical return of Jesus as the Christ and this was not what He was speaking about. What He was speaking about was that we need to all let the I AM presence be so clearly within each one of us that His Spirit would be again with us. That indeed, with the right amount of personal attention, could be at any point in time, yet He was wise enough to say it might be a long time, knowing how long it takes for the consciousness to oblige. I think that is all we need to say here because I have made it fairly clear what is referred to by the taking on the whole Body of Christ, the Garment of Light, in my further discourses.

FIRST THESSALONIANS 2

2 *For yourselves, brethren, know our entrance in unto you, that it was not in vain:*

2 But even after that we had suffered before, and were shamefully entreated, as ye know, at Philippi, we were bold in our God to speak unto you the gospel of God with much contention.

3 For our exhortation was not of deceit, nor of uncleanness, nor in guile:

4 But as we were allowed to God to be put in trust with the gospel, even so we speak; not as pleasing men, but God, which trieth our hearts.

5 For neither at any time used we flattering words, as ye know, nor a cloke of covetousness; God is witness:

6 Nor of men sought we glory, neither of you, nor yet of others, when we might have been burdensome, as the apostles of Christ.

7 But we were gentle among you, even as a nurse cherisheth her children:

8 So being affectionately desirous of you, we were willing to have imparted unto you, not the gospel of God only, but also our own souls, because ye were dear unto us.

9 For ye remember, brethren, our labour and travail: for labouring night and day, because we would not be chargeable unto any of you, we preached unto you the gospel of God.

10 Ye are witnesses, and God also, how holily and justly and unblameably we behaved ourselves among you that believe:

11 As ye know how we exhorted and comforted and charged every one of you, as a father doth his children,

12 That ye would walk worthy of God, who hath called you unto His kingdom and glory.

2 (1-8) You are aware of the impact that was made upon you. We are happy that you saw the truth, that there was no guile or deceit in us (especially after the unfortunate way that we were treated when we visited Philippi), and that we were empowered by God to speak the good news.[1] Even as God entrusted us to tell you the good news, so did we speak to you. We seek not to please man, but to please God before Whom all hearts are known. As that same God is our witness, we did not ever seek to flatter, we were not covetous, and sought no glory for ourselves, as Apostles of Christ. We have always dealt gently with you in the same way that a nurse would deal with a child. This being so, and holding a great affection for you, we not only shared the true teachings of God with you, but we bared our very souls to you.

(9-12) We have worked endlessly to bring the message of truth and hope to you, because we do not wish to be charged with failure.[2] You, our friends are witness, as well as God is our witness, that we have been just, holy and blameless in our dealings with you. We have treated you as a father would treat his own children. We have trusted that you would from that time, walk worthily before God who has given you His Kingdom and His Glory.

First Thessalonians 2

13 For this cause also thank we God without ceasing, because, when ye received the word of God which he heard of us, ye received it not as the word of men, but as it is in truth, the word of God, which effectually worketh also in you that believe.

14 For ye, brethren, became followers of the churches of God which in Judaea are in Christ Jesus; for ye also have suffered like things of your own countrymen, even as they have of the Jews:

15 Who both killed the Lord Jesus, and their own prophets, and have persecuted us; and they please not God, and are contrary to all men:

16 Forbidding us to speak to the Gentiles that they might be saved, to fill up their sins alway: for the wrath is come upon them to the uttermost.

17 But we, brethren, being taken from you for a short time in presence, not in heart, endeavored the more abundantly to see your face with great desire.

18 Wherefore we would have come unto you, even I Paul, once and again; but Satan hindered us.

19 For what is our hope, or joy, or crown of rejoicing? Are not even ye in the presence of our Lord Jesus Christ at his coming?

20 For ye are our glory and joy.

(13) We give thanks endlessly that this is so, because the Truth has not come from our mouths alone, but is the word of God. This can be attested to by the very power which comes with your belief.

(14-20) You have become part of that same Community of Christ which exists in Judea, and you have suffered the same persecution from your own countrymen as have they from theirs. Those who persecuted the prophets of God and who crucified Jeshua ben Joseph have also persecuted us (your correspondents).[3] They are unpleasing to God and men alike. They forbade us to speak to Gentiles and have put all kinds of obstacles in our way. Although we are not with you in person, we are much with you in spirit and long to see you all again. Rejoice though, for we are all one in Christ who is ever present with us all.

DISCOURSE CHAPTER TWO

1. Q: Were the Romans the ones who were leveling the charges of guile against your character and that of your associates in 2:3?

    A: Yes, you see the thing was that Rome remembered and Jerusalem remembered that I had erstwhile been an employee of those who sought to rid themselves of this strange new cult as it has been called, and here, in their eyes, was a turncoat who had on the one hand been very heavy in his persecution of these people, and now suddenly for what was regarded as his own best interest, was now in the opposite camp. This is something which has never been very well received in the eyes of a Roman soldier whose work it is to be forever a Roman soldier and none other. Therefore they found it very difficult to understand the one who is now Paul; fed, of course, by the citizens of Greece who were Jewish. We had in miniature a similar situation to the one in Jerusalem at the time of the trial of Jesus – pockets of people who were trying to create a case against Paul so that he too could be made an example in an attempt to eradicate once and for all this strange cult. I think that answers.

2. Q: You left out a verse in 2:9 of the King James and Revised Standard where you refer to your own work so that you would not be a burden to the people there. I know that people refer to this as a warm, personal statement that you and Timothy worked hard to provide your own keep so that you were not a burden on people. Why did you leave it out?

    A: I did perhaps leave it out at this point because it is mentioned again later and I saw no point in saying it twice but it is in there. I did make a very clear statement of the fact that we earned our own keep and were not a burden upon anyone. This I clearly recall saying.

3. Q: In 2:14-20, you refer to the opposition and persecution and tribulations that everyone went through. Particularly, the charges that Paul and his associates were facing. Could you say more about this opposition? Was it from within or without the Church?

    A: When we were in Thessaly we had just passed through Philippi where we encountered a great deal of personal difficulty. There was within that area a very strong Roman garrison, the leaders of which were still feeling very sore around the whole issue of the Nazar-Essenes, the zealots, the trial and eventual execution of the One Jeshua, Jesus, and this was perhaps the worst opposition we had found in any of our travels at that particular moment in time. We were, in fact, arrested and tried and it was only the fact that I was a Roman citizen that allowed our freedom. So we had to, what one might now call, beat a hasty retreat from that area which gave me course to be very cautious for quite some time. Not because

Discourse Chapter Two continued:

we were, any of us, afraid for our physical persons, but because we felt that it would be wise to be discreet in order that our work might carry on without undue impedance. After we left the mainland of Greece, we did not choose to journey back in that same direction and went rather by ship to Ephesus.

4. Q: In 2:18 of the King James and RSV, you dropped the word "Satan". Are we doing away with Satan?

    A: There is no such person as Satan. Why do we need to mention him. Do we want a discourse at this moment as to who or what is Satan?

    Q: Paul, in the various versions uses the term Satan and you are dropping it. Perhaps something should be said.

    A: I am dropping it because Paul did not use that word. Each being passes in his evolutionary pattern through all of the twelve constellations of the zodiac. Each is born at one point in his pattern or another into the sign which is called or sometimes ruled by one of those great Elohim. Hercules gave us, by his own example, the picture of what each of the signs offers to the soul in its learning. These energies reflect into our own immediate planetary family and it is the work, the overlighting force field of certain planets, within our group, our solar system, to offer certain frequencies with which the soul in its passage through the evolutionary process may learn. I will not go into the roles of the other planets, it will simply suffice to say that the role of the planet Saturn is that of allowing humanity to see itself. The symbolic energy of Saturn is "man know thyself". He is indeed the tempter who showed to Jeshua all the kingdoms of earth and said "These can be yours if you wish". It was not an embodiment with the name Satan to which the initiate may answer. It was a statement of recognition that Saturn is the governing principle behind all of our discernment. It is the planet Saturn which allows us to know ourselves. It is not the devil or Satan, there is no such person.

FIRST THESSALONIANS 3

3 Wherefore when we could no longer forbear we thought it good to be left at Athens alone;

2 And sent Timotheus, our brother, and minister of God, and our fellow labourer in the gospel of Christ, to establish you, and to comfort you concerning your faith:

3 That no man should be moved by these afflictions: for yourselves know that we are appointed thereunto.

4 For verily, when we were with you, we told you before that we should suffer tribulation; even as it came to pass, and ye know.

5 For this cause, when I could no longer forbear, I sent to know your faith, lest by some means the tempter have tempted you, and our labour be in vain.

6 But now when Timotheus came from you unto us, and brought us good tidings of your faith and charity, and that ye have good remembrance of us always, desiring greatly to see us, as we also to see you:

7 Therefore, brethren, we were comforted over you in all our affliction and distress by your faith.

8 For now we live, if ye stand fast in the Lord.

9 For what thanks can we render to God again for you, for all the joy wherewith we joy for your sakes before our God;

10 Night and day praying exceedingly that we might see your face, and might perfect that which is lacking in your faith?

11 Now God Himself and our Father, and our Lord Jesus Christ, direct our way unto you.

12 And the Lord make you to increase and abound in love one toward another, and toward all men, even as we do toward you:

13 To the end He may establish your hearts unblameable in holiness before God, even our Father, at the coming of Our Lord Jesus Christ with all His saints.

3 (1-6) I decided to stay in Athens at this time, and I therefore sent Timothy, our brother, to be with you. He too is a Minister of God, and our fellow worker carried the good news of Christ to comfort and strengthen you. No one should worry about affliction, for you know well that we brought them to ourselves, all of us. We warned you that you, as well as we, would be sorely tried. I had heard so much concerning you, however, that I could not wait longer to contact you. I do not want the work we did to be in vain, and I desired that you remain steadfast. It was therefore a great relief when Timothy returned with the news that all was well.

(7-10) We are happy to know that you remember us kindly and that you want to see us again as much as we wish to see you. Your own faith has comforted us much during times of distress and adversity. Our lives are blessed as you stand fast in the Lord. What thanks can we possibly render to God for your steadfastness? We pray daily that we may soon come to be with you to encourage this.

(11-13) May God and His Son, our Lord Christ so assist us. May the Lord increase your love for each other and for all humanity – may it abound even as our love toward you. May your hearts be unblemished before God when Christ comes again with all His saints.[1]

DISCOURSE CHAPTER THREE

1. Q: In 3:13 you refer to Christ coming back and with all His saints. Who are all these saints?

   A: If you will, all of His angels, all of those beings who have passed through the earthly plane who have learned all that the earthly plane has to offer and who have the option to pass into some of those other many mansions, but who have exercised their option to stay, "We will remain to help this earth until all have passed through those gates". Some there are at all times in physical embodiment upon the earthly plane. Others there are who are in other dimensions and yet from those other dimensions monitor and assist. It shall be those who are in those other frequencies monitoring and assisting who will come in His train when He comes. Those may still be in the classification of adept, initiate, in the mortal sense in which case they would be what the church would call saints. Or, they might have passed beyond that into the angelic force field and be counted among the hosts of Michael. Either way, they will be there.

FIRST THESSALONIANS 4

4 *Furthermore then we beseech you, brethren, and exhort you by the Lord Jesus, that as ye have received of us how ye ought to walk and to please God, so ye would abound more and more.*

2 For ye know what commandments we gave you by the Lord Jesus.

3 For this is the will of God, even your sanctification, that ye should abstain from fornication:

4 That every one of you should know how to possess his vessel in sanctification and honour;

5 Not in the lust of concupiscence, even as the Gentiles which know not God:

6 That no man go beyond and defraud his brother in any matter: because that the Lord is the avenger of all such, as we also have forewarned you and testified.

7 For God hath not called us unto uncleanness, but unto holiness.

8 He therefore that despiseth, despiseth not man, but God, who hath also given unto us His Holy Spirit.

9 But as touching brotherly love ye need not that I write unto you: for ye yourselves are taught of God to love one another.

10 And indeed ye do it toward all the brethren which are in all Macedonia: but we beseech you, brethren, that ye increase more and more;

11 And that ye study to be quiet, and to do your own business, and to work with your own hands, as we commanded you;

12 That ye may walk honestly toward them that are without, and that ye may have lack of nothing.

13 But I would not have you to be ignorant, brethren, concerning them which are asleep, that ye sorrow not, even as others which have no hope.

4 (1-8) We have spent much time teaching how one might walk in the light of truth before God. We have told you what were the words of Jesus who was the Christ. We would remind you again of those words: Keep your bodies honorable and sanctified; abstain from excess fleshly desire; do not entertain desire like some of those Gentiles who are as yet unaware;[1] do not defraud anyone in any way. You have been warned that the Lord attributes the just effects of karmic law to such behavior. We are required to keep ourselves clean and holy. Anyone despising this truth despises God therefore, not humanity, for goodness is of the Holy Spirit.

(9-10) I do not need to remind you about love, for everyone is taught through that Holy Spirit of God, to love one another. We have noted that the strength of your love has reached out to all Macedonia, and that is good. But we also ask that you reach out even further, for the love of God knows no boundaries.

(11-12) We ask also that you spend time in quiet contemplation and meditate. Work also with your hands and conduct your own affairs, in order that you lack nothing, and create respect among your fellow men.

(13-18) Now we would like to address a subject which you have asked about. What of those who died without hearing the word of the Lord? The Lord was crucified, yet rose again in order to demonstrate life's most important lesson, that lesson being Life Eternal. Those who are increasing our awareness at this time are not a limited few. All of life is a continuum in

First Thessalonians 4

14 For if we believe that Jesus died and rose again, even so them also which sleep in Jesus will God bring with him.

15 For this we say unto you by the word of the Lord, that we which are alive and remain unto the coming of the Lord shall not prevent them which are asleep.

16 For the Lord Himself shall descend from heaven without a shout, with the voice of the archangel, and with the trump of God: and the dead in Christ shall rise first:

17 Then we which are alive and remain shall be caught up together with them in the clouds, to meet the Lord in the air: and so shall we ever be with the Lord.

18 Wherefore comfort one another with these words.

which we move through endless rounds of death and rebirth. One day we shall all be fully enlightened, and shall stand with Christ as His family. All those in whom the lesser self has died – all who have attained divinity within themselves shall stand with Christ, no matter whether they be embodied or in other realms when He comes. Be a comfort to others with this truth.

DISCOURSE CHAPTER FOUR

1. Q: In 4:3-4, there is the sentence "Keep your bodies honorable and sanctified, abstain from fornication, do not entertain carnal desire as some of those Gentiles who are as yet unaware". The RSV did not use the term fornication, they used the word immorality.

    A: I have no objection whatsoever to exchanging that word. Immorality is better.

    Q: Carnal is an antiquated term. Maybe a word like lustful would be more appropriate?

    A: Lustful and carnal are not the same. Carnal means fleshly desire. Fleshly desires might not necessarily be lustful, they are simply the desires of the flesh. Therefore, one might say do not entertain desires of the flesh or physical desires. I think we might look carefully at this because I don't want to give the impression that I say "don't entertain any physical desires at all". I am speaking to excess rather than that which is natural. Perhaps we can devise some way to change that sentence so that it reflects the fact that excessive fleshly desires are not to be entertained. What is natural is absolutely correct. You have my absolute concurrence in using your editorial discretion.

FIRST THESSALONIANS 5

5 *But of the times and the seasons, brethren, ye have no need that I write unto you.*

2 For yourselves know perfectly that the day of the Lord so cometh as a thief in the night.

3 For when they shall say, Peace and safety; then sudden destruction cometh upon them, as travail upon a woman with child; and they shall not escape. But ye, brethren, are not in darkness that the day should overtake you as a thief.

4 But you are not in darkness, brethren, for that day to surprise you like a thief.

5 Ye are all the children of light, and the children of the day: we are not of the night, nor of darkness.

6 Therefore let us not sleep, as do others; but let us watch and be sober.

7 For they that sleep sleep in the night; and they that be drunken are drunken in the night.

8 But let us, who are of the day, be sober, putting on the breastplate of faith and love; and for an helmet, the hope of salvation.

9 For God hath not appointed us to wrath, but to obtain salvation by our Lord Jesus Christ.

10 Who died for us, that, whether we wake or sleep, we should live together with Him.

11 Wherefore comfort yourselves together, and edify one another, even as also ye do.

12 And we beseech you, brethren, to know them which labour among you, and are over you in the Lord, and admonish you;

13 And to esteem them very highly in love for their work's sake. And be at peace among yourselves.

14 Now we exhort you, brethren, warn them that are unruly, comfort the feeble-minded, support the weak be patient toward all men.

5 (1-11) I do not need to tell you of the time or season when Christ shall come again. You know as well as we that this day will come as quietly as does a thief in the night to those who walk in darkness. Of this we may be well assured, that if we fall into a habit of complacency and think all is peace and safety, we may find ourselves destroyed by the kind of travail that besets a woman in labor at childbirth. But you, our brethren, are not the children of darkness that walk in the night. Stay awake and alert, don't fall asleep in your faith. Let those who want to, fall asleep and be in darkness. Let those who wish, be drunken. It is for us to remain sober. It is for us to put on the armor of God; the breastplate of faith and love, and for our helmet we have the hope of salvation. God has given us this salvation through our Lord the Christ. By His act of mercy, we shall live with Him, no matter what is our state.

(12-15) Finally, we would ask that you acknowledge those who are your teachers and superiors in the Lord. Hold them in high esteem because of their work, and be at peace. Please be of comfort to those who are weak minded; be firm with the unruly; support the weak in body; and above all, be patient to all people. See to it that no one repays evil with evil, but follow only goodness, both among your own kind and in the world at large.

First Thessalonians 5

15 See that none render evil for evil unto any man; but ever follow that which is good, both among yourselves, and to all men.

16 Rejoice evermore.

17 Pray without ceasing.

18 In everything give thanks: for this is the will of God in Christ Jesus concerning you.

19 Quench not the Spirit.

20 Despise not prophesyings.

21 Prove all things; hold fast that which is good.

22 Abstain from all appearance of evil.

23 And the very God of peace sanctify you wholly; and I pray God your whole spirit and soul and body be preserved blameless unto the coming of our Lord Jesus Christ.

24 Faithful is he that calleth you, who also will do it.

25 Brethren, pray for us.

26 Greet all the brethren with an holy kiss.

27 I charge you by the Lord that his epistle be read unto all the holy brethren.

28 The grace of our Lord Jesus Christ be with you. Amen.

(16-22) Rejoice always. Pray unceasingly. Give thanks for everything, for these are matters in accord with the teachings of Jesus the Christ. Do nothing that will quench the Holy Spirit; do not despise those who are able to prophesy; hold fast to all things which you have proven to your own satisfaction to be good; abstain from all that you feel to be not good.

(23-28) I, Paul, pray that your whole being, body, mind and spirit, be preserved blameless so that you reach your inner Divinity. Accept also that others there are, of like mind, who call you to do as they do. Therefore our brothers, pray for us. Greet all of the brethren with a Holy kiss, and please read this letter to them.

May the Grace of our Lord Jesus Christ be with you.

Written from Athens in the year of Our Lord 50 AD.

INTRODUCTION TO THE SECOND LETTER OF PAUL TO THE THESSALONIANS

Let us now move to the translation of the second letter to the Thessalonians. I wish first of all to make a brief statement as to the reason for writing this second letter. Some little time after Timothy had returned from delivering the first letter, it came to our attention that some of the group there were becoming so obsessed with the idea of the "Second Coming" that they were totally unable to think about anything else. Some had even given up their normal lives in anticipation of the event. It therefore seemed necessary to send an urgent message to them in hope of putting them right. The letter was written in Corinth, where we stayed after our visit to Athens.

SECOND LETTER OF PAUL TO THE THESSALONIANS

1 *Paul, and Silvanus, and Timotheus, unto the church of the Thessalonians in God our Father and the Lord Jesus Christ:*

2 Grace unto you, and peace, from God our Father and the Lord Jesus Christ.

3 We are bound to thank God always for you, brethren, as it is meet, because that your faith groweth exceedingly, and the charity of every one of you all toward each other aboundeth;

4 So that we ourselves glory in you in the churches of God for your patience and faith in all your persecutions and tribulations that ye endure:

5 Which is a manifest token of the righteous judgement of God, that ye may be counted worthy of the Kingdom of God, for which ye also suffer.

6 Seeing it is a righteous thing with God to recompense tribulation to them that trouble you;

7 And to you who are troubled rest with us, when the Lord Jesus shall be revealed from heaven with His mighty angels,

1 (1-2) Greetings from Paul, Silvanus and Timothy. The Grace of Father-Mother God and the Lord Christ be with you, and peace.

(3-6) We are deeply grateful to see the way in which your love to one another increases as your faith grows. Indeed we delight in the way that we see the communities of God develop in patience and faith despite all the vicissitudes that you have to endure. We should say, though, that this is normal, for when we declare ourselves a part of the Light, we shall expect to be sorely tested. It is only by passing through all our tests, that we grow further into the Light.

(7-12) We may all rest assured as to the matter of the Revelation. We simply ask you, earnestly, that you maintain the true teachings of faith. It is the task of all of us to walk daily on the path toward enlightenment, that when the day does come that the Christ shall again descend with all His Angels, into this earthy plane,

Second Thessalonians 1

8 In flaming fire taking vengeance on them that know not God, and that obey not the gospel of our Lord Jesus Christ:

9 Who shall be punished with everlasting destruction from the presence of the Lord, and from the glory of His power;

10 When He shall come to be glorified in His saints, and to be admired in all them that believe (because our testimony among you was believed) in that day.

11 Wherefore also we pray always for you, that our God would count you worthy of this calling, and fulfill all the good pleasure of His goodness, and the work of faith with power:

12 That the name of our Lord Jesus Christ may be glorified in you, and ye in him, according to the grace of our God and the Lord Jesus Christ.

we shall all be ready and worthy to be counted among the Righteous. We shall have plenty of opportunity to work toward this. The karmic laws are such that the Angels of Destiny place us always into situations that will try to test us, that we shall walk in the light, unafraid. The fires of purification must be passed through by all Souls in order that they shall ultimately attain. Those fires are for purging all that is of darkness, and can be wrathful indeed to assist us to true realization.

The good news spoken by Jesus the Christ attested to this – that we may all attain His Glory through that same power which He held. It is always our hope that we shall each attain His Perfection that we may be counted among His Saints, and be worthy of His calling. Let the name of Christ be glorified in you, and you in Him, according to His Grace.[1]

DISCOURSE CHAPTER ONE

1. Q: In 1:7-12 you again leave out the references to vengeance and judgement. My question is: could you describe why this desire or this belief in vengeance, punishment and harsh judgement came to be so prominent among these early Christians?

    A: It really did not become so prominent at that point in time. You will remember there were not any churches as such at this time, merely communities of people coming together with a common cause. Churches become prominent after the disputes between Rome and Byzantium. Rome, of course, became the dominant force and in order to keep that domination, a doctrine was propounded which was a doctrine of fear and suppression. The church of Rome decided that there was only one way to God and it should be through Rome. In order that the people be kept in a state of apprehension, fear, suppression and all of those other iniquities, such words were infiltrated into the New Testament by the clerics who were, by this time, thoroughly inculcated in the methods of Rome. Therefore, this was their manner of thinking. It was not the manner of thinking during the time when Paul wrote his letters to those communities. The main purpose in any one of Paul's letters and messages was to hold the little communities of the true faith within the tenets of that faith. Paul therefore was saying to those communities, do not entertain emotions of negativity, whatever they might be. Rather, live within the tenets of the law as set forth by Jesus Christ, love being the most important. It is argued that such negative principles were the motivation of the rabbinical elders. I would say not. In the main the Hebraic faith is not one of fear in the same sense as the Church of Rome. The Rabbi has a desire to uphold the law, whatever his interpretation of the law might be. Theirs is not a religion of fear, that honor goes to the Catholic Church.

SECOND THESSALONIANS 2

2 *Now we beseech you, brethren by the coming of Our Lord Jesus Christ, and by our gathering together unto Him.*

2 That ye be not soon shaken in mind, or be troubled, neither by spirit, nor by word, nor by letter as from us, as that the day of Christ is at hand.

3 Let no man deceive you by any means: for that day shall not come, except there come a falling away first, and that man of sin be reveled, the son of perdition;

4 Who opposeth and exalteth himself above all that is called God, or that is worshipped; so that he as God sitteth upon in the temple of God, shewing himself that he is God.

5 Remember ye not, that, when I was yet with you, I told you these things?

6 And now ye know what with-holdeth that He might be revealed in His time.

7 For the mystery of iniquity doth already work: only he who now letteth will let, until he be taken out of the way.

8 And then shall that Wicked be revealed, whom the Lord shall consume with the spirit of His mouth, and shall destroy with the brightness of His coming:

9 Even him, whose coming is after the working of Satan with all power and signs and lying wonders,

10 And with all deceivabless of unrighteousness in them that perish; because they received not the love of the truth, that they might be saved.

11 And for this cause God shall send them strong delusion, that they should believe a lie:

12 That they all might be damned who believeth not the truth, but had pleasure in unrighteousness.

2 (1-12) We need to make something very clear to you. That is, that you should not think the second coming is close at hand, for it is not. Do you not recall the words that I said to you in person when I was last with you? Do you not remember my saying that a great deal of time will pass, and much shall happen before that momentous occasion? Do not let anyone deceive you into thinking that it is otherwise. Jesus Himself was asked the same question, and gave the same answer. There shall be raised Temples in His name that shall not be of Him, but of all that stands opposed to Him. There will be those who exalt themselves and who will be worshipped as though God's Holy Messenger, and they will in reality be the Dark Forces. These iniquities are already beginning, as people begin to create those things in the so-called name of Christ, that are not of Him. Even as Jesus said, Brother shall rise against brother, and there will be all kinds of iniquity before the Light shall again descend in all Glory. These things must all be, for they are all within the Divine Plan, so that over the course of time, all will discover the truth. Each soul will tread the path of delusion until each one works out through love what is the real truth. There is only one religion, and that is Truth.[1]

Second Thessalonians 2

13 But we are bound to give thanks alway to God for you, brethren, beloved of the Lord, because God hath from the beginning chosen you to salvation through sanctification of the Spirit and belief of the truth:

14 Whereunto he called you by our gospel, to the obtaining of the glory of our Lord Jesus Christ.

15 Therefore, brethren, stand fast, and hold the traditions which ye have been taught, whether by word, or our epistle.

16 Now our Lord Jesus Christ Himself and God, even our Father, which hath loved us, and hath given us everlasting consolation and good hope through grace,

17 Comfort your hearts, and stablish you in every good word and work.

(13-17) There is only one Truth – that all are part of the One Body of God, in Christ. Therefore, stand firmly in your beliefs after the teachings we passed on to you, which were based on the message of Jesus the Christ. May those same teachings, whether given verbally or in letters, be of great comfort to you, and establish you firmly on the path of Truth.[2]

DISCOURSE CHAPTER TWO

1. Q: In 2:1-12, in the King James version there is reference to rebellion, the lawless one who has been restrained who will come down and show real lawlessness. You have left that out.

   A: I do refer to this whole issue in some length in the discourse around the second coming when the question was raised when will that be? and I have answered to quite some extent referring to Jesus' own words in those latter days and what might happen in those days. It is therefore possible that during the time of the translation I found it necessary not to include it at that point. It is covered in the overall text of the letter and discourses thereafter.

2. Q: At the end of chapter two in the King James and RSV there was a prayer on 2:16-17. Again, you left that short prayer out.

   A: I left it out because I did not find it necessary in a translation which is stating a correction. To a very large extent, I have been careful to move along chapter by chapter and verse by verse in order that one might keep an eye on the text and its translation. However, there are places where one might find that I have missed out completely that which I do not feel relevant to the modern translation. The slipping in of a small prayer in the middle of the text, I feel, is not relevant at this point. If one therefore treats, in a short letter such as this, the whole context, and if you still find that something such as the one mentioned earlier, is missed erroneously, then we will look at it again.

SECOND THESSALONIANS 3

3 Finally, brethren, pray for us, that the word of the Lord may have free course, and be glorified, even as it is with you.

2 And that we may be delivered from unreasonable and wicked men: for all men have not faith.

3 But the Lord is faithful, who shall stablish you, and keep you from evil.

4 And we have confidence in the Lord touching you, that ye both do and will do the things which we command you.

5 And the Lord direct your hearts into the love of God, and into the patient waiting for Christ.

6 Now we command you, brethren, in the name of our Lord Jesus Christ, that ye withdraw yourselves from every brother that walketh disorderly, and not after the tradition which he received of us.

7 For yourselves know how ye ought to follow us: for we behaved not ourselves disorderly among you;

8 Neither did we eat any man's bread for nought; but wrought with labour and travail night and day, that we might not be chargeable to any of you:

9 Not because we have not power, but to make ourselves an ensample unto you to follow us.

10 For even when we were with you, this we commanded you, that if any would not work neither should he eat.

11 For we hear that there are some which walk among you disorderly, working not at all, but are busy bodies.

12 Now them that are such we command and exhort by our Lord Jesus Christ, that with quietness they work and eat their own bread.

3 (1-12) Please also remember us in your prayers so that the good news will be received as equitably by others as it was by you, and so that we shall be delivered from those who are unreasonable. We have great trust that you have been touched by the hand of the Lord, and that you will do the things we ask of you. The Lord will continue to keep you in His way, and protect you. May He direct your hearts while you work diligently for Him. Please stay clearly within your own circles and avoid dealings with un-believers and those who do not love the Lord. We set a clear example for you to follow. Also we worked for all that we received, and did not expect charity. This was not because we are powerless but on the contrary, we did this in order to set the right example. People who do not work, should not expect to eat.[1]

(13-16) Never become weary in well-doing, but walk at all times in the Way. When you come across those who walk not in the way, do not stay with them. That is not to say that you consider such people as enemies, but it is simply not to your best interests to mingle with people who are not as you are. (This is a part of the Universal Law – for like attracts to like).

Second Thessalonians 3

13 But ye, brethren, be not weary in well doing.

14 And if any man obey not our word by this epistle, note that man, and have no company with him, that he may be ashamed.

15 Yet count him not as an enemy, but admonish him as a brother.

16 Now the Lord of peace Himself give you peace always by all means. The Lord be with you all.

17 The salutation of Paul with mine own hand, which is the token in every epistle: so I write.

18 The grace of our Lord Jesus Christ be with you all. Amen.

(17-18) May the Lord of Peace be with you. I have written this letter personally, and in closing, I wish you the Blessing and Grace of our Lord also.

Written from Corinth in the year of Our Lord, 51 A.D.

DISCOURSE CHAPTER THREE

1. Q: In 3:10, you make a statement that will give a lot of moderns trouble. The statement is "people who do not work should not expect to eat".

    A: Yes indeed, it will give them trouble won't it. The statement however stands, even in these modern times.

    Q: I think the situation that would bother people are the phenomena of the tremendous number of unwed mothers our society creates, the elderly and many others unable to work.

    A: Ah, yes, thank you for calling that to my attention. I am speaking, when I say that, directly to those who are of working capacity, working age. Of course I am not referring to the elderly or to young mothers whose task it is to look after their children. I am speaking of an honourable estate, one which should be self respecting and one which commands respect: young people who are fit to work until the time of their old age. The elderly, the infirm and mothers with young children are part of society and should be cared for, for their estate is also honorable. Let us make no mistake of my meaning. One also needs to remember that society at that time took more account of the family than is so now.

INTRODUCTION TO THE LETTER OF PAUL TO THE GALATIANS

I sojourned for quite some time in Athens, my purpose there having to do with the Areopagus. In the Greek world of that time the Areopagitae were the learned judges (this was traditional since the founding of Athens, there being the Areopagus at the time of Pericles, founded upon that hill of Athens known as the Hill of Mars [ref. Acts 17:22]). The Areopagitae have existed since the time of Solon and the number of judges in the assembly was variable according to the reason for the gathering together.

Since Athens forms part of the Sacred Triangle within the Greek "Mysteries" any seeker after the Ancient Wisdoms, including Jeshua, spent time there. Many of the older Areopagitae remembered the visit, and were interested to hear from my own lips what I knew of the message that the Christos (as they had heard Him called) had imparted. Such men as Dionysus recognized and understood that message. Others found it more difficult to assimilate.

Immediately after leaving Athens, we journeyed to Corinth where we remained for nearly two years. My earlier plans had been to journey from thence to Rome and Southern Italy. However, this had to be changed because of the tension existing, making it difficult, if not dangerous, to visit Rome. Most people born Jewish were by this time unwelcome, and in fact many had been ordered out of Rome altogether. Even though I held Roman citizenship, I did not wish to endanger my mission by deliberately, at that time, seeking to visit places that could be considered dangerous, particularly since my "reputation" had gone before me following the misfortunes at Phillipi.

After we had remained in Corinth long enough to establish a firm community there, and I had personally attended to my own inner quest, we returned to Ephesus. Close friends that I had made during my sojourn in Corinth came with me. These were Aquila and his wife Priscilla, who became citizens of Ephesus.

Using Ephesus for some time as a base of operations, I journeyed throughout Phrygia, Galatia and Syria, for a period of approximately four years. It was during the latter part of this time in Ephesus that I wrote the letter recorded as "To the Galatians". There were at the time a number of small communities of faith in the province of Galatia, and it was to all of them that I addressed my words.

THE LETTER OF PAUL TO THE GALATIANS

1 *Paul, an apostle, (not of men, neither by man, but by Jesus Christ, and God the Father, who raised him from the dead;)*

2 And all the brethren which are with me, unto the churches of Galatia:

3 Grace be to you and peace from God the Father, and from our Lord Jesus Christ.

4 Who gave Himself for our sins, that He might deliver us from this present evil world, according to the will of God and our Father:

5 To whom be glory for ever and ever. Amen.

6 I marvel that ye are so soon removed from him that called you into the grace of Christ unto another gospel:

7 Which is not another; but there be some that trouble you, and would pervert the gospel of Christ.

8 But though we, or an angel from heaven, preach any other gospel unto you than that which we have preached unto you, let him be accursed.

9 As we said before, so say I now again, If any man preach any other gospel unto you than that ye have received, let him be accursed.

10 For do I now persuade men, or God? Or do I seek to please men? For if I yet pleased men, I should not be the servant of Christ.

11 But I certify you, brethren, that the gospel which was preached of me is not after man.

12 For I neither received it of man, n either was I taught it, but by he revelations of Jesus Christ.

1 (1) Written by myself, Paul;[1] I consider myself now an apostle of God, in that line of Apostolic Succession[2] through Christ, whom the Father raised "from the dead".

(5-5) All of the Brethren of the Faith who are at this time with me in Ephesus, send greetings to the Churches in Galatia. Grace and peace be with you from God and from Our Lord Jesus Christ, that same Christ who gave us all such a demonstration that we might live according to His message among us, and in accord with the will of God, to Whom be glory for ever, Amen.

(12-12) I am writing to you in some degree of sorrow, because I have learned that there are those among you who attempt to pervert the true message of Christ. Truly, I am amazed that you could be so far removed from the Truth in so short a time. It matters not whether the message purports to come from the mouth of angels or men, if that message is not the true gospel of Christ, then ignore it. I did not receive that good news from the lips of mere humankind; that message which I, Paul, brought to you was the Revelation of Christ as it was given to me. It is not the message of man; it is the Word of God.

Galatians 1

13 For ye have heard of my conversation in time past in the Jews' religion, how that beyond measure I persecuted the church of God, and wasted it:

14 And profited in the Jews' religion above many my equals in mine own nation, being more exceedingly zealous of the traditions of my fathers.

15 But when it pleased God, who separated me from my mother's womb, and called me by His grace,

16 To reveal His Son in me, that I might preach Him among the heathen; immediately I conferred not with flesh and blood:

17 Neither went I up to Jerusalem to them which were apostles before me; but I went into Arabia, and returned again unto Damascus.

18 Then after three years I went up to Jerusalem to see Peter, and abode with him fifteen days.

19 But other of the apostles saw I none, save James the Lord's brother.

20 Now the things which I write unto you, behold, before god, I lie not.

21 Afterwards I came into the regions of Syria and Cilicia;

22 And was unknown by face unto the churches of Judea which were in Christ:

23 But they had heard only, That he which persecuted us in times past now preacheth the faith which once he destroyed.

24 And they glorified God in me.

(13-16) Do you not remember how that I was the one who started out persecuting those first followers of the Truth? Do you not recall how that I was converted from that path of error into the path of Truth? How I wasted my time persecuting God's only True Way, believing that the words I had learned in the past from the traditional sources were the only way. Why, I was even more zealous of that way than my elders! That is, until the intervention of Christ, who showed me the Real Truth.

(17-24) You may recall when I received that wonderful message on the way to Damascus, I gave up my intent and I did not, in fact, return to Jerusalem. Rather I stayed for awhile in Damascus and then went into Arabia to learn more. It was not until three years (and much instruction) had passed that I finally returned to Jerusalem. At that time I went to confer with Peter and James, the brother of Jeshua. I tell you before God, that this is the truth and that I do not lie. After that time I came into the areas of Syria and Cilicia and was not known by appearance to the churches of Judea. Simply they had heard how the one who had erstwhile been the persecutor of their brethren in times past now was preaching the faith that he had once endeavored to disrupt. Therefore they glorified God because of me.

DISCOURSE CHAPTER ONE

1. Q: There has been considerable discussion of where in Galatia you are talking about; was it north or south?

   A: In fact it was both north and south. I have made a short statement to the effect that there were a number of small pockets of followers across the whole area which was at that time known as Galatia. If you take a map you will see that the area of land that lies immediately to the east of the coastal area is known as Phrygia and behind that is the area known as Galatia. It was not, of course, so thickly populated with cities as the areas closer to the coastal waters. Since the geographical area is much more widely dispersed and far more sparsely populated, it was not to the large areas of the cities to which I refer so much as to these smaller communities around the greater geographical location. There is one particular city, in order to not to be confused with that which is regularly known as Antioch, more northerly, also called Antioch which has the double title of Phebian Antioch. It was around there, more particularly, where the groups were clustered and out in an easterly direction from there. This is quite a different part of the world from what was known as the Roman region of Galatia.

2. Q: In the very first sentence in 1:1, you have added a phrase that will cause considerable discussion. You use the phrase "apostolic succession."

   A: I have entertained quite a sizeable discourse within the introduction as to what exactly was an apostle. The church has somewhat glibly christened all those members of the discipleship apostles; Peter, myself, etc. The use of that term being rather ambiguously put forth by the church, I have therefore discussed at some length what, in fact, is an apostle: one who has become aposted to the world. There was quite a distinction made in the initiatory path of the disciple. One must remember that in the path of initiation, first one is a seeker. When one is accepted into the lodge or ashram of a master teacher, one then is known as a disciple. It is only when one has passed completely through the preliminary and probationary period of discipleship that one eventually sets oneself upon the path of initiation. At the point in time when one indeed becomes a seeker along the path of initiation, there are many levels within that initiatory process. The first level is when it suddenly dawns upon the individual that he/she is not here for himself/herself alone and he/she begins to look toward the path of enlightenment and the return of the soul toward a more conscious state; in other words, integration between the physical and spiritual levels. The second degree is a little further along that path. The third degree is when the disciple accepts the path of service and recognizes that the movement toward enlightened consciousness requires that one serve one's fellow man, humanity. The fourth degree is when one takes that service to humanity beyond all thought of self – the

Discourse Chapter One continued:

point of total renunciation. It is likened in some schools to the crucifixion; in effect, the crucifixion of all that is of the material plane of form. When the initiate passes through that fourth degree and it is fully realized that he has renounced the world in all its material sense and seeks only the path of true service in a state of enlightened consciousness, then and only then, is one apostate, having renounced the world. Only then is one entitled to be called an Apostle of God. My argument is against any title thereto which is incorrect. The apostolic succession is the succession of those souls who have thus progressed and who are entitled to bear that name. Even now there are still few in number.

Q: The apostolic succession is one of the foundations of the Catholic belief in the infallibility of the pope.

A: There are many things, my friend, about the Catholic church which is founded in error, that being not the least of them. If any being achieves the office within the church of Rome of Holy Father, it is to be preferred that indeed he has arrived at a time within his own being of total apostacy and indeed, that he is of the line of apostolic succession. The history of the Church and the records of the rest of humanity historically are well enough pinpointed as to the truth of that. I repeat, few there are, even now.

(Comment aside): This particular question will be perhaps the least of our worries in the overall work. I think that by the time we are done, there will not be very much left directly concerning the Catholic church that we have not turned around. This is part of the overall intent. I should again here repeat also that it is not the intention to create any kind of situation or thought form which would implicate or place blame before any one segment of religious thought. In the evolutionary progress of humanity as it stood at the time of the writing of this work originally, and in the 2,000 years that have passed since then, we must be filled with respect for much of the great good that all parts have given in their evolutionary state. We are however now, for this next phase which might be called the New Dispensation, endeavoring to upgrade and clarify.

We are not intending to attack and in that respect I do not hold myself blameless for many of the errors. As I have said earlier, I too, at that point in time, was merely beginning and much that I transmitted was an exchange of views coming from my own progress along the path and the thoughts that I entertained at that moment in time.

Overshadowed by the personality which Paul had of the Scorpionic nature, having been born a Scorpio, and being very aware of the work which that particular influence brings about,

Discourse Chapter One continued:

I went through my own period of what might be called death and rebirth, resurrection. Not being the Master that Jeshua was, and therefore, being unable to take upon myself the Christ energy to the degree that He did, much of my own communication with others was, at that time, part of my own search, in an exchange with those who were also seeking – at times coming from the standpoint of one who had gone before and therefore knew a little better, and at other times being filled with self doubt and wonderment at the whole process.

GALATIANS 2

2 Then fourteen years after I went up again to Jerusalem with Barnabas, and took Titus with me also.

2 And I went up by revelation, and communicated unto them that gospel which I preach among the Gentiles, but privately to them which were of reputation, lest by any means I should run, or had run, in vain.

3 But neither Titus, who was with me, being a Greek, was compelled to be circumcised:

4 And that because of false brethren unawares brought in, who came in privily to spy out our liberty which we have in Christ Jesus, that they might bring us into bondage:

5 To whom we gave place by subjection, no, not for an hour; that the truth of the gospel might continue with you.

6 But of these who seemed to be somewhat, (whatsoever they were, it maketh no matter to me: God accepteth no man's person:) for they who seemed to be somewhat in conference added nothing to me:

7 But contrariwise, when they saw that the gospel of the uncircumcision was committed unto me, as the gospel of the circumcision was unto Peter;

8 (For he that wrought effectually in Peter to the apostleship of the circumcision, the same was mighty in me toward the Gentiles:)

9 And when James, Cephas, and John, who seemed to be pillars, perceived the grace that was given unto me, they gave to me and Barnabas the right hands of fellowship; that we should go into the heathen, and they unto the circumcision.

10 Only they would that we should remember the poor; the same which I also was forward to do.

11 But when Peter was come to Antioch, I withstood him to the face, because he was to be blamed.

2 (1-4) It was fourteen years later that I returned to Jerusalem, at which time Barnabas and Titus were with me. At that time I went by guidance and I talked with various people in private about the message which I had been giving to the Gentiles. Titus, being Greek, was of course uncircumcised. There were a number of spies sent to come among us as we talked in an attempt to trick us into something which might be accountable at the legal level. (In the hope of having us committed to prison presumably).

(5-10) I might say that we deferred to no one, no matter who they appeared to be. God had given to me the task of speaking the message of Christ to those called Gentiles, and He had committed to Peter the task of speaking that same message to the apostleship within the Jewish tradition. You need to be aware that John, James and Cephas (who are the very pillars of the Faith) recognized the Grace that had been bestowed on me, they extended to me the same right hand of Fellowship (as they would have extended to Barnabas) and it was decided that we (Barnabas and I) would go forth and preach to the people who are not of the Jewish tradition, and they themselves would continue to talk to the circumcised. The only thing that John asked in particular was that we sustain the poor and needy along the way. That was ever something I was willing to do anyhow.

Galatians 2

12 For before that certain came from James, he did eat with the Gentiles: but when they were come, he withdrew and separated himself fearing them which were of the circumcision.

13 And the other Jews dissembled likewise with him; insomuch that Barnabas also was carried away with their dissimulation.

14 But when I saw that they walked not uprightly according to the truth of the gospel I said unto Peter before them all, thou, being a Jew, livest after the manner of Gentiles, and not as do the Jews, why compellest thou the Gentiles to live as do the Jews?

15 We who are Jews by nature, and not sinners of the Gentiles,

16 Knowing that a man is not justified by the works of the law, but by the faith of Jesus Christ, even we have believed in Jesus Christ, that we might be justified by the faith of Christ, and not by the works of the law: for by the works of the law shall no flesh be justified.

17 But if while we seek to be justified by Christ, we ourselves also are found sinners, is therefore Christ the minister of sin? God forbid.

18 For if I build again the things which I destroyed, I make myself a transgressor.

19 For I through the law am dead to the law, that I might live unto God.

20 I am crucified with Christ: nevertheless I live; yet not I, but Christ liveth in me: and the life which I now live in the flesh I live by the faith of the Son of God, who loved me, and gave himself for me.

21 I do not frustrate the grace of God: for if righteousness come by the law, then Christ is dead in vain.

(11-13) When Peter arrived in Antioch and we again met personally, I took him somewhat to task because of the predicament he had put me into. Peter himself had indeed been keeping company with Gentiles, until James and others met up with him, and then he refrained, for fear of what they might think. That kind of action set us at odds, even to the extent that Barnabas disputed with me. I therefore challenged Peter to his face to live according to the very teachings and truth that Christ gave us:

(14-21) I told him straight, that he had no business saying one thing and doing another. We lived in accord with what Judaism taught, and which we believed as the Law, until the time when Jeshua showed us a Higher Law. I said firmly that if we seek to be justified[1] as followers of that Higher Law, in Christ, then we have no business trying to please followers after that lesser law. Did the message of Christ lie? God forbid. We cannot try to rebuild the things which we have worked to destroy. We are now as though dead to those old laws, now that we know the Truth in God's Law. If that lesser self has "died" into the knowledge of Christ, then I live from henceforth in that new knowledge. We must not frustrate the working of that knowledge, or else it has been given to us in vain.

DISCOURSE CHAPTER TWO

1. Q: The man who wrote the exegesis in the *Interpreter's Bible* makes an interpretation of the whole concept of being justified in a way that I am not sure that you would. He takes the word "justified", which you use in 2:16 where you are taking Peter to task, to mean that man was acquitted or saved as in a court of law*. This implies a sinful, unruly or criminal state prior to justification. I do not get that same implication from what you stated; that justification meant saving someone from a sinful criminal state.

   A: I am not quite sure what is the actual context at the moment, however, I think I might answer the whole subject by again pointing to the laws of cause and effect. No, one would not be justified, in the sense that having been a criminal or a perpetrator of some kind of grave error, simply by coming to that point of baptism and being recognized as from this point forth a follower after the True Way. This is a little similar to the modern concept of the Catholic church whereby one goes to a priest and confesses and is given certain penance, in which case, having done the penance, all is justified. Perhaps I should eradicate the word "modern" in this sense, because it is far less a problem now than in the middle ages when one could purchase anything by paying for it, including pardon. One does not free oneself from the law of cause and effect at the point in time when one determines to accept the message of Christ. It is hoped that from this point onward one will pay more attention and do things differently but we may rest assured that whatever we have done previously which is in error, shall incur the necessary working out of that error for that individual concerned.

   Q: I think he was also implying that Paul was saying that everyone was unworthy until they were justified in the faith.

   A: In a sense this is a correct statement, even now. For what this actually is getting at is that so long as we, as individuals, continue to go our own way and fail to recognize the unity of all life and fail to recognize also our own divinity, we walk in the shadow. Until the time when it becomes obvious to us that we must follow after the path which brings us into the light, until we cease to be the prodigal and set our feet back along the path to our Father's home, then we are all in that state of error. Everyone of us. The subject of justification by Christ's message is that we too, must become as He demonstrated. That is for each being within themselves. There is no way to do otherwise and become part of the Body of Christ.

---

*Stamm, Raymond T., *Interpreter's Bible*, Vol. 10, p. 483. Abingdon Cokesbury Press, Nashville, *1953*

GALATIANS 3

3 O foolish Galatians, who hath bewitched you, that ye should not obey the truth, before whose eyes Jesus Christ hath been evidently set forth, crucified among you?

2 This only would I learn of you, Received ye the Spirit by the works of the law or by the hearing of faith?

3 Are ye so foolish? Having begun in the Spirit, are ye now made perfect by the flesh?

4 Have ye suffered so many things in vain? If it be yet in vain.

5 He therefore that ministereth to you the Spirit, and worketh miracles among you, doeth he it by the works of the law, or by the hearing of faith.

6 Even as Abraham believed God, and it was accounted to him for righteousness.

7 Know ye therefore that they which are of faith, the same are the children of Abraham.

8 And the scripture, foreseeing that God would justify the heathen through faith, preached before the gospel unto Abraham, saying In thee shall all nations be blessed.

9 So then they which be of faith are blessed with faithful Abraham.

10 For as many as are of the works of the law are under the curse: for it is written, Cursed is every one that continueth not in all things which are written in the book of the law to do them.

11 But that no man is justified by the law in the sight of God, it is evident: for, The just shall live by faith.

12 And the law is not of faith: but, The man that doeth them shall live in them.

13 Christ hath redeemed us from the curse of the law, being made a curse for us: for it is written, Cursed is every one that hangeth on a tree:

3 (1-5) Foolish Galatians! Who has bewitched you so that you cannot obey these truths? What I want to know from you is this: did you receive the Power of the Holy Spirit from the following of those old laws, or did you receive that Grace because of following the New Message? Foolish ones, having received this power of the Spirit, will you enhance that power by following once again the things of the flesh? Did you suffer all of those trials you went through for nothing? (If indeed what I hear is right.) Do those who worked miracles among you do so by faith, or through the human adherence to law?

(6-9) I tell you that those who have the faith of Abraham shall be counted even as he. Because of His total faith, God promised that through His example all generations would be blessed. So then, those who have the kind of faith He had, will be blessed ever as He was.

(10-23) Christ has given us a new concept which has relieved us from the drudgery of those old and misunderstood laws. Those laws were not interpreted by the True Faith, and no one has yet been saved by them, while laboring under misapprehension. I tell you now, the Covenant which was affirmed to us all through Christ is not different than that which was earlier given through Abraham. Christ re-affirmed the truth which we had long forgotten. We have been held prisoner by laws that have been falsely interpreted and we have been led to believe that the establishments of the law are the mediators between us and God. The priesthood thereby has held us all

Galatians 3

14 That the blessing of Abraham might come on the Gentiles through Jesus Christ; that we might receive the promise of the Spirit through faith.

15 Brethren, I speak after the manner of men; Though it be but a man's covenant, yet if it be confirmed, no man disannulleth, or addeth thereto.

16 Now to Abraham and his seed were the promises made. He saith not, And to seeds, as of many; but as of one, And to thy seed, which is Christ.

17 And this I say, that the covenant, that was confirmed before of God in Christ, the law, which was four hundred and thirty years after, cannot disannul, that it should make the promise of none effect.

18 For if the inheritance be of the law, it is no more of promise: but God gave it to Abraham by promise.

19 Wherefore then serveth the law? It was added because of transgressions, till the seed should come to whom the promise was made; and it was ordained by angels in the hand of a mediator.

20 Now a mediator is not a mediator of one, but God is one.

21 Is the law then against the promises of God. God forbid: for if there had been a law given which could have given life, verily righteousness should have been by the law.

22 But the scripture hath concluded all under sin, that the promise by faith of Jesus Christ might be given to them that believe.

23 But before faith came, we were kept under the law, shut up unto the faith which should afterwards be revealed.

24 Wherefore the law was our schoolmaster to bring us unto Christ, that we might be justified by faith.

in thraldom, for it has been by their interpretation that we have been kept in fear of retribution.[1]

(24-29) Jesus spoke truly when He said that no one would come before God except by baptism into the True Faith.[2] We are no longer children in school. We must now realize that we are all united as one family in God, through Christ who takes no account of whether we are Jew, Greek, bondservant, freeman, male or female. Everyone of us is regarded as the seed of Abraham and every one is party to that same promise by God to the faithful.

Galatians 3

25 But after that faith is come, we are no longer under a schoolmaster.
26 For ye are all the children of God by faith in Christ Jesus.
27 For as many of you as have been baptized into Christ have put on Christ.
28 There is neither Jew nor Greek; there is neither bond nor free, there is neither male nor female: for ye are all one in Christ Jesus.
29 And if ye be Christ's, then are ye Abraham's seed, and heirs according to the promise.

DISCOURSE CHAPTER THREE

1. Q: In 3:23 you use the phrase "the priesthood thereby have held us all in thraldom, for it has been by their interpretation that we have been kept in fear of retribution." Is this something Paul would have said? Would he have used the term "priesthood?"

    A: Yes, I would think that term quite reasonable, even then. In later times during the Christian Church it had, of course, more specific connotation. But even in historic earlier times, most religions had their priesthood. The Judaic was perhaps a minor exception, although even they had the High Priest. So yes, the phrase is quite in order.

2. Q: You also added a phrase in 3:24 and 3:25: "Jesus spoke truly when He said that no one would come before God except by baptism into the true faith." As you can see, that is a problematic statement for modem times.

    A: It is indeed one of those areas that require far more than a cursory statement such as the one you have read. What in fact was being said here was not referring to baptism into a state which later became called Christianity. There is no hidden implication that Christianity is the only true faith, because, of course, there was not a Christian Church in those days. And even in modern times this would still not be a reference to the Christian Church being the only true way to what one terms God. It is, however, a statement that for any seeker after righteousness – which is another way of saying "heightening one's consciousness" – there comes a time, even as the Christ through Jesus declared, when one must go through a

Discourse Chapter Three continued:

baptism. It is in fact, if we want to get into a discourse at this moment, what one might term the second degree of initiation. The first degree is that of rebirth, or re-entry; it is the moment in time when soul discovers that such a one is not simply following that one's own course, but is, in fact, seeking to place the feet back upon the path to the Creator, to become a co-creator with that divinity.

Having set one's feet firmly back upon the path of return, the second degree of initiation is then that of baptism, which point in the Christian gospel is extremely important, for it was, in fact, the point when the man Jesus surrendered his prepared body for the entry of the Divine Christos. In effect, every aspirant shall pass through that same degree and for some the baptism shall be literal, immersing in water, which is symbolic of the emotional body or state and is a statement that such a one is ready to take command of that emotional vehicle. The emotions no longer control the man; from here on out the man is in control of the emotions. That is a very distinct initiatory degree and statement and is vital along the path to what might be termed the True Faith, which in any instance is the path of return back to the Creator. I will not, at this point, go on to enumerate the other degrees, suffice it that this answers the question.

GALATIANS 4

4 Now I say, That the heir, as long as he is a child, differeth nothing from a servant, though he be lord of all;

2 But is under tutors and governors until the time appointed of the father.

3 Even so we, when we were children, were in bondage under the elements of the world:

4 But when the fullness of the time was come, God sent forth His son, made of a woman, made under the law,

5 To redeem them that were under the law, that we might receive the adoption of sons.

6 And because ye are sons, God hath sent forth the Spirit of His Son into your hearts, crying, Abba, Father.

7 Wherefore thou art no more a servant, but a son; and if a son, then an heir of God through Christ.

8 Howbeit then, when ye knew not God, ye did service unto them which by nature are no gods.

9 But now, after that ye have known God, or rather are known of God, how turn ye again to the weak and beggarly elements, whereunto ye desire again to be in bondage?

10 Ye observe days, and months, and times and years.

11 I am afraid of you, lest I have bestowed upon you labour in vain.

12 Brethren, I beseech you, be as I am; for I am as ye are: ye have not injured me at all.

13 Ye know how through infirmity of the flesh I preached the gospel unto you at the first.

14 And my temptation which was in my flesh ye despised not, nor rejected; but received me as an angel of God, even as Christ Jesus.

4 (1-7) I say to you that anyone's son, be that son heir to everything the parents possess, is still no different than a servant in the household while yet a child. The children have to study under tutors and governors until they come of age. We all as children are under the bondage of the elements of the world. This is true also of the human race, until in the right timing God sent forth His Messenger. That One chose to be born after the manner of mortal flesh, into a human family of earthly Mother and Father. He was born within the law (that means to legal parents). That one prepared himself to receive the Christ Spirit, and to reveal to all the True Law, so that we need no longer be in bondage, but adopted also as true Sons of God. If we believe this, then we too, can become Children of God, through the example and message of the Christ.

(8-12) How is it then, that when you knew not the True God, you did service to those who are not the True God? How can you, having recognized the truth, turn back to that old way? I am sorry for you, if I have labored in vain. You observe the passage of the seasons do you not? I beseech you, brothers and sisters, be also as I AM, for the I AM in you is the same in us all.

(13-16) You are well aware that when I first came to you to speak, I was a mere beginner, and so you have done me no injustice. All of my weaknesses[1] were accepted by you, and you still regarded me as a messenger of God, even as of Christ in Jeshua (some even thought me an angel). Some there were among you who

Galatians 4

15 Where is then the blessedness ye spake of? For I bear you record, that, if it had been possible, ye would have plucked out your own eyes, and have given them to me.

16 Am I therefore become your enemy, because I tell you the truth?

17 They zealously affect you, but not well; yea, they would exclude you, that ye might affect them.

18 But it is good to be zealously affected always in a good thing. and not only when I am present with you.

19 My little children, of whom I travail in birth again until Christ be formed in you,

20 I desire to be present with you now, and to change my voice; for I stand in doubt of you.

21 Tell me, ye that desire to be under the law, do ye not hear the law?

22 For it is written that Abraham had two sons the one by a bondmaid, the other by a freewoman.

23 But he who was of the bond woman was born after the flesh; but he of the freewoman was by promise.

24 Which things are an allegory: for these are the two covenants; the one from the mount Sinai, which gendereth to bondage, which is Agar.

would have given me their eyes, if they could be like me. I now ask therefore, what happened? Am I suddenly your enemy?

(16-21) It is good to be strongly affected by something (if that which affects you is the truth) and it is good to stay that way even when I am not with you. It is as though you were children, and I am going through the pangs of birth again for you to bring the message of Christ back to you. I wish I could be there with you, and that I might speak to you differently, for I am afraid that I have doubt of your faithfulness. Tell me, what is it that you want? Do you not hear the true Law?

(22-25) I remind you that Abraham had two sons. One was born while he was still "of the flesh" and following after those things. The other came from the Holy Spirit, being conceived when Abraham was initiated into the things of a higher nature. This historic reference is actually an allegory, for they refer to the actual process of Initiation. The name "Agar" is not a woman but is a place of high initiation in Arabia.*

---

* Agar (also spelled Hagar) means in Arabic – Flight. In the great desert of Sinai there are two mountains – Jebel Musa and Jebel Serbal. The former is the Mount to which Moses repaired to learn of his future work. The lands were, at the time of Abraham, governed by the Arabs of Peta, as an outpost from the land of Egypt. The land of Egypt in those days included a greater part of the Sinai desert. The two great mountains were high places of Initiation. Allegorically speaking, after Sara bore Isaac and Hagar bore Ishmael, the Lord said that both sons were "The Seed of Great Nations", the one being Hebraic, the other being Arabic. It is noted in Genesis that the same "Angel of the Lord" cared for Hagar and her son upon the mountain. Be it therefore understood from this that Arab and Jew were alike in the eyes of God and His angels.

Galatians 4

25 For this Agar is mount Sinai in Arabia, and answereth to Jerusalem which now is, and is in bondage with her children.

26 But Jerusalem which is above is free, which is the mother of us all.

27 For it is written, Rejoice, thou barren that bearest not; break forth and cry, thou that travailest not: for the desolate hath many more children than she which hath an husband.

28 Now we, brethren, as Isaac was, are the children of promise.

29 But as then he that was born after the flesh persecuted him that was born after the Spirit, even so it is now.

30 Nevertheless what saith the scripture? Cast out the bond woman and her son: for the son of the bondwoman shall not be heir with the son of the freewoman.

31 So then, brethren, we are not children of the bond woman, but of the free.

(26-27) The "True Jerusalem" is above bondage, for She dwells within the freedom of the True Laws of God and is Mother to us all. It is written: "Rejoice thou barren that beareth not. Break forth and cry, thou that travailest not, for the desolate hath many more children than she which hath an husband".

(28-31) Again, this is allegoric in nature. Rejoice that you do not bear seed of flesh only, for that is bondage. Rather, be glad that "she that hath a husband" *(they who know the true law)* have fewer seed.[2] The seed of the flesh is travail. Those that are born of the flesh persecute those that are born of spirit – it was always so. Therefore, let us "cast out" the seed which is merely of the flesh in order to be free. We are, as Isaac was, children of the Promise of the Holy Spirit.

DISCOURSE CHAPTER FOUR

1. Q: In 4:13-16, you speak about the weakness you had when visiting the Galatians. There has been much speculation as to what illness you had when you were with the Galatians.

    A: First of all, it was not epilepsy. In the period of almost 20 years, because of all the things on the many levels which I had assimilated – the complete change around of my spiritual outlook, the striving to learn for myself and at the same time all of the travelling that had been undertaken (one must remember that in those days also under very difficult conditions), had resulted in my physical being becoming depleted and the effects particularly upon my central nervous system, to the degree that I often was sufficiently depleted to be almost in a state of paralysis. This is perhaps what gave people the impression that Paul had epilepsy, he did not. It was simply a continual process of regeneration and like so many Scorpio subjects, one does not take care of oneself and regenerate until it suddenly hits one that unless one does, there might be serious problems. We tend to go on until something hits. I was not an exception to that rule in those days.

2. Q: In 4:28-31, you state "rejoice that you do not bear the seed of flesh only for that is bondage, rather be glad that she that hath a husband hath fewer seed". Now you inserted a parenthetical phrase "they who know the true law". That doesn't make sense, to my mind, because you are saying be glad that she that hath a husband have fewer seed because that is of the flesh. I couldn't put that together.

    A: The phrase "she that hath a husband" is referring to the somewhat obscure and allegorical allusion to Jerusalem. The statement "she that hath a husband hath fewer seed" and the admonition that that is something we might rejoice about means that those who know the law, those who abide by the law, and therefore those who are cared for, nurtured and secured by the knowledge of being with their husbands likely to make fewer mistakes, are likely to transgress to a lesser extent than those who are outside of that atmosphere of nourishment. We are speaking here to the whole issue of knowing the Divine Law and abiding thereby in which case one creates fewer errors which must then be rectified as opposed to the one who is still following after things of the material plane.

    Q: So "seed" is referring there to the things of the material plane. Up above there was reference to children and I was confused that "seed" might refer to children.

    A: No it does not.

GALATIANS 5

5 *Stand fast, therefore in the liberty wherewith Christ hath made us free, and be not entangled again with the yoke of bondage.*

2 Behold, I Paul say unto you, that if ye be circumcised, Christ shall profit you nothing.

3 For I testify again to every man that is circumcised, that he is a debtor to do the whole law.

4 Christ is become of no effect unto you, whosoever of you are justified by the law; ye are fallen from grace.

5 For we through the Spirit wait for the hope of righteousness by faith.

6 For in Jesus Christ neither circumcision availeth any thing nor uncircumcision; but faith which worketh by love.

7 Ye did run well; who did hinder you that ye should not obey the truth?

8 This persuasion cometh not of Him that calleth you.

9 A little leaven leaveneth the whole lump.

10 I have confidence in you through the Lord, that ye will be none otherwise minded: but he that troubleth you shall bear his judgement, whosoever he be.

11 And I, brethren, if I yet preach circumcision, why do I yet suffer persecution? Then is the offence of the cross ceased.

12 I would they were even cut off which trouble you.

13 For, brethren, ye have been called unto liberty; only use not liberty for an occasion to the flesh, but by love serve one another.

14 For all the law is fulfilled in one word, even in this; Thou shalt love thy neighbour as thyself

15 But if ye bite and devour one another, take heed that ye be not consumed one of another.

5 (1-10) Stand fast therefore in the liberty with which Christ has made us free. Do not get tangled up again in that which makes you slaves. I have just said that it does not make any difference in Christ whether you are circumcised or not. If you still continue to observe the old traditions, then the message of Christ is to no effect, and you are fallen from that Grace. Through the gift of the Holy Spirit (as He told us) we can be love, and we can maintain faith, and in that hope of righteousness we can live in truth. This is not governed by whether or not we are "circumcised", it is governed by our faith and our love. You began well. What hindered you, that you did not continue so? Whatever you believe, a little yeast makes the whole bread rise. I have confidence in you to make the right choice.

(11-17) If I were to continue myself to observe the old ways, then the message of the crucifixion means nothing. You have been given the message of freedom; do not use that as a means of self glorification. Use it as a means to serve one another. Remember that in order to fulfill the true law, you must love each other even as though each was your own self. If you consume each other with anger and negativity, then be assured that this will reflect back to you. Walk always in the things of spiritual value and not those things which are material. Material things keep us from following after things of the Spirit. You cannot follow both at the same time.

Galatians 5

16 This I say then, Walk in the Spirit, and ye shall not fulfill the lust of the flesh.

17 For the flesh lusteth against the Spirit, and the Spirit against the flesh: and these are contrary the one to the other: so that ye cannot do the things that ye would.

18 But if ye be led of the Spirit ye are not under the law.

19 Now the works of the flesh are manifest, which are these: Adultery, fornication, uncleanness, lasciviousness,

20 Idolatry, witchcraft, hatred, variance, emulations, wrath, strife, sedition, heresies,

21 Envyings, murders, drunkenness, revelings, and such like: of the which I tell you before, as I have also told you in time past, that they which do such things shall not inherit the kingdom of God.

22 But the fruit of the Spirit is love, joy, peace, longsuffering, gentleness, goodness, faith,

23 Meekness, temperance: against such there is no law.

24 And they that are Christ's have crucified the flesh with the affections and lusts.

25 If we live in the Spirit, let us also walk in the Spirit.

26 Let us not be desirous of vain glory, provoking one another, envying one another.

(18-21) When Spirit guides, you are no longer bound by lesser law. Avoid idolatry, adultery, lack of hygiene, lewdness, sorcery,[1] hatred, deviousness, wrath, strife, trying to copy others, sedition, heresy, excessive sexual practices, envy, murder, drunkenness, and the revelling that goes with it. I have told you strictly before that these are not Godly.

(22-26) The things that are Godly are: love, joy, peace, longsuffering, gentleness, goodness, faith, meekness and temperance; and against these there are no laws. They that are of the Body of Christ no longer follow after the former things. If we think we live according to the Holy Spirit, then let this be seen in the way we live. That does not include being envious of one another and being full of vainglory, nor should we provoke one another.

DISCOURSE CHAPTER FIVE

1.   Q: Later on in 5:18-21, you list the many things which are not of the spirit – adultery, idolatry, etc. You originally mentioned witchcraft and then used a phrase "black" rather than white, so I was wondering if you could explain.

    A: In this modern age if I were to condemn witchcraft without differentiation, we would open Pandora's box because there are many, many people upon the earth plane at this present time who would be most offended if Paul were to continue to condemn witchcraft. It is rather unfortunate that the word "witchcraft" was ever used at all. It would be better if one should stay with the terminology which refers to the ability to follow the path of the white magician. One must understand that anyone who has followed the path of true occultism and is therefore a white magician is not in any way being condemned. Unfortunately, so much superstition has been attracted around the word "witchcraft" that in the minds of so many people, and most of all the Catholic church, that needs must be now clarified. Perhaps it might be better to omit the word "witchcraft" from the list completely. The word "witchcraft" was something that was coined within the thinking of the medieval period (by the clerical people within the church).

    Q: The Revised Standard Version uses the term "sorcery" but I don't think that is much of an improvement.

    A: Oh, yes, indeed, that would be better. Sorcery is black magic and does differentiate between the art of the occult and the black magic. Let us use that.

GALATIANS 6

6 *Brethren, if a man be overtaken in a fault, ye which are spiritual, restore such an one in the spirit of meekness; considering thyself, lest thou also be tempted.*

2 Bear ye one another's burdens, and so fulfill the law of Christ.

3 For if a man think himself to be something when he is nothing, he deceiveth himself

4 But let every man prove his own work and then shall he have rejoicing in himself alone, and not in another.

5 For every man shall bear his own burden.

6 Let him that is taught in the word communicate unto him that teacheth in all good things.

7 Be not deceived; God is not mocked: for whatsoever a man soweth, that shall he also reap.

8 For he that soweth to his flesh shall of the flesh reap corruption; but he that soweth to the Spirit shall of the Spirit reap life everlasting.

9 And let us not be weary in well doing: for in due season we shall reap, if we faint not.

10 As we have therefore opportunity, let us do good unto all men, especially unto them who are of the household of faith.

11 Ye see how large a letter I have written unto you with mine own hand:

12 As many as desire to make a fair shew in the flesh, they constrain you to be circumcised; only lest they should suffer persecution for the cross of Christ:

13 For neither they themselves who are circumcised keep the law; but desire to have you circumcised, that they may glory in your flesh.

6 (1-5) My brothers and sisters, if we see such faults in others, recall that all is part of self, and do your best to set the feet of each other along the way of righteousness. If we think we are above others, we deceive ourselves. Let everyone prove their own worth to themselves.

(6-10) Let those who wish to learn, discover the right teachers, and do not be deceived in that – for God will not be mocked. Whatever we sow, so do we reap. Sow good things of the Spirit, so that you also reap everlasting life, rather than corruption. Do not become tired of goodness, for it is only goodness that allows progress. Let us do good to all, following especially in the way of those who also do good.

(11-15) What a long letter this has been for me to write myself. Finally, remember that those who demand that you become one of them, do so only for show, and in order to save their own comfort. They want to see you be as them, so they will not need to listen to the good news of the Christ (or suffer for their beliefs). God forbid that I should be so! I have renounced the world and everything it stands for, and now follow only in the Way that the Christ showed. Nothing else is of any further importance to me. I am a new person for that message of Christ.

Galatians 6

14 But God forbid that I should glory, save in the cross of our Lord Jesus Christ, by whom the world is crucified unto me, and I unto the world.

15 For in Christ Jesus neither circumcision availeth any thing, nor uncircumcision, but a new creature.

16 And as many as walk according to this rule, peace be on them, and mercy, and upon the Israel of God.

17 From henceforth let no man trouble me: for I bear in my body the marks of the Lord Jesus.

18 Brethren, the grace of our Lord Jesus Christ be with your spirit. Amen.

(16-18) Peace be with all who walk in accordance with that, also mercy. Peace and mercy also is with the true Is-ra-el which is of God. From this time forward nothing of a human nature shall trouble me, for I have now within me the true Nature of Christ (and my body bears the marks of the Lord Jeshua).*

Brothers in Christ, I commend to Him, your spirits, and may His Grace be with you always, Amen.

(The King James bears at the end of this text that the letter was written from Rome. This is incorrect. The letter, forwarded just before departure for Rome, came from Ephesus in the year 56 A.D.)

During the last part of Paul's sojourn in Ephesus, he went into a period of personal retreat. During that time, the Revelation of the Truth was so great before Paul, that he went through the Fourth Initiation. As with Francis of Assisi, from that point Paul bore upon his physical person the "Stigmata". Not so physically visible as with John (Francis) but nonetheless there (as is often so after the 4th degree).

INTRODUCTION TO THE FIRST LETTER OF PAUL TO THE CORINTHIANS

In the course of my Apostolic ministry, several letters were written to the brethren at Corinth. The New Testament contains what in fact were but two of these.

Corinth at that time was one of the largest cities in the eastern Mediterranean and a place with much traffic, both as a seaport and as a garrison city for Roman legionnaires. As such, there was a greatly mixed population, from the higher Greek and Roman nobility and well-to-do down to what one might call (without judgement) the dregs of humanity. Out of this very mixed bag came forth one of the strongest and largest of the Communities of the "New Faith". It was to those developing community members that Paul wrote frequently. To Paul the person, this area of Greece was also very important (and a further reason for the exchange of several messages over a number of years). It was a center where many of the teachings of the early "wisdoms" could be discovered, not only those with a particularly Greek flavor, but also certain of the Egyptian and Celtic teachings. It was a place of particular interest, therefore, for the "seeker after truth".

Perhaps it would serve at this point to give a chronological sequence to events and journeys during the years from A.D. 33 (which we use empirically as a starting point, though I have stated earlier that the whole timing of this period which bridges from "B.C." to "A.D." is incorrect).

After the Damascus event Paul remained in Antioch for some time, and then travelled to Arabia, to join one of the Essene Communities where he stayed for approximately three years. In the year 36 he made his way to Jerusalem where he visited with Peter and James, the brother of Jesus. From 36 to 50 – fourteen years in all – Paul studied the deeper esoteric wisdoms and pursued the life of an ascetic, seeking the Path of Initiation. During those years he spent time in Persepolis and thence travelled to the Mount Sinai area and eventually Egypt, where he stayed for a time at Gizeh and On (Heliopolis). Here Paul concerned himself with the recapitulation from earlier lives of the message of the Schools of Wisdom – those of the Persio/Arabic, and those of the Egyptian.

When visiting Greece, Paul was particularly interested in the Orpheic Mysteries and in visiting the Temples of Apollo at Delphi and the Aesculapian at Epidaurus. In pursuit of those same Wisdoms he travelled to the Greek Isles of Cos, Rhodes and Crete, and eventually spent time on Samos in contemplation of the work of Pythagoras.

In the year 50 Paul returned to Corinth and Athens where he remained through 51, from there travelling back to Ephesus. This area was used as a "base" during the next four years. From there Paul journeyed to areas throughout Syria, Phrygia and Galatia.

In the year 56 it was decided that the problems in Rome had settled enough that a visit might be contemplated. Paul therefore left Ephesus and went again via Corinth to journey to Rome. Later that year he travelled back through Macedonia, visiting Phillipi.

The letter addressed to the Corinthians which is enumerated "First" in the New Testament, is so called because it is considered as the first written in (what might be termed) an "official" capacity as one who is at this time considered by the groups of the faithful a "teacher". Sosthenes was the bearer of that letter (which is what is meant by "Through the will of God and Sosthenes"). In fact, the brethren present with me at the time of writing were Timothy, Stephanus and Fortunatus, as is indicated.

In reference to the interplay of the two names Saul of Tarsus and Paul, it might be worthwhile at this point to clarify a misconception. Saul was the name given by the family at birth and was retained throughout life when addressing members of personal family to whom Saul was known. It was also the name on official records of that day, both in Tarsus and Rome. It was therefore the name used in signature of any official matter. To the Brethren of the New Faith, and more particularly in Greece and Rome, the name Paul was more often used (Paulinus as the Romanized name in that area).

FIRST LETTER OF PAUL TO THE CORINTHIANS

1 *Paul, called to be an apostle of Jesus Christ through the will of God, and Sosthenes our brother.*

2 Unto the church of God which is at Corinth, to them that are sanctified in Christ Jesus, called to be saints, with all that in every place call upon the name of Jesus Christ our Lord, both theirs and ours:

3 Grace be unto you, and peace, from God our Father, and from the Lord Jesus Christ.

4 I thank my God always on your behalf for the grace of God which is given you by Jesus Christ.

5 That in every thing ye are enriched by Him in all utterance, and in all knowledge;

6 Even as the testimony of Christ was confirmed in you:

7 So that ye come behind in no gift; waiting for the coming of our Lord Jesus Christ:

8 Who shall also confirm you unto the end, that ye may be blameless in the day of our Lord Jesus Christ.

9 God is faithful, by whom ye were called unto the fellowship of His Son Jesus Christ our Lord.

10 Now I beseech you, brethren, by the name of our Lord Jesus Christ, that ye all speak the same thing. and that there be no divisions among you; but that ye be perfectly joined together in the same mind and in the same judgement.

11 For it hath been declared unto me of you, my brethren, by them which are of the house of Chloe, that there are contentions among you.

12 Now this I say, that every one of you saith, I am of Paul; and I of Apollos; and I of Cephas; and I of Christ.

1 (1-8) From Paul, who was called to be an Apostle through the will of God, and through the offices of the Lord Christ, addressed to the Community of God at Corinth. This letter is carried to you by our brother Sosthenes. Grace be to you all, and Peace, to all who are called through the message of Christ to become even as He. I thank God always for that Grace which is given to you by means of that Christ consciousness, that in all things you are enriched, in everything you know (and therefore, speak), and which is a testimonial of the Christ within you. You are not backward in any gift, because you wait for that consciousness to come. I trust that this will always be so, that you may remain blameless through that same consciousness.

(9-18) That same God who called you to this fellowship, keeps His faith, and therefore, I beseech you that you do also. Stay together in the same mind, not divided among yourselves. It has come to my ears that there has been dissent among you, coming from the house of Chloe.[1] All I have to say to that, is that it does not serve to say I am Paul, or I am Apollos, or I am Cephas, or even I am of the Christ.[2,3] I remind you that it was not I, Paul, who was crucified, and that you were not baptized in the name of Paul. You were so baptized in the company of Christ, who is not divided. In case there are those who say I have baptized in my own name, rather than that of Christ, I am grateful that I only performed baptism for Crispus and Gaius, and the household of Stephanas. Christ did not send me to perform baptisms, but to preach the good news and not with the wisdom of mere

First Corinthians 1

13 Is Christ divided? Was Paul crucified for you? Or were ye baptized in the name of Paul?

14 I thank God that I baptized none of you, but Crispus and Gaius;

15 Lest any should say that I had baptized in mine own name.

16 And I baptized also the household of Stephanas; besides, I know not whether I baptized any other.

17 For Christ sent me not to baptize, but to preach the gospel; not with wisdom of words, lest the cross of Christ should be made of none effect.

18 For the preaching of the cross is to them that perish foolishness; but unto us which are saved it is the power of God.

19 For it is written I will destroy the wisdom of the wise, and will bring to nothing the understanding of the prudent.

20 Where is the wise? Where is the scribe? Where is the disputer of this world? Hath not God made foolish the wisdom of this world?

21 For after that in the wisdom of God the world by wisdom knew not God, it pleased God by the foolishness of preaching to save them that believe.

22 For the Jews require a sign, and the Greeks seek after wisdom;

23 But we preach Christ crucified, unto the Jews a stumbling block and unto the Greeks foolishness;

24 But unto them which are called, both Jews and Greeks, Christ and the power of God, and the wisdom of God.

25 Because the foolishness of God is wiser than men; and the weakness of God is stronger than men.

26 For ye see your calling brethren, how that not many wise men after the flesh, not many mighty not many noble, are called:

words, but with the power of that cross of Christ. This is indeed the power which is of God though this might seem a foolish statement to people who are dying.

(19-25) It has been written "I will destroy the wisdom of the wise and will bring to nothing the understanding of the prudent." Has not God made the wisdom of this world seem foolish? Where then is the wisdom of the scribe, the orator? The world never knew God by this kind of wisdom; it has therefore become apparent that what some call foolish preaching, is the means to convey the message of salvation. The Jews are still seeking a sign. The Greeks seek for Wisdom. Therefore that which we preach, the message of the Christ crucified, is to the Jew as a stumbling block, and to the Greek is foolishness. But to any who truly hear the message, whether Jew or Greek, it is the power and wisdom of God through Christ. God's foolishness is wiser than any man; God's weakness is stronger than men.

First Corinthians 1

27 But God hath chosen the foolish things of the world to confound the wise; and God hath chosen the weak things of the world to confound the things which are mighty;

28 And base things of the world, and things which are despised, hath God chosen, yea, and things which are not, to bring to nought things that are:

29 That no flesh should glory in His presence.

30 But of Him ye are in Christ Jesus, who of God is made unto us wisdom, and righteousness, and sanctification, and redemption:

31 That, according as it is written, He that glorieth, let him glory in the Lord.

(26-31) You see, therefore, do you not, that few so called wise men (fleshly wise, that is) and few who are noble, or mighty, are called. God has chosen those the world calls foolish, in order to confound the wise. God has chosen the weak things, to confound those that are mighty. Those which are despised and considered base, God has chosen, things which the world considers as nothing, in order to negate things that the world thinks real. This is in order that nothing of the flesh is glorified in the presence of God, only those who glorify the Christ, who is the means to wisdom, righteousness, sanctification and redemption. It has been truly written: those who glory, let them glory in the Lord.

DISCOURSE CHAPTER ONE

1.   Q: 1:11 Who were Chloe's people? One of the scholars says he thought they might have been slaves who were not going to go back and who therefore would not be subject to any kind of retribution for tattling on the people in Corinth.*

   A: I think that fairly well sums it up. Chloe was a dear friend to many of the Community of the Faith who herself had been enslaved and who had received her freedom and in that freedom had become part of a nuclear family. There was, to a great extent, what might have been considered subversion coming from people like herself and not a little from Paul who were not at all favorably inclined toward the whole aspect of slavery and who spoke very strongly against it. So, yes, your comments, I think, are a good summation of what in fact was happening at that time.

2.   Q: In 1:12 Clarence Craig, who is the person who does the exegesis in the *Interpreter's Bible* for First Corinthians, comments on the fact that he believes there were many factions in the church at Corinth, not just the factions of the followers of Paul and Cephas and Apollo. He lists factions like the Gnostic Libertines, and the emancipated group of women and former slaves and factions on food and speaking in tongues. Is he accurate on saying that the Church at Corinth was split into many factions? **

   A: He is accurate. I regret that he chooses to call Gnostics Libertines. I have made comment concerning my stay in Athens and in Corinth as being a great part of my own research into the more ancient mysteries – Greece, of course, being a profound center. There were quite a few people who came within the brotherhood of the new faith after Jesus the Christ who were well acquainted with the ancient schools and who came forth firmly upon the teachings of the Nazar-Essenes of which Jesus was a part, and gladly added their weight to the teachings which the new groups were beginning to recognize. They constituted, as it were, a bridge between the ancient wisdom schools and the more universal aspects of those wisdoms which the Christ, through the embodiment in Jesus, had taught, and which it was Paul and his group of messengers charge to continue to teach. And so, in that sense, there were among those communities quite an interesting collection of thinkers as well as numbers of people who had no earlier path of any kind and therefore were seekers.

---

* Craig, Clarence T.; *Interpreter's Bible*, Vol. X, p.7 Abingdon-Cokesbury, Nashville, 1953

** Ibid, p.7

Discourse Chapter One continued:

3.	Q: In 1:12 You said you didn't particularly care for that linkage of the Gnostic with the Libertine and when we were discussing Romans you said that at that time the Gnostic development had not yet occurred. Is it true here that among the people at Corinth "Gnostic" was not a term they were yet familiar with?

A: Absolutely not and they were certainly not Libertines. Gnosticism was more widely acknowledged around the turn of the 4th century. Prior to that I think the word was not known. I think in the time of the coming together of the groups in Paul's day, they would have been regarded by the more conservative members as pagan, certainly not as Gnostic. However, there were very few, even then, who would refer to paganism, for the Catholic Church of Rome did not have such pronouncements at that time. Many of these judgments came in the early church of Rome, mostly coming from about, I would say, 300 A.D. onward. In Paul's time certainly these pronouncements would not have been couched in the same phraseology.

FIRST CORINTHIANS 2

2 *And I, brethren, when I came to you, came not with excellency of speech or of wisdom, declaring unto you the testimony of God.*

2 For I determined not to know any thing among you, save Jesus Christ, and him crucified.

3 And I was with you in weakness, and in fear, and in much trembling.

4 And my speech and my preaching was not with enticing words of man's wisdom, but in demonstration of the Spirit and of power:

5 That your faith should not stand in the wisdom of men, but in the power of God.

6 Howbeit we speak wisdom among them that are perfect: yet not the wisdom of this world, nor of the princes of this world, that come to nought:

7 But we speak the wisdom of God in a mystery, even the hidden wisdom, which God ordained before the world unto our glory:

8 Which none of the princes of this world knew: for had they known it, they would not have crucified the Lord of glory.

9 But as it is written, Eye hath not seen, nor ear heard, neither have entered into the heart of man, the things which God hath prepared for them that love Him.

10 But God hath revealed them unto us by His spirit: for the Spirit searcheth all things, yea, the deep things of God.

11 For what man knoweth the things of a man, save the spirit of man which is in him? Even so the things of God knoweth no man, but the Spirit of God.

12 Now we have received, not the spirit of the world, but the spirit which is of God; that we might know the things that are freely given to us of God.

2 (1-8) And what of me, Paul? When I came to you, it was not with practiced speech or words of wisdom concerning the knowledge of God. I was filled with my own fears and weaknesses, and trepidation, seeking those of you who, like myself, wished to serve the Christ. Anything that I might have said was because of the strength given to me through that power. It was my hope that seeing this in me, you too would recognize that power, rather than power attributed to men. We do not talk of the wisdom of this world, or of the princes of this world; this is meaningless to those who seek the perfection of Christ. Indeed, we are alluding to the inner secrets of the Ageless Wisdoms which are unknown to the princes of this world (if indeed they had known, they would never have crucified the One who came to reveal those secrets to humanity).

(9-13) It is written in truth "Eye hath not seen, nor ear heard, neither have entered into the heart of man the things which God has prepared for those who love Him". But in fact God has revealed those things by means of Spirit, for Spirit is able to know all things, including the ways of God. What man can truly say that he knows even man, except by the revelation of Spirit within man? That Spirit knows not only the things of man, but also the things of God. Know that we have received that Spirit, so that we might become aware of those gifts which are freely given of God. This is the Holy Ghost, the power which teaches us of things spiritual.

First Corinthians 2

13 Which things also we speak, not in the words which man's wisdom teacheth, but which the Holy Ghost teacheth; comparing spiritual things with spiritual.

14 But the natural man receiveth not the things of the Spirit of God: for they are foolishness unto him: neither can he know them, because they are spiritually discerned.

15 But he that is spiritual judgeth all things, yet he himself is judged of no man.

16 For who hath known the mind of the Lord, that he may instruct him? But we have the mind of Christ.

(14-16) The baser nature of humans does not receive the things which are of God, because that baser nature deems them foolish. The spiritual man sees all things through the eyes of discernment, judging for himself, and not being judged by any other person. When we think with the mind of Christ, we can become aware, even as He.

FIRST CORINTHIANS 3

3 And I, brethren, could not speak unto you as unto spiritual, but as unto carnal even as unto babes in Christ.

2 I have fed you with milk, and not with meat: for hitherto ye were not able to bear it, neither yet now are ye able.

3 For ye are as yet carnal: for whereas there is among you envying and strife, and divisions, are ye not carnal and walk as men?

4 For while one saith I am of Paul; and another, I am of Apollos; are ye not carnal?

5 Who then is Paul and who is Apollos, but ministers by whom ye believed, even as the Lord gave to every man?

6 I have planted, Apollos watered; but God gave the increase.

7 So then neither is he that planteth anything, neither he that watereth; but God that giveth the increase.

8 Now he that planteth and he that watereth are one: and every man shall receive his own reward according to his own labour.

9 For we are laborers together with God; ye are God's husbandry, ye are God's building.

10 According to the grace of God which is given unto me, as a wise master builder, I have laid the foundation, and another buildeth thereon. But let every man take heed how he buildeth thereupon.

11 For other foundation can no man lay than that is laid, which is Jesus Christ.

12 Now if any man build upon this foundation gold, silver, precious stones, wood, hay, stubble;

13 Every man's work shall be made manifest: for the day shall declare it, because it shall be revealed by fire; and the fire shall try every man's work of what sort it is.

14 If any man's work abide which he hath built thereupon, he shall receive a reward.

3 (1-4) There are many among you still who think after the fashion of the lower mind, and dwell on things of carnal nature. Because of this, I have been unable to tell you yet the deeper message; I have had to be content to feed you as babes, with milk; I cannot give you the "meat" for you would be unable to digest it. So long as you continue to bicker among yourselves as to who is the greatest, you still give away the fact that you are unready.

(5-9) Who is Paul? Who is Apollos? We are all ministers of the Word, equal in the eyes of the Lord. I planted, Apollos watered, but it was God who caused the seed to grow and increase, and God alone. We who labor do so as one, for we are laborers together with God – God's husbandry, God's building – and each shall reap the reward he deserves.

(10-15) I have laid the foundations after the fashion of a wise master builder, according to that grace which is God given. It will be for others to build onto those foundations. Take heed how you do that! You cannot lay other foundations than those which are of Christ. Rest assured we are all subject to trial by fire, and that trial shall reveal the nature of our work, be it gold or silver, precious stones, wood, hay or stubble. The work itself might be burned in that fire, but by the testing of it, we are saved.

First Corinthians 3

15 If any man's work shall be burned, he shall suffer loss, but he himself shall be saved; yet so as by fire.

16 Know ye not that ye are the temple of God and that the Spirit of God dwelleth in you?

17 If any man defile the temple of God, him shall God destroy; for the temple of God is holy, which temple ye are.

18 Let no man deceive himself. If any man among you seemeth to be wise in this world let him become a fool, that he may be wise.

19 For the wisdom of the world is foolishness with God. For it is written, He taketh the wise in their own craftiness.

20 And again, the Lord knoweth the thoughts of the wise, that they are in vain.

21 Therefore let no man glory in men. For all things are yours;

22 Whether Paul of Apollos or Cephas, or the world, or life, or death, or things present, or things to come; all are yours;

23 And ye are Christ's; and Christ is God's.

(16-17) Do you not know that you are, each, the temple of God, and that the Spirit of God dwells therein? If you defile that temple, that very Spirit within you shall destroy you. The temple of God is holy; you are that temple.

(18-23) Let no one deceive himself. If anyone among you wishes to become wise, then be simple, for the so-called wisdom of the world is but foolishness. It is written "He taketh the wise in their own craftiness" and "The Lord knoweth the thoughts of the wise, that they are vain. Do not, therefore, glory in the ways of humankind, remember rather that all things are yours. Whether you be Paul or Apollos or Cephas or any other, remember that life, death, the present and the future are all yours; and that you are Christ's; and Christ is God's.

FIRST CORINTHIANS 4

4 *Let a man so account of us, as of the ministers of Christ, and stewards of the mysteries of God.*

2 Moreover it is required in stewards, that a man be found faithful.

3 But with me it is a very small thing that I should be judged of you, or of man's judgement: yea, I judge not mine own self

4 For I know nothing by myself, yet am I not hereby justified: but He that judgeth me is the Lord.

5 Therefore judge nothing before the time, until the Lord come, who both will bring to light the hidden things of darkness, and will make manifest the counsels of the hearts: and then shall every man have praise of God.

6 And these things, brethren, I have in a figure transferred to myself and to Apollos for your sakes; that ye might learn in us not to think of men above that which is written, that no one of you be puffed up for one against another.

7 For who maketh thee to differ from another? And what hast thou that thou didst not receive? Now if thou didst receive it, why dost thou glory, as if thou hadst not received it?

8 Now ye are full, now ye are rich, ye have reigned as kings without us: and I would to God ye did reign, that we also might reign with you.

9 For I think that God hath set forth us the apostles last, as it were appointed to death: for we are made a spectacle unto the world, and to angels and to men.

10 We are fools for Christ's sake, but ye are wise in Christ; we are weak but ye are strong; ye are honorable, but we are despised.

4 (1-5) Be accountable to us as ministers of Christ, and stewards of God's mysteries. Remember it is required of stewardship that we remain faithful. To me, it counts for little what you judge me to be – I don't judge myself. Of myself I know nothing, yet at the same time I am justified because I am justified by the Lord. Judge nothing without the wisdom of the Lord, for in that wisdom shall be revealed the hidden things of darkness. He shall make manifest the innermost wisdom of the heart and then you will have reason to praise God indeed!

(6-10) In a manner of speaking, my brothers and sisters, I have taken these things onto myself, and so has Apollos, for your sakes so that you can learn what is the truth and what is not, and in order that you do not set one another up. For who is it that makes you different from others – and if you are not different from others, why act as though you have superiority? You are full of self importance as though you were rich and prosperous rulers. I would that you were, and then we might come and reign with you! I sometimes feel that we who have become apostles are counted the least among you, for it sometimes feels as though we are made spectacles of before men, before the world, and even before the angels. We are fools for the sake of Christ, but you are wise for Christ. We are weak and despised, while you are strong and honorable.

First Corinthians 4

11 Even unto this present hour we both hunger, and thirst, and are naked, and are buffeted, and have no certain dwelling place;

12 And labor, working with our own hands: being reviled, we bless; being persecuted, we suffer it;

13 Being defamed, we entreat: we are made as the filth of the world, and are the off-scouring of all things unto this day.

14 I write not these things to shame you, but as my beloved sons I warn you.

15 For though ye have ten thousand instructors in Christ, yet have ye not many fathers: for in Christ Jesus I have begotten you through the gospel.

16 Wherefore I beseech you, be ye followers of me.

17 For this cause have I sent unto you Timotheus, who is my beloved son, and faithful in the Lord, who shall bring you into remembrance of my ways which be in Christ, as I teach every where in every church.

18 Now some are puffed up, as though I would not come to you.

19 But I will come to you shortly, if the Lord will, and will know, not the speech of them which are puffed up, but the power.

20 For the kingdom of God is not in word, but in power.

21 What will ye? Shall I come unto you with a rod, or in love, and in the spirit of meekness?

(11-13) Even now, we hunger and thirst, we are naked and buffeted around, with no home; we labor with our own hands and are ridiculed; but though we are thus persecuted, we bless it. Even though we are reduced to the dregs of the world, and being thus defamed, we still go on.

(14-21) I do not tell you of these things in order to make you feel ashamed, but as beloved sons, by way of warning. You might have ten thousand people who call themselves instructors after Christ, but you do not have many fathers. I am as a spiritual father,[1] begotten through the gospel of Christ Jesus. I therefore beseech you to follow my ways. For this cause I am sending Timothy to you who is also as a beloved son, and faithful to the Lord. He will remind you of me, and that my message is of Christ, as I teach everywhere I go. Some are worried that I will not come to you, but I will do so, if the Lord wills it. When I do, I shall recognize those who truly have the Power. The Kingdom of God is in that power, not in words. What do you wish? That I come to you with a rod, or that I come in love and meekness?[2]

DISCOURSE CHAPTER FOUR

1. Q: In 4:15 you make a statement to the fact that you would be willing to be their spiritual father and that the people could seek a spiritual father. In this day and time, speaking to modern people, the father image is not always a very positive one because of paternalistic abuses and a lot of feeling that the Bible over-emphasized the father figure and gives practically no mention to the mother, the Mother-God or the mother energy. It is just not a figure of speech that people are going to particularly like. People are not looking for a spiritual father, they are maybe looking for a spiritual teacher or guide, but they would not use the term father. Would you like to comment on that?

A: The term was used, I think, in pretty much the same sense. I was using spiritual father in the same way that our Lord before myself had used it, that I AM in the father and He in me. It is a little different than calling oneself a spiritual teacher.

There were quite a number of people around at that time who called themselves teachers. They were not, however, in quite the same sense, relating to being a direct channel of the God force; the I Am presence. This was the differentiation that I was attempting to make and I need to say that again; the concentration upon the masculine aspect was something which was at that time – and had been for some time, and continued for some time – to be the prevalent thought.

In the mind of those who are truly aware there is no exclusion of the feminine principle. I recognize in modern times that womankind has made a very serious attempt to have the fact recognized that the masculine and the feminine principle are equal and therefore co-equal in importance. However, I could not speak of myself as a spiritual father-mother obviously and I was addressing myself in that instance. Had there been a woman who had been my consort and equal at that time then I would quite well have referred to her and me as being a spiritual mother and father. But I was single and alone and could, in that context, only refer to myself as the masculine principle. But let us again be very clear that all reference which will seek in any way to exclude womankind or to make woman any less than man, is a concept founded upon total error. The masculine and the feminine principles – therefore, male and female – are fully equal.

Discourse Chapter Four continued:

2. Q: In 4:21 you are talking about your coming to Corinth again and you say "What do you wish, that I come to you with the rod or that I come in love and meekness?" Craig* deduces from second Corinthians that your choice on arrival was the rod rather than love, spirit and gentleness; that the factions were going from bad to worse. He said your choice was the rod.

    A: Indeed so. Corinth was perhaps one of the most challenging areas because it was very close to Pireus and a place where there were so many different people with so much difference of opinion. As with many seaports there was what might be described as the "dregs of humanity" rubbing shoulders with nobles of Greece and Rome, merchants, every class of humankind that you care to imagine. I had frequently, therefore, admonished that it is doubly difficult in such surroundings to remain centered within oneself and to carry on a straight course toward one's purpose. I had admonished many times that in order to do this one must be very careful how one lived one's own life and be careful of those with whom one had social intercourse and it seemed that my words were falling upon deaf ears. And so yes, when I did eventually meet with them it was in order to very strictly pull them back on course. I had made it very clear that what each individual being chooses for himself or herself is between that one and his or her own process. It is between that one and whatever he or she calls God and is not for others to judge. However, when such a one decides to move in circles or community in the coming together of a brotherhood – and I use the male term not to exclude females – when those individuals no longer seek only their own process but choose to come together to work together toward common goals, then I had to remind each one that they then do have a responsibility to those others within their community. I am my brother's keeper. What I do reflects to those who are with me at all times. It was difficult then to have people understand and it is still difficult in the world today.

---

* Ibid., p. 59

FIRST CORINTHIANS 5

5 It is reported commonly that there is fornication among you, and such fornication as is not so much as named among the Gentiles, that one should have his father's wife.

2 And ye are puffed up, and have not rather mourned, that he that hath done this deed might be taken away from among you.

3 For I verily, as absent in body, but present in spirit, have judged already, as though I were present, concerning him that hath so done this deed,

4 In the name of our Lord Jesus Christ, when ye are gathered together, and my spirit, with the power of our Lord Jesus Christ,

5 To deliver such an one unto Satan for the destruction of the flesh, that the spirit may be saved in the day of the Lord Jesus.

6 Your glorying is not good. Know ye not that a little leaven leaveneth the whole lump?

7 Purge out therefore the old leaven, that ye may be a new lump, as ye are unleavened. For even Christ our passover is sacrificed for us:

8 Therefore let us keep the feast, not with old leaven, neither with the leaven of malice and wickedness; but with the unleavened bread of sincerity and truth.

9 I wrote unto you in an epistle not to company with fornicators:

10 Yet not altogether with the fornicators of this world, or with the covetous, or extortioners, or with idolaters; for then must ye needs go out of the world.

11 But now I have written unto you not to keep company, if any man that is called a brother be a fornicator, or covetous, or an idolater, or a railer, or a drunkard, or an extortioner; with such an one no not to eat.

5 (1-5) I would address the matter that has come to my attention, being common knowledge – namely, that there is much sexual promiscuity among you. Basically, that of incest; relationships for instance, with the wife of one's father.[1] You are so full of yourselves that you have not even noticed these things going on and required that the perpetrators of these things leave you. I tell you that even though I am not with you in person, I am with you in spirit and am well aware that these things are happening, and of what this can do to you. I urge that whenever you gather together to pray, that you join with me on the level of Spirit to request that such people be delivered from their wrong doing. Pray that they be released from lusts of the flesh and that they discover the way of Spirit, through the grace of Christ. Know that your own power is not sufficient of itself to combat wrong doing.

(6-8) I tell you, a little yeast is all it takes to make the whole dough rise. Purge out all sour yeast, so that the whole dough may be renewed. Remember that you are part of the Sacrament of the Bread, which is the Body of Christ, broken for you before the Passover, when the Body of Christ was sacrificed for us. Therefore, let us keep the Covenant of that Feast, not with old yeast, and not with the yeast of malice and wickedness, but with the Bread of Life, which is of sincerity and truth.

First Corinthians 5

12 For what have I to do to judge them also that are without? Do not ye judge them that are within?

13 But them that are without God judgeth. Therefore put away from among yourselves that wicked person.

(9-13) I wrote to you in an earlier letter not to keep company with wrongdoers, and I was not referring only to the wrongdoers in this world's opinion – namely the sexually promiscuous. I refer also to the covetous, the extortioners, the idolatrous, liars and drunkards, and urge that you take yourselves apart from them. Have nothing to do with them, do not sit down to eat with them. Put them away from you, and leave them to their karma.[2,3]

DISCOURSE CHAPTER FIVE

1. Q: In 5:1, there is a reference to the man who has been living with his father's wife. There has been a lot of discussion about that one. First of all, let me check a couple of assumptions, because we don't know: was the father dead, and were they married? That partly is based upon old Rabbinical law. If they were new converts and they were married and the father was dead, it might not be such a bad thing. Under modern definitions that would not necessarily be incest.

   A: It is not incest because they are not of the same blood family, or the wife is not. I am not quite sure that I understand your question here.

   Q: You use the term incest which was also in the King James. The question comes up, was it in fact incest and were these other assumptions correct that the father was dead and they were married? It is the biblical scholars debating the fine points of what they don't know.

   A: The letter refers to an incestuous liaison in the case of one living with the father's wife when the father is, in fact, still alive. Were the father to be dead and the woman to be a widow and the two to be remarried, then according to Rabbinical law and any other law, there is no incest; there is no blood tie with the woman. But when the man chooses to have relationship with the wife of the father, the father being still alive, then it is tantamount to an incestuous relationship. It is not strictly so because the woman is still not blood but it is tantamount to being so as long as the father is still living.

Discourse Chapter Five continued:

I think that perhaps one might say here that there is a stronger line of definition between someone committing adultery with another person's wife or husband and, in this case, the adultery being between two people who are of the same family. So long as the father still lives, the wife is a member of the same family.

2. Q: You made reference to this issue in the past, but I want to raise it more specifically. In 5:9-13 you make the statement about the fact that the people should not have anything to do with people who are seen as "sexually promiscuous, covetous, extortioners, idolaters, drunkards, liars and that you keep yourselves apart from them" and not have anything to do with them. The problem that raises for some is that it seemed like the message of Jesus was that these are exactly the people that the ministry should be to, that in a sense, one should go out and deal with all of the people that are in need. It is the essence of the message of salvation and love. For instance, in my own ministry when I was in the Tenderloin in San Francisco, my whole congregation was composed of pimps, prostitutes, drug users, etc. So you can see the issue.

A: The issue here is of a finer point than the letter would disclose. It is therefore good that we have the opportunity to enlarge upon it. So much of that which is within the confines of the Christian Bible is so condensed that it does, of course, give rise to these problematic areas. Of course you ministered to the needy, whatever that need was. That was and is the whole message of Christian ministry. Of course Jesus went out to minister to the halt, the lame, the blind and the beggars. That is ministry. That was the ministry of Paul and is the ministry of all elders who make it their choice to serve humanity and shall be so as long as there is any one member of humanity who still has the need to be helped; let that be clear. However, it must also be noted that Jesus did not admit those to the Twelve. The Twelve kept themselves apart in order to do the inner work that each as individuals had to do and in order to hold firm the brotherhood which they as a total unit expressed.

When I was admonishing the young group which had come together there, it was in regard to their meetings which were pursuant to their work of ministry. It was in regard to the building up of their own strength as a vehicle of service that this strength not be dissipated by bringing into their ranks those who were not ready to be admitted – even as did the Twelve with Jesus. Eventually as the strength of that inner cause was such, then it is possible to increase. But the young community in Corinth at the point of my statement was not ready and had to be extremely discerning as to whom they would admit into their inner work. That is the difference.

Discourse Chapter Five continued:

3. Q: That answers that very clearly. Today in this time the above list of problems would please the fundamentalist Christians to no end. The liberal Christians, as I would term it, might have difficulty in the fact that they see much greater problems on the horizon. They see the problems of nuclear war, pollution of the planet, terrorism, oppression, the poor, the hungry and the homeless as much more important than some of the ones you are listing. Do you think if Paul were writing today that he would have a slightly different priority list?

    A: I am not too sure that he would. The list went on endlessly then as it does now. One uses a set of examples which is intended to cover the major points of human frailty. No matter how grave the world situation is in this modern day – and we do have threats of nuclear extinction – it still comes back to the same basic frailty within that human nature which is the frailty of materialism. So long as humankind attaches so much vast importance to the acquisition of the material plane to the exclusion of or to the detriment of the realms of spirit, then we shall always have these problems. The list certainly might not have covered every single aspect of frailty any more than it would now.

FIRST CORINTHIANS 6

6 *Dare any of you, having a matter against another, go to law before the unjust, and not before the saints?*

2 Do ye not know that the saints shall judge the world? And if the world shall be judged by you, are ye unworthy to judge the smallest matters?

3 Know ye not that we shall judge angels? How much more things that pertain to this life?

4 If then ye have judgments of things pertaining to this life, set them to judge who are least esteemed in the church.

5 I speak to your shame. Is it so, that there is not a wise man among you? No, not one that shall be able to judge between his brethren?

6 But brother goeth to law with brother, and that before the unbelievers.

7 Now therefore there is utterly a fault among you, because ye go to law one with another. Why do ye not rather take wrong? Why do ye not rather suffer yourselves to be defrauded?

8 Nay, ye do wrong and defraud, and that your brethren.

9 Know ye not that the unrighteous shall not inherit the kingdom of God? Be not deceived: neither fornicators, nor idolaters, nor adulterers, nor effeminate, nor abusers of themselves with mankind,

10 Nor thieves, nor covetous, nor drunkards, nor revilers, nor extortioners, shall inherit the kingdom of God.

11 And such were some of you: but ye are washed, but ye are sanctified, but ye are justified in the name of the Lord Jesus, and by the Spirit of our God.

6 (1-6) If any of you have something against another person, are you so righteous yourself that you would take them to be tried by law?[1] Do you not know that we are all tried before a higher law, which is the law of karma, before which we deem ourselves unworthy to judge others, even in the smallest of matters? Know you not that all things come before the Lords of Karma? If then, you really feel that you have things in this life that need to be remedied, let those least of your brothers in the church be the mediators. I speak to your shame. Is it true that there is no one among you who is able to mediate between you in your disputes? Are you in such a way that people take their own brothers before the courts of law? (And those very courts run by people who are not of our Faith?)

(7-11) This is a serious fault among you. Why are you unable to accept those wrongs which others do to you, recalling that there are times when you have done wrong to others? The Kingdom of God shall not be inherited by wrongdoers, whoever they may be. Do not deceive yourselves, the Kingdom of God shall not include the sexually promiscuous, idolaters, adulterers, thieves, drunkards, the covetous, those who revile others, extortioners and the like. Some of you were as such, but you have now been baptized, washed clean and sanctified and are therefore now accepted into the community of those who follow the way of Spirit, through our Lord, Jesus.

First Corinthians 6

12 All things are lawful unto me, but all things are not expedient: all things are lawful for me, but I will not be brought under the power of any.

13 Meats for the belly, and the belly for meats: but God shall destroy both it and them. Now the body is not for fornications, but for the Lord; and the Lord for the body.

14 And God hath both raised up the Lord, and will also raise up us by His own power.

15 Know ye not that your bodies are the members of Christ? Shall I then take the members of Christ, and make them the members of an harlot? God forbid.

16 What? Know ye not that he which is joined to an harlot is one body? For two, saith he, shall be one flesh.

17 But he that is joined unto the Lord is one spirit.

18 Flee fornication. Every sin that a man doeth is without the body; but he that committeth fornication sinneth against his own body.

19 What? Know ye not that your body is the temple of the Holy Ghost which is in you, which ye have of God, and ye are not your own?

20 For ye are bought with a price: therefore glorify God in your body and in your spirit, which are God's.

(12-16) I could say that all things may be lawful, but not all things are expedient; all things may be lawful, but I will not be subject to their power. The belly is made for food and food for the belly, but the day shall come when they will both be gone (according to the cycles of God). God created that body not to be abused, but in order to be a vehicle for his Holy Law. The God that raised the Lord Christ will also raise each one of us by that same power. Do you not yet know that each one of your bodies is part of the body of Christ?[2] Shall we then take Christ's members, and give them to a prostitute? God forbid! Do you still not understand that what you join with a prostitute is one body, that the two of you become as one flesh?[3] One who is joined to the Lord is one spirit.

(17-20) Shun abuse of the body therefore. All other laws which you break, do not affect the body so much as sexual excess. When you permit sexual wrongdoing, you do wrong against your own body, which is the Temple wherein Spirit dwells. That Holy Spirit is given by God, not to be abused, for the giving has been at great cost. Therefore, glorify that very God with your body, who paid that price.

DISCOURSE CHAPTER SIX

1. Q: In 6:1, you are taking them to task for evidently they have brought law suits against each other and are taking them to an outside court. Was this partly Paul's belief in the parousia that there was no use to use outside court; the church ought to deal with its own internal things because the end was coming soon.

    A: It had very little to do with any "end" as it were. It had everything to do with Paul's astonishment that a brotherhood supposedly dealing with its own growth and with service each to the other, would have any reason for recourse to law courts.

2. Q: You make the statement toward the end of chapter 6:15, "do you not yet know that each one of your bodies is part of the body of Christ?" How are our bodies part of the, body of Christ? It is one thing to conceive the body as being the temple of the spirit, but what did Paul really mean?

    A: One is here addressing the oneness of all things. If one truly believes that we are, every single one of us, part of that allness, then indeed we are literally part of the body of Christ. We are indeed literally part, each of the other. This is the same thing as I said in my last statement that I am my brother's keeper; it could not be otherwise. His or her difficulty is my difficulty. That which I do reflects in them. And that which they do affects me. This is again a very vast subject and is perhaps one that we might wish to enter more into in the suggested appendix. For the flow of the text here I would simply stress that yes, indeed, I did mean literally that we are a part of that body of Christ and He part of us; then and now.

3. Q: You state in 6:16 "Do you still not understand that what you join with the harlot is one body; that the two of you become as one flesh"? How does the becoming one flesh with the prostitute differ from becoming one flesh in the marriage relationship?

    A: It differs in motivation. In the marriage relationship the two are coming together in accord with that which was set forth by what we might term divine command. And there is within the joining together of the male and female the opportunity during that act of love for the two as one whole to raise each other into a very high level of spiritual bliss. In the case of using a prostitute for sexual gratification, one is simply satisfying the flesh and it is very different.

FIRST CORINTHIANS 7

7 Now concerning the things whereof ye wrote unto me: It is good for a man not to touch a woman.

2 Nevertheless, to avoid fornication, let every man have his own wife, and let every woman have her own husband.

3 Let the husband render unto the wife due benevolence: and likewise also the wife unto the husband.

4 The wife hath not power of her own body, but the husband; and likewise also the husband hath not power of his own body, but the wife.

5 Defraud ye not one the other, except it be with consent for a time, that ye may give yourselves to fasting and prayer; and come together again, that Satan tempt you not for your incontinency.

6 But I speak this by permission, and not of commandment.

7 For I would that all men were even as I myself. But every man hath his proper gift of God, one after this manner, and another after that.

8 I say, therefore to the unmarried and widows, It is good for them if they abide even as I.

9 But if they cannot contain, let them marry: for it is better to marry than to burn.

10 And unto the married, I command, yet not I, but the Lord, Let not the wife depart from her husband:

11 But and if she depart, let her remain unmarried, or be reconciled to her husband: and let not the husband put away his wife.

12 But to the rest speak I, not the Lord: If any brother hath a wife that believeth not, and she be pleased to dwell with him, let him not put her away.

7 (1-5) Concerning those matters about which you wrote to me: It is good for a man or woman to be continent and abstain from sex at times. It is at all times necessary to avoid immorality. There have been certain rules (since the sexes were divided).[1] Each man must have his own wife, and each wife her husband, and each should be good to the other. Let neither husband nor wife use their body to create power over the other. You must not defraud one another by withdrawal except under due consent of the other. There are times when one may wish to withdraw in order to fast and pray. Then you must come together again, in order that you be not tempted to other things through incontinence.

(6-7) Abstinence is not a matter of commandment, it is a matter of permission. Personally, it is my wish that all may attain to spiritual continence, even as I; but everyone has his own gift, given by God and in due time after his own persuasion.[2]

(8-11) I would say, however, that the unmarried and the widowed would be better to remain continent. If they cannot, then they should marry, rather than be consumed with sexual desire. To those who are already married, I say this: let not the wife leave her husband, nor husband leave wife. If they do, then they should remain single (or go back to their husband or wife). This is the Lord's command, not mine.[3]

First Corinthians 7

13 And the woman which hath an husband that believeth not, and if he be pleased to swell with her, let her not leave him.

14 For the unbelieving husband is sanctified by the wife, and the unbelieving wife is sanctified by the husband: else were your children unclean; but now are they holy.

15 But if the unbelieving depart, let him depart. A brother or a sister is not under bondage in such cases: but God hath called us to peace.

16 For what knowest thou, O wife, whether thou shalt save thy husband? Or how knowest thou, O man, whether thou shalt save thy wife?

17 But as God hath distributed to every man, as the Lord hath called every one, so let him walk And so ordain I in all churches.

18 Is any man called being circumcised: Let him not become uncircumcised. Is any called in uncircumcision? Let him not be circumcised.

19 Circumcision is nothing and uncircumcision is nothing but the keeping of the commandments of God.

20 Let every man abide in the same calling wherein he was called.

21 Art thou called being a servant? Care not for it: but if thou mayest be made free, use it rather.

22 For he that is called in the Lord, being a servant, is the Lord's freeman: likewise also be that is called, being free, is Christ's servant.

23 Ye are bought with a price; be not ye the servants of men.

24 Brethren, let every man, wherein he is called, therein abide with God.

(12-17) To the rest of you, I speak (and this is I, Paul, not the Lord): If you are a member of the community of the faith, and your wife or husband is not of that same belief, then do not let this be reason to desert them. The partner who is not a believer is held sanctified by the partner who does believe. If this were not so, then your children would be born without the blessing of our faith. However, if the unbeliever leaves, let him do so.[4] One cannot be held in bondage in such a case. God has called us to be at peace. Neither wife nor husband is able to know that they can help the other, therefore as God has moved each person, and as the Lord has called them, so must they do. I have told all the communities this.

(18-24) Whoever is called that is circumcised, or whoever is not circumcised it is the same. It is not circumcision that calls, it is the knowing and keeping of the laws of God. Let everyone therefore stay with that to which they were called. It does not matter if you are called to serve Spirit while you are a servant of others (though it would be preferable if you could be free). Even though a servant, you are a free man before God, and those who consider themselves free, are the servants of the Lord, who bought you at great price. Be not therefore, slaves to men. Let each one abide in God, no matter what his station in life.

First Corinthians 7

25 Now concerning virgins I have no commandment of the Lord: yet I give my judgement, as one that hath obtained mercy of the Lord to be faithful.

26 I suppose therefore that this is good for the present distress, I say, that it is good for a man so to be.

27 Art thou bound unto a wife? Seek not to be loosed. Art thou loosed from a wife? Seek not a wife.

28 But and if thou marry thou hast not sinned; and if a virgin marry, she hath not sinned. Nevertheless such shall have trouble in the flesh: but I spare you.

29 But this I say, brethren, the time is short: it remaineth, that both they that have wives be as though they had none;

30 And they that weep, as though they wept not; and they that rejoice, as though they rejoiced not; and they that buy, as though they possessed not;

31 And they that use this world, as not abusing it: for the fashion of this world passeth away.

32 But I would have you without carefulness. He that is unmarried careth for the things that belong to the Lord, how he may please the Lord:

33 But he that is married careth for the things that are of the world, how he may please his wife.

34 There is difference also between a wife and a virgin. The unmarried woman careth for the things of the Lord, that she may be holy both in body and in spirit: but she that is married careth for the things of the world, how she may please her husband.

(25-28) To those who are still virgins I have no special comments, except to say stay faithful. If this state distresses you, I would say that it is good to be so. To those who are married I would say, stay so. To those who are not, I would say there is nothing wrong. You are not committing wrong by marrying, and a virgin who marries is not committing wrong.

(29-31) I need to say this, that before too long there will be such travail on the earthly plane that those who have wives will act as though they had none; they that weep will be as if they did not; they that rejoice shall act as if they had nothing to rejoice about; those that make purchases shall be as if they possessed nothing. The people who use this world shall change, for the fashion of this world will pass away.[6]

(32-34) I would have you live without worldly cares; be not married to the world. One who is not married to the world is better able to care for the things that are of the Lord. This is also true of unmarried women. Most unmarried women tend more easily to the things of the Lord, that they may stay pure in Spirit, whereas a married woman tends to care more for the things of the world, and how she may please her husband.

First Corinthians 7

35 And this I speak for your own profit; not that I may cast a snare upon you, but for that which is comely, and that ye may attend upon the Lord without distraction.

36 But if any man think that he behaveth himself uncomely toward his virgin, if she pass the flower of her age, and need so require, let him do what he will, he sinneth no: let them marry.

37 Nevertheless he that standeth stedfast in his heart, having no necessity but hath power over his own will, and hath so decreed in his heart that he will keep his virgin, doeth well.

38 So then he that giveth her in marriage doeth well; but he that giveth her not in marriage doeth better.

39 The wife is bound by the law as long as her husband liveth; but if her husband be dead, she is at liberty to be married to whom she will; only in the Lord.

40 But she is happier if she so abide, after my judgemen: and I think also that I have the Spirit of God.

(35-38) I do not say this to cast any problems before you, but so that you may profit by it, and do more of the things that are of worthiness for the Lord, with fewer distractions. If any man is concerned about his virginity, and feels he is getting past his prime, then let him marry without feeling ashamed. Nevertheless, one who has power over his own will, and who has decided in his heart to stay virgin, is also well to accept it. The one who releases his virginity in marriage is acceptable, and the one who decides to remain continent is acceptable also.[7]

(39-40) In marriage, a wife is bound to her husband so long as he lives, and is at liberty to remarry after his death, only in the teachings of the Lord. I feel that I agree with this.[8]

DISCOURSE CHAPTER SEVEN

1. Q: You insert a phrase in 7:2 that opens up pandora's box. You use the parenthetical phrase "since the sexes were divided"; do you want to get into that?

   A: In what way do you pose this question?

   Q: This is something that you added; it is not in the other text and so immediately someone is going to catch it and say "Oh, when were the sexes divided?" Then the question arises, do you want to give an explanation of that phrase?

   A: Could we recap on the context here.

   Q: "Concerning those matters about which you wrote to me, it is good for a man or woman to be continent and abstain from sex at times. It is at all times necessary to avoid immorality; (Since the sexes were divided) there have been certain rules. Each man must have his own wife and each wife her husband and each should be good to the other."

   A: This is a subject which is rather lengthy and would be a little distracting to entertain in this particular point. What we should do, I think, is earmark that subject as one for the appendix. I shall be very happy to enlarge upon it; it is required I think. I shall look to you to put forward suggestions concerning these matters which are extremely important for the general understanding of people. Such a subject as homosexuality, sexuality in the main, vicarious atonement, original sin; they are such vital issues that it is important that they be entered into rather more than is possible within the flow of the context here and I shall be very interested to do this. It will be for your careful study to produce a list of those subjects including the ones that I just listed.

2. Q: In chapter 7:1-7, you are giving advice about marriage and Craig makes a comment. He is coming from the viewpoint of most New Testament scholars that Paul believed firmly in the second coming happening soon. Craig says "Paul's own point of view inevitably lent encouragement to those who felt that marriage should be repudiated entirely. The whole chapter is dominated just as are other sections by the expectations of the immanent parousia. Responsibility to our children and the generations to come does not enter into the apostle's calculations, for he thought of himself as living not in the first century, but in the last century. Marriage was a doubtful wisdom because it might divert from undivided attention to the work of the Lord." *

   A: I think I have lost your question.

   Q: The basic question is: Is he right in assuming that Paul did think that he was

Discourse Chapter Seven continued:

living in the last century instead of the first; that anything that might divert one from true spirituality should be done away with because the end was coming soon, and therefore marriage was something for people who could not handle it otherwise? It was better to stay single because of this view of the Second Coming. Is he interpreting Paul right? He represents many people who believe that is where Paul was.

A: I think he is rather approaching the correct assumption that is to a great extent where Paul was. One has to at all times remember that Paul was also a learner. It was within his own great hope that indeed, the Christ would come again quite soon. Although we think about the state of the world at this present time as being somewhat catastrophic, one must recall that in the limited experience of the traveler in those countries at that time and the suppression by the Roman empire, matters were no less serious and catastrophic then. Indeed, has this not always been the case in the world? And so, those who had the ardor of Paul indeed did entertain the hope that the Christ had not gone away for very long. I might say at this point, he never ever left, but that is another matter. It was the hope within the hearts of Paul and the other apostles indeed, that the Beloved would soon return. And that with his return, would come that glorious golden age about which humanity has been taught down the ages. It was not at that time in Paul's own sphere of reference to recognize cosmic timing.

3. Q: That answer will satisfy many people. This whole section on marriage (7:1-11) and what the single person should do so that they shouldn't be consumed by sexual desire, raised a question from a friend of mine who is deeply involved in the urban scene. Is it possible that there can be a religion for single people? He feels that so often all of the faiths emphasize the family so much that for all those who are single and in the urban scene, they cannot find a place. It is hard for them to find a place in a family oriented religion. Isn't there a religion for single people?

---

*Ibid., p. 76

Discourse Chapter Seven continued:

A: Oh, but of course there is. It is the Universal Religion; the only religion indeed. It is the knowledge of the Christ within and the struggle within each individual to attain that state. We have said that when one arrives at a certain time in his own evolution the need for laws, per se, upon that vehicle are no longer a point of stress, for obedience to the law is then automatic and in that sense there are no longer written laws. In order to impress upon human evolution the fact that each being must work upon itself in order to raise the consciousness beyond the fleshly limitations to the point when that one is able to unite with the All Consciousness, the All Being, the Ten Commandments – and indeed all of the laws – are set forth as guidelines. One who is for any reason a single person upon the earthly plane is no less, is no different in any way to others who choose family relationships. It is simply that the one who is single is so because that is soul's choice for the learning process that this soul is undertaking at this given time. And it matters not in the progress of that soul whether outwardly he/she choose to be a Christian, a Muslim, a Buddhist, whether he follows the Judaic laws, or whatever the choice. It matters not if he profess to be an atheist or anything else. That is a stage in the moment where that soul is. And all are making progress toward universality no matter what their state upon the physical plane, and in the end, there are no religions. We all make our individual soul choice to walk whatever path we choose toward divinity. The God self, the Kingdom of Heaven, the Divine Spark, whatever words we choose, are in us and it is our responsibility to attain.

4. Q: I am raising a question now from 7:16. This is in the discussion of mixed couples where one member of the couple is a believer and the other is not. The statement had been made that if the unbeliever wishes to stay in the relationship that it was fine, being sanctified by the believer; but if he or she wanted to leave, that was okay; that if an unbeliever leaves, the husband or wife should let the other go, whichever it may be. Is it okay for the believer to remarry after the unbeliever has left the couple relationship?

A: As always, there is a situation which is the ideal and there is the situation which is less than ideal. When one deals in generalities one expresses the ideal. And the ideal is that one should be very certain before marriage that the one whom one is marrying is the right partner. And one marries in the hope that this will be a lifetime of mutual support. However, the world is well aware now, as it was then, that such ideal situations are not very prevalent. Does one therefore advocate that the two remain together despite differences which can create anguish, lack of harmony, pain, suffering? My response is no, one does not advocate such.

Discourse Chapter Seven continued:

The particular case in point would appear to suggest that a good reason for separation would be difference in beliefs. One must assume that such a pair would come together in the hope that one of that couple would move away from their belief system and adopt the one which the other is following. If in due time that simply does not work out, then my suggestion in that case was that it were better to separate than to cause all of the negative emotions listed, which in the end serve to no good purpose. Does that then mean that for the rest of the lifetime of those individuals, one is not allowed to remarry? The answer is obviously no, it does not.

Marriage, as such, is an earthbound institution and if those who are separated from one marriage, because for many reasons that marriage does not work out, should the individuals at some future time come together with another who is more suited and with whom mutual harmony can be established, then I say there is nothing within the universal laws of God that says they must not come together. There were certain laws set forth in those biblical times in order to arrive at a degree of order. The laws were such to provide a means to reduce immorality, but these laws are earthbound.

As has been reiterated by many sources, the ultimate coming together between male and female is in order to assist in the growth toward unconditional love. If there is no hope within a present coupling of such, and belief systems do appear to be a considerable stumbling block in that regard, then it is better that the ones in question separate and let the future take its course.

5. Q: That's good. You use the word "churches" in 7:17; do we want to do that? That is a word the KJ version uses too.

A: Perhaps not. I think it might be less confusing were we to fix on one particular term of reference and I believe that in the main I have used the word "community". Church, in the modern age, is rather difficult because of the number of different sectarian religions and offshoots. In the time of that earlier translation, it was a word which would have had more meaning than now. Yes, I think perhaps we should use something else.

Q: I think you are right on the confusion about churches. In Romans we talked about the fact that they really had not formed anything like what we now know as a church, that it was a community of people gathering together for support and teaching. They may not have even had a building at that time.

Discourse Chapter Seven continued:

    A: No, no they did not. "Community" I think is the best word here. Let us therefore be consistent with that.

6.   Q: I think you have partly answered this already, but there is a section in 7:29, where Paul sounds like he is talking about the end of the age: "I need to say this, that before too long there will be much travail on the earthly plane, that those who have wives will act as though they had none, they that weep will be as if they did not, they that rejoice shall act as if they had nothing to rejoice about, those that make purchases shall be as if they possess nothing, the people who use this world shall change, for the fashion of this world will pass away". That sounds very much as if he was expecting the second coming rather soon.

    A: There have been prophesies concerning the end of the world as we know it down through many centuries and the ministers of that day were no more certain of the precise timing of that forecast which is contained in all of the mythology of the world, than they are now. Perhaps we are a little closer now. I think that subject is covered.

7.   Q: Again, at the end of chapter 7:38, you say "The one who releases his virginity in marriage is acceptable and the one who decides to remain continent is doing better". Do you really want to use the term "better"?

    A: No.

    Q: We could change it to the phrase to match the other one, "also acceptable."

    A: Read the whole sentence again please.

    Q: "If any man is concerned about his virginity and feels he is getting to be past his prime, then let him marry without feeling ashamed, nevertheless, one who has power over his own will and has decided in his heart to stay virgin, is also well to accept it. The one who releases his virginity in marriage is acceptable and the one who elects to remain continent is doing better".

    A: Yes, I think we should change it to "is acceptable also". In other words, either one is acceptable.

8.   Q: I found this last sentence in 7:40 confusing: "In marriage a wife is bound to her husband so long as he lives and is at liberty to remarry after his death, only in the teachings of the Lord. I feel that I agree with this however, but in my judgment I feel that this is correct and it is better" That last sentence doesn't make sense.

Discourse Chapter Seven continued:

A: It is rather badly worded, isn't it. What in fact is being said here is that the Lord has set forth teachings to the effect that a widow or widower is perfectly at liberty to remarry; in fact, in some cases it were better that she or he did. I specify that this is in accordance with the teachings set forth by Jesus because there are many religions that do not feel remarriage to be a good thing. Some religions stipulate that when one's marriage partner has died, one should remain single until the end of life. This subject was addressed from the standpoint of the teachings of our Lord. Does that clarify? Perhaps the sentence needs to be redone so that it is clearer. I do agree that it was very ambiguous.

Q: Yes, I think it could be shortened; we could say "I feel that I agree with this."

FIRST CORINTHIANS 8

8 Now as touching things offered unto idols, we know that we all have knowledge. Knowledge puffeth up, but charity edifieth.

2 And if any man think that he knoweth anything he knoweth nothing yet as he ought to know.

3 But if any man love God, the same is known of him.

4 As concerning therefore the eating of those things that are offered in sacrifice unto idols, we know that an idol is nothing in the world, and that there is none other God but one.

5 For though there be that are called gods, whether in heaven or in earth (as there be gods many, and lords many,)

6 But to us there is but one God, the Father, of whom are all things, and we in him; and one Lord Jesus Christ, by whom are all things, and we by him.

7 Howbeit there is not in every man that knowledge: for some with conscience of the idol unto this hour eat it as a thing offered unto an idol; and their conscience being weak is defiled.

8 But meat commendeth us not to God: for neither, if we eat, are we the better; neither, if we eat not, are we the worse.

9 But take heed lest by any means this liberty of yours become a stumbling block to them that are weak.

10 For if any man see thee which has knowledge sit at meat in the idol's temple, shall not the conscience of him which is weak be emboldened to eat those things which are offered to idols;

11 And through thy knowledge shall the weak brother perish, for whom Christ died?

12 But when ye sin so against the brethren, and wound their weak conscience, ye sin against Christ.

8 (1-6) I wish to address now the issue concerning eating of things which have been offered in sacrifice to idols. There are many things which, as yet, we do not understand (even though many of us think we do). Let me remind you that there is only One First Cause or Supreme Godhead, that is God the Father, God the Son which is Christ, and God the Holy Spirit; even though there are many lesser gods and lords (and those who are called "gods" which are not). [1,2]

(7-13) In any case, everyone is not aware of the difference. Some who until this moment have only been aware of idols are conscience stricken at the thought of eating meat that has been sacrificed. Do you not understand that it is not what we eat that raises our consciousness; for it really makes little difference whether we eat or not. Be very careful lest this issue become a stumbling block to others who are unsure of themselves. If others were to see you who now have a better understanding (of the Teachings), sitting down to eat sacrificial meat, shall not their own conscience be appeased in doing the same? When you carry out these kinds of heedless actions, you harm others, you harm yourselves, and above all, you repudiate the Teachings of Christ. For myself, if I find that such eating causes offense to others, I would refrain from partaking to the end of the world, rather than give offense.

First Corinthians 8

13 Wherefore, if meat make my brother to offend, I will eat no flesh while the world standeth, lest I make my brother to offend.

DISCOURSE CHAPTER EIGHT

1. Q: In 8:6, in the RSV it is stated "hence as to the eating of food offered to idols, we know that an idol has no real existence and that there is no God but one. For all those so called Gods in heaven or on earth, as indeed there are many gods and many lords, yet for us there is one God the father from whom all things..." In the way you worded it, you do not put the word "yet" at the end so that it reads: "Let me remind you that there is only one First Cause or Supreme Godhead, that is God the Father, God the Son, which is Christ the God and only Spirit, even though there are many lesser gods and lords, and those who are called gods which are not". Basically what you have done is to say "even though there are many lesser gods". In the old version it states "yet for us there is one God". That is going to raise some questions.

    A: The basic difficulty has arisen from the use of the word God. Throughout the evolution of humanity there has been the recognition of certain forces which man has chosen to call gods. There has been then confusion in the monotheistic religions which advocate one God as the supreme God. The confusion arises out of the fact that the lesser devic forces are called god by many other religions. Let us therefore assume that the First Cause, or that which the Christian looks upon as the only God, is in fact God. In the three-fold energy of God the Father, God the Son, and God the Holy Ghost or Holy Spirit which is the feminine aspect of that Godhead, we therefore equate that supreme source of all things – call it what we will – with the one and only God.

    What then do we do with all of the powers besides the throne – the co-creators; what do we do with the planetary logoi; what do we do with the devic and the nature spirits and all of the multitudes of forces which work in hierarchic sequence down into this earthly plane? It is unfortunate that the very God referred to in the Old Testament is one such; is not the Supreme Godhead. He was, rather, a racial god; one of the gods of this world. We must therefore recognize that to use the same word to describe something which is of this earth and then to also attempt to describe that which cannot be named, indeed, is very confusing, and has been

Discourse Chapter Eight continued:

confusing since man was created. However, let us here make no mistake that there are many, many levels. There are many force fields which move down from that first supreme creator of all things, the One, and step down their frequencies until they come into created form, and then in the realms of created form meet again many more forces that are all part of the creative urge; yet, again, all part of the One. If we know above all things that we are all part of the One, then yes, we recognize one supreme deity but this does not discount all of the forces that assist that Supreme Cause.

2. Q: This other question from 8:6 is likely to need a long answer also. In your version you left out a phrase that was in the KJ and RVS version which I think reflects your belief but you left it out.

    A: Are you saying that something was omitted from the translation of the King James version?

    Q: Yes. It is a whole verse containing the phrase "and one Lord Jesus Christ by whom are all things and we by Him". The RSV states it "Through whom we are all things and through whom we exist". The problem for the biblical people is that they are concerned that this is one of the few phrases that confirms the pre-existence of Christ. Craig responds to it in this way: "It is improbable that we shall ever be in a position to explain exactly how Paul came to affirm this pre-existence. Had he ground for belief that Jesus Himself had taught it? Was it a development of the Jewish belief in wisdom as the means by which God created? Did it arise from the influence of Greek popular philosophy on the speculative Judaism with which Paul had contact? Was it due to the influence of Egyptian beliefs that a lord had sway over the world as well as within the cult? It is unlikely that research will ever demonstrate a genealogy satisfactory to all specialists in the field because of our very fragmentary evidence from the ancient world, we can only know in part. But it is perfectly clear that Paul wanted to affirm a pre-existence of Christ."

---

* Ibid., p.94

Discourse Chapter Eight continued:

A: My commentary surrounding the last question does, to some extent, answer this one also. The new Paul, the one who is now initiated into the meanings of the deeper wisdoms, recognizes full well that Christ, the Universal Christ, of course pre-existed the birth of Jesus the Master. The difficulty within the minds of the formative Christian Church and the continuing difficulty in the progress of that church down through the centuries has been the differentiation between Jesus the man and Jesus the Christ. And in referring to the one being as Jesus Christ, what the Christian Church has done is make of that one human being a supreme deity which is incorrect. First there was the man, born of human parents and fully of the flesh; Jeshua ben Joseph, or Jesus. At a point within His own progress, that one, having prepared so lovingly a body into which part of the Supreme Godhead – the Christ – could fully enter and therefore come down into the world of form at that point, Jeshua and the Christ became one being, and yes, from that point on He was Jesus the Christ. And yes, in the recognition of that truth, Paul the man also recognized and admitted that first and always there was and is The Christ.

It comes from the error set down within the annals of the Christian Church. The error, I repeat, that the Supreme Godhead in the form of the Christ has only ever come to this earthly plane once through the body of our Lord Jesus. This is not founded in truth. The supernal being has come to this earthly plane many, many times in many other bodies; Jesus the Master being one only; perhaps the greatest, yet none the less one of many.

FIRST CORINTHIANS 9

9 *Am I not an apostle? Am I not free? Have I not seen Jesus Christ our Lord? Are not ye my work in the Lord?*

2 If I be not an apostle unto others, yet doubtless I am to you: for the seal of mine apostleship are ye in the Lord.

3 Mine answer to them that do examine me is this,

4 Have we not power to eat and to drink?

5 Have we not power to lead about a sister, a wife, as well as other apostles, and as the brethren of the Lord, and Cephas?

6 Or I only and Barnabas, have not we power to forbear working?

7 Who goeth a warfare any time at his own charges? Who planteth a vineyard, and eateth not of the fruit thereof? Or who feedeth a flock and eateth not of the milk of the flock?

8 Say I these things as a man? Or saith not the law the same also?

9 For it is written in the law of Moses, Thou shalt not muzzle the mouth of the ox that treadeth out the corn. Doth God take care for oxen?

10 Saith He it altogether for our sakes? For our sakes, no doubt, this is written: that he that ploweth should plow in hope; and that he that thresheth in hope should be partaker of his hope.

11 If we have sown unto you spiritual things, is it a great thing if we shall reap your carnal things?

12 If others be partakers of this power over you, are not we rather? Nevertheless we have not used this power; but suffer all things, lest we should hinder the gospel of Christ.

13 Do ye not know that they which minister about holy things live of the things of the temple. And they which wait at the altar are partakers with the altar?

9 (1-3) I am the Apostle of Christ and in that freedom, having recognized the power of Christ, you are my chosen work, and you are the seal of that apostleship in the Lord. I may not be an apostle to others, but I am to you.

(4-7) And to those who question me, I say, Do we not have the right to our food and drink? Do we not have the right to be accompanied by a wife, as the other apostles and the brothers of the Lord and Cephas? Or is it only Barnabas and I who have no right to refrain from working for a living? Who serves as a soldier at his own expense? Who plants a vineyard without eating any of its fruit? Who tends a flock without getting some of the milk?[1]

(8-12) Do I say this on human authority? Does not the law say the same? For it is written in the law of Moses, "You shall not muzzle an ox when it is treading out the grain." Is it for oxen that God is concerned? Does He not speak entirely for our sake? It was written for our sake, because the plowman should plow in hope and the thresher thresh in hope of a share in the crop. If we have sown spiritual good among you, is it too much if we reap your material benefits? If others share this rightful claim upon you, do not we still more?

(13-14) Nevertheless, we have not made use of this right, but we endure anything rather than put an obstacle in the way of the gospel of Christ: Do you not know that those who are employed in the temple service get their food from the temple, and those who serve at the altar share in the sacrificial offerings?

First Corinthians 9

14 Even so hath the Lord ordained that they which preach the gospel should live of the gospel.

15 But I have used none of these things: neither have I written these things, that it should be so done unto me: for it were better for me to die, than that any man should make my glorying void.

16 For though I preach the gospel I have nothing to glory of for necessity is laid upon me; yea, woe is unto me, if I preach not the gospel!

17 For if I do this thing willingly, I have a reward: but if against my will a dispensation of the gospel is committed unto me.

18 What is my reward then? Verily that, when I preach the gospel I may make the gospel of Christ without charge, that I abuse not my power in the gospel.

19 For though I be free from all men, yet have I made myself servant unto all that I might gain the more.

20 And unto the Jews I became as a Jew, that I might gain the Jews; to them that are under the law, as under the law, that I might gain them that are under the law;

21 To them that are without law as without law, (being not without law to God, but under the law to Christ,) that I might gain them that are without law.

22 To the weak became I as weak that I might gain the weak: I am made all things to all men, that I might by all means save some.

23 And this I do for the gospel's sake, that I might be partaker thereof with you.

In the same way, the Lord commanded that those who proclaim the gospel should get their living by the gospel.

(15-18) However, I have not pressed any of these matters for provisions, for I would rather die than have anyone think I am vainglorious. Though I am a preacher of the gospel, I am myself as nothing. I would simply feel the worse, were I not to spend my life preaching the good news. When I do this with good will, it is its own reward. Were I to do it unwillingly, it might seem like a commission, in expectation of reward. What is my reward then? This is it: that when I bring the gospel of Christ, I do so without any personal charge upon it, thus not expecting results.

(19-23) Thus I do not abuse that power, for in being free, spiritually, I become a server of all, and thus gain the more. To those who are Jews, I spoke as a Jew that I might gain their attention. To those who know the law, I speak of the law, that I might gain theirs also. To those who are outside of the law, I speak as one outside (being not outside of God's laws, in Christ) that I might also gain the lawless among you. To the weak, I was weak, and so tried to be all things to all men, that I might gain some of them. This I do for the sake of the Good News, that I might share it with you.

First Corinthians 9

24 Know ye not that they which run in a race run all, but one receiveth the prize? So run, that ye may obtain.

25 And every man that striveth for the mastery is temperate in all things. Now they do it to obtain a corruptible crown; but we are incorruptible.

26 I therefore so run, not as uncertainly; so fight I, not as one that beateth the air;

27 But I keep under my body, and bring it into subjection: lest that by any means, when I have preached to others, I myself should be a castaway.

(24-27) Realize that all who are in the race, run that race, but only one receives the prize. Run then, that you may obtain. Everyone who strives for self-mastery must be temperate in all things. People do this to obtain the crown which is perishable,[2] but we do it for a reward which is imperishable. I therefore also run the race and fight, but not like someone beating the empty air. Rather, I keep my own things of the body under control, so that people do not accuse me of doing the things I speak against, and cast me out.

DISCOURSE CHAPTER NINE

1. Q: In the beginning of 9:3-15, there is a marked difference between the K.J version and the RSV. Our scholars say that the KJ in that section was using an inferior text and that the RSV version is more accurate. It changes the meaning. Since you were following the KJ version, you tend to have the meaning that it conveys as compared to the RSV. I will read the two sections.

   A: Before you do this, there is an interesting comment here. Whose text was inferior? There is only one letter written by Paul. Therefore, if there were several texts, obviously only one is the wording of Paul. Please proceed.

   Q: I don't think they have an original letter at all. What they have are two or three copies and they are making some judgments on which copy is most accurate.

   A: Exactly so, making judgments. Shall we proceed.

   Q: The King James version reads: "Mine answer to them that do examine me is this, Have we not power to eat and to drink, have we not power to lead about a sister, a wife as well as other apostles as the brethren of the lord and Cephas or is it I only and Barnabas, have not we power to forebear working? Who goeth the warfare any time at his own charges. Who planteth the vineyard and eateth not of the fruit thereof. . . " The RSV states: "This is my defense to those who would examine me; do we not have the right to our food and drink, do we not have the

Discourse Chapter Nine continued:

right to be accompanied by a wife as the other apostles and the brothers of the Lord as Cephas, or is it only Barnabas and I who have no right to refrain from working for a living? Who serves as a soldier at his own expense. Who plants a vineyard without eating any of its fruit. Who tends the flock without getting some of the milk?" In other words, the RSV is much clearer in regards to the fact that Paul is writing about their rights to be taken care of. Then he goes on to use the argument that he and Barnabas have not done that, that they have not taken that right which was due them. You wrote, "I may not be an apostle to others, but I am to you. To those who question me I say, have we not power to eat and drink, have we not the power to be guides to others, sisters, wives, other apostles, and such as Cephas, all of whom are brethren of the Lord. Or do you think it is only Barnabas and I who have the power to do as we wish."

A: I am not sure I understand your question here, although in contemplation of the text, I do recognize that it is a little obscure. What is your question?

Q: That is my question; that it is a little obscure and I thought that the RSV is clearer in this instance. Do you wish to re-dictate it?

A: No, I really do agree with you here that the RSV does, in that particular section, express it far more clearly. Rather than going over it again, why don't we just use that for that section. Indeed, it does express quite clearly what I was saying. In effect Paul was saying here what the RSV indicates. Even a soldier does not go to war with his own money, people plant vineyards and are allowed to eat the fruits, etc.

2. Q: This is a minor one; at the end of 9:24-27, it is talking about the runners and the crown. In the Greek races the winner would get a crown of laurel leaves. In the KJ they use the word "corruptible", that the crown is "corruptible". The RSV uses the word "perishable".

A: Corruption is very different than perishable indeed. Let us use perishable.

FIRST CORINTHIANS 10

10 *Moreover, brethren, I would not that ye should be ignorant, how that all our fathers were under the cloud, and all passed through the sea;*

2 And were all baptized unto Moses in the cloud and in the sea;

3 And did all eat the same spiritual meat;

4 And did all drink the same spiritual drink for they drank of that spiritual Rock that followed them: and that Rock was Christ.

5 But with many of them God was not well pleased: for they were overthrown in the wilderness.

6 Now these things were our examples, to the intent we should not lust after evil things, as they also lusted.

7 Neither be ye idolaters, as were some of them; as it is written, The people sat down to eat and drink, and rose up to play.

8 Neither let us commit fornication, as some of them committed, and fell in one day three and twenty thousand.

9 Neither let us tempt Christ, as some of them also tempted, and were destroyed of serpents.

10 Neither murmur ye, as some of them also murmured, and were destroyed of the destroyer.

11 Now all these things happened unto them for ensamples: and they are written for our admonition, upon whom the ends of the world are come.

12 Wherefore let him that thinketh he standeth take heed lest he fall.

13 There hath no temptation taken you but such as is common to man: but God is faithful, who will not suffer you to be tempted above that ye are able; but will with the temptation also make a way to escape, that ye may be able to bear it.

10 (1-5) I would remind you of our forefathers who accompanied Moses (out of Egypt) and were guided through the desert by the cloud. They crossed the sea, and were, so to speak, "baptized" to Moses by this experience. They all partook of the same spiritual food and drink which was the Rock that followed them. That Rock was the Christ. But even so there were some that offended and were overthrown in the desert.

(6-13) These things should be a lesson to us, that we do not fall by the same means. Do not you be idolaters either, as were some of them. I remind you that twenty three thousand people fell in a single day because of immorality. Some defied the Christ and were killed by serpents.[1] Some that dissented fell as a result of their dissent. All these things are for good example, and recorded for our warning in the records of all time. Therefore, let those who think they are upright look to themselves lest they fall. The temptations that beset you are the same for all humanity. God is all wise and does not submit any to temptations greater than their ability to overcome.

(14-22) Therefore dear friends, stay away from idolatry. I speak wisely – hear me. When we drink the Blessed Cup and break the Bread, we partake in the blood and the body of Christ, in the sacrament of His Holy Communion. We are therefore all one body, for we participate in that one bread which is Life. Take a look at the practice of Israel, are not the very ones who eat sacrificial flesh those who serve at the altar? Does this make anything out

First Corinthians 10

14 Wherefore, my dearly beloved, flee from idolatry.

15 I speak as to wise men; judge ye what I say.

16 The cup of blessing which we bless, is it not the communion of the blood of Christ? The bread which we break, is it not the communion of the body of Christ?

17 For we being many are one bread, and one body: for we are all partakers of that one bread.

18 Behold Israel after the flesh: are not they which eat of the sacrifices partakers of the altar?

19 What say I then? That the idol is any thing, or that which is offered in sacrifice to idols is any thing?

20 But I say, that the things which the Gentiles sacrifice, they sacrifice to devils, and not to God: and I would not that ye should have fellowship with devils.

21 Ye cannot drink the cup of the Lord, and the cup of devils: ye cannot be partakers of the Lord's table, and of the table of devils.

22 Do we provoke the Lord to jealousy? Are we stronger than He?

23 All things are lawful for me, but all things are not expedient: all things are lawful for me, but all things edify not.

24 Let no man seek his own, but every man another's wealth.

25 Whatsoever is sold in the shambles, that eat, asking no question for conscience sake:

26 For the earth is the Lord's and the fullness thereof

27 If any of them that believe not bid you to a feast, and ye be disposed to go; whatsoever is set before you, eat, asking no question for conscience sake:

of the idol, or out of the flesh that is sacrificed? I say this, those things which the Gentiles sacrifice, they at least sacrifice to devils, and not to "God". I do not advocate that you keep company with devil worshippers.[2] One cannot partake of the Communion given by the Lord, while at the same time partaking of sacrificial meat. Do we disprove what the Lord taught us? Do we know better than He?

(23-30) All things might be regarded as lawful but they are certainly not therefore expedient, nor do they raise our consciousness. In this, let us not look only for our own, but also for the raising in consciousness of others. That which is sold to you in the market, accept in good faith, for the trust in others, remembering that the Earth is the Lord's and the fullness thereof. If you are invited to a feast with those of a different faith, and you accept, eat whatever is placed before you – with a blessing, so that you do not offend.[2] On the other hand, if someone informs you that this is food which has been offered to idols, then do not eat it (for the sake of your own consciousness) in deference to your informant, even though again the Earth is the Lord's and its fullness. What I say is that you are thus putting the feelings of others before your own, remembering that if you partake with grace in what is offered, then no ill can possibly come of it.

First Corinthians 10

28 But if any man say unto you, This is offered in sacrifice unto idols, eat not for his sake that shewed it, and for conscience sake: for the earth is the Lord's, and the fullness thereof.

29 Conscience, I say, not thine own, but of the other: for why is my liberty judged of another man's conscience?

30 For if I by grace be a partaker, why am I evil spoken of for that for which I give thanks?

31 Whether therefore ye eat, or drink, or whatsoever ye do, do all to the glory of God.

32 Give none offence, neither to the Jews, nor to the Gentiles, nor to the church of God:

33 Even as I please all men in all things, not seeking mine own profit, but the profit of many that they may be saved.

(31-33) Whatever you eat, drink or do, do it all for God's glorification and give offense to none – neither Jew, Gentile, or the Community of faith. This is what I try to do, seeking nothing which is a gain for myself, but pleasing all, that all might gain.

DISCOURSE CHAPTER TEN

1. Q: In 10:8-10, it reads "I remind you that 23,000 people fell in a single day because of immorality". I think you are referring to the time in the wilderness. "Some defied the Christ and were killed by serpents". My response is that this sounds like the old, wrathful, jealous God and seems like the Old Testament concept. Paul is using this as an example. Does this need comment?

    A: No, it is not equating with the Old Testament God who is a jealous warlike individual. It is simply admonishing the people of that time by statement of what was an historic fact, that because of their stupidity during that period of history known as the Exodus, many people perished who need not have done so had they heeded. Really, the passage is not altogether simply an injunction against immorality. It is saying that if one goes blindly ahead with one's ignorance, then this can have dire results – both individually and collectively. Not so much threatening calamity on a mass scale – as was the case in Exodus – but endeavoring

Discourse Chapter Ten continued:

to point out that what we do certainly brings about its effect, again harking back to the Law of Cause and Effect; and that what each individual creates does have a repercussion upon the group, upon the community, and upon the race. It had nothing to do with calling down the wrath of a jealous God; it had everything to do with again attempting to convince the mind of the hearer that all actions pre-date effect.

2. Q: There are some questions regarding 10:20 and 10:27. The context of 10:20 is "I say this, those things which the gentiles sacrificed, they at least sacrificed to devils and not to God"; and then, "I do not advocate that you keep company with devil worshippers". A little further down in verse 27; "If you are invited to a feast with those of a different faith, then you eat whatever is placed before you with a blessing so that you do not offend. On the other hand, if someone informs you that this is food which has been offered to idols, then do not eat it". In one case you are saying don't keep company with the gentiles in the area who worship idols, and in the next you say that if you are invited to a feast with them, be gracious and fit in with them. These seem contradictory.

    A: No, not quite. They are not contradictory, but the amount of discourse within the text is a little too simplistic. There was at that period in history a great deal of what one could only call devil worship – the practice of what is today more commonly regarded as "black magic". There were many cults who sacrificed to those occult practices – of the black variety, that is. On the one hand, the first reference is that one must indeed avoid such at all costs. However, one must also remember that one of the things that our Lord had tried to eradicate from the Jewish faith was the sacrifice of animals; ritual sacrifice of animals is not correct no matter who does it. But because of the centuries of inbred belief, one could not classify the latter as devil worship; it was simply an erroneous concept which Jesus tried very hard to set straight and of course, was not heard. In this instance where one has an otherwise upright citizen, then certainly if one sits down at table with such a one, one is not doing anything outside of the law. However, since it became Paul's conviction, as it had been Jesus' conviction, that the ritual slaughter of animals was incorrect, and was tantamount to being sacrificed to idols, then in such a case it would be quite correct within the conscience of the individual to refuse such food.

Discourse Chapter Ten continued:

Q: Can you name some of those satanic or black magic cults; the historians might be very interested if you named some of them.

A: I think not within the context we are currently speaking about; there are many, many such.

Q: In that sentence where it states "if you are invited to sit with someone of another faith", you are primarily referring to Jewish people.

A: Exactly, or any legitimate path, the citizens of which are upright people, but who have been subjected to erroneous illusions.

FIRST CORINTHIANS 11

11 Be ye followers of me, even as I also am of Christ.

2 Now I praise you, brethren, that ye remember me in all things, and keep the ordinances, as I delivered them to you.

3 But I would have you know, that the head of every man is Christ; and the head of the woman is the man; and the head of Christ is God.

4 Every man praying or prophesying, having his head covered, dishonoureth his head.

5 But every woman that prayeth or prophesieth with her head uncovered dishonoureth her head: for that is even all one as if she were shaven.

6 For if the woman be not covered, let her also be shorn: but if it be a shame for a woman to be shorn or shaven, let her be covered.

7 For a man indeed ought not to cover his head, forasmuch as he is the image and glory of God: but the woman is the glory of the man.

8 For the man is not of the woman; but the woman of the man.

9 Neither was the man created for the woman; but the woman for the man.

10 For this cause ought the woman to have power on her head because of the angels.

11 Nevertheless neither is the man without the woman, neither the woman without the man, in the Lord.

12 For as the woman is of the man, even so is the man also by the woman; but all things of God.

13 Judge in yourselves: is it comely that a woman pray unto God uncovered?

14 Doth not even nature itself teach you, that, if a man have long hair, it is a shame unto him?

11 (1-17) Be followers of my example, even as I follow that of Christ. I thank you for trying to stay faithful to these concepts as I have delivered them to you and I remind you that Christ stands at the head of us all, and God above Him. Touching on the subject of head covering it is said that when a man meditates or preaches he should do so with head uncovered since that is more honorable, whereas woman should keep her head covered so that she does not dishonor man. To be uncovered is (for woman) tantamount to being a man, and she should therefore shave her head as a man. If she feels shame at shaving the head, then let her head remain covered while praying or preaching or making prophesy, because of the presence of the angels. There are all kinds of contentions concerning such things (even the length of a man's hair) and I tell you that the Community of God has no such contentions or customs. Those who contend simply make their difficulties worse.[1]

First Corinthians 11

15 But if a woman have long hair it is a glory to her: for her hair is given her for a covering.

16 But if any man seem to be contentious, we have no such custom, neither the churches of God.

17 Now in this that I declare unto you I praise you not, that ye come together not for the better, but for the worse.

18 For first of all, when ye come together in the church, I hear that there be divisions among you; and I partly believe it.

19 For there must be also heresies among you, that they which are approved be made manifest among you.

20 When ye come together therefore into one place, this is not to eat the Lord's supper.

21 For in eating every one taketh before other his own supper: and one is hungry, and another is drunken.

22 What? Have ye not houses to eat and to drink in? Or despise ye the church of God and shame them that have not? What shall I say to you? Shall I praise you in this? I praise you not.

23 For I have received of the Lord that which also I delivered unto you. That the Lord Jesus the same night in which He was betrayed took bread:

24 And when He had given thanks, He brake it and said, "Take, eat: this is My body, which is broken for you: this do in remembrance of Me."

25 After the same manner also He took the cup, when He had supped, saying "This cup is the new testament in My blood: this do ye, as oft as ye drink it, in remembrance of Me."

26 For as often as ye eat this bread, and drink this cup, ye do shew the Lord's death till He come.

(18-22) I am hearing that even when you come together to the Lord's Table for the Sacrament, there is contention among you, and I am inclined to believe it. There must be some heresy which creates these divisions. You cannot come to the Lord's table each looking for your own fulfillment and go away replete while another is left in hunger. Do you not have your own homes in which to indulge yourselves? Do you so despise God's congregation that you act in this way? Will you shame others who are needy? Do you think I should be happy with such actions? I tell you, I am not!

(23-26) I receive the sacrament of the Lord, which I pass on to you. At the Last Supper, that night in which He was betrayed, the Lord Jesus took bread; and when He had given thanks, He broke it, saying: "Take, eat; this is My Body which is broken for you; this do in remembrance of Me." After the same manner He then took the cup, and when He had drunk, said: "This cup is the New Covenant in My blood; this do you, as often as you drink it in remembrance of Me." For as often as you eat this bread and drink this cup, you shall do so in knowledge of the Lord's sacrifice until He comes.[2]

First Corinthians 11

27 Wherefore whosoever shall eat this bread, and drink this cup of the Lord, unworthily, shall be guilty of the body and blood of the Lord.

28 But let a man examine himself and so let him eat of that bread, and drink of that cup.

29 For he that eateth and drinketh unworthily, eateth and drinketh damnation to himself not discerning the Lord's body.

30 For this cause many are weak and sickly among you, and many sleep.

31 For if we would judge ourselves, we should not be judged.

32 But when we are judged, we are chastened of the Lord, that we should not be condemned with the world.

33 Wherefore, my brethren, when ye come together to eat, tarry one for another.

34 And if any man hunger, let him eat at home; that ye come not together unto condemnation. And the rest will I set in order when I come.

(27-34) Whoever does this with unworthy heart is shamed in that Body and that Blood. Therefore, examine your consciousness and be sure that you partake worthily. Those who do not, bring condemnation to themselves, and that state can create sickness and imbalance in you; for it means you are spiritually asleep. If we would judge ourselves, then we would not be judged. By this we are chastened so that we are not seen in the eyes of the world as worthy of condemnation. I urge that when you meet together, that you are there for each other. If anyone wishes to attend only his own needs, then let that one stay at home. I will speak to other matters when I come to be with you.[3,4]

DISCOURSE CHAPTER ELEVEN

1. I was in two minds about this chapter, from verse three through sixteen. The reason for inclusion in the letter in the first place, of comment regarding concern for head covering was this: According to Judaic law, a man entering the Temple covered the head (women also, even though in later history they were confined to the outer precincts). According to the laws of many gentile countries the man does not cover the head, though women still do. Dissent arose as to which was correct, and also concerning the length of hair worn by men.

    I was hastening to inform the dissenters that there is no such law before God. However, there is a deeper esoteric law, which at this point might be referred to, because verse ten touches on "woman having power on her head because of the angels..."

Discourse Chapter Eleven continued:

In order to understand the significance of this, one needs to have basic knowledge concerning the human aura and the head. One also is required to have basic knowledge of what is the Akasha. The mind is a sphere of intangible substance responsive to the slightest impulse from either inside or outside of that entity whose mind it is. Each impression gives rise to countless images by these stimuli; that is, from association of ideas, or from objects we feel with our senses. All of these things, whether material or astral, are formed from the substance of that which is called "Akasha". The brain, mind and head are, in fact, a small world, or sphere of Akasha. The Akashic substance penetrates the human brain and head, and can carry with it images, carried by currents of force or thoughts projected onto it by another mind. These thoughts carry for thousands of miles from the point of generation, and, according to their nature, can be a hindrance, or an assistance. Akasha then, can be said to correspond to a great extent, to the head, to the pituitary body of the brain, and to the senses of sight, hearing and speech. The impulses are also conveyed to the heart and to the generative organs, affecting the fires of creation. Akasha is particularly attractive to the germinal spot in the egg or seed. It corresponds to the emotional surge of Love, and particularly potent in women, to the passive side of nature and to the soil in which the seed is planted. Akasha corresponds in matter, to Ether, to sound, (vibrating to the color Indigo and the keynote A in the tonic scale) and touches Universal Mind. It is recorded by the great Recording Angel, and responds to the negative pole (the left hand, the receptor). In the true Church Universal, it is said to be the Bride, that is, the channel through which Universal Light and Love-Wisdom may flow without interruption.

Knowing these facts, the Ancient Wisdom Schools required that a woman cover the head on entering a place of power, dedicated to the Universal Wisdoms, because of the particular energy being received and transmitted by the Feminine Principle, more especially when contained in the physical vehicle of a woman. Only the more advanced woman Initiate was admitted to the Inner Sanctum of such places of power because she must exercise great personal discernment on two causes: (a) that she not project her powerful thoughts to the detriment of others not so powerful; and (b) that she not bring with her into the Inner Place, any negative frequencies. All frequencies surrounding the head are attractive to the denizens of the subtle realms, which are loosely termed "angels" in Christian theology. These may be of a positive or of a negative nature. It is advisable for man also to cover the head if intending to go into a deeper meditational state in order to receive transmitted wisdom from those other realms.

Discourse Chapter Eleven continued:

This whole subject was taken by the translators in the Church of Rome as an excuse to prolong and exacerbate the denigration of women to the rank of servility which, of course, is an absolute miscarriage of the truth.

2. Q: In chapter 11:18-32, I have a general comment here. Since this chapter deals with Communion, can you comment more about what the Communion meal was. It sounds very different from what we do with Communion today. We assume it was probably in a home, which means it wasn't a very large gathering, and was it always a full meal? Were class distinctions becoming a problem as implied, and was there anyone to lead it?

A: There are a number of questions in that. I will try to answer all the questions that were put together there. First of all, no, there was not in any way considered to be any kind of class distinction any more than there was any kind of class distinction in the choice of those who were the disciples. The Twelve came from many different walks of life as you well know. What has been generally called the last supper was such for the obvious reason that this was indeed the last time that all came together to participate in a collective meal. The collective meal had been something which the group had enjoyed together many times and this was to be the last.

Since it was also to be the last time that the Lord Jesus would be with all of those people together, the group chosen to participate was select; not because of any kind of class distinction, but because there was a final message of great importance that He desired to impart to all present while the opportunity still existed. The meal itself was more in nature of the Passover meal that would be enjoyed throughout the land and I believe, would have conformed to the traditional and is very likely to have been bread, wine, and lamb. Since down through the ages, the bread which comes from the wheat, has been regarded as the stuff of life, and the wine, which comes from the grape, has been regarded also as the support of vitality, our Lord took this as an opportunity to express a much older concept than what became the sacrament of the Last Supper.

First of all, He reminded those present of the passage of the seasons, of the festivals of the passage of the seasons. He spoke of the planting, of the preparing of the soil. He spoke of the bursting forth of the plants, of their coming to maturity, and of the harvest which is the giving of the life of the plant and its return of the seed back into the earth in order to perpetuate life. In other words, He spoke of the age-old mystery which is the precession of the equinoxes and which is significant as the giver of life upon this planet.

Discourse Chapter Eleven continued:

And in so doing, He demonstrated the meaning in the washing of the disciples' feet, speaking of the sacrifice made by Mother Earth in order that the Spring shall come. He spoke of the service to other, and admonished all present that those who would seek to be teachers, leaders, masters, must also be of service in humility to others. And when finally He had spoken of all of these things, He reminded those present of the bread of life which is the result of all that has been sacrificed. And in taking the bread and breaking it, He reminded those present, "I too am now come to that point in My life when I am sacrificed, therefore, eat this bread now with Me and whenever you do so again, remember this time". Then He took the wine which is the stuff of life, equivalent from the plant to the blood in the human body, and He said "That which is sacrificed, that which gives of itself in sacrifice, gives its blood, falling upon the earth, in order to insure that all of life will continue. This I too shall do. When you drink, remember that. And whenever you drink the wine again, remember that".

There were many lessons of which Our Lord reminded those present in those last hours. Those teachings were the mysteries and ageless wisdoms. Therefore, the ones who were chosen to be present were those who carried in their hearts the knowledge: the Twelve, the Magdalene, the sisters of Bethany, Mary His mother, and others, all of whom were initiates upon the path and to whom He could entrust the message. Where it was, in whose home, is really quite immaterial.

Q: I am glad I garbled my question enough so that you did something else and it came out very well. I think that is a beautiful thing to add to the description in chapter 11 but what I was asking is how was it practiced in Corinth? You were writing to the fact that they were having some problems about it, some people eating too much, some going away hungry, and that you were trying to admonish them, and you were describing to them what the service ought to be like. I want to find out more about what was going on in Corinth, how was it practiced?

A: Ah yes. No, in fact, my comments were not intended to register a feast in the normally accepted sense. It was not that people were coming together and sitting down at a banquet where some people feasted while others remained hungry. It was more in the sense that the continuums of the blessing of the bread and the wine eventually became the tradition within the church itself. It was that the participants entered into the spirit as though consuming in the same sense as one might be a glutton at a feast, taking all of the energy to oneself while leaving another to remain hungry, which is not in accord with the spirit of the Last Supper. Our Lord first demonstrated by the washing of the feet that service, that humility, in which the Eucharist is a matter of service to others, is not a question of going to the table in order to be personally satiated. Do you understand the difference? That is what I meant. I was not referring to the act of eating.

Discourse Chapter Eleven continued:

3. Q: This was the assumption. I presume these took place in a home. One of the questions was, had yet the office of someone leading the Lord's Supper developed, or was this kind of a community affair?

    A: No, it had developed in the sense that someone did actually administer. From the point of the Supper until modern times someone took over the act of administration and others participated.

4. Q: Did Paul, at that time, view the Lord's Supper or communion as a Sacrament, much as the church has for centuries dealt with it as a Sacrament?

    A: Oh, absolutely, absolutely. What I have endeavored to elaborate upon was that Jesus was not creating a new institution which has been down the centuries called the Eucharist, or the breaking of the bread. This was not something which was new. The symbolic breaking of the bread and the drinking of the wine was something which has existed in different forms down through the ages in the mystery schools of the Universal Wisdoms, and was something of which he was reminding those present, not something that he was newly teaching them. And yes, indeed, it was, and has always been very much of extremely significant nature and a Sacrament.

The only difference which I would add now for modern generations is that we do not come to the table on our knees begging for mercy. We come, as members all in the body of Christ by our own right to do so. And we celebrate not with tears and wailing; we celebrate with infinite joy. All who bear within themselves, within the heart, the Divine Spark and the recognition of the brotherhood of Christ, are celebrants. Then let us celebrate.

FIRST CORINTHIANS 12

12 *Now concerning spiritual gifts, brethren, I would not have you ignorant.*

2 Ye know that ye were Gentiles, carried away unto these dumb idols, even as ye were led.

3 Wherefore, I give you to understand, that no man speaking by the Spirit of God calleth Jesus accursed: and that no man can say that Jesus is the Lord, but by the Holy Ghost.

4 Now there are diversities of gifts, but the same Spirit.

5 And there are differences of administrations, but the same Lord.

6 And there are diversities of operations, but it is the same God which worketh all in all.

7 But the manifestation of the Spirit is given to every man to profit withal.

8 For to one is given by the Spirit the word of wisdom to another the word of knowledge by the same Spirit.

9 To another faith by the same Spirit; to another the gifts of healing by the same Spirit;

10 To another the working of miracles; to another prophecy; to another discerning of spirits; to another diverse kinds of tongues; to another the interpretation of tongues;

11 But all these worketh that one and the self-same Spirit, dividing to every man severally as he will.

12 For as the body is one, and hath many members, and all the members of that one body, being many, are one body: so also is Christ.

13 For by one Spirit are we all baptized into one body, whether we be Jews or Gentiles, whether we be bond or free; and have been all made to drink into one Spirit.

12 (1-7) Concerning spiritual gifts, brothers and sisters, I would not have you remain ignorant. You know that you were previously Gentiles worshipping idols, even as you had been led to believe. I told you that no one who speaks from the Holy Spirit will condemn Jesus, and I also say that no one will understand that Jesus is that Lord unless he has the Holy Spirit. There are (within us) diverse gifts, but only one Spirit and there are differences in belief systems, but only One Lord. There are diverse human activities, but only One God which works through them all. The Divine Spirit is given to all seekers that they may raise their consciousness.

(8-11) To some may be given words of wisdom, to others words of knowledge, to others faith; to yet others, the gift of healing; to another may be given the ability to work miracles and to another, prophesy; to another may be the ability to discern the nature of spirits; another may have the gift of tongues; and to others, the interpretation of those tongues. But all of these work through that same Divine Spirit, working within each as It will.

(12-13) Even as our bodies are one, yet containing many parts (all parts of that same body), so too is Christ. In that One Spirit we are all baptized to become one body whether we are Jews or Gentiles, whether we are in bondage or free. We have all been made to drink in that One Spirit.

First Corinthians 12

14 For the body is not one member but many.

15 If the foot shall say, Because I am not the hand, I am not of the body; is it therefore not of the body?

16 And if the ear should say, Because I am not an eye, I do not belong to the body, that would not make it any less a part of the body.

17 If the whole body were an eye, where were the hearing? If the whole were hearing, where were the smelling?

18 But now hath God set the members every one of them in the body, as it hath pleased him.

19 And if they were all one member, where were the body?

20 But now are they many members, yet but one body.

21 And the eye cannot say unto the hand, I have no need of thee: nor again the head to the feet, I have no need of you.

22 Nay, much more those members of the body, which seem to be more feeble, are necessary:

23 And those members of the body which we think to be less honourable, upon these we bestow more abundant honour; and our uncomely parts have more abundant comeliness.

24 For our comely parts have no need: but God hath tempered the body together, having given more abundant honour to that part which lacked;

25 That there should be no schism in the body; but that the members should have the same care for one another.

26 And whether one member suffer, all the members suffer with it; or one member be honored, all the members rejoice with it.

(14-26) The body itself is not one great whole, but composed of many parts. Can a foot say that because it is not a hand, it is not part of the body? If the ear say that because it is not an eye, then how would there be a way of hearing? If all were hearing, then how would we smell? God has fashioned the body to be perfect; how would it be so if everything was one large part? So there are many parts but only one whole body. The eye cannot say to the hand that it has no need of it, or the head to the feet. Even those parts of the body which appear not very useful, are necessary, and those parts of the body which we feel less honorable. We should be proud of these less comely parts, and regard them all as perfect. God has made all of the body to be perfect, even those parts which appear less so, so that there is no imbalance within that body. If one part of the body is sick, the whole body is sick. If one part of the body is beautiful, then the whole body may rejoice.

First Corinthians 12

27 Now ye are the body of Christ, and members in particular.

28 And God hath set some in the church, first apostles, secondarily prophets, thirdly teachers, after that miracles, then gifts of healings, helps, governments, diversities of tongues.

29 Are all apostles? Are all prophets? Are all teachers? Are all workers of miracles?

30 Have all the gifts of healing? Do all speak with tongues? Do all interpret?

31 But covet earnestly the best gifts: and yet shew I unto you a more excellent way.

(27-31) You and we are all the body of Christ, and each are parts of that same Body. God has given us cause to set forth a group of whom some are apostles, some prophets, some teachers, some to work miracles, others to be healers, helpers, government officials and speakers. Can we all be apostles? Can we all be prophets? Are we all teachers, all workers of miracles? Do we all have the gift of healing, or do all speak in diverse tongues? Do we all have the ability to interpret? Take care of whatever gifts you possess. Yet even so, I can tell you there is a better way.[1]

DISCOURSE CHAPTER TWELVE

1. Q: In chapter 12:27-31 which is the one where you spend time listing the various tasks that are needed with the fellowship of the Community, some of the scholars want to know whether it was hierarchical or not. It starts out listing the Apostles, then the teachers and on down through miracle workers, healers and government officials and speakers. Is this hierarchical?

   A: No, not at all. It was simply a listing of various possibilities of service.

FIRST CORINTHIANS 13

13 Though I speak with the tongues of men and of angels, and have not charity, I am become as sounding brass, or a tinkling cymbal.

2 And though I have the gift of prophecy, and understand all mysteries, and all knowledge; and though I have all faith, so that I could remove mountains, and have not charity, I am nothing.

3 And though I bestow all my goods to feed the poor, and though I give my body to be burned. and have not charity, it profiteth me nothing.

4 Charity suffereth long and is kind; charity envieth not; charity vaunteth not itself, is not puffed up,

5 Doth not behave itself unseemly, seeketh not her own, is not easily provoked, thinketh no evil;

6 Rejoiceth not in iniquity, but rejoiceth in the truth;

7 Beareth all things, believeth all things, hopeth all things, endureth all things.

8 Charity never faileth: but whether there be prophecies, they shall fail; whether there be tongues, they shall cease; whether there be knowledge, it shall vanish away.

9 For we know in part, and we prophesy in part.

10 But when that which is perfect is come, then that which is in part shall be done away.

11 When I was a child. I spake as a child. I understood as a child. I thought as a child; but when I became a man, I put away childish things.

12 For now we see through a glass, darkly; but then fac to face: now I know in part; but then shall I know even as also I am known.

13 And now abideth faith, hope, charity, these three; but the greatest of these is charity.

13 (1-3) Though I had the language of both men and angels, if I did not also have love, I might as well be as sounding brass or tinkling symbol. Even if I could speak prophetically and understand all mysteries and have all knowledge; even though I professed great faith so that I could move mountains, if I did not also have love, I would be nothing. Even if I gave all of my goods to feed the poor, and even if I gave my life to sacrificial fire, if I did not do it with love, it would be of no consequence.

(4-7) Love suffers long and is kind. Love does not entertain envy; love does not set itself above others, is not anxious to impress, does not behave in an unseemly manner, is not selfish, is not easily provoked, and does not think evil of others. Love rejoices not in wrongdoing, but rejoices in the Truth. Love bears all things, believes in good things, sets no limits on hope or the extent of endurance.

(8-13) For love never fails, but prophesies may not happen, tongues may become silent, knowledge may be forgotten. For we can only know part of the Truth, we can only forecast part of the future. But when all things are come to perfection, then all of these imperfections shall be dispensed with. When I was a child, I acted as a child, for I understood things through the mind of that child. When I became a man, I grew out of childish things.

First Corinthians 13

At the moment we can only see things as through a dark mirror, but one day we will all see clearly. For now, we only know a part (of the Truth) but one day we shall know, even as we too are known. There are three lasting qualities which are faith, hope and love. The greatest of them is love.[1]

DISCOURSE CHAPTER THIRTEEN

1. Q: In chapter 13, I do not have a specific question. I want to comment that this is probably the most famous of all the passages and one of the most beautiful. It is one I used in my wedding ceremony with Ronda and wanted to know if you would like to make any further comment on it. This is the one about love.

   A: Yes, indeed. I think it is not possible to add to what was then and still is now a very inspired moment. There is, in the final analysis, in all of our striving, that same truth: without love as one's motivation, anything we do may as well be left not done. There is nothing one can add to what was stated there. It is an eternal truth.

FIRST CORINTHIANS 14

14 *Follow after charity, and desire spiritual gifts, but rather that ye may prophesy.*

2 For he that speaketh in an unknown tongue speaketh not unto men, but unto God: for no man understandeth him: howbeit in the spirit he speaketh mysteries.

3 But he that prophesieth speaketh unto men to edification, and exhortation, and comfort.

4 He that speaketh in an unknown tongue edifieth himself; but he that prophesieth edifieth the church.

5 I would that ye all spake with tongues, but rather that ye prophesied: for greater is he that prophesieth than he that speaketh with tongues, except he interpret, that the church may receive edifying.

6 Now, brethren, if I come unto you speaking with tongues, what shall I profit you, except I shall speak to you either by revelation, or by knowledge, or by prophesying, or by doctrine?

7 And even things without life giving sound, whether pipe or harp, except they give a distinction in the sounds, how shall it be known what is piped or harped?

8 For if the trumpet give an uncertain sound, who shall prepare himself to the battle?

9 So likewise, ye, except ye utter by the tongue words easy to be understood, how shall it be known what is spoken? For ye shall speak into the air.

10 There are, it may be, so many kinds of voices in the world, and none of them is without signification.

11 Therefore if I know not the meaning of the voice, I shall be unto him that speaketh a barbarian, and he that speaketh shall be a barbarian unto me.

14 (1-12) Follow therefore after love and desire gifts of the Spirit. Seek to speak clearly, for those who speak in unknown, words say nothing to humanity, only to God. No one understands what you are saying, for you address only the soul. Let those who wish to speak to humanity, do so for their betterment, and for their comfort. He who speaks in unknown words does so only for his own sake; but he who preaches the Word, does so for the betterment of the community. I am happy if you all can speak to the Soul, but would be happier if you also preached the Word. This is the greater mission. If I had come to you speaking with tongues, what good would it have done you? The only thing of value is that I tell you of my revelations and knowledge, through preaching of the Good News. Even musical instruments have to be discerned by the nature of their sound. A harp sounds as a harp. A pipe as a pipe. If the trumpeter is uncertain, how will the troops muster for battle. The same goes for you. Unless you talk to people in words they understand plainly, how are you doing any good? You might as well cry in the wind! There are many voices raised in the world, and all of them have their own merit, so unless you speak a common language, the one will sound like a foreigner to the other. Use all of your spiritual gifts to edify yourselves, so that you are of value in the community.

First Corinthians 14

12 Even so ye, forasmuch as ye are zealous of spiritual gifts, seek that ye may excel to the edifying of the church.

13 Wherefore let him that speaketh in an unknown tongue pray that he may interpret.

14 For if I pray in an unknown tongue, my spirit prayeth, but my understanding is unfruitful.

15 What is it then? I will pray with the spirit, and I will pray with the understanding also: I will sing with the spirit, and I will sing with the understanding also.

16 Else when thou shalt bless with the spirit, how shall he that occupieth the room of the unlearned say Amen at thy giving of thanks, seeing he understandeth not what thou sayest?

17 For thou verily givest thanks well, but the other is not edified.

18 I thank my God, I speak with tongues more than ye all:

19 Yet in the church I had rather speak five words with my understanding, that by my voice I might teach others also, than ten thousand words in an unknown tongue.

20 Brethren, be not children in understanding: howbeit in malice be ye children but in understanding be men.

21 In the law it is written, With men of other tongues and other lips will I speak unto this people; and yet for all that will they not hear me, saith the Lord.

22 Wherefore tongues are for a sign, not to them that believe, but to them that believe not: but prophesying serveth not for them that believe not, but for them which believe.

23 If therefore the whole church be come together into one place, and all speak with tongues, and there come in those that are unlearned, or unbelievers, will they not say that ye are mad?

(13-19) Let he who has been given the ability to speak in tongues also ask that he be able to interpret the words, so that he is not only addressing his inner self, but so that his understanding will give him more wisdom. Pray with both wisdom and understanding. Sing with spirit and with understanding. Otherwise, how will anyone ever agree with what you say? You might know, but it will not help anyone else. I, too, speak with tongues and am grateful for that gift, yet when I address others, I would rather speak five words with proper understanding, than ten thousand words that no one can interpret, so that by my own better wisdom, I can also teach others.

(20-25) Brothers, do not be childish. When you keep up your malice you are children. When you act with understanding, you are adults. It is written in Isaiah, "With men of other tongues and other lips will I speak unto this nation, yet for all that, they will not hear me, saith the Lord." From this is inferred that tongues are for people who do not believe, not for those that do. Preaching the Good News serves those who do believe, not those who do not. Therefore if the whole community were to meet together, and everyone spoke with tongues, should someone enter who is learned, yet an unbeliever, would that person not think you all mad? But if everyone is talking of the Good News and such a one comes, he can listen to it all. In this way the secret places of his own heart can be recognized and he will kneel and thank God, realizing that truly, the Divine Spirit is in you all.

First Corinthians 14

24 But if all prophesy and there come in one that believeth not, or one unlearned, he is convinced of all, he is judged of all:

25 And thus are the secrets of his heart made manifest; and so falling down on his face he will worship God, and report that God is in you of a truth.

26 How is it then, brethren? When ye come together, every one of you hath a psalm, hath a doctrine, hath a tongue, hath a revelation, hath an interpretation. Let all things be done unto edifying.

27 If any man speak in an unknown tongue, let it be by two, or at the most by three, and that by course; and let one interpret.

28 But if there be no interpreter, let him keep silence in the church; and let him speak to himself and to God.

29 Let the prophets speak two or three, and let the other judge.

30 If any thing be revealed to another that sitteth by, let the first hold his peace.

31 For ye may all prophesy one by one, that all may learn, and all may be comforted.

32 And the spirits of the prophets are subject to the prophets.

33 For God is not the author of confusion, but of peace, as in all churches of the saints.

34 Let your women keep silence in the churches; for it is not permitted unto them to speak; but they are commanded to be under obedience, as also saith the law.

35 And if they will learn any thing let them ask their husbands at home: for it is a shame for women to speak in the church.

36 What? Came the word of God out from you? Or came it unto you only?

(26-33) Albeit, when you meet, each one of you has a psalm, a message, a miracle, a revelation, a way of interpreting; let it all be done for upliftment. If anyone does receive the gift of tongues, confine this to two, or at the most three, and let someone be interpreter. However, if no one present is able to interpret, then it were better for the gifted one to stay quiet, allowing the tongues to speak within himself, to God. Let only two or three people testify the Good News, and let others hear what they say.[1] If anything comes as a revelation to one person, then let the others stay quiet. You will all get your turn, and in this way will you each find satisfaction. The inner message of the Good News comforts the receiver, for God is not the author of confusion but of peace.

(34-40) The communities of the faithful should be at peace. The old laws have said that women are not allowed to speak in gatherings of the church, but that they should confine their speech and questions to their husbands. It is said that for a woman to speak in church is shameful and that they shall be obedient. Did this come from God, or did this error come from you?[2]

First Corinthians 14

37 If any man think himself to be a prophet, or spiritual, let him acknowledge that the things that I write unto you are the commandments of the Lord.

38 But if any man be ignorant, let him be ignorant.

39 Wherefore, brethren, covet to prophesy, and forbid not to speak with tongues.

40 Let all things be done decently and in order.

If any man think that he bears the Good News, or that he is a spiritual person, let him acknowledge that the things of which I have spoken are the things of the Lord. Those who wish to remain in ignorance, let them be. I say that telling of Good News is to be encouraged, and *forbidden to no one*. Let all things be done according to decency.[3]

DISCOURSE CHAPTER FOURTEEN

1. Q: In 14:29, there is a difference between the KJ and RSV which influenced the way you put it. In the RSV they make use of a phrase, that instead of just listening, that you listen and discern, or the concept which Paul puts out later that the hearer of prophecy should discern whether it is right or not. What you said was more like the King James: "And let others hear what they say." It doesn't imply at all discernment or weighing what they say.

    A: Would you be kind enough to read more?

    Q: The RSV states "Let two or three prophets speak and let the others weigh what is said." The KJ says, "Let the prophets speak, two or three, and let the others judge." What you say is, "Let two or three people testify the Good News and let others hear what they say." You have dropped out either the sense of weighing or judgement.

    A: Would you continue for a little longer.

    Q: "If anything comes as a revelation to one person, then let the other stay quiet. You will all get your turn, and in this way will you all find satisfaction. The inner message of the Good News comforts the receiver for God is not the author of confusion but of peace."

    A: The thing that needs to be avoided at that particular point is the suggestion that Paul was in any way continuing what had been already a somewhat delicate

Discourse Chapter Fourteen continued:

situation. What was occurring among the groups in Corinth and one of the major reasons for writing this particular letter was a great deal of dissent as to who had the truth, who had the authority; and many of the statements he made in the letter were to try to have the people of Corinth recognize that each one has an element of that truth within his own being, and not to continue the error which was that some have, others have not. To place into the text at that particular moment something which suggests that one be discerning against other members of one's own small group would have perpetuated the very thing I was trying to eliminate and, therefore, is best not stated at that point.

I am not advocating lack of discernment on any occasion. One should always have discernment. However, there was very good reason at that particular moment why Paul would not have required that the members each hear the other with the suggestion that there be discernment as to who might be right and who might not; this would have been injurious to the cause at hand. You see, one must remember that I had stated a possibility of my return in person. Questions such as personal discernment I think need to be left to admonition on a personal level, if you follow.

Q: In 14:34-35, you make the statement, "The old laws have said that women are not allowed to speak in gatherings of the church but that they should confine their speech and questions to their husbands. It is said that for a woman to speak in church is shameful and that they shall be obedient. Did this come from God or from you?" I understand what you are trying to say. I am wondering if you would like to say it more strongly. Craig states "There is no question but that Paul believed in the definite subordination of women and was convinced that the emancipation of women from this subjection would be a violation of the Divine Order."*

A: Utter rubbish!

Q: I know what you mean, but I am hoping that you might like to word it more strongly where you say "Did this come from God or did it come from you?" This leaves the meaning ambiguous.

---

* Ibid., p. 213

Discourse Chapter Fourteen continued:

A: Yes it does, doesn't it. I had stated very, very clearly earlier in my discourses, and I shall state equally clearly again: Paul entertained no such nonsense and was asking "Do you really believe that such nonsensical statements come from God or is this nonsense of your own?" Women always were and always will be totally equal to men. One of the things which I attempt at this moment is that the conflict that has been apparent within many faiths for thousands of years concerning the stature of women finally now be clarified. The Creator created men and women as equal. By the time that Paul became an Apostle of God, despite his upbringing, which had taught him to the contrary, Paul the Apostle was well aware of the fact and made it very clear that women and men are equal. That which has perpetuated this nonsense down through the ages is the inability of either the Christians or the Jews to hear what was said and, of course, the Muslims now and the Hindu. It goes on and on. Whether humanity wishes to hear it now any more than then is beside the point. The point remains that women and men are and always were equal. Is that strong enough.

Q: I love it. Can I make a suggestion that in the text where it says or did it come from you" could you agree to say "or did this nonsense come from you" because that makes it really clear.

A: Certainly. It is however, I must admonish at this point, interjecting a very modern word. What I am endeavoring to do in the actual translation is render a little more accurate that which was translated. To interject the word "nonsense" tends to take out of context what we are doing in that moment.

Q: Is there another word?

A: I think error would be better. In the discourses let me just say we can use whatever words we wish because we are in the now. But one should be rather careful in the translations not to stretch them too far out of the idiom in which they would have been. Otherwise we will have another hundred years of scholars asking why is the word nonsense in there, there was no such word. You see?

3. Q: There is an overall question for this chapter which describes the meetings and the kind of behavior that you suggest in the meetings. People are curious about what those community meetings were like. People would like to know: more about how often did the community get together; did someone preside at the meetings; were they like Quaker meetings where everyone participates?

A: It would be extremely difficult and misleading to try to generalize and say what kind of meeting this particular one was because they were so very different from one small group to the next. And even in some larger areas like Corinth,

Discourse Chapter Fourteen continued:

there were more than one group. When I write to the Corinthians or to the Romans, I am not writing only to one little group in one person's home; I am addressing the whole community of those who have accepted the teachings of Christ. By the years 56 and 57 when these letters were written, there were several such. In earlier times when one was writing, one might have been addressing only one such in somebody's house or in a small meeting room but by the time Corinthians and Romans were written this was no longer so. How the groups in question conducted themselves was very much a matter for the groups in question. Those that were being conducted in Rome, according to my own observation while visiting, were quite different from those conducted in Corinth or Philippi or even more, in Ephesus; for, to some extent, they were governed by the nature of the person who did, in effect, adopt leadership. By this time each of the communities was beginning to accept one particular person or perhaps two or three individuals as the obvious leaders and the way that procedure would take place was very much a thing to be decided by that person who had been accepted as the leader. Therefore, it would not be a good service for me to offer statements as to how these meetings were; this was very individual.

Q: I think that is very helpful. You made one comment that raised a question in my mind and that was something to the effect that by the year 56 or 57 they were no longer meeting in homes or in meeting rooms. Is that what you intended. Did they have someplace else to meet?

A: No, no, certainly in Rome as is well known historically, such fear and secrecy surrounded the meetings that quite often the groups could not happen within the family home but had to be taken to areas which were much more secretive. That is very unfortunate. In the main, however, if the home was large enough, the group would meet there. If not, then places would be chosen which were larger, in the same way that one would today find a hall where more people could gather together.

FIRST CORINTHIANS 15

15 *Moreover, brethren, I declare unto you the gospel which I preached unto you, which also ye have received, and wherein ye stand;*

2 By which also ye are saved, if ye keep in memory what I preached unto you, unless ye have believed in vain.

3 For I delivered unto you first of all that which I also received, how that Christ died for our sins according to the scriptures;

4 And that He was buried, and that He rose again the third day according to the scriptures:

5 And that He was seen of Cephas, then of the twelve:

6 After that, He was seen of above five hundred brethren at once; of when the greater part remain unto this present, but some are fallen asleep.

7 After that, He was seen of James; then of all the apostles.

8 And last of all He was seen of me also, as of one born out of due time.

9 For I am the least of the apostles, that am not meet to be called an apostle, because I persecuted the church of God.

10 But by the grace of God I am what I am: and His grace which was bestowed upon me was not in vain; but I laboured more abundantly than they all; yet not I, but the grace of God which was with me.

11 Therefore whether it were I or they so we preach, and so ye believed.

12 Now if Christ be preached that He rose from the dead, how say som among you that there is no resurrection of the dead?

13 But if there be no resurrection of the dead, then is Christ not risen:

14 And if Christ be not risen, then is our preaching vain, and your faith is also vain.

15 (1-11) I commend to you that good news which I had spoken to you, and which you also were aware of, and believe in. This shall be your salvation if you will stay firm in the believing and keep what I said in mind; for I conveyed to you that same message which I myself received that being that Christ made sacrifice of Himself for us, and that He rose again from that ordeal.[1] Cephas, of course, saw Him, and so did the Twelve.[2] After that, He was seen by more than five hundred people. Many of those people are still alive today, though others have died. James also saw Him, and then all the apostles, and finally me. It was as though I was quite out of my time, for I am the least of all, and not fit to be called an apostle, after the way I persecuted those who believed in Him. But I am what I am through the Grace of God. That Grace which was given to me, was not given in vain. I have labored more earnestly than all the rest. Yet it has not been I who have worked, but the Grace working in me. So whether it was I who spoke, or others, it is the same message.

(12-19) If it had been Christ Himself who spoke to you of "coming back from the dead" how then would you have denied this possibility? If there were no resurrection from the dead, then Christ would not have done so. And if He did not do so, then we are all speaking in vain. We would be false witnesses of God because we would be saying that God raised up Christ when He did not, and the truth being that the dead do not arise! If the dead cannot arise, then is Christ not risen – and we would all be still as we were before, and all

First Corinthians 15

15 Yea, and we are found false witnesses of God; because we have testified of God that He raised up Christ: whom He raised not up, is so be that the dead rise not.

16 For if the dead rise not, then is not Christ raised:

17 And if Christ be not raised, your faith is vain; yea are yet in your sins.

18 Then they also which are fallen asleep in Christ are perished.

19 If in this life only we have hope in Christ, we are of all men most miserable.

20 But now is Christ risen from the dead, and become the first fruits of them that slept.

21 For since by man came death, by man came also the resurrection of the dead.

22 For as in Adam all die, even so in Christ shall all be made alive.

23 But every man in his own order: Christ the firstfruits; afterward they that are Christ's at His coming.

24 Then cometh the end, when He shall have delivered up the kingdom to God, even the Father; when He shall have put down all rule and all authority and power.

25 For He must reign, till He hath put all enemies under His feet.

26 The last enemy that shall be destroyed is death.

27 For He hath put all things under His feet. But when He saith, all things are put under Him, it is manifest that He is excepted, which did put all things under Him.

28 And when all things shall be subdued unto Him, then shall the Son also Himself be subject unto Him that put all things under Him, that God may be all in all.

29 Else what shall they do which are baptized for the dead?

30 And why stand we in jeopardy every hour?

of those who have died remain dead. If it were true that there is only one life, then what a miserable one that would be.[3]

(20-28) But Christ is arisen and is shown as the fruit of all that has gone before. Because the body does die, it is also true that the Divine Spark of Life reincarnates.[4] Even since Adam, all have died. Yet even as Christ demonstrated, all relive. Everyone to their own ordering, Christ being the first, and all we who are of Him, will follow. There will eventually be a time when He will return all of us through His Grace to that Divinity, even the Godhead, when all other power and authority have ceased. Christ shall stand supreme over all other, even that, last enemy which we call death of Spirit. Even the Son (of this Earth) shall eventually be called back to the One Source.

(29-34) Why else would we have taken our baptism in acknowledgement of this faith, if what we do is not the truth? I tell you by that same token that I "die" daily to all temptations of the flesh. What good would it have done me if I had gone into the ring and fought with wild beasts at Ephesus?[4] Why would those people die, except in the belief that they will live again? Otherwise we might say (quoting the Romans) "Let us eat, drink and be merry, for tomorrow we die!" Do not mistake me, such wrong messages do nothing for our thinking. Stay awake to the truth and do not fall into error. There are still many who do not have any knowledge of the Truth. I am sorry to have to say this.

First Corinthians 15

31 I protest by your rejoicing which I have in Christ Jesus our Lord, I die daily.

32 If after the manner of men I have fought with beasts at Ephesus, what advantageth it me, if the dead rise not? Let us eat and drink; for tomorrow we die.

33 Be not deceived: evil communications corrupt good manners.

34 Awake to righteousness, and sin not; for some have not the knowledge of God: I speak this to your shame.

35 But some man will say How are the dead raised up? And with what body do they come?

36 Thou fool, that which thou sowest is not quickened, except it die:

37 And that which thou sowest, thou sowest not that body that shall be, but bare grain, it may chance of wheat, or some other grain:

38 But God giveth it a body as it hath pleased Him, and to every seed His own body.

39 All flesh is not the same flesh: but there is one kind of flesh of men, another flesh of beasts, another of fishes, and another of birds.

40 There are also celestial bodies, and bodies terrestrial: but the glory of the celestial is one, and the glory of the terrestrial is another.

41 There is one glory of the sun, and another glory of the moon, and another glory of the stars: for one star differeth from another star in glory.

42 So also is the resurrection of the dead. It is sown in corruption; it is raised in incorruption:

43 It is sown in dishonour; it is raised in glory: it is sown in weakness; it is raised in power.

(35-44) There will be those who will question, "How are the dead raised, and which body are they raised in?" This is foolishness. Of course, it is not that the body which has undergone physical death comes back. That which is in you as a seed, comes back again in other flesh – not the same flesh. (By this I do not mean that humans come as animals; for humans are humans, animals are animals, fishes are fishes, birds are birds.) There are, however, also celestial bodies, and earthly, terrestrial ones. That which is of the highest in the celestial spheres is different from that which is of the highest in the earthly planes. The sun has a different radiance than the moon; some stars have differing radiances from others stars.

(42-50) Just so is the resurrection. On the mortal plane, the seed is sown after the fashion of that which decays. On the higher planes, the seed does not decay. That which (on this plane) seems less honorable, is, on the higher planes, not so. That which is sown in weakness can be raised into power. The seed which is sown begets a natural body, within which is the Spirit. So it is written that the first Adam was created as a living being (with a soul) and the "last Adam" is become quickened by the Spirit. How, you say, is it that it was not the other way around: the first Adam being spiritual and the last becoming of the earth? that first Adamic man was of the Earth. The "Second Adam" was the Lord, of the higher realms. The things of earthly, material form, stay that way. Things that are of the finer realms also. We who are of humanity have both the stamp of the material plane, and that of the higher planes.

First Corinthians 15

44 It is sown a natural body; it is raised a spiritual body. There is a natural body, and there is a spiritual body.

45 And so it is written. The first man Adam was made a living soul; the last Adam was made a quickening spirit.

46 Howbeit that was not first which is spiritual, but that which is natural; and afterward that which is spiritual.

47 The first man is of the earth, earthy: the second man is the lord from heaven.

48 As is the earthy, such are they also that are earthy: and as is the heavenly, such are they also that are heavenly.

49 And as we have borne the image of the earthy, we shall also bear the image of the heavenly.

50 Now this I say, brethren, that flesh and blood cannot inherit the kingdom of God; neither doth corruption inherit incorruption.

51 Behold, I shew you a mystery; We shall not all sleep, but we shall all be changed.

52 In a moment, in the twinkling of an eye, at the last trump: for the trumpet shall sound, and the dead shall be raised incorruptible, and we shall be changed

53 For this corruptible must put on incorruption, and this mortal must put on immortality.

54 So when this corruptible shall have put on incorruption, and this mortal shall have put on immortality, then shall be brought to pass the saying that is written, Death is swallowed up in victory.

55 O death, where is thy sting? O grave, where is thy victory

56 The sting of death is sin; and the strength of sin is the law.

However, it is still a fact that while we remain attached to material things, we will not gain those higher realms because that which is subject to decay cannot do anything other than decay.

(51-58) Look, I am disclosing to you what has been considered a mystery. This is how it has been stated: We shall not all sleep, but we shall be changed. In a moment, in the twinkling of an eye at the last trump: for the trumpet shall sound and the dead shall be raised incorruptible, and we shall be changed. For this corruptible must put on incorruption and this mortal must put on immortality. And when all this has come to pass, then shall have occurred that which is written, "Death is swallowed up in victory. O death, where is thy sting? O grave, thy victory?" Through the message of Jesus, the Lord Christ, we now realize what this all means, and in that knowledge lies our true strength. We can all overcome the fear of death through that which He has shown to us.[7]

First Corinthians 15

57 But thanks be to God, which giveth us the victory through our Lord Jesus Christ.

58 Therefore, my beloved brethren, be ye stedfast, unmovable, always abounding in the work of the Lord, forasmuch as he know that your labour is not in vain in the Lord.

DISCOURSE CHAPTER FIFTEEN

1. Q: In 15:4, you make the statement "For I convey to you that same message which I myself received, that being that Christ made sacrifice of Himself for us and that He rose again from that ordeal." The phrase that was in KJ is a phrase used often and you substituted "ordeal" for the phrase "dead, buried and on the third day rose." Did you want to eliminate that traditional phrase and substitute ordeal?

    A: I simply wish to eliminate the phrase and I felt that "ordeal" was the best way to do it. The statement that the Christ died, descended into Hell and on the third day came out of that state and rose again from the dead; is a cannon which has too long been perpetuated. I have no desire to continue its perpetuation.

2. Q: Good. Now we have the woman issue again in 15:5. When Paul describes who Jesus showed Himself to, He only describes the men; He completely leaves out the fact that He first may have shown Himself to Mary Magdalene and Mary. Was this part of Paul's subjugation of women? Since you were using the KJ version, you did the same thing where you say, "Cephas, of course saw him and so did the twelve and after that He was seen by more than 500 people." There is no mention of the women at the beginning.

    A: You see, we are talking about a different chain of events here. You have noticed, have you not, that Cephas is named fairly regularly throughout my letters, as being one of the companions. In mentioning him at that particular point, I was admonishing, "Do you still not believe in all of this when your own companion Cephas actually saw, and is stating what it was he saw?" It is not intending to leave out the earlier fact. It is simply an admonition to those people that your own brother saw this very thing with his own eyes, do you therefore say you do not believe him? It is very different; it is not from an intent to leave out the women and above all, the Magdalene and mother of Jesus. That is, I think, such a

Discourse Chapter Fifteen continued:

touchy issue in the minds of the scholars that they will latch on to any particular area where they think "Oh yes, Paul has done it again." But it was entirely out of context there, for the reason I have just given.

3. Q: In chapter 15:19, you make the statement "If it were true that there is only one life, then what a miserable one that would be. The Christ is risen and is shown as the fruit of all that has gone before." My question regards the word "miserable". We have had this problem throughout Christian history of looking upon the current life as being "miserable" in contrast to the life of the spirit. Are we perpetuating the physical life as being a miserable life?

    A: I can think of other words which might be interchangeable, but I think that they would be equally negative. One might think, for instance, of the word "pathetic". Because you see, if one agrees with the principle of only one opportunity, one life in which to get it all straight, and that at the end of that one life we face a judgement which, according to some, would send us into some kind of eternal purgatory or would elevate us to a position along with the angels; then such a mind set is miserable indeed. In the first place, it removes all power from that which we believed to be the Creator. It allows people to ask the age-old questions, "what about children, what about people who for no apparent reason die violent or cruel deaths?" In the face of such alternatives in the living of only one life as opposed to the truth which is the continuum of life and its attention to the laws of cause and effect, then I would say certainly the use of the word "miserable" is correct indeed.

4. Q: Right near that, in 15:21, there is a phrase that, at least for me, is a little confusing. It says "Because the body does die, it is also true that it reincarnates." Is there a tendency there to imply that the physical body dies and that the physical body will reincarnate?

    A: Oh no, no. That is a misleading statement. The physical body is the physical body; it is a shell. In that sense this body will only live once; there is only one life for this particular shell or frame. In the same sense as the seed; the seed is only in existence once but the life force of the seed becomes a plant; the plant bears more seeds. Those seeds again fall into the ground, die, are buried and their life force comes forth again. This is very much the nature of how we too are. It is not the same seed coming forth again, it is the product of the first seed being perpetuated.

Discourse Chapter Fifteen continued:

Q: Is there a word that we could substitute for "it" where you say "Because the body does die, it is also true that 'it' reincarnates?"

A: I think one might say the Divine Spark of Life reincarnates, or the Divine Essence.

5. Q: In 15:32 you make the reference that "what good would it have done me if I had gone into the ring and fought with wild beasts at Ephesus?" To me the question comes to mind, had the Christians already been thrown to the lions at this stage?

A: Not so much the Christians, but you will recall that the games – if one could call them games – of the gladiators in the Roman Arena already were very well established before someone thought of Christian martyrdom as an event for public amusement. There was, even at that point in time, some distinct possibility of this kind of event happening.

One of the reasons why many of the people who had adopted the new faith indeed left Rome, and why it was rather dangerous to remain for any length of time too close to the Roman legions was that one never knew how they might act. When Paul made this reference it was indeed because of that fear and that possibility.

Q: Did Ephesus have an arena?

A: Oh yes, all of the outposts of the Roman Legion had them to a lesser or smaller degree. And of course, the idea of human sacrifice in this way was one that the Roman emperor Caligula particularly enjoyed.

6. Q: In 15:50, this is the phrase you have, "However, it is still a fact that while we remain attached to material things, we will not gain those higher realms, because that which is subject to decay cannot do anything other than decay." In the KJ and RSV they use "the Kingdom of God" instead of "higher realms." Are you equating higher realms to the Kingdom of God?

A: Well indeed, of course I am. The problem is that First Cause does not have a kingdom. There isn't any such place as the Kingdom of God. To be more correct, therefore, when speaking of other dimensions than the earth plane, one might say other dimensions or one might say higher realms. I use the latter in order to differentiate between other dimensions which might not necessarily be of a finer quality.

Discourse Chapter Fifteen continued:

7. Q: In 15:51-58 there is the affirmation that is famous in which Paul says, "Look, I am disclosing to you what has been considered a mystery. This is how it is since David. We shall not all sleep but we shall be changed in a moment in the twinkling of an eye at the last trumpet. For the trumpet shall sound and the dead shall be raised incorruptible and we shall be changed. For this corruption was put on in corruption and this mortal must put on immortality and when all this has come to pass then shall have occurred that which is written: 'Death is swallowed up in victory, Oh death where is thy sting, oh death where is thy victory?' " This is a statement that is very colored by Paul's notion of the immanent approach of the "second coming".

As we discussed previously, Paul at that time had this view. I wondered if we were to look at that and someone were to say, "What has happened in the interim"? It has been 2,000 years, what has been happening during that time? Would he say it any differently?

A: That is a tricky question, because the fact is that we are not dealing in that particular context now. As I have stated quite clearly many times, the whole subject would require not a discourse here but . . . I think that we have covered the issue of what was meant, we have covered incarnation, reincarnation, we have covered what was meant by the "second coming", we have covered the fact that Paul did entertain at that time that the second coming would be immanent. Paul, who was writing at that time, did not have the clarity of the one who speaks now. And I think we shall leave it there, for the whole subject is an extremely vast one which has been covered as much as we may cover it in a work of this kind.

FIRST CORINTHIANS 16

16 *Now concerning the collection for the saints, as I have given order to the churches of Galatia, even so do ye.*

2 Upon the first day of the week let every one of you lay by him in store, as God hath prospered him, that there be no gatherings when I come.

3 And when I come, whomsoever ye shall approve by your letters, them will I send to bring your liberality unto Jerusalem.

4 And if it be met that I go also. they shall go with me.

5 Now I will come unto you, when I shall pass through Macedonia: for I do pass through Macedonia.

6 And it may be that I will abide, yea, and winter with you, that ye may bring me on my journey whithersoever I go.

7 For I will not see you now by the way; but I trust to tarry a while with you, if the Lord permit.

8 But I will tarry at Ephesus until Pentecost.

9 For a great door and effectual is opened unto me, and there are many adversaries.

10 Now if Timotheus come, see that he may be with you without fear: for he worketh the work of the Lord, as I also do.

11 Let no man therefore despise him: but conduct him forth in peace, that he may come unto me: for I look for him with the brethren.

12 As touching our brother Apollos, I greatly desired him to come unto you with the brethren: but his will was not at all to come at this time; but he will come when he shall have convenient time.

13 Watch ye, stand fast in the faith, quit you like men, be strong.

14 Let all your things be done with charity.

16 (1-4) Now I would like to address the concern for the people of the New Faith, and the collections on their behalf. I have given instructions to the communities in Galatia, and suggest the same to you. On the first day of each week, be in the habit of putting aside a tithe so that there will be no need to start collecting when I come.

(5-12) When I do come, whomever you appoint as the bearer shall take your offerings to those people in Jerusalem. If at that time, it seems good that I too shall go (to Jerusalem) then your ambassador shall travel with me. I shall visit with you when next I pass through Macedonia. I will try to winter with you, and this will sustain me for the rest of my journey. I cannot see you at the moment, but will hope to do so soon. I plan to remain in Ephesus until Pentecost, for many revelations are coming to me at present, and I also have a lot of adversaries. It is likely that Timothy will soon be with you. Make sure that he is able to rest unafraid, for he too is a worker for God.[1] Do not let anyone think badly of him, and send him on his way in peace, so that he can join me; I look forward to that. Concerning Brother Apollos, I wanted him to visit you but he did not wish to do so right now. He will do that when it is more convenient to him.

(13-24) Meantime, be on your guard that you act like men, strong in faith, and all things do with love. I beg of you (you know the house of Stephanas those first converted to the Faith in Achaia, that they have become quite obsessed with the ministry to the faithful), to respect such people and all who

First Corinthians 16

15 I beseech you, brethren, (ye know the house of Stephanas, that it is the firstfruits of Achaia, and that they have addicted themselves to the ministry of the saints,)

16 That ye submit yourselves unto such, and to every one that helpeth with us, and laboureth.

17 I am glad of the coming of Stephanas and Fortunatus, and Achaicus: for that which was lacking on your part they have supplied.

18 For they have refreshed my spirit and yours: therefore acknowledge ye them that are such.

19 The churches of Asia salute you. Aquila and Priscilla salute you much in the Lord, with the church that is in their house.

20 All the brethren greet you. Greet ye one another with an holy kiss.

21 The salutation of me Paul with mine own hand.

22 If any man love not the Lord Jesus Christ, let him be Anathema Maranatha.

23 The grace of our Lord Jesus Christ be with you.

24 My love be with you all in Christ Jesus. Amen.

assist us, and who also work. I am glad of the arrival of Stephanus, Fortunatus and Achaicus, for they have been able to make up for anything that others lacked. They have truly refreshed my spirit and yours; acknowledge them for it. The communities in Asia send their greetings. Aquila and Priscilla send much love in the Lord, together with the community that meets in their home. All the brothers and sisters send you warm greeting. Give each other a Holy Kiss for us, and I add to all that my own hand in salute. May the grace of Our Lord be with you, as my love is with you all in Christ. Amen.

Written from Philippi in the year of Our Lord 57 AD.

DISCOURSE CHAPTER SIXTEEN

1. Q: In chapter 16:10, you make the comment indicating that you hope Timothy will be treated well and that he be not put in danger. What was the problem; was this a problem of outside forces or acceptance within the community?

    A: It was a problem with outside forces which I have touched upon in other parts of the discourse. By now, in the year 56 or 57 A.D. it was becoming increasingly difficult to move around in areas where one enc ountered the legions of Rome, to openly express one's attachment to the New Faith, without creating a certain amount of danger; and I was asking that the communities in Corinth be very careful that they did not expose Timothy to that difficulty.

INTRODUCTION TO THE SECOND LETTER OF PAUL TO THE CORINTHIANS

The first letter to the Corinthians was written in Philippi and dispatched back to the Corinthians in early 57 A.D.

It will be recalled that Paul had finally paid a brief visit to Rome after much waiting, in 56. The reason for that waiting was this: After the death of the Roman Emperor Tiberius, his successor, Caligula, began a campaign to terrorize anyone, Roman or Jew, who professed the Christ as a teacher. This persecution lasted throughout Caligula's (fortunately) brief reign.

After succession, Claudius Caesar decreed that all people professing to be of the Christian persuasion – whether or not Roman citizens – must leave Rome and return to their native country. It therefore became difficult, if not impossible, for Paul to visit Rome between the years 50 and 54. Nero became Emperor in the year 54, approximately, and for a short while things relaxed. Therefore, in 56 Paul decided to take the opportunity to go to Rome. Under Nero, however, terrorism did again begin to affect the small Christian communities which eventually had to go into hiding to conduct their meetings. As the years of Nero's reign wore on, that terrorism grew to obscene cruelty and the Arena of the Gladiator a commonly attended occurrence.

During his travels through Macedonia and along the coast of Asia Minor, Paul had to be extremely careful, as did all of the Apostles and Teachers who continued the Ministry of Christ. On leaving Rome after the short visit, Paul journeyed to Corinth in route via Philippi to return to Asia Minor. From Corinth the letter to the Romans was sent in the form of a dispatch in the closing weeks of 56. The first letter to Corinth (the first recorded that is) was in early 57. Paul at this time was back in Philippi and none too certain of his reception. It will be recalled that on the first visit to Philippi with Silas, the two of them were scourged and after being beaten were put in prison. While in prison there was an earthquake and the two of them managed to escape and retreat to more hospitable territory.

Paul had journeyed briefly to Rome, as has been previously stated. The reason for the fleeting visit was of a personal nature. There had been a rising concern for the people in Rome, particularly, for some years. During the time of Claudius, friends of the Faith had left and settled elsewhere. Among them were Aquila and Priscilla, who were devoted friends of Paul and his colleague, Luke. During the years between 33 when they first met (and were at enmity) and all that ensued in the intervening period, Paul and Luke established a very deep connection and often travelled in company. Luke's mother was Greek and his stepfather a Roman. People had arrived in Ephesus with dispatches from Rome to Lucanus – a Roman – which required him to return to the court. (There was some suggestion of his assisting the Emperor as a physician of no mean repute.) This was seen as an opportunity for Paul, his close friend, and also Roman Citizen, to accompany him with, as it were, diplomatic immunity.

Aquila and Priscilla accompanied also since they too were citizens of Rome. The only one in the party who was a non-Jew therefore, was Luke. It was found on arrival in Rome that things were extremely difficult, and that Luke's position was itself somewhat precarious. He had to be extremely careful and eventually it was considered that Paul might be better off not to stay. He therefore left, having only been in Rome a short time, and had no time to do the things he went there to do. He therefore wrote his dispatches to contain what would have been his theology had he shared it in person.

At great risk to themselves, Priscilla and Aquila stayed on, intending to leave Rome when Luke did so. However, for reasons not now known, Luke journeyed to join Paul some while afterwards and met with Titus in Corinth. Chapter 8:18 is a direct reference to Luke, variously known as Lucanus or Lucas.

Now, once again, braving the "elements" Paul is writing back to Corinth, the Second Letter to the Corinthians.

THE SECOND LETTER OF PAUL TO THE CORINTHIANS

1 *Paul, an apostle of Jesus Christ by the will of God, and Timothy our brother, unto the church of God, which is at Corinth, with all the saints which are in Achaia:*

2 Grace be to you and peace from God our Father, and from the Lord Jesus Christ.

3 Blessed be God, even the Father of our Lord Jesus Christ, the Father of mercies, and the god of all comfort;

4 Who comforteth us in all our tribulation, that we may be able to comfort them which are in any trouble, by the comfort wherewith we ourselves are comforted of God.

5 For as the sufferings of Christ abound in us, so our consolation also aboundeth by Christ.

6 And whether we be afflicted, it is for your consolation and salvation, which is effectual in the enduring of the same sufferings which we also suffer: or whether we be comforted, it is for your consolation and salvation.

7 And our hope of you is stedfast, knowing that as ye are partakers of the sufferings, so shall ye be also of the consolation.

8 For we would not, brethren have you ignorant of our trouble which came to us in Asia, that we were pressed out of measure, above strength, insomuch that we despaired even of life:

9 But we had the sentence of death in ourselves, that we should not trust in ourselves, but in God which raiseth the dead:

10 Who delivered us from so great a death, and doth deliver: in whom we trust that he will yet deliver us;

11 Ye also helping together by prayer for us, that for the gift bestowed upon us by the means of many persons thank may be given by many on our behalf.

1 (1-7) Letter from Paul, an apostle of Christ by the will of God, being sent by our brother Timothy to the people of God's community at Corinth (and to all of the believers throughout Achaia), Grace unto you and the peace of God our Father, and also that of Christ our Lord. Blessed be that God who is the Father of our Lord, the Father of all mercies and the God of all comfort. He it is that comforts us all in our tribulations so that we too can comfort those who are in any kind of trouble, in that same way that we ourselves receive comfort through our trust in God. For let us be assured that the same comfort that we receive through our trust in Christ, was the comfort that Christ Himself received of God. If we are persecuted, let it be known that it is on your behalf. If we are comforted, it is also on your behalf. We continue to hold steadfast to our hopes for you knowing that even though you too are being persecuted, you will equally be consoled and remain strong.

(8-11) It would be well for you to be aware that when we were travelling in Asia, things came to such a pressure that we went in fear of our very lives, but we had ever confidence in God.[1] Even though we might have had a death sentence hanging over us, we know beyond doubt that we live again in God, who has delivered us from the worst of all deaths. In Him we trust, and He continues to watch over us. You are also helping us greatly by your prayers for us.

Second Corinthians 1

12 For our rejoicing is this, the testimony of our conscience, that in simplicity and godly sincerity, not with fleshly wisdom, but by the grace of God, we have had our conversation in the world, and more abundantly to you-ward.

13 For we write none other things unto you than what ye read or acknowledge; and I trust ye shall acknowledge even to the end;

14 As also ye have acknowledged us in part, that we are your rejoicing, even as ye also are ours in the day of the Lord Jesus.

15 And in this confidence I was minded to come unto you before, that ye might have a second benefit;

16 And to pass by you into Macedonia, and to come again out of Macedonia unto you, and of you to be brought on my way toward Judea.

17 When I therefore was thus minded, did I use lightness? Or the things that I purpose, do I purpose according to the flesh, that with me there should be yea, yea, and nay, nay?

18 But as God is true, our word toward you was not yea and nay.

19 For the Son of God, Jesus Christ, who was preached among you by us, even by me and Silvanus and Timotheus, was not yea and nay, but in him was yea.

20 For all the promises of God in Him are yea, and in Him Amen, unto the glory of God by us.

21 Who hath also sealed us, and given the earnest of the Spirit in our hearts.

22 Who hath also sealed us, and given the earnest of the Spirit in our hearts.

23 Moreover, I call God for a record upon my soul, that to spare you I came not as yet unto Corinth.

24 Not for that we have dominion over your faith, but are helpers of your joy: for by faith ye stand.

(12-14) For that gift, coming from so many people, we give thanks to them all. Be it known to you all that not by our wisdom, but by the very simplicity of our lives and by simple faith and trust in God's Grace, we are continuing our work, and are able to send more of that confidence also to you. We cannot write to you any differently than we know – which it is my hope you will continue to acknowledge even to the last. It is good that you have acknowledged us even if only in part, that which we have given you is something for you to rejoice over, even as we also rejoice daily in the Lord Jesus.

(15-24) It was in that confidence that I last visited you, so that you would have the added strength – and to travel via yourselves through into Macedonia as I go back making for Judaea. Did I speak of this lightly? Did I address those things only as thought from a standpoint of earthly matters, that you think I vacillate? As before God I say to you that I did not vacillate. Christ who was in Jesus did not vacillate, all things through Him were affirmed; for through His Office, all things of God are affirmed, Amen. And God is glorified through even me and Sylvanus and Timothy. That very God has anointed us also, and has used our offices to bring the message to you. He has given us the very gift of the Holy Spirit in our hearts. May God record this upon my Soul that I came not to Corinth in order to establish any power over your expression of faith, but in order to strengthen and share your joy. For it is by your own faith that you stand.

DISCOURSE CHAPTER ONE

1. Q: In 1:8-9, you refer to an event in Asia that evidently threatened your very life and those with you. Do you want to say what that was?

    A: You know, I honestly do not recall. During this time, at the point when this letter was written, there were so very many events. It was becoming extremely dangerous to move around from place to place carrying the ministry of the gospel of Christ. All who did so were in extreme danger and I must have been referring at that time to one of those events which were singularly difficult.

    Q: You referred to the fact that you were traveling in Asia at the time. If one looks at the list you described later, one can understand why you may have forgotten some, it seems to me that you experienced a number of dangerous incidents.

    A: Yes, one must recall here, that in addition to the government of Rome being opposed to the new movement, there was a further difficulty around Byzantine relationships with Rome which were not at all happy. That whole region was strife ridden for many reasons, mostly political, and to be a messenger of something which was so different was always suspect, no matter what that difference was; even at the best of times one had to be extremely careful.

SECOND CORINTHIANS 2

2 *But I determined this with myself that I would not come again to you in heaviness.*

2 For if I make you sorry, who is he then that maketh me glad, but the same which is made sorry by me?

3 And I wrote this same unto you, lest, when I came, I should have sorrow from them of whom I ought to rejoice; having confidence in you all, that my joy is the joy of you all.

4 For out of much affliction and anguish of heart I wrote unto you with many tears; not that ye should be grieved, but that ye might know the love which I have more abundantly unto you.

5 But if any have caused grief he hath not grieved me, but in part: that I may not overcharge you all.

6 Sufficient to such a man is this punishment, which was inflicted of many.

7 So that contrariwise ye ought rather to forgive him, and comfort him, lest perhaps such a one should be swallowed up with overmuch sorrow.

8 Wherefore I beseech you that ye would confirm your love toward him.

9 For to this end also did I write, that I might know the proof of you, whether ye be obedient in all things.

10 To whom ye forgive any thing I forgive also: for if I forgave any thing, to whom I forgave it, for your sakes forgave I it in the person of Christ;

11 Lest Satan should get an advantage of us: for we are not ignorant of his devices.

12 Furthermore, when I came to Troas to preach Christ's gospel, and a door was opened unto me of the Lord,

13 I had no rest in my spirit, because I found not Titus my brother: but taking my leave of them, I went from thence into Macedonia.

2 (1-4) I convince myself though, that I should not be heavy with you, for if I upset you, will you make me happy? I say this so that when I do come to visit you again, I will not have sorrow from those with whom I should rejoice. I have confidence in you, and your joy is my joy. At one time I wrote to you with much anguish and many tears, not in order to grieve you, but in order that you would realize how much I love you all.[1]

(5-11) If there were any who caused grief, it was only partial, and I do not hold it against you. It is enough for such a one that they suffered the annoyance of the brethren there. Therefore, forgive it, so that they do not suffer too much for it. Be loving. That was another reason why I wrote, so that I can be assured that you walk truly and that you forgive one another even as we are all forgiven by Christ. We are all well aware of the temptations that beset us.

(12-17) Let me tell you that when I came to Troas with the message of Christ, the Lord opened up doors for me, but I was unable to discover the whereabouts of Titus my brother, so I left Troas and came speedily back to Macedonia.

Second Corinthians 2

14 Now thanks be unto God, which always causeth us to triumph in Christ, and maketh manifest the savour of His knowledge by us in every place.

15 For we are unto God a sweet savour of Christ, in them that are saved, and in them that perish:

16 To the one we are the savour of death unto death; and to the other the savour of life unto life. And who is sufficient for these things?

17 For we are not as many, which corrupt the word of God: but as of sincerity, but as of God, in the sight of God speak we in Christ.

I thank God that I did so. The inner promptings of Christ work always for our good and direct our ways. It seems that before God we are to be trusted with the message of Christ no matter how people see us. For some we speak of death but for others we speak of life, and who is truly the judge of these things? We are not like many who have been known to corrupt the word of God, but we speak sincerely of our faith, and the message of Christ which is the truth before God.

DISCOURSE CHAPTER TWO

1. Q: This leads us to the issue of the latter part of the letter and it comes up here in the last part of chapter one and the beginning of chapter two, concerning your not visiting Corinth. The biblical scholars* are making the assumption that you wrote several letters, four of which they know about – one which was written before First Corinthians, one which was written in between which they title the "stern letter" and then the Second Corinthians. You may have written others, but they only have reference to those. They are assuming that this "stern letter" which got lost may have included the three chapters of Second Corinthians. The first nine chapters are much more positive and joyous about the reconciliation; the latter chapters implying that there hadn't been a reconciliation yet. They think it was Titus that carried the "stern letter" to them in fear and trepidation and the stern letter worked. Could we have your response to that?

---

*Filson, Floyd V.; *Interpreter's Bible,* Vol. 10, p.270-271.
Abingdon-Cokesbury Press, Nashville, TN, 1953

Discourse Chapter Two continued:

A: The commentators are correct. There were, of course, several letters to the Corinthians and the sequence in which they were dispatched was correct as surmised; the one reportedly the First Corinthians was more accurately the last of many. There was indeed another "stern letter" between what is recorded as First and Second. In other words, in sequence as recorded, there was letter #1, and letter #2 with what one might call 1-A in between.

The surmise that there was only one earlier letter is incorrect; there were several which have not been recorded, or not necessarily letters per se, because letters implies writing. It might perhaps be more accurate to say messages, many of which were sent by mouth and which as a result, were not too accurate in their delivery. This is partially the reason for the confusion around what appears to be tacked on to the second letter as recorded.

Those last chapters were indeed sent in a box of dispatches, and contained in that was another written letter which is the one now called the Second. It had also been reported to me that the middle letter, which I am now calling 1-A, the "stern letter", had indeed been given in entirety as I had sent it. But certain of its content had been lost and certain of the words which had been relayed to the Corinthians earlier than my first epistle, had been relayed incorrectly. That which came back to me as having been said by me was, in fact, not what I had intended.

Therefore, I wrote in the second letter what one might, in more recent times, call a post script. It was part of the letter, but it was pertaining to what I had sent to them before in earlier times and it was another of my famous "oh, and by the way, this is what I said to you earlier and which you seem to have mislaid or misremembered."

That is why what is said appears to be so very different in context; it was very different in context, but it was in form of what one might call a memorandum, simply to remind the receivers in writing, of my more correct statements since the delivery in words had not been as careful as I might have hoped.

SECOND CORINTHIANS 3

3 *Do we begin again to commend ourselves? Or need we, as some others, epistles of commendation to you, or letters of commendation from you?*

2 Ye are our epistle written in our hearts known and read of all men:

3 Forasmuch as ye are manifestly declared to be the epistle of Christ ministered by us, written not with ink, but with the Spirit of the Living God; not in tablets of stone, but in fleshy tablets of the heart.

4 And such trust have we through Christ to God-ward:

5 Not that we are sufficient of ourselves to think any thing as of ourselves; but our sufficiency is of God;

6 Who also hath made us able ministers of the new testament; not of the letter, but of the spirit: for the letter killeth, but the spirit giveth life.

7 But if the ministration of death, written and en graven in stones, was glorious, so that the children of Israel could not stedfastly behold the face of Moses for the glory of his countenance; which glory was to be done away:

8 How shall not the ministration of the spirit be rather glorious?

9 For if the ministration of condemnation be glory, much more doth the ministration of righteousness exceed in glory.

10 For even that which was made glorious had no glory in this respect, by reason of the glory that excelleth.

11 For if that which is done away was glorious, much more that which remaineth is glorious.

12 Seeing then that we have such hope, we use great plainness of speech:

3 (1-3) Do we again have to justify ourselves? Do we need letters of recommendation from others to you, or to others from you? You are our letters, written in our hearts, to be read by all. Our words are not merely the words written in ink, but are the very Spirit of the living God. We do not write only on stone tablets, we write with the very substance of our heart.

(4-6) Such trust comes only through faith in God. Such strength comes only through God. We are not ministers of letters, but of Spirit. Words are dead things, Spirit is life!

(7-11) If that which was written on the Tablets of Stone through Moses had such effect on him that the children of Israel could not look upon his countenance because of its radiance (and which passed) should not that which is written in Spirit also be glorious? For if those Commandments given as laws for a judgement, were none-the-less glorious, then should not the new ministration coming from greater consciousness, be even more glorious?

(12-18) In this hope, we speak plainly; not as did Moses whose face was so radiant that no one could look upon it.

Second Corinthians 3

13 And not as Moses, which put a vail over his face, that the children of Israel could not stedfastly look to the end of that which is abolished:

14 But their minds were blinded: for until this day remaineth the same vail in the reading of the old testament; which vail is done away in Christ.

15 But even unto this day, when Moses is read, the vail is upon their heart.

16 Nevertheless, when it shall turn to the Lord, the vail shall be taken away.

17 Now the Lord is that Spirit: and where the Spirit of the Lord is, there is liberty.

18 But we all, with open face beholding as in a glass the glory of the Lord, are changed into the same image from glory to glory even as by the Spirit of the Lord.

It was their minds that were blinded. To this very day in the reading of the Old Testament, that same blindness is perpetuated. That blindness was done away in the New Testament of Christ. Even now though, whenever the words of Moses are read, that same blindness descends upon the heart of the hearer. Nevertheless, when the words of Christ are heard, that blindness is removed. Wherever our Lord Christ's Spirit is, there also is freedom. All who recognize, even as though through a darkened mirror, the Glory of Christ, are become as part of that glory, which grows through that Spirit.

SECOND CORINTHIANS 4

4 Therefore seeing we have this ministry, as we have received mercy we faint not;

2 But have renounced the hidden things of dishonesty, not walking in craftiness, nor handling the word of God deceitfully; but by manifestation of the truth commending ourselves to every man's conscience in the sight of God.

3 But if our gospel be hid, it is hid to them that are lost.

4 In whom the god of this world hath blinded the minds of them which believe not, lest the light of the glorious gospel of Christ, who is the image of God, should shine unto them.

5 For we preach not ourselves, but Christ Jesus the Lord; and ourselves your servants for Jesus' sake.

6 For God, who commanded the light to shine out of darkness, hath sinned in our hearts, to give the light of the knowledge of the glory of God in the face of Jesus Christ.

7 But we have this treasure in earthen vessels, that the excellency of the power may be of God, and not of us.

8 We are troubled on every side, yet not distressed; we are perplexed, but not in despair.

9 Persecuted, but not forsaken; cast down, but not destroyed.

10 Always bearing about in the body the dying of the Lord Jesus, that the life also of Jesus might be made manifest in our body.

11 For we which live are always delivered unto death for Jesus' sake, that the life also of Jesus might be made manifest in our mortal flesh.

12 So then death worketh in us, but life worketh in you.

4 (1-6) Therefore, because we have received this strength, we faint not in our ministry. We have renounced all things which are hidden in dishonesty. We do not use craftiness or deceit. We speak what we know to be the truth, and commend ourselves to all on that basis, in the sight of God. It may be lost on those who have been blinded by the god of this world lest the real truth of Christ be revealed to them.[1]

(7-12) We are your servants for the sake of Christ, and it is His message, not our own, that we convey. The Light of God shines in our hearts so that we can pass on the Light of Knowledge to you. We still carry this knowledge in our earthly persons, that the greatness of the power shall be known as that of God, not ourselves. Even though we are troubled on every side, we are not distressed. We are sometimes perplexed, but we never despair. We may be persecuted, but we know we are not forsaken. We remember what Jesus suffered, and ask for that same strength. We all must go through those trials, and we all hope that we shall bear them as He did.

Second Corinthians 4

13 We having the same spirit of faith, according as it is written, I believed, and therefore have I spoken; we also believe, and therefore speak.

14 Knowing that He which raised up the Lord Jesus shall raise up us also by Jesus, and shall present us with you.

15 For all things are for your sakes, that the abundant grace might through the thanksgiving of many redound to the glory of God.

16 For which cause we faint not; but though our outward man perish, yet the inward man is renewed day by day.

17 For our light affliction, which is but for a moment, worketh for us a far more exceeding and eternal weight of glory.

18 While we look not at the things which are seen, but at the things which are not seen: for the things which are seen are temporal; but the things which are not seen are eternal.

(13-15) We have that same spirit of faith, so that even if we died it would give you renewed life (hope); to this we speak because we believe. In the knowledge that He who raised the Lord Jesus shall also raise us, we speak to you. All things are for your sakes that the abundance of grace which you witness might cause many to give thanks, so shall God be glorified.

(16-18) For this very reason we hold fast to our purpose. We may die outwardly to all appearances, but inwardly we are daily renewed. Even that small affliction which we suffer, works toward that increase of glory. We do not look at what is on the surface, but what is not seen. Things seen are only temporal, the things which are not seen are eternal.

DISCOURSE CHAPTER FOUR

1. Q: In 4:4, you have used the phrase "the God of this world" which people will see as a reference to Satan. I wondered if you want to change it or deal with it. It reads, "It may be lost on those who have been blinded by the God of this world, lest the real truth of Christ be revealed to them."

   A: Is there any reason for it to be changed? People will think I am referring to Lucifer or to Satan or whatever else they call the Prince of Darkness; I think it really does not matter, for it is that force to which I refer.

SECOND CORINTHIANS 5

5 *For we know that if our earthly house of this tabernacle were dissolved, we have a building of God, an house not made with hands, eternal in the heavens.*

2 For in this we groan, earnestly desiring to be clothed upon with our house which is from heaven:

3 If so be that being clothed we shall not be found naked.

4 For we that are in this tabernacle do groan, being burdened: not for that we would be unclothed, but clothed upon, that mortality might be swallowed up of life.

5 Now He that hath wrought for us the selfsame thing is God, who also hath given unto us the earnest of the Spirit.

6 Therefore we are always confident, knowing that, whilst we are at home in the body, we are absent from the Lord:

7 (For we walk by faith, not by sight.)

8 We are confident, I say, and willing rather, to be absent from the body, and to be present with the Lord.

9 Wherefore we labour, that, whether present or absent, we may be accepted of Him.

10 For we must all appear before the judgement seat of Christ; that every one may receive the things done in his body, according to that he hath done, whether it be good or bad.

11 Knowing therefore the terror of the Lord, we persuade men; but we are made manifest unto God; and I trust also are made manifest in your consciences.

12 For we commend not ourselves again unto you, but give you occasion to glory on our behalf that ye may have somewhat to answer them which glory in appearance, and not in heart.

5 (1-5) We know well that if this earthly vessel is dissolved, we still have a house of God. This is not made with mortal hands, but is eternal and of the heavens. For this, we earnestly seek, requiring to be clothed with things of heaven; for with this kind of covering, we shall never be naked. As long as we are in this fleshly form, we shall seek that which is of the heavenly realms. God has made us all for that purpose; that we seek after things of the Spirit.[1]

(6-10) We are confident that whilst in the body, we do not see God, yet still know Him by faith. For that reason, we do not attach to things of the body, but seek God's presence. We work on ourselves so that we are acceptable before God for we are aware that we all shall receive according to the way we ourselves have worked, be those things good or bad.

(11-13) We trust that you understand and seek within your own consciences for we are aware that nothing we do escapes God. Again, we do not say this for our own sakes, but so that you might have reason to rejoice. This will give you something to answer to those who put much in appearances, rather than seeking what is in the heart. The love of Christ is what keeps us on track, and if we seem to be sober-minded, it is for your sakes.

Second Corinthians 5

13 For whether we be beside our-selves, it is to God: or whether we be sober, it is for your cause.

14 For the love of Christ constraineth us; because we thus judge, that if one died for all, then were all dead:

15 And that He died for all, that they which live should not hence-forth live unto themselves, but unto Him which died for them, and rose again.

16 Wherefore henceforth know we no man after the flesh: yea, though we have known Christ after the flesh, yet now henceforth know we Him no more.

17 Therefore, if any man be in Christ, he is a new creature: old things are passed away; behold, all things are become new.

18 And all things are of God, who hath reconciled us to Himself by Jesus Christ, and hath given to us the ministry of reconciliation;

19 To wit, that God was in Christ, reconciling the world unto Himself not imputing their trespasses unto them; and hath committed unto us the word of reconciliation.

20 Now then we are ambassadors for Christ, as though God did beseech you by us: we pray you in Christ's stead, be ye reconciled to God.

21 For He hath made him to be sin for us, who knew no sin; that we might be made the righteousness of God in Him.

(14-21) If any man recognize the truth of Christ, then that man is a new creature who no longer lives for himself alone. Because of the message of Christ, all things become new. All things are of God, who has shown us the Truth in Christ. His is the Message of Truth; that is, God was in Christ, and they, not considering our wrongdoings, appointed us, and committed us to that Truth.[2] We are therefore ambassadors for Christ, and it is as though God calls you through us. We speak on behalf of Christ, asking you to accept God's Truth. He caused Christ to take on worldly form, who Himself was perfect, that we too, might become perfect in that knowledge.

DISCOURSE CHAPTER FIVE

1. Q: In 5:1-8, we have an issue we have talked about before, but I am putting it in a new way just to see what kind of response you might give. In the first verses of Chapter Five, just to refresh our memories, "We know well that if this earthly vessel is dissolved, we still have a house of God. This is not made with mortal hands, but is eternal and of the heavens. For this we earnestly seek, requiring to be clothed with things of heaven, for with this kind of covering, we shall never be naked. As long as we are in this fleshly form, we shall seek that which is of the heavenly realms. God has made us all for that purpose: that we seek after things of the Spirit." You have changed it slightly from the KJ and RSV into what I personally think is a change for the better, but it still raises the question about Paul's view of the fleshly or the body. How did Paul really feel about the body, and especially his own body? It seems in those comments that Paul was anxious to get out of his body so that he could be totally in the Spirit. It is as though he was anxious to leave his fleshly body; it was a hindrance to him.

   A: Good question. You have summed it up quite with insight. I think one might correctly say that Paul did, in fact, have such feelings. It is ever so. I think more particularly with the Scorpio person, as my channel herself will freely agree, that having come so very closely into the field of radiation which one enters at a certain point in evolution, there is a very strong surge always of recognition that being in the fleshly body has serious limitations. While it is part of the path of growth to be in the material world, and although one recognizes that when in the material world one must have the feet firmly planted upon the earth and one must maintain balance between the things of the body and the things of Spirit, there is nonetheless – particularly with the Scorpio person – an ardent desire to fly as the eagle; to not be bound upon the earthly plane.

   It was a part of that voyage of Paul's own discovery to recognize that so long as the being chafes against the body and its limitations, that one is calling to Self even more challenges, even more limitations, until finally the message is accepted by that one that action must not create reaction. Paul was struggling with that lesson, as do we all, and there were times in his messages to others when that struggle was extremely obvious to others. During his life span as Paul he came very close to loving that which he knew as God with all of his soul, all of his mind, and all of his strength, as indeed, the first commandment has said. But he did not succeed very well in the second part which admonishes to "Love thy neighbor as thyself," for he had not yet learned to love himself.

Discourse Chapter Five continued:

2.   Q: We dealt with the issue of reconciliation in Romans, but I felt we should touch on it again. In 5:18-20, there are classic statements of the Christian Faith: You stated in a previous discourse that "it could be said that mankind was in darkness and lost until the coming of Jesus the Christ who showed the way and the love of God for humankind." Is this not a form of reconciliation?

A: Yes, I suppose it could be considered in that light. It is in effect, reference to the return of the prodigal, of which Our Lord spoke. However, the point which I was endeavoring to make in our past discourse on this subject is that the use of an expression of reconciliation in too many references, in too many occasions, implies a basic separation. One can only be reconciled to that from which one is separated. Is that not so? And what I am trying to impart at this time, which might not have been possible to impart in earlier ages, is that we are not in any way separate from that which we regard as God. That is the only thing which I think needs to be made quite clear.

SECOND CORINTHIANS 6

6 *We then, as workers together with Him, beseech you also that ye receive not the grace of God in vain.*

2 (For He saith, I have heard thee in a time accepted, and in the day of salvation have I succoured thee: behold, now is the accepted time; behold, now is the day of salvation.)

3 Giving no offence in any thing, that the ministry be not blamed:

4 But in all things approving ourselves as the ministers of God, in much patience, in afflictions, in necessities, in distress.

5 In stripes, in imprisonments, in tumults, in labours, in watchings, in fastings;

6 By pureness, by knowledge, by longsuffering, by kindness, by the Holy Ghost, by love unfeigned,

7 By the word of truth, by the power of God, by the armour of righteousness on the right hand and on the left,

8 By honour and dishonour, by evil report and good report: as deceivers, and yet true;

9 As unknown, and yet well known; as dying, and, behold, we live; as chastened, and not killed;

10 As sorrowful, yet always rejoicing; as poor, yet making many rich; as having nothing, and yet possessing all things.

11 O ye Corinthians, our mouth is open unto you, our heart is enlarged.

12 Ye are not straightened in us, but ye are straightened in your own bowels.

13 Now for recompense in the same, (I speak as unto my children,) be ye also enlarged.

6 (1-2) We then, who work with God, beseech you that you have not received that grace in vain. For He says: "I have heard thee in a time accepted and in the day of salvation have I succored thee". Behold, now is the accepted time, behold now the time of salvation.

(3-10) We do not give offence in anything, so that the ministry will not be blamed. But, in all things, we approve of our own actions as ministers of God, with much patience in the face of discouragements. We act with pureness of knowledge and are longsuffering, we act with kindness through the Holy Spirit, and by love that is not pretended. We speak the word of Truth by the Power of God; we have the armor of righteousness on our right hand and on our left; through honor or dishonor, through good report or ill, through truth (even though people might call us deceivers); though well known or unknown, as though dying, yet look – we live! As though chastened, but not killed, as sorrowful yet always rejoicing, as though ourselves poor, yet making many people rich; as though we had nothing, yet possessing all things.

(11-13) Oh you people of Corinth, our words are spoken to you, and our heart is large. We do not make constrictions for you; the stoppages are in your own bowels! I speak as to children, open them up! Enlarge your hearts.

Second Corinthians 6

14 Be ye not unequally yoked together with unbelievers: for what fellowship hath righteousness with unrighteousness? And what communion hath light with darkness?

15 And what concord hath Christ with Belial? Or what part hath he that believeth with an infidel?

16 And what agreement hath the temple of God with idols? For ye are the temple of the living God: as God hath said, I will dwell in them, and walk in them; and I will be their God, and they shall be my people.

17 Wherefore come out from among them, and be ye separate, saith the Lord, and touch not the unclean thing; and I will receive you.

18 And will be a Father unto you, and ye shall be my sons and daughters, saith the Lord Almighty.

(14-18) Do not spend time with unbelievers so that you are classed with them. What communion does Light have with darkness? What would Christ have in common with Belial and what does the Temple of God have in common with idols?[1] You are the Temple of the Living God, and He has said that He will "dwell with them and walk with them and they will be My people." Therefore, stay apart from all that is unclean, as God has said, that He may be a Father to you, and you shall be His sons and daughters.

DISCOURSE CHAPTER SIX

1. Q: In 6:15, I have an editorial question. You use the word in this phrase "what would Christ have in common with Belial?" The scholars say that it is a kind of hybrid word between the Greek and the Hebrew and they wondered if you coined a word. What did you mean by "Belial"?

   A: It is, in fact, a hybrid word. It is the masculine and the feminine equivalent of that same dark force which is combined. The dark force has variously been called Baal, and the feminine aspect Lelis, and the Belian force is the masculine and feminine, or the negative and positive aspects of that same force.

SECOND CORINTHIANS 7

7 *Having therefore these promises, dearly beloved, let us cleanse ourselves from all filthiness of the flesh and spirit, perfecting holiness in the fear of God.*

2 Receive us; we have wronged no man, we have corrupted no man, we have defrauded no man.

3 I speak not this to condemn you: for I have said before, that ye are in our hearts to die and live with you.

4 Great is my boldness of speech toward you, great is my glorying of you: I am filled with comfort, I am exceeding joyful in all our tribulation.

5 For, when we were come into Macedonia, our flesh had no rest, but we were troubled on every side; without were fightings, within were fears.

6 Nevertheless God, that comforteth those that are cast down, comforted us by the coming of Titus;

7 And not by his coming only, but by the consolation wherewith he was comforted in you, when he told us your earnest desire, your mourning, your fervent mind toward me; so that I rejoiced the more:

8 For though I made you sorry with a letter, I do not repent, though I did repent: for I perceive that the same epistle hath made you sorry, though it were but for a season.

9 Now I rejoice, not that ye were made sorry, but that ye sorrowed to repentance: for ye were made sorry after a godly manner, that ye might receive damage by us in nothing.

10 For godly sorrow worketh repentance to salvation not to be repeated of; but the sorrow of the world worketh death.

7 (1-4) Having therefore these promises, dearly beloved, let us keep ourselves clean and pure in both body and spirit, let us perfect our holiness out of respect for the Creator. Hear our words, for we have done nothing which shall corrupt anyone (I do not say this to condemn you, for I have said before that you are much in our hearts that we would willingly live or die with you). I have been very bold of speech with you, because I do hold you in such high esteem. I am comforted and joyous, even through all our tribulations.

(5-7) When we last came through Macedonia we were weary, with nowhere to rest, and troubled on all sides. There was fighting on the outside, and fears on the inside: Nevertheless, God, who is the comforter of all, was indeed our strength, and Titus' arrival was a great comfort, especially because of the way in which you received him: When he conveyed to me your feelings, your earnestness, your high esteem of me personally, your sorrow for things that were not right – these things were all great comfort to me.

(8-11) Although I realize that my earlier letter somewhat upset you, I do not regret having written it (in a sense I can say that I regret it upset you, but I am still not sorry I wrote it, for it only upset you a short time). Now it is cause for me to be glad, not that it upset you, but that it caused you to stop and think; you were thus made sorry for a good reason.

Second Corinthians 7

11 For behold this selfsame thing, that ye sorrowed after a godly sort, what clearing of yourselves, yes, what indignation, yea, what for, yea, what vehement desire, yea, what real, yea, what revenge! In all things ye have approved yourselves to be clear in this matter.

12 Wherefore, though I wrote unto you, I did it not for his cause that suffered wrong, but that our care for you in the sight of God might appear unto you.

13 Therefore we were comforted in your comfort: yea, and exceedingly the more joyed we for the joy of Titus, because his spirit was refreshed by you all.

14 For if I have boasted any thing to him of you, I am not ashamed; but as we spake all things to you in truth, even so our boasting, which I made before Titus, is found a truth.

15 And this inward affection is more abundant toward you, whilst he remembreth the obedience of you all, how with fear and trembling ye received him.

16 I rejoice therefore that I have confidence in you in all things.

Thus what I wrote did not do any damage. To be upset in a just cause, creates the means to repeat the errors. Look then, you were upset for a just reason, and this helped you to straighten things out. What a cleansing effect all this had. All the indignation, all the fear, all the zeal – it all amounted to a purgation, that you would arrive at a clearing within yourselves.

(12-16) It could now therefore be seen that what I wrote to you then was not wrong, nor in a manner to put you in the wrong; but so that you would eventually see how much we care for you. Therefore our comfort is our comfort, your joy our joy. Now I am even more rejoicing in Titus' report, because I can see that he has been refreshed by you all. I can now see that all the good things I said to him about you were justified. His inward feelings of affection toward you all has been greatly increased. He recalled to me how you first received him with fear and trembling, and how eager you all were to obey his wishes. All this gives me reason to be very confident in you.

SECOND CORINTHIANS 8

8 Moreover, brethren, we do you to wit of the grace of God bestowed on the churches of Macedonia;

2 How that in a great trial of affliction the abundance of their joy and their deep poverty abounded unto the riches of their liberality.

3 For to their power, I bear record, yea, and beyond their power they were willing of themselves;

4 Praying us with much entreaty that we would receive the gift, and take upon us the fellowship of the ministering to the saints.

5 And this they did, not as we hoped, but first gave their own selves to the Lord, and unto us by the will of God.

6 Insomuch that we desired Titus, that as he had begun, so he would also finish in you the same grace also.

7 Therefore, as ye abound in every thing, in faith, and utterance, and knowledge, and in all diligence, and in your love to us, see that ye abound in this grace also.

8 I speak not by commandment, but by occasion of the forwardness of others, and to prove the sincerity of your love.

9 For ye know the grace of our Lord Jesus Christ, that, though He was rich, yet for your sakes He became poor, that ye through His poverty might be rich.

10 And herein I give my advice: for this is expedient for you, who have begun before, not only to do, but also to be forward a year ago.

11 Now therefore perform the doing of it; that as there was a readiness to will, so there may be a performance also out of that which ye have.

12 For if there be first a willing mind, it is accepted according to that a man hath, and not according to that he hath not.

13 For I mean not that other men be eased, and ye burdened:

8 (1-7) Moreover, brethren, this calls me to mind the other communities in Macedonia, and the grace of God which they have received. During great trials and affliction, their joy has remained constant. In much poverty have they remained rich in spirit. I can attest to their strength, and their willingness. They were received into the fellowship of the Lord first of all, and then they requested us most earnestly, that we would continue to minister unto them in the name of God. That was why we had requested that Titus visit and assist in that strengthening. As you stay constant in your faith, in your inner knowledge and in the things that you speak so you stay constant in that Grace.[1]

(8-15) I do not say this as a command, but as a recommendation. You know that our Lord Christ took a vow of poverty and gave up worldly wealth; that His Grace might be assured also in you. I said to you a year ago that it would be well to abide by His example, now I again advise that you would be well to do it. There was then an apparent readiness to take the vow of poverty and perhaps there might be some who are ready to do this. Where there is a willing mind, you will see that it is not what a person possesses but what they are, that is important. I suggest that your abundance may be a supply for the needs of others, and the things that others might have (which you do not) can be a supply to you.

Second Corinthians 8

14 But by an equality, that now at this time your abundance may be a supply for their want, that their abundance also may be a supply for your want: that there may be equality:

15 As it is written, He that had gathered much had nothing over, and he that had gathered little had no lack.

16 But thanks be to God, which put the same earnest care into the heart of Titus for you.

17 For indeed he accepted the exhortation; but being more forward of his own accord he went unto you.

18 And we have sent with him the brother whose praise is in the gospel throughout all the churches;

19 And not that only, but who was also chosen of the churches to travel with us with this grace, which is administered by us to the glory of the same Lord, and declaration of your ready mind:

20 Avoiding this, that no man should blame us in this abundance which is administered by us:

21 Providing for honest things, not only in the sight of the Lord, but also in the sight of men.

22 And we have sent with them our brother, whom we have oftentimes proved diligent in many things, but now much more diligent, upon the great confidence which I have in you.

23 Whether any do inquire of Titus, he is my partner and fellow helper concerning you; or our brethren be inquired of they are the messengers of the churches, and the glory of Christ.

24 Wherefore shew ye to them, and before the churches, the proof of your love, and of our boasting on your behalf.

In this way equality is created. It has been written: "He that hath gathered much had nothing over; he that gathered little had no lack." [2]

(16-24) I thank God that Titus cared for you so well. He accepted my charge, and being of good courage, came to you. We also sent with him our dear brother who has set forth praise in the gospel which is being heard in all the communities. He has chosen to travel everywhere with us; through Grace, we serve the same Lord. I tell you this that no one will have a wrong impression of the abundance of faith which we display, for we build up this abundant grace through honest application in the sight of God and men. The other brother who travels with us has proved extremely diligent in all things, and he is now even more careful of the great trust which I have placed in you all.[3] To any who should inquire of Titus, he is indeed my partner and fellow helper concerning you, or our other brothers, if they be questioned; yes, they too are the messengers to the communities and to the Glory of Christ. Therefore be good to them, demonstrate your lovingness, and justify our confidence in you.

DISCOURSE CHAPTER EIGHT

1.   Q: In 8:2 and 8:4, the KJ and RSV are very specific in regards to the collection. You have taken some of that specificity out and made it more general than the old text, referring to the wealth of liberality that the Macedonian church showed, and hoping that this is a good example for the Corinthians to follow. Paul has boasted again about Corinth and he hopes they will not disappoint his boasting. You eliminated some of those specific references which changes the meaning slightly. Do you wish to comment?

A: Would you care to remind me of the difference?

Q: This is what you say in the new text, "Moreover brethren, this calls me to mind the other communities in Macedonia and the grace of God which they have received. During great trials and affliction their joy has remained constant. In much poverty have they remained rich in Spirit (a change there). I can attest to their strength and their willingness. They were received into the fellowship of the Lord first of all, and then they requested most earnestly that we would continue to minister unto them in the name of God." The RSV states, "The churches of Macedonia, for in a severe test of affliction, their abundance of joy and their extreme poverty have overflowed in a wealth of liberality on their part, for they gave according to their means, as I can testify, and beyond their means of their own free will, begging us earnestly for the favor of taking part in the relief of the saints. Accordingly, we have urged Titus that he has already made a beginning, he should also complete among you this gracious work." They were talking very specifically about going back and taking the collection. Later on you do get specific again. It is only this first section that is more general.

A: The part of the letter to which we are speaking does concern the actual gathering of alms. If in referring to richness of spirit, there is a degree of ambiguity as to what was meant here, then perhaps it might be good to specify we are speaking about alms, and it does take richness of Spirit in order to give when the giver is himself poor materially, that is. So please, if you think that creates ambiguity, then let us alter accordingly.

Q: I don't think it needs to be changed; I think your comment is all that is necessary. That makes it very specific.

A: I tend in the now to be of fewer words. Where the clarity is obtained in a later sentence it is not necessary to say it twice, in my opinion.

Discourse Chapter Eight continued:

2.   Q: There is no specific reference in either chapter 8 or 9; we are assuming though that this is the collection for the saints in Jerusalem. The question arose as to whether other collections were ever taken for other people other than the saints in Jerusalem.

    A: Oh, by all means. During the whole of my own personal ministry, and I am quite sure the ministry of the other apostles and eventually bishops, it was always part of that ministry to make collection of tithing which was always very strongly encouraged, and to take help into areas where help was needed. I must say that to a very large extent it was needed more particularly in Jerusalem in the earlier days, but in later times it became very much more needed in Rome itself than anywhere else.

3.   Q: Toward the end of 8:22, there is reference to Titus and the two who accompanied him; one of whom you identified as Luke. Do you want to identify the other one.

    A: Of course, Timothy was the third person to whom the reference was made.

SECOND CORINTHIANS 9

9 *For as touching the ministering to the saints, it is superfluous for me to write to you:*

2 For I know the forwardness of your mind, for which I boast of you to them at Macedonia, that Achaia was ready a year ago; and your zeal hath provoked very many.

3 Yet have I sent the brethren, lest our boasting of you should be in vain in this behalf; that, as I said, ye may be ready:

4 Lest haply if they of Macedonia come with me, and find you unprepared, we (that we say not, ye) should be ashamed in this same confident boasting.

5 Therefore I though it necessary to exhort the brethren, that they would go before unto you, and make up beforehand your bounty whereof ye had notice before, that the same might be ready, as a matter of bounty, and not as of covetousness.

6 But this I say, He which soweth sparingly shall reap also sparingly; and he which soweth bountifully shall reap also bountifully.

7 Every man according as he purposeth in his heart, so let him give; not grudgingly, or of necessity: for God loveth a cheerful giver.

8 And God is able to make all grace abound toward you; that ye, always having all sufficiency in all things, may abound to every good work:

9 (As it is written, He hath dispersed abroad; he hath given to the poor: His righteousness remaineth for ever.

10 Now he that ministereth seed to the sower both minister bread for your food, and multiply your seed sown, and increase the fruits of your righteousness;)

11 Being enriched in every thing to all bountifulness, which causeth through us thanksgiving to God.

9 (1-5) For touching on the subject of ministry to the faithful, I thought it superfluous for me to write to you, for I know that you are very conscious (I boasted of this throughout Macedonia – that the Achaians were ready a year ago). Your zeal has been a good example to many. Nevertheless, I have sent my colleagues to you, to make quite certain that you are ready and my praise of you is not unwarranted. I felt this necessary, because if the people here in Macedonia should come themselves to visit you to be helped, and they find you not living up to my praise, then we shall both be the worse for it. Therefore I sent my messengers on ahead so that you could put together all that you are willing to give to help these people.

(6-10) Be bountiful, for I say those who sow sparingly shall reap sparingly. Let each one give according to the abundance he feels in his heart, not grudgingly or from a sense of duty, for God loves a cheerful giver. God gives to all with equal grace, that you always have sufficient, and that you may rejoice in all good work. It is written: "He hath dispersed abroad; He hath given to the poor, His righteousness remaineth forever. Now that He ministereth seed to the sower both minister bread for your food, and multiply your seed sown and increase the fruits of your righteousness."

Second Corinthians 9

12 For the administration of this service not only supplieth the want of the saints, but is abundant also by many thanksgivings unto God;

13 While by the experiment of this ministration they glorify God for your professed subjection unto the gospel of Christ, and for your liberal distribution unto them, and unto all men;

14 And by their prayer for you, which long after you for the exceeding grace of God in you.

15 Thanks be unto God for his unspeakable gift.

(11-15) Being enriched in every way, we should give thanks to God, for by supplying the needs of others who spend their time in ministry, you are also showing your thanks to God. During their ministry they glorify God, bringing you into the fold of those who accept Christ, and in so doing, request distribution of help not only for themselves, but for those in need everywhere. The strength of their prayers is also to your comfort, increasing the grace of God in you. God be thanked for this immeasurable gift.[1]

DISCOURSE CHAPTER NINE

1. Q: In chapter nine, you exhorted the Corinthians to use the people in Macedonia as an example, you have exhorted them to share their abundance because they are the strong and the wealthy. Were you successful; did they come through in the collections?

   A: Oh, yes indeed they did. The Greeks were ever generous if one could speak to them in the right vein.

   Q: So your boasting was in good order.

   A: Yes.

SECOND CORINTHIANS 10[1]

10 *Now I Paul myself beseech you by the meekness and gentleness of Christ, who in presence am base among you, but being absent am bold toward you:*

2 But I beseech you, that I may not be bold when I am present with that confidence, wherewith I think to be bold against some, which think of us as if we walked according to the flesh.

3 For though we walk in the flesh, we do not war after the flesh:

4 (For the weapons of our warfare are not carnal, but mighty through God to the pulling down of strong holds;)

5 Casting down imaginations, and every high thing that exalteth itself against the knowledge of God; and bringing into captivity every thought to the obedience of Christ;

6 And having in a readiness to revenge all disobedience; when your obedience is fulfilled.

7 Do ye look on things after the outward appearance? If any man trust to himself that he is Christ's, let him of himself think this again; that, as he is Christ's, even so are we Christ's.

8 For though I should boast somewhat more of our authority, which the Lord hath given us for edification, and not for your destruction, I should not be ashamed:

9 That I may not seem as if I would terrify you by letters.

10 For His letters, say they, are weighty and powerful; but His bodily presence is weak and His speech contemptible.

11 Let such an one think this, that, such as we are in word by letters when we are absent, such will we be also in deed when we are present.

10 (1-6) I Paul, personally beg of you through the gentleness and meekness of Christ – I who am bold when I write from a distance, but when among you feel the least of you. I try to remain mild when I am with you personally, lest people might think that we follow only after the conceits of the flesh. For in truth, though we are in the body, we care not for it. Our weapons are not of the body, but of the Spirit, that through Godliness we may cast down anything that sets itself up in authority against God. Through adherence to the message of Christ, we can bring about change. Being changed ourselves, we can hope to assist you.

(7-12) It is not the outward appearance that counts. If anyone think that he has the Spirit of a Christ, then let him be Christ-like. If I were to boast of the authority given to me by Christ, for your edification, (not for your destruction) I should not be ashamed. If my letters seem to you to be very strong, yet when I am among you I seem to be mild, then I remind you that this was true of our Lord also. His letters too are weighty and powerful, yet He preserves a very mild appearance and His speech is not particularly impressive.[2] Perhaps one might think that the way we appear from our letters, should be the way we are in person. We do not count ourselves among those numbers that commend their own measure, or seek to compare themselves with others. These are not wise ones.

Second Corinthians 10

12 For we dare not make ourselves of the number, or compare ourselves with some that commend themselves: but they measuring themselves by themselves, and comparing themselves among themselves, are not wise.

13 But we will not boast of things without our measure, but according to the measure of the rule which God hath distributed to us, a measure to reach even unto you.

14 For we stretch not ourselves beyond our measure, as though we reached not unto you: for we are come as far as to you also in preaching the gospel of Christ:

15 Not boasting of things without our measure, that is, of other men's labours; but having hope, when your faith is increased, that we shall be enlarged by you according to our rule abundantly.

16 To preach the gospel in the regions beyond you, and not to boast in another man's line of things made ready to our hand.

17 But he that glorieth, let him glory in the Lord.

18 For not he that commendeth himself is approved, but whom the Lord commendeth.

(13-18) We do not boast of ourselves, only do we measure ourselves according to the Laws of God, who has given us all the means to attainment. We do not put ourselves above the level that we are aware. We are at about the same level as you in that awareness, and in our ability to spread the Message of Christ. We cannot boast through the labors of others, we can only hope that as we grow ourselves in awareness, we shall be able to speak with that greater awareness, and it is our hope that we will be enriched by you in equal abundance, perhaps speaking of the gospel in those regions that lie beyond you (yet not to boast of things gained only through others). Let all who glory, glory in the Lord. It is not the one who commends himself that is approved, but the one whom the Lord commends.[3]

DISCOURSE CHAPTER TEN

1. Q: Just to review quickly: chapters 10-13 are part of the "stern letter" which never got read to the Corinthians for some reason; either it didn't get delivered, or it was lost, etc. and you added it on to the end of the other nine chapters.

   A: That is so.

   Q: When you did that, since there was no particular transition in the writing, did you assume that the messenger would convey the fact or that they would understand that this was an addendum from the past?

   A: It was, in fact, something that had back by the same messenger, Timothy, it document. The lack of separation has recorded historically but which was not so been requested and when taken was in fact given as a separate been something which has been at the time of writing.

2. Q: That is helpful. In 10:10, you have changed the meaning slightly here and it is intriguing. There are two or three references to "his letters are weighty and strong" and the assumption in the past was that Paul was referring to his letters in the sense that people were quoted as saying "His letters are weighty and strong." You have changed that to referring to "his" as Lord Jesus, and that His letters were well known. We have never heard of any letters written by Jesus.

   A: No, we didn't did we? Nonetheless, as has been said by Jesus Himself in His contribution to the appendices, there were letters written by Him and these also were conveyed by messenger to the communities and my translation in the present time states quite clearly that I am likening myself to Our Lord wherein His letters are considered to be rather weighty and strong, and yet, when one is in the Presence, that Presence is extremely mild.

3. Q: That will give food for thought to many people. This is a question I have after reading chapters 10-13. Would you care to talk about who these troublemakers were, or false prophets who were coming from the outside and stirring up the Corinthians? What were they doing?

   A: Greece, being geographically located as it is, was a clearinghouse, I should say. It was a stopping point for many travellers coming from the western Mediterranean – the western Mediterranean being the Iberian peninsula which is now known as Spain – coming down from the northern Celtic countries, coming indeed from that which is now Russia, coming across from Italy, and from Asia Minor, and in particular, Byzantium. Therefore, Greece has always, to a large extent, been a melting pot, and sometimes the pot boils with all kinds of rumor, opinion, cults and practices.

Discourse Chapter Ten continued:

To the Greek of that day in particular, the many ideas, theologies, practices, were confusing in the extreme and here is another one, to some extent speaking of something totally new, and yet contained in that very newness, there is an essence, a thread, of many of the theologies being practiced and believed by those different groups. Therefore, one can imagine, with not too much difficulty, just how challenging the message which Paul and his group were delivering was to the people of Achaia, particularly the Corinthians, more so than the people of Macedonia, because it has to be remembered that Corinth and Athens were very close to one of the major ports at that time, or any time; it still is.

It took a great deal of application and clarity not to speak of understanding in order for the mind of the majority of people to sort out from all of these theologies and practices, which one is the Truth. Down through the ages there had been many hierophants in the different sects, each of whom were very powerful, were able to speak in a very eloquent and often grandiose manner. Part of my statement was that I, too, in my letters – Our Lord, too, in His letters – spoke equally powerfully. The challenge then, as always, was that the crowds will behave with certain limitations of skepticism toward those whom they do not consider to be as powerful as a Hercules in their physical being as well as in their art of oratory. We were not all so blessed.

SECOND CORINTHIANS 11

11 *Would to God ye could bear with me a little in my folly: and indeed bear with me.*

2 For I am jealous over you with godly jealousy: for I have espoused you to one husband, that I may present you as a chaste virgin to Christ.

3 But I fear, lest by any means, as the serpent beguiled Eve through his subtility, so your minds should be corrupted from the simplicity that is in Christ.

4 For if he that cometh preacheth another Jesus, whom we have not preached, or if ye receive another spirit, which ye have not received, or another gospel, which ye have not accepted, ye might well bear with him.

5 For I suppose I was not a whit behind the very chiefest apostles.

6 But though I be rude in speech, yet not in knowledge; but we have been thoroughly made manifest among you in all things.

7 Have I committed an offence in abasing myself that ye might be exalted, because I have preached to you the gospel of God freely?

8 I robbed other churches, taking wages of them, to do you service.

9 And when I was present with you, and wanted, I was chargeable to no man; for that which was lacking to me the brethren which came from Macedonia supplied: and in all things I have kept myself from being burdensome unto you, and so will I keep myself

10 As the truth of Christ is in me, no man shall stop me of this boasting in the regions of Achaia.

11 Wherefore? Because I love you not? God knoweth.

11 (1-6) If what I say at first appears foolish, please bear with me, for I am ever mindful of your welfare; it is as though I have recommended you in marriage to a husband, and now I want to present that husband with a chaste virgin for a wife. (The husband being Christ). It is my constant fear though, that the same temptations that have beset us since Eve shall keep you from recognizing the very simplicity of the message of Christ. If certain people come to you speaking of a different Jesus than the one of whom we speak, or if you hear other stories, other rumors (which you have not accepted) you might well also bear with the bringer. I might be halting in my speech, but I am not so in knowledge, and that has been given to you fully in all things.

(7-11) Have I done the wrong thing in putting myself into a position of humility that you might be exalted, or because I have fully shared with you concerning these things? If so, then I have robbed other communities by taking payment from them in order to come to you. And when I was there with you and in need, I asked nothing of you for the people of Macedonia had given me supply. In all things I have refrained from being a burden to you, and shall continue that way. As Christ is with me, nothing shall prevent me from the way I feel in the regions of Achaia. Why is this? Certainly not that I do not love you.

Second Corinthians 11

12 But what I do, that I will do, that I may cut off occasion from them which desire occasion; that wherein they glory, they may be found even as we.

13 For such are false apostles, deceitful workers, transforming themselves into the apostles of Christ.

14 And no marvel; for Satan himself is transformed into an angel of light.

15 Therefore, it is no great thing if his ministers also be transformed as the ministers of righteousness; whose end shall be according to their works.

16 I say again, let no man think me a fool; if otherwise, yet as a fool receive me, that I may boast myself a little.

17 That which I speak, I speak it not after the Lord, but as it were foolishly, in this confidence of boasting.

18 Seeing that many glory after the flesh, I will glory also.

19 For ye suffer fools gladly, seeing ye yourselves are wise.

20 For ye suffer, if a man bring you into bondage, if a man devour you, if a man take of you, if a man exalt himself if a man smite you on the face.

21 I speak as concerning reproach, as though we had been weak. Howbeit whereinsoever any is bold, (I speak foolishly,) I am bold also.

22 Are they Hebrews? So am I. Are they Israelites? So am I. Are they the seed of Abraham? So am I.

23 Are they ministers of Christ? (I speak as a fool) I am more; in labours more abundant, in stripes above measure, in prisons more frequent, in deaths oft.

24 Of the Jews five times received I forty stripes save one.

(12-15) What I continue to do, I do. I cut short those who seek personal glorification because they are only like the rest of us. False apostles are deceitful in what they do; because they profess to be apostles of Christ. This is not so marvelous; even Lucifer was an angel of Light, therefore it is no great thing if his ministers do the same. Their end shall be according to their works.

(16-21) I am not a fool; if any man think me a fool, then let him receive me as one. If what I speak about is truly not of Christ, then it shall have its own recompense. Are you yourselves so wise that you suffer fools gladly? You suffer only if what someone does, makes a prisoner of you, or if they consume you, or rob you, or if they hit you in the face in their conceit. I address the subject of reproach as though we were thought weak. How is it that when anyone is thought bold, I am bold?

(22-28) Are they also Hebrews, as I? Are they Israelites? So am I. Are they descendants of Abraham: So am I. Are they ministers of Christ (remember, it is the fool speaking!), I am the more. In works more abundant, in beatings beyond measure, in prison more frequently, in dying a death, often.

Second Corinthians 11

25 Thrice was I beaten with rods, once was I stoned, thrice I suffered shipwreck a night and a day I have been in the deep;

26 In journeyings often, in perils of waters, in perils of robbers, in perils by mine own countrymen, in perils by the heathen, in perils in the city, in perils in the wilderness, in perils in the sea, in perils among false brethren;

27 In weariness and painfulness, in watchings often, in hunger and thirst, in fastings often, in cold and nakedness.

28 Beside those things that are without, that which cometh upon me daily, the care of all the churches.

29 Who is weak and I am not weak? Who is offended, and I burn not?

30 If I must needs glory, I will glory of the things which concern mine infirmities.

31 The God and Father of our Lord Jesus Christ, which is blessed for evermore, knoweth that I lie not.

32 In Damascus the governor under Aretas the king kept the city of the Damascenes with a garrison, desirous to apprehend me:

33 And through a window in a basket was I let down by the wall, and escaped his hands.

From those very Jews I have been beaten with forty lashes on five occasions. On three occasions I was beaten with the rod. Once I was stoned. I have three times been shipwrecked (one time in the sea a night and a day). In my travels I have often been in much peril on the sea, from robbers, from my own countrymen, from the heathen, in the cities and in the wilderness, and from false brothers. Often in weariness or in pain, often in hunger or thirst, often through fastings, and in cold and nakedness. And through all these outward tribulations I have cared for the young communities of the faithful.[1]

(29-33) Who is weak, am I? Who is offended? Not I. If I needed glory, I would glory in my infirmities through God, the Father of our Lord Christ who knows that I do not lie. When I was in Damascus, the then governor under Aretas the King,[2] kept that city garrisoned. They were trying to catch me, and I escaped by being let down through a window in the city wall in a basket.

DISCOURSE CHAPTER ELEVEN

1. Q: This is a commentary from 11:22-28. All through my seminary days and my acquaintance with the New Testament, I don't think I have ever looked carefully at the rather awesome list of trials and tribulations that Paul went through. I looked at it again, and was awed – the number of beatings and imprisonments, and of course, this list is not complete, because more trouble happened after Second Corinthians was written. I wanted you to know that it is possible for someone to know the Bible fairly well and just not have ever come to grips with that list of tribulations. It is impressive and awesome.

    A: It should not be something impressive. Did you take heed of what was said by Our Lord concerning this? If there had not been something in Judas which attracted the energy of betrayal, that would never have arisen for him. Yes, indeed, awesome, but do not be impressed with that which Paul attracted to himself in order to learn what it was he needed. This is something that we all do and continue to do until soul decides that the lesson is clearly learned. There was, in Paul the man, a great deal of self flagellation.

2. Q: Thank you for that. We have a question in 11:32-3 for the biblical detectives.* You make a reference to King Aretus as having been governor of Damascus. The biblical scholars are saying that they cannot find any evidence that Damascus was ever in the kingdom of Aretus. They go through long explanations, that maybe it was a representative of the king, or maybe you would say that they have not found the evidence yet.

    A: The latter.

    Q: We will let them chew on that.

    A: That is something they apparently enjoy.

---

* Ibid, p. 404

SECOND CORINTHIANS 12

12 *It is not expedient for me doubtless to glory. I will come to visions and revelations of the Lord.*

2 I knew a man in Christ above fourteen years ago, (whether in the body, I cannot tell; or whether out of the body, I cannot tell: God knoweth;) such an one caught up to the third heaven.

3 And I knew such a man, (whether in the body, or out of the body, I cannot tell: God knoweth;)

4 How that he was caught up into paradise, and heard unspeakable words, which it is not lawful for a man to utter.

5 Of such an one will I glory; yet of myself I will not glory, but in mine infirmities.

6 For though I would desire to glory, I shall not be a fool; for I will say the truth: but now I forbear, lest any man should think of me above that which he seeth me to be, or that he heareth of me.

7 And lest I should be exalted above measure through the abundance of the revelations, there was given to me a thorn in the flesh, the messenger of Satan to buffet me, lest I should be exalted above measure.

8 For this thing I besought the Lord thrice, that it might depart from me.

9 And He said unto me, "My grace is sufficient for thee: for My strength is made perfect in weakness." Most gladly therefore will I rather glory in my infirmities, that the power of Christ may rest upon me.

10 Therefore, I take pleasure in infirmities, in reproaches, in necessities, in persecutions, in distresses for Christ's sake: for when I am weak then am I strong.

12 (1-6) It is not expedient that I glory. I will speak only of the visions and revelations of the Lord.[1] More than fourteen years ago I knew personally a man who was in Christ. I was not sure whether in the body or out of it; only God knows. I tell you that I knew that man whether bodily or not, who was of the third heaven, or paradise as we know of it wherein he knew of things that cannot be understood on this earth. Of that One I shall glory, never of myself. I can only recognize my infirmities and though at times I might want to be caught up in ego, I will not be so foolish, but I shall tell the truth. I must forbear much, lest people think me more than I really am and lest they set me up to be higher than I deserve because of the revelations I give, (as they were given to me).

(7-10) There was also given to me that which is a thorn in my side; the temptations of "Satan" to constantly try me, so that my ego does not get above me. I have three times asked the Lord to relieve me, and his answer is that the Grace of Christ is sufficient for me, for it is in these trials that I shall become strong. Most gladly therefore will I continue to accept these trials and tribulations, if through them, I shall attain enlightenment with Christ's power. In this way, when I seem weakest, I can become the stronger.

Second Corinthians 12

11 I am become a fool in glorying; ye have compelled me: for I ought to have been commended of you: for in nothing am I behind the very chiefest apostles, though I be nothing.

12 Truly the signs of an apostle were wrought among you in all patience, in signs, and wonders, and mighty deeds.

13 For what is it wherein ye were inferior to other churches, except it be that I myself was not burdensome to you? Forgive me this wrong.

14 Behold, the third time I am ready to come to you; and I will not be burdensome to you: for I seek not yours, but you: for the children ought not to lay up for the parents, but the parents for the children.

15 And I will very gladly spend and be spent for you; though the more abundantly I love you, the less I be loved.

16 But be it so, I did not burden you: nevertheless, being crafty, I caught you with guile.

17 Did I make a gain of you by any of them whom I sent unto you?

18 I desired Titus, and with him I sent a brother. Did Titus make a gain of you? Walked we not in the same spirit? Walked we not in the same steps?

19 Again, think ye that we excuse ourselves unto you? We speak before God in Christ: But we do all things, dearly beloved, for your edifying.

20 For I fear, lest, when I come, I shall not find you such as I would, and that I shall be found unto you such as ye would not: lest there be debates, envyings, wraths, strifes, backbitings, whisperings, swellings, tumults:

(11-13) All this talk has made me foolish. You have compelled this in me. I should really have had your confidence, for I am in no way less than other apostles, though I am, of myself, nothing. In truth the sign of an apostle is that of great patience, miracles and good deeds. In what way did you feel inferior to any of the other churches, unless it was that I myself was a burden on you? This seems folly; forgive me.

(14-18) For the third time I have made ready to visit you, and again I will not be a burden. I do not want anything you possess; I want only to be with you. Children do not look after parents, it is the parents that look after children. I am glad to expend my time and energy on you, that is how much I love you. This would be true even though the more I seem to love you, the less I am loved. However, be it so. I did not want to so burden you, but it seems that I caught you out. Did I seek to gain from you by those whom I sent to you? I sent Titus and my other Brother in Christ. Did they take from you? Did we all not walk the same path of Spirit?

(19-21) We do not make excuses for ourselves, for we do all things in the name of Christ. I do begin to be afraid though, that when I return I might not find this to be the case, and I might find you in endless debates, filled with envy, wrath, backbiting and other strife, even in tumult.

Second Corinthians 12

21 And lest, when I come again, my God will humble me among you, and that I shall bewail many which have sinned already, and have not repented of the uncleanness and fornication and lasciviousness which they have committed.

In case this is so, I shall find myself crying out against the many who have fallen by the wayside.

DISCOURSE CHAPTER TWELVE

1. Q: In 12:1-6, you say that after the Damascus experience, you had many visions. Can you say more about that. This is something that people pay much attention to.

    A: While in the fleshly body it is difficult in the extreme for the average human to communicate and see into those other realms that are ever present – working in parallel manner, side by side if you will, and often integrated with the physical manifest form. The ability of retention of awareness of those realms for the average human is rare. In very rare circumstances, some are born with that; all children are born with that ability which lasts only for a very short time. Others, in rare circumstances, retain that ability.

    But in the main, the ability of sight usually comes with a death experience. When a person has died to the fleshly vehicle and then for some reason returns into that vehicle, or perhaps, I should say, when the Spirit returns into that vehicle, it is usually possible and very likely that the person in question has a greater ability to retain knowledge of those other spheres of existence. This might be likened to enlightenment. One is certainly based in the pure light of that which lies beyond the physical form and one can say with true certainty that from that point, one's life is changed, and there is no return to what was before that event.

    I do not say that one immediately thereafter becomes a high degree initiate or adept; those are circumstances that must be won over rigorous and long disciplines, but there is, however, a change, and a knowledge that cannot be eradicated, no matter what the circumstances from that point onward. These people are quite frequently totally misunderstood. For they have a knowing that

Discourse Chapter Twelve continued:

cannot be conveyed to others. They are thought of as arrogant, withdrawn, many things. The man Paul, could answer to all of that and particularly in light of his earlier record. It was this event, in fact, which reconciled Luke and Paul because of Luke's intimate understanding of such an event.

2.   Q: Going on in 12:7-8. you mention the thorn that was in your side that was there for Paul to learn from. Is that a reference to the illness we have discussed in an earlier letter?

A: Yes, indeed. Paul did not suffer gladly the fact that his physical body often gave him a great deal of concern.

SECOND CORINTHIANS 13

13 *This is the third time I am coming to you. In the mouth of two or three witnesses shall every word be established.*

2 I told you before, and foretell you, as if I were present, the second time; and being absent now I write to them which heretofore have sinned, and to all other, that, if I come again, I will not spare:

3 Since ye seek a proof of Christ speaking in me, which to you-ward is not weak, but is mighty in you.

4 For though he was crucified through weakness, ye He liveth by the power of God. For we also are weak in Him, but we shall live with Him by the power of God toward you.

5 Examine yourselves, whether ye be in the faith; prove your own selves. Know ye not your own selves, how that Jesus Christ is in you, except ye be reprobates?

6 But I trust that ye shall know that we are not reprobates.

7 Now I pray to God that ye do no evil; not that we should appear approved, but that ye should do that which is honest, though we be as reprobates.

8 For we can do nothing against the truth but for the truth.

9 For we are glad, when we are weak, and ye are strong: and this also we wish, even your perfection.

10 Therefore I write these things being absent, lest being present I should use sharpness, according to the power which the Lord hath given me to edification, and not to destruction.

11 Finally, brethren, farewell. Be perfect, be of good comfort, be of one mind, live in peace; and the God of love and peace shall be with you.

12 Greet one another with an holy kiss.

13 All the saints salute you.

14 The grace of the Lord Jesus Christ, and the love of God, and the holy communion of the Holy Ghost, be with you all. Amen.

(1-4) This is my third visit as I said. All my words can be borne out even by two or three. I tell you again, were I to make that visit and find the things mentioned, I should not spare you my feelings. Since you seek to prove that it is Christ who speaks through me, you will find it powerful towards you, not weak. Although the Lord was crucified through apparent weakness, He lived by the power of God. We are all weak beside Him, but we shall live as He, through the power of God.

(5-10) Look carefully at yourselves, to assure that you abide in that faith. Prove yourselves to yourselves. How can you know that Christ lives in you unless you seek it in yourselves? I trust that each of us shall know where we stand. I pray to God that we do not perpetrate evil, but that we shall be honest with ourselves. We cannot live against that inner truth. We can be glad in our weakness if we see that you are strong, for we seek no better result (for our ministry) than your perfection. Therefore I write these things in absentia lest being with you in person I might be too sharp with you (it is the power which the Lord gave me, and it is to educate people, not destroy them).

(11-14) Finally, farewell. Be perfect, be of good cheer, be in unity together, and live in peace, and the God of Love and Peace shall go with you. Greet one another with a holy kiss. All the minsters salute you. The Grace of our Lord Christ, and the love of God the Father, God the son and God the Holy Spirit be with you all. Amen.

Taken in Corinth from Philippi by Timothy in the year of our Lord *57* A.D.

INTRODUCTION TO THE LETTER OF PAUL TO THE PHILIPPIANS

After the brief visit to Rome described earlier, when Paul spent his whole time in the Palace and was therefore unable to visit personally with the brethren there, he journeyed through Philippi back to Asia. Here, a further period of four years in total is spent before he is finally once again in Rome.

Paul journeyed first to Alexandria Troas and stayed there for some time as a base from where to discover the "climate" of the northern Asian scene. It was not, however, possible to gain much real truth about events in Jerusalem from that part and therefore Paul determined that he would eventually make the trip himself in order to see once again the many people in areas en route, and to see Jerusalem for, possibly, the last time.

By ship Paul continued down the coast of that country which is now Turkey, visiting Assos, Nitylene and the island of Chios. After Chios he went to Samos where he remained for some time. Resuming his journey, Paul intended to skirt the city of Ephesus because he was aware that there was still much animosity toward himself from certain factions.* A visit there would, it was ascertained, be still rather precarious and since he now had reason to hasten to Jerusalem, he did not wish to jeopardize the trip. A message was therefore sent across the narrow strip of water for the people of the Faith (or at least the elders) to rendezvous with Paul. On meeting, Paul conveyed to the Elders that he was intent on going to Jerusalem, and not knowing what he would have to face there, he wished to assure these friends of his continued trust in them. He wished also to assure them of his own steadfastness no matter what might happen. In view of what he had suffered in Ephesus in the last visit, Paul stressed that they must remain faithful no matter what vicissitudes might come, even as he, Paul was intent to do. He then bade them a fond personal farewell, for his inner Being knew that this would be the last time he would see any of them in life. Before leaving, he spent much time in prayer with them, asking that they be strong. They then took a tearful leave of each other before Paul departed finally.

Paul and his travelling companions then went via Cos to Rhodes. After a stay in Rhodes the route was via Patara on the mainland of Pamphylia. Here they connected with a ship making for Tyre in Phoenicia. Paul bade farewell to his travelling in Tyre with the faithful there. Many there were who begged him not to travel to Jerusalem, for they feared for his life.

Nothing, however, would dissuade him. He continued via Ptolemais to Caesarea and there stayed awhile with Philip the Evangelist. Again, many tried to convince Paul not to continue to Jerusalem but his answer was the same – he was determined to see the faithful there, personally, no matter what.

---

*On the last visit to Ephesus, Paul was in serious trouble because of some of the artisans in that city. There is little need to elaborate here; the story is told with fair accuracy in Acts 19.

The result of Paul's arrival in Jerusalem is also well recorded in Acts. He first visited James and other Elders of the brethren there. He spoke much of his ministry since he last saw them in person, and they were filled with happiness to hear all that he had to tell.

Since the time of year was that now called Pentecost, Paul had his own special reason for happiness. He spent time in personal purification and then went with some of the brothers to the temple. Here he was discovered and taken prisoner. After a brief so-called trial before the elders present, they took him forth to be stoned to death as was the customary execution. However, the Roman captain heard the noise and came to see what was going on. They took Paul in chains to the fortress and there began to interrogate him. Paul informed the captain that he was a citizen of Tarsus, "No Mean City", a Jew born, but also a Roman citizen. They demanded to know what it was that the people had against Paul, and so he gave them a full account of his upbringing, and his work prior to his conversion. He then went on to let them know of his activity since conversion as an Apostle of Christ. Upon this statement the Romans were prepared to lash Paul until he renounced. However, he was able to demand his right as a Roman citizen. The captain recognized that he himself had earned his freedom, whereas Paul was born a freeman. This is no mean status at that time in history and cause enough for action to be stayed.

It was eventually decided to get Paul out of Jerusalem and bring him to Felix the Governor of the Province at Caesara. The Governor heard Paul and he listened to those of his accusers who spoke. Paul demanded to be tried before Caesar if necessary, as a Roman citizen. The Jewish Elders demanded that he be tried before their own highest authority – King Agrippa. Much of these accounts are recorded in Acts.

Paul eventually set sail under guard for Rome and in route the ship was wrecked off the Island of Malta. The people of Malta were very kind to all those who were in the ship and washed ashore. During the three month period spent there, much was recorded of the Apostle. He, in turn, learned a great deal about the ancient Isle that added to his knowledge. When the weather was felt sufficiently settled the travellers resumed their journey by first stopping at Syracuse in Sicily; and then, crossing to the mainland, the long journey to Rome was eventually completed.

At this point in time, because of the earlier short visit there, Paul was not kept a strict prisoner in chains as would have normally been the case. He was, rather, under what one might again call "house arrest". All his movements had to be accounted for during a specific period. Nero had no alternative than to hear the case against Paul, but as a friend of Luke and already somewhat familiar, the Emperor did not pay particular attention. He had "better things" on his mind at that time to trouble over. Eventually Paul was allowed to go loosely free, but under observation. He found a house to rent and lived there for a period.

During his house arrest Paul wrote to the Philippians to let them know how things were with him. The year was 62. He also sent a brief note to the Ephesians to let them know what transpired in Jerusalem and in the journey to Rome. The letter attributed to Paul addressed to the Colossians was not actually one written personally; though for a very strong reason, I now propose to deal with this particular letter.

LETTER TO THE PHILIPPIANS

1 *Paul and Timotheus, the servants of Jesus Christ, to all the saints in Christ Jesus which are at Philippi, with the bishops and deacons:*

2 Grace be unto you, and peace, from God our Father, and from the Lord Jesus Christ:

3 I thank my God upon every remembrance of you,

4 Always in every prayer of mine for you all making request with joy,

5 For your fellowship in the gospel from the first day until now;

6 Being confident of this very thing, that he which hath begun a good work in you will perform it until the day of Jesus Christ:

7 Even as it is meet for me to think this of you all, because I have you in my heart; inasmuch as both in my bonds, and in the defence and confirmation of the gospel, ye all are partakers of my grace.

8 For God is my record, how greatly I long after you all in the bowels of Jesus Christ.

9 And this I pray, that your love may abound yet more and more in knowledge and in all judgement;

10 That ye may approve things that are excellent; that ye may be sincere and without offence till the day of Christ;

11 Being filled with the fruits of righteousness, which are by Jesus Christ, unto the glory and praise of God.

12 But I would ye should understand, brethren, that the things which happened unto me have fallen out rather unto the furtherance of the gospel;

13 So that my bonds in Christ are manifest in all the palace, and in all other places;

1 (1-11) From Paul and Timothy, the servants of Jesus Christ, to all the faithful at Philippi, and the elder brothers and sisters of the faith also;[1] grace and peace to you through Christ. I thank God each time I remember you all. I give thanks for you and pray joyfully for you because of your faithfulness to the gospel since the beginning. The confidence which this creates in those who bring the message to you, will allow its continuance as long as we live. Even as it is a good thing to think of you, having you all at heart, I can be of good cheer even though a prisoner; it attests to the strength of that message we bear, that you are all participants in the same grace. God knows how much I have yearned for you all as with the very nature of Jesus Christ. I pray most earnestly that your love may abound through the power of God that your knowledge and judgement may help you to affirm those things which are right; that you may be sincere and not give offence until the Day of Christ. Be filled with goodness through His power, to God's glory and praise.

(12-18) I want you to understand, brothers, that what has happened to me is to the advantage of the gospel; my imprisonment makes me a prisoner of Christ, whether at the palace or anywhere else. Many of the faith have been more confident, as a result, to speak out without fear.

Philippians 1

14 And many of the brethren in the Lord, waxing confident by my bonds, are much more bold to speak the word without fear.

15 Some indeed preach Christ even of envy and strife; and some also of good will:

16 The one preach Christ of contention, not sincerely, supposing to add affliction to my bonds:

17 But the other of love, knowing that I am set for the defence of the gospel.

18 What then? Notwithstanding every way, whether in pretence, or in truth, Christ is preached; and I therein do rejoice, yea, and will rejoice.

19 For I know that this shall turn to my salvation through your prayer, and the supply of the Spirit of Jesus Christ,

20 According to my earnest expectation and my hope, that in nothing I shall be ashamed, but that with all boldness, as always, so now also Christ shall be magnified in my body, whether it be by life, or by death.

21 For me to live is Christ, and to die is gain.

22 But if I live in the flesh, this is the fruit of my labour; yet what I shall choose I know not.

23 For I am in a straight betwixt two, having a desire to depart, and to be with Christ; which is far better;

24 Nevertheless to abide in the flesh is more needful for you.

25 And having this confidence, I know that I shall abide and continue with you all for your furtherance and joy of faith;

26 That your rejoicing may be more abundant in Jesus Christ for me by my coming to you again.

Some speak out of personal envy I dare say, but most speak from goodwill. The former are motivated by contention and are not sincere. They seek merely to add to my afflictions; but the latter are motivated by love, knowing how rigorously I defend the true faith. It really makes little difference, for whichever way it comes, the message of Christ is being spoken and that gives me cause for gladness.

(19-26) I know that this will be my saving: the strength of your prayers together with the power of the Spirit of Christ. I shall at all times stand firm, knowing that I have nothing to fear or be ashamed of, and Christ shall be magnified through my being, whether I shall live or die. For me, I only have life if it is in Christ, and to die is to gain more life. I do not care either way. If I continue to live in the flesh, it shall only be as the just fruits of my work. Sometimes I have a hard time to choose between the two, for if I leave this world, I shall be nearer to Christ, which is better. However, if I stay in the body, I can continue to be of service to you all. With this fact to strengthen my resolve, I can continue in the body to help you gain deeper faith and joy. Bearing this in mind, you can look forward to my coming to be with you again.

Philippians 1

27 Only let your conversation be as it becometh the gospel of Christ: that whether I come and see you, or else be absent, I may hear of your affairs, that ye stand fast in one spirit, with one mind striving together for the faith of the gospel;

28 And in nothing terrified by your adversaries: which is to them an evident token of perdition, but to you of salvation, and that of God.

29 For unto you it is given in the behalf of Christ, not only to believe on him, but also to suffer for his sake;

30 Having the same conflict which ye saw in me, and now hear to be in me.

(27-30) Let your thoughts and words be as fitting to the believer in Christ, so that whether I visit you again in the body or not, I shall still hear of you that you are steadfast in one spirit and mind, striving together always to uphold the true faith. Do not be ashamed by adversity. Adversity to those who seek it is their own failing. To you, it can be salvation through the power of God. For Christ gave you the strength not only to believe in the truth, but to be strengthened through suffering. Stand firm and continue to fight, even as you saw me doing (and am still doing).

DISCOURSE CHAPTER ONE

1. Q: In the beginning of the letter to the Philippians, for the first time, you make specific reference to bishops and deacons. Many people will want to know why this had just developed and what does it mean; what were the roles of the bishops and deacons of that time?

    A: One has to first of all look at the passage of time. The later letters, as recorded, marked a passage of several years and also witnessed the increase of membership within the new movement. As with all membership, if one leaves the masses of people to their own devices, there is a certain amount of disintegration of energy rather than an accumulation thereof. In order to maintain an impetus and to bring about an increase in energy, there has to be in all things a discipline. In order to maintain discipline, as in all sections of group work, one has to have a form of government. Therefore, it was found to be necessary in those times to create an appointed body of those who were felt to be trustworthy because of the personal progress that had been made within their own lives.

    They were not called bishops or deacons in those days; these are words which have been introduced in later translations of the Bible. They were elders – elder brothers and elder sisters holding specific roles in order to carry out certain tasks. Those tasks were primarily to hold together the faithful and to see to it very carefully that the message of the faith was maintained in its purity. The secondary

Discourse Chapter One continued:

part of their work was to attend to the more practical issues and the designation of the work of the people in spreading not just the message, but the underlying meaning in healing, in helping the sick, assisting the poor, and all of the works that any true faith upholds. In other words, the elders were carrying out the basic roles of what would be called a pastor and his lay assistants, but the names given, I repeat, are modern additions.

Q: Would you be open to the idea – since the terms bishop and deacon were probably picked up from the King James – of substituting elder brothers and elder sisters for bishops and deacons?

A: Certainly. One has to accept that by the time of the translation in the James point in history, the Catholic brotherhood, out of its own necessity, had already begun to appoint abbots and bishops and these titles were placed onto the earlier historic account simply because they have no other name to substitute. One was attempting to give a similar picture to that which pertained in one's own mind at the time of translation.

PHILIPPIANS 2

2 If there be therefore any consolation in Christ, if any comfort of love, if any fellowship of the Spirit, if any bowels and mercies,

2 Fulfil ye my joy that ye be like minded, having the same love, being of one accord, of one mind.

3 Let nothing be done through strife or vainglory; but in lowliness of mind let each esteem others better than themselves.

4 Look not every man on his own things, but every man also on the things of others.

5 Let this mind be in you, which was also in Christ Jesus;

6 Who, being in the form of God, thought it not robbery to be equal with God:

7 But made himself of no reputation, and took upon him the form of a servant, and was made in the likeness of men:

8 And being found in fashion as a man, he humbled himself and became obedient unto death, even the death of the cross.

9 Wherefore God also hath highly exalted him, and given him a name which is above every name:

10 That at the name of Jesus every knee should bow, of things in heaven, and things in earth, and things under the earth;

11 And that every tongue should confess that Jesus Christ is Lord, to the glory of God the Father.

12 Wherefore, my beloved, as ye have always obeyed, not as in my presence only, but now much more in my absence, work out your own salvation with fear and trembling.

13 For it is God which worketh in you both to will and to do at His good pleasure.

14 Do all things without murmurings and disputings:

15 That ye may be blameless and harmless, the sons of God, without rebuke, in the midst of a crooked and perverse nation, among whom ye shine as lights in the world;

2 (1-11) If there is any consolation in Christ, if any comfort of love or fellowship through the Spirit, any mercy and strength of purpose, then allow my hopes of you to be fulfilled by being as one in mind and accord. Let all things be done for love and not in contention. Be humble and think of others before self. Be of the same mind as that of Christ in Jesus, who being filled with Godliness, thought nothing of stating His equality with God. Yet He did not set Himself up, rather did He behave as a servant in humility and He was born and lived after the manner of humanity. He was humble even to death on the cross – and being so has been exalted to the highest in God; higher indeed than all others, that before Jesus all shall bow, whether of heaven or on earth, or within the earth. Because of what He attained, all should acknowledge Jesus the Christ as Lord, to the glory of God the Father.[1]

(12-18) For this reason, beloveds, work diligently; each at your own salvation, whether I should be there among you or not. For it is really that same God that works in you to raise yourselves in consciousness and to do those things which are of goodness. Do them without dispute and contention so that you can progress and not build up negative karma. In the midst of a perverse and wayward generation, stand forth as shining lights in the world.

Philippians 2

16 Holding forth the word of life; that I may rejoice in the day of Christ, that I have not run in vain, neither laboured in vain.

17 Yea, and if I be offered upon the sacrifice and service of your faith, I joy, and rejoice with you all.

18 For the same cause also do ye joy, and rejoice with me.

19 But I trust in the Lord Jesus to send Timotheus shortly unto you, that I also may be of good comfort, when I know your state.

20 For I have no man like minded, who will naturally care for your state.

21 For all seek their own, not the things which are Jesus Christ's.

22 But ye know the proof of him, that, as a son with the father, he hath served with me in the gospel.

23 Him therefore I hope to send presently, so soon as I shall see how it will go with me.

24 But I trust in the Lord that I also myself shall come shortly.

25 Yet I supposed it necessary to send to you Epaphroditus, my brother, and companion in labour, and fellow soldier, but your messenger, and he that ministered to my wants.

26 For he longed after you all, and was full of heaviness, because that ye had heard that he had been sick.

27 For indeed he was sick nigh unto death: but God had mercy on him; and not on him only, but on me also, lest I should have sorrow upon sorrow.

28 I sent him therefore the more carefully, that, when ye see him again, ye may rejoice, and that I may be the less sorrowful.

29 Receive him therefore in the Lord with all gladness; and hold such in reputation:

30 Because for the work of Christ he was nigh unto death, not regarding his life, to supply your lack of service toward me.

Hold fast and speak of the Word of Life and in this will be my joy, for then I shall know that I did not labour in vain. Yes, even if I too will be put to death, I will die joyfully; and for that matter, you will be able to rejoice with me.

(19-24) God willing, I am hoping that I shall be able to send Timothy soon after this letter, and it will comfort me a lot to know how you are. I have no one as trustworthy as he is to look at your needs. So many there are who are intent on looking after themselves, rather than doing Christ's work. But you know the truth concerning Timothy, how well he has served and stood by me. I therefore hope to send him soon – soon as it is known how things shall go with me. I can but trust that I will also be soon free to travel to you.

(25-30) For the moment I found it expedient to send Epaphroditus who has also been a good companion and help. He longed to be with you all, and was sorry that you were distressed because he was sick. Indeed, he was ill and almost died. God was merciful and he recovered, which was a mercy to me too, as I could not have borne anything else I think. I sent him with an admonition to be very careful of himself so that you will find him well and be glad. Welcome him therefore with much gladness and recall that he nearly died, having no thought for his own life, in order to do things for me which you could not, being too far away.

DISCOURSE CHAPTER TWO

1.   Q: In chapter two I have a comment coming from the man who does the exegesis in the *Interpreter's Bible* (Scott)* who refers to 2:5-11 as one of the great soaring passages of Paul. He indicates that some even see it as a poem or song inserted by Paul to remind the Philippian faithful of how lofty indeed is the mind of Christ compared to the petty conflicts of humans. Would you like to say more about that passage and was it a song or poetic verse or was Paul soaring into the heights himself?

A: One of the attributes of the Scorpio nature is the desire within the heart to soar to the heights. We are indeed getting to the point in that statement. I have talked earlier of the peaks and the valleys in the life of Paul, even the same as is with most of all of our lives upon this earth; and yes, that was one of my personal peaks giving expression. One might consider it eulogy, poetry, whatever. Part of the upliftment in soaring to those heights is the ability to wax poetic. Even my dour nature had its moments, you know.

---

* Scott, Ernest F., *Interpreter's Bible,* Volume XI, p.46, Abingdon Press, Nashville, 1953.

PHILIPPIANS 3

3 Finally, my brethren, rejoice in the Lord. to write the same things to you, to me indeed is not grievous, but for you it is safe.

2 Beware of dogs, beware of evil workers, beware of the concision.

3 For we are the circumcision, which worship God in the spirit, and rejoice in Christ Jesus, and have no confidence in the flesh.

4 Though I might also have confidence in the flesh. If any other man thinketh that he hath whereof he might trust in the flesh, I more:

5 Circumcised the eighth day, of the stock of Israel, of the tribe of Benjamin, an Hebrew of the Hebrews; as touching as the law, a Pharisee;

6 Concerning zeal, persecuting the church; touching the righteousness which is in the law, blameless.

7 But what things were gain to me, those I counted loss for Christ.

8 Yea doubtless, and I count all things but loss for the excellency of the knowledge of Christ Jesus my Lord: for whom I have suffered the loss of all things, and do count them but dung, that I may win Christ.

9 And be found in Him, not having mine own righteousness, which is of the law, but that which is through the faith of Christ, the righteousness which is of God by faith:

10 That I may know Him, and the power of His resurrection, and the fellowship of His sufferings, being made conformable unto His death;

11 If by any means I might attain unto the resurrection of the dead.

12 Not as though I had already attained, either were already perfect: but I follow after, if that I may apprehend that for which also I am apprehended of Christ Jesus.

3 (1-3) Finally brethren, rejoice in the Lord. It does not trouble me to keep repeating this for it is sound counsel. Beware of other counsel that is not of God, coming from the mouth of dogs and those who work evil.[1] Circumcision, I tell you, is not the mark of truth, for we are equal in spirit and rejoice in Christ when we do God's will.

(4-12) I myself came of the Israeli stock and was duly circumcised on the eighth day as is customary. I was of the Tribe of Benjamin, as Hebrew as anyone can be, and a Pharisee at that! You know how I zealously persecuted the new faith, insisting that the law was blameless, but what did I know in my ignorance. What was then my gain was loss for Christ. I now count all that folly and am content in the excellency of my true knowledge, revealed through Christ. For Him I have since suffered the loss of all things and gladly regard them as refuse for what I may win in the name of Christ. In His sight I have nothing, despite all that I knew of the law. Yet I have everything in the true knowledge and faith which is of God. In the full assurance of the truth through His resurrection, God has given me the genuine value which comes from faith. Now I long to die as He died so that I might rise as He did.[2]

Philippians 3

13 Brethren, I count not myself to have apprehended: but this one thing I do, forgetting those things which are behind, and reaching forth unto those things which are before,

14 I press toward the mark for the prize of the high calling of God in Christ Jesus.

15 Let us therefore, as many as be perfect, be thus minded: and if in any thing ye be otherwise minded, God shall reveal even this unto you.

16 Nevertheless, whereto we have already attained, let us walk by the same rule, let us mind the same thing.

17 Brethren, be followers together of me, and mark them which walk so as ye have us for an example.

18 (For many walk, of whom I have told you often, and now tell you even weeping that they are the enemies of the cross of Christ:

19 Whose end is destruction, whose God is their belly, and whose glory is in their shame, who mind earthly things.)

20 For our conversation is in heaven; from whence also we look for the Saviour, the Lord Jesus Christ.

21 Who shall change our vile body, that it may be fashioned like unto His glorious body, according to the working whereby He is able even to subdue all things unto Himself

(13-16) Yet brothers, I do not profess to have arrived, but this one thing I do know, I have put aside the past and look only to the future and press ever onward toward the goal of attainment through Christ. All who wish to attain must do the same and if you are not of like mind, you will know it through God. Let us abide by those truths which we have already attained, and try to be an example to others, even as I too try to do.

(17-21) Let me tell you as I have said before, that there are many who are the enemies of Christ and the demonstration of the Cross. They are seekers after self glorification and are aware only of things of this earth. Christ came to demonstrate that earthly things are temporal and they pass. He taught us to transcend earthly things in order to attain the life of spirit. Even as He conquered all things, so too may we.

DISCOURSE CHAPTER THREE

1. Q: Speaking of your dour nature, in 3:2 there is a rather uncharacteristic outburst for Paul where you say, "Beware of other counsel that is not of God; coming from the mouth of dogs and those who work evil." Was there something specific you had in mind to come out so strongly?

   A: Philippi was ever, to the one Paul, a testing ground; a place dear to my heart because it was, in fact, one of the centers where the first known Christian movement became apparent. As is the case wherever the center is focussed for the light, one must be aware that with equal strength there will be a balancing focus for that which could be called the negative polarity. Phihppi was an area where I and my brothers first found a great deal of violence. Much of the violence was directed against myself and indeed, included imprisonment; yet, it was also the place where, because of that very violence, the greatest test of the power of love and the strength of Christ was to be demonstrated. Therefore, yes, at the same time as I could eulogize and wax poetic and soar to those heights of bliss, my Scorpio nature also could sink to the depths of frustration and annoyance. It was not entirely uncharacteristic of the personality of Paul to speak those kinds of words. It is perhaps simply one of the rare accounts.

2. Q: In 3:12 there is the statement "In the full assurance of the truth through His resurrection, God has given me the genuine value which comes from faith. How I long to die as He died so that I might rise as He did." This sentence is a bit confusing, since Paul already has believed in reincarnation; this sounds like a different element than the belief in reincarnation.

   A: This is not addressing my uncertainty as to the possibility of reincarnation. It is a simple statement, "Oh that I too might become so Christed within myself that I might die to self in order to obtain total mastery and become also as a Christ". I felt to be some distance from that goal at that time.

PHILIPPIANS 4

4 Therefore, my brethren, dearly beloved and longed for, my joy and crown, so stand fast in the Lord my dearly beloved.

2 I beseech Euodias, and beseech Syntyche, that they be of the same mind in the Lord.

3 And I entreat thee also, true yokefellow, help those women which laboured with me in the gospel with Clement also, and with other of my fellow labourers, whose names are in the book of life.

4 Rejoice in the Lord always; and again I say Rejoice.

5 Let your moderation be known unto all men. The Lord is at hand.

6 Be careful for nothing; but in every thing by prayer and supplication with thanksgiving let your requests be made known unto God.

7 And the peace of god, which passeth all understanding, shall keep your hearts and minds through Christ Jesus.

8 Finally, brethren, whatsoever things are true, whatsoever things are honest, whatsoever things are just, whatsoever things are pure, whatsoever things are lovely, whatsoever things are of good report; if there be any virtue, and if there be any praise, think on these things.

9 Those things, which ye have both learned and received, and heard, and seen in me, do: and the God of peace shall be with you.

10 But I rejoiced in the Lord greatly, that now at the last your care of me hath flourished again; wherein ye were also careful but ye lacked opportunity.

11 Not that I speak in respect of want: for I have learned, in whatsoever state I am, therewith to be content.

4 (1-7) Therefore, beloveds, whom I long for, who are my joy and crown, stand fast in our dear Lord. I beg you, Euodia and Syntyche to stand firmly as of one mind and I also earnestly ask all of you who laboured with me to be of help to these women who worked so hard with me to spread the faith; with Clement also, and other fellow workers whose names are recorded in the Book of Life. Rejoice in the Lord always, and again I say, Rejoice. Let your gentleness be a byword. The Lord is near. Do not spend time on anything except thanksgiving, and pray to God that He will attend you in peace which passes all human understanding. He will keep your minds through the knowledge of Christ.

(8-9) Finally, those things that are true, honest, just, pure, lovely and of good conversation, think only of such things. Those things which you have witnessed in me, try also to do. The God of peace shall go with you.

(10-23) I am happy that you have sent word to me again and that you are concerned for my welfare. I do not mean that you neglected me earlier, it was just that you had no opportunity to contact me. I do not speak of need, for I have no needs.[1]

Philippians 4

12 I know both how to be abased, and I know how to abound: every where and in all things I am instructed both to be full and to be hungry both to abound and to suffer need.

13 I can do all things through Christ which strengtheneth me.

14 Notwithstanding ye have done well, that ye did communicate with my affliction.

15 Now ye Philippians know also, that in the beginning of the gospel, when I departed from Macedonia, no church communicated with me as concerning giving and receiving but ye only.

16 For even in Thessalonica ye sent once and again unto my necessity.

17 Not because I desire a gift: but I desire fruit that may abound to your account.

18 But I have all, and abound: I am full, having received of Epaphroditus the things which were sent from you, an odour of a sweet smell, a sacrifice acceptable, well pleasing to God.

19 But my God shall supply all your need according to His riches in glory by Christ Jesus.

20 Now unto God and our Father be glory for ever and ever. Amen.

21 Salute every saint in Christ Jesus. The brethren which are with me greet you.

22 All the saints salute you, chiefly they that are of Caesar's household.

23 The grace of our Lord Jesus Christ be with you all. Amen.

I know how to accept whatever condition I find myself in, for I can do all things through Christ, who is my strength. I am not diminishing your concern for me however. People of Philippi, you should also know that in the beginning of my ministry when I departed from Macedonia, no one kept in touch with me for a time, except you. Even in Thessalonica you sent me help when I was needing it. Not that I wanted to count on your help, but it is the fact that you gave help that enriches you. At this time I have everything I might need, thanks to Epaphroditus for bringing your gifts. They came as sweet perfume, an acceptable offering well pleasing to God. That same God shall supply all your needs also according to His riches in Christ. Now unto Father, Mother God, be all glory, Amen. Give greetings to all the faithful. Those who are here with me send their greetings also. (In the main, these are the people in Caesar's household.) The Grace of our Lord be with you all, Amen.

(This letter was dispatched via Epaphroditus from Rome where I was under "House Arrest" in the Palace of Nero. It was sent along with letters also to be transmitted to the faithful in Colossae in central Phrygia in the year of Our Lord 62 A.D.)

DISCOURSE CHAPTER FOUR

1. Q: In 4:11, regarding the time you were in prison in Rome, you say that Paul states he has no needs and because of this some think that Paul may have come into some kind of family inheritance. How were you able to be sustained during those years of detainment?

    A: The term "spent in prison" is misleading. One might be considered to be detained and guarded and yet allowed to live in a certain amount of physical comfort in which all of one's bodily needs were fully met by those who were willing so to do. Or, one was cast into the dungeons which was a sorry state indeed. It was my own physical good fortune to be in the former state. One here must remember that Paul had, especially in the family of Luke, friends in high places. My imprisonment was not the sorry condition that might have been the case for many others.

INTRODUCTION TO THE LETTER OF PAUL TO THE COLOSSIANS

There were a number of letters written to the peoples, indeed the whole area of the near East, by my brothers who were with me at that time. It was not possible for many reasons for me to write all of them myself. However, where it was permissible because of my circumstances, for me to approve the letters and therefore give them my seal of approval, I did so. This particular letter, if one looks at it rather carefully, is not my own personal style; however, that is not the point I am making. The point that I am here making is that there have been erroneous accounts of this letter which have been extremely damaging.

Scholars and Christian theologians down through the centuries have tended to consider that it was Paul's intention in the context of this letter to clearly condemn certain practices which were prevalent, particularly in that part of Asia. The reason why they were prevalent in that particular geographical area was because many Essene communities were there. The attitude of the Christian theologian was that I was condemning the Essene communities because of their angel worship and ritual observances of the festivals of the year and the practice of meditation at the point of the full moon, and that Paul was speaking out very strongly against these so-called pagan practices. My point at this particular time is that I was doing no such thing. Jesus and His family were Essenes.

This is a very important issue within the modern Christian community which still believes that meditation at the time of the full moon, belief in communion with angels and all of these things are pagan, and therefore not a part of Christian theology Some even at this point go so far as to say it is of the devil. One might go into a major theological discourse to explain many of the deeper esoteric truths but I feel quite deeply that the point is well made that this is not devil worship; it is a truthful part of life of all who believe in God and therefore should not be in any way negated or condemned by those who call themselves Christians. It were wiser if the Christian church of this day might seek a deeper truth and cease to condemn those who have beliefs that would appear to be different.

LETTER OF PAUL TO THE COLOSSIANS

1 *Paul, an apostle of Jesus Christ by the will of God, and Timotheus our brother,*

2 To the saints and faithful brethren in Christ which are at Colossae; Grace be unto you, and peace, from God our Father and the Lord Jesus Christ.

3 We give thanks to God and the Father of our Lord Jesus Christ, praying always for you,

4 Since we heard of your faith in Christ Jesus, and of the love which ye have to all the saints,

5 For the hope which is laid up for you in heaven, whereof ye heard before in the word of the truth of the gospel;

6 Which is come unto you, as it is in all the world; and bringeth forth fruit, as it doth also in you, since the day ye heard of it, and knew the grace of God in truth:

7 As ye also learned of Epaphras our dear fellow servant, who is for you a faithful minister of Christ;

8 Who also declared unto us your love in the Spirit.

9 For this cause we also, since the day we heard it, do not cease to pray for you, and to desire that ye might be filled with the knowledge of His will in all wisdom and spiritual understanding;

10 That ye might walk worthy of the Lord unto all pleasing, being fruitful in every good work, and increasing in the knowledge of God;

11 Strengthened with all might, according to His glorious power, unto all patience and long-suffering with joyfulness;

12 Giving thanks unto the Father, which hath made us meet to be partakers of the inheritance of the saints in light:

13 Who hath delivered us from the power of darkness, and hath translated us into the kingdom of His dear Son:

1 (1-3) From Paul, an apostle of Christ by the will of God and witnessed by Timothy. (This letter is actually written by Tychicus, and Onesimus also had a little to say.) We send greetings to the faithful in Colossae and neighbouring cities. May the Grace of God and the Lord Christ be with you. We give thanks to that same God and remember you always in our prayers.

(4-8) We have heard via Epaphras from whom you have received the Ministry, that you have been most faithful, and we are most thankful to hear this from him (he himself has been imprisoned for his faith, on arrival in Rome). We can tell you that we know your faith will bear fruit. We shall continue to pray that your strength will stay strong in Christ.

(9-14) Give thanks to that same God that His Grace allowed you to be participants in the true faith. He has delivered us all from the power of darkness, and we now have the chance to attain the True Light, through the message of Christ, in whom we have total redemption.

Colossians 1

14 In whom we have redemption through His blood, even the forgiveness of sins:

15 Who is the image of the invisible God, the firstborn of every creature:

16 For by Him were all things created, that are in heaven, and that are in earth, visible and invisible, whether they be thrones, or dominions, or principalities, or powers: all things were created by Him, and for Him:

17 And He is before all things, and by Him all things consist.

18 And He is the head of the body, the church: who is the beginning the firstborn from the dead; that in all things He might have the pre-eminence.

19 For it pleased the Father that in Him should all fullness dwell;

20 And, having made peace through the blood of His cross, by Him to reconcile all things unto Himself, by Him, I say, whether they be things in earth, or things in heaven.

21 And you, that were sometimes alienated and enemies in your mind by wicked works, yet now hath He reconciled,

22 In the body of His flesh through death, to present you holy and unblameable and unreproveable in his sight:

23 If ye continue in the faith grounded and settled, and be not moved away from the hope of the gospel, which ye have heard, and which was preached to every creature which is under heaven; whereof I Paul am made a minister;

24 Who now rejoice in my sufferings for you, and fill up that which is behind of the afflictions of Christ in my flesh for His body's sake, which is the church:

25 Whereof I am made a minister, according to the dispensation of God which is given to me for you, to fulfill the word of God;

26 Even the mystery which hath been hid from ages and from generations, but now is made manifest to His saints:

(15-17) He who is made in the image of that invisible Creator, the creator of all things, by whom all things were made that are seen and unseen, in the earth or in other realms. All things were created in the same way, whether they be called principalities, powers, thrones; and He came before all of His creation. He is head of that very Body of His creation, and with God is the Christ as the Firstborn.[1]

(18-23) Christ is the Head of that body, the firstborn from the Void that in all things He might have pre-eminence.[2] For it pleased The Godhead that in Him should be seen the true nature of all things. And now Christ has shown that truth through His earthly Ministry and the cross that the wisdom of Earth and beyond Earth be shown through His example. You who were enemies, or alienated from each other, you who have entertained wicked thoughts, all are shown this same example. You may all attain the same wisdom by remaining grounded and centered in that faith of which I too, Paul, as His minister, am part. Do not let anything daunt you or keep you away from that hope which lies in the message we have brought to you.

(24-29) We rejoice in the suffering that we have had to experience in order that the message of Christ may be more widely heard. (For did not He suffer those same afflictions?) In the same strength He demonstrated, we are ministers of His word, and with the Grace of God. The great mysteries have been hidden from the world down through the ages but are now being made manifest through those who have the faith. God shall reveal to such the true

Colossians 1

27 To whom. God would make known what is the riches of the glory of this mystery among the Gentiles; which is Christ in you, the hope of glory:

28 Whom we preach, warning every man, and teaching every man in all wisdom; that we may present every man perfect in Christ Jesus:

29 Whereunto I also labour, striving according to His working, which worketh in me mightily.

nature of those mysteries, and they shall know the richness of God's True Glory. Christ in you is the hope of glory. This we speak of, setting before everyone the truth of the wisdoms, that all may have the chance to perfection, through that wisdom of Christ. Thereto do we, His ministers, labour, striving in accordance with His teachings and that power that works in us mightily.

DISCOURSE CHAPTER ONE

1. Q: In 1:15-18, going back to the *Interpreter's Bible,* the exegesis writer (Francis Beare)* says "In the earlier Pauline epistles, only one passage (in First Corinthians) can be cited which even faintly suggests that the apostle even indulged in speculation about the cosmic significance of Christ. Two parallels to this Colossian passage are to be found only in Hebrews and the Fourth Gospel, i.e. in works of the second Christian generation." Would you care to comment about that?

   A: What in fact is the question underlying all of this is did Paul believe in the Cosmic Christ or did Paul subscribe to the belief of the man Jesus as the Christ. The truth of that is that Paul, from the point of time of his conversion was totally aware of the office of Cosmic Christ and was totally aware that the man Jesus was not the only son of God in the sense that the Christian church gives it, but that the one who was/is Jesus became totally overlighted by the Cosmic Christ and therefore became Christ incarnate. Paul, from the moment of his ministry, knew it and taught it. This is the most important part of the whole message, why would he not deliver it? Perhaps if it is not apparent in earlier texts, it is because words written are almost invariably translated by the mind of the reader into the meaning that each one desires to see. I think that certainly in this current work we have made it very clear from the beginning, is that not so?

2. Q: Yes, that is true. In 1:18 the statement reads "Christ is the head of that body." In the old KJ they put in the phrase that "Christ was the head of the body, the church." You have dropped the term "the church". Do we need a description of what is meant by body or is that going to be confusing?

---

* Beare, Francis W., *The Interpreter's Bible,* Vol. XI, p. 162 Abingdon Press, Nashville 1953.

Discourse Chapter One continued:

A: Would you please expand the context a little.

Q: "Christ is the head of that body, the firstborn from the void that in all things he might have pre-eminence." What is meant by body?

A: It has nothing to do with the church. The church put that in. This is a very profound esoteric subject for indeed as we have the Trinity, from that supreme body of which he does indeed stand the firstborn and therefore the head, comes all other created forms – the body of the whole creation, not the body of the Christian church. The body of creation does not exclude those who do not in this life believe in the Christian church; the Christian church does and therefore creates a very different situation.

Q: That certainly gives a lot of people something to chew on. I like that.

A: Before we pass on, I am going to put in another Paulian "By the way". If one studies very carefully all of the great overlighting spirits who have come to this earthly plane, one will see very clearly in their own words and the message of their lives that they did not require a church to be built around their message. The Christ, through Jesus, was no different than the Buddha or any of the others in that He said repeatedly and most clearly, "The kingdom of heaven is within you, the individual. The holy temple is the body wherein the Spirit dwells." The temple body is the body of man, not a stone building. We cannot repeat this too often. This is the church, not some edifice where people go to worship something outside of themselves; and there is no form of dogma or religion that will bring the Christ into that temple, only each one working in themselves.

When one is fully able to accept that there is one body, one mind, one Spirit, and that all of humanity – whether they call themselves Christians, Buddhists, or anything else, is a part of that Oneness, then shall it be accepted that Christ reigns. Then shall it be accepted that the kingdom of God is here on Earth. All of the religions, including the Christian, have done great service; we do not discount that service, but we can no longer allow the misconception that there is only one path to God and that it is either through the Christian church or any other institution created in the name of a god. There is only one path to God and it lies inside each and every single member of that body which came from God.

Q: Down south they have a term that "You've gone to preachin", and it is great.

A: My little postscript turned out to be quite a sermon, didn't it?

COLOSSIANS 2

2 For I would that ye knew what great conflict I have for you, and for them at Laodicea, and for as many as have not seen my face in the flesh;

2 That their hearts might be comforted, being knit together in love, and unto all riches of the full assurance of understanding, to the acknowledgement of the mystery of God, and of the Father, and of Christ;

3 In whom are hid all the treasures of wisdom and knowledge.

4 And this I say, lest any man should beguile you with enticing words.

5 For though I be absent in the flesh, yet am I with you in the spirit, joying and beholding your order, and the steadfastness of your faith in Christ.

6 As ye have therefore received Christ Jesus the Lord, so walk he in him:

7 Rooted and built up in Him, and stablished in the faith, as ye have been taught, abounding therein with thanksgiving.

8 Beware lest any man spoil you through philosophy and vain deceit, after the tradition of men, after the rudiments of the world, and not after Christ.

9 For in Him dwelleth all the fullness of the Godhead bodily,

10 And ye are complete in Him, which is the head of all principality and power.

11 In whom also ye are circumcised with the circumcision made without hands, in putting off the body of the sins of the flesh by the circumcision of Christ:

12 Buried with Him in baptism, wherein also ye are risen with Him through the faith of the operation of God, who hath raised Him from the dead.

13 And you, being dead in your sins and the uncircumcision of your flesh, hath He quickened together with him, having forgiven you all trespasses;

2 (1-5) We would like you to know how concerned Paul has been for the people in Laodicea, and those many who have never met him personally. He wishes their hearts to be comforted, their strength united in Love. To you all may come the richness of true understanding in acknowledgement of the true mysteries of God the Father, and of the Christ in whom are hidden all the treasures of wisdom and knowledge.[1] Paul's message to you now is a warning, lest you be beguiled by other words that seem enticing. Though not with you in the body, he is with you in spirit, filled with joy at your order, and the steadfastness of the faith which you are reported to possess in Christ.

(6-15) You have obviously received the message of the True Christ, therefore walk steadfastly in His way. Be rooted firmly in Him, and be established in the true wisdoms as you have been instructed, and be filled with thanksgiving. Be wary of those who come with other philosophies and so called wisdom, which is not of the real truth, but only following human tradition, rudimentary and of the world – not that of the Christ. In Christ truly dwells all the fullness of the Godhead manifest. You are fully complete in that wisdom, which is above all the power of the kingdoms of this earth. His "circumcision" is not of the flesh, but is of the Holy Spirit. By baptism in the true knowledge of Christ, you are also set upon the way to the same consciousness which He has, through the same power of God who was able to raise Him, though dead. You also, being as dead because of worldly attachments, can now be raised in consciousness even as He. We have the means

Colossians 2

14 Blotting out the handwriting of ordinances that was against us which was contrary to us, and took it out of the way, nailing it to the cross;

15 And having spoiled principalities and powers, He made a shew of them openly, triumphing over them in it.

16 Let no man therefore judge you in meat, or in drink, or in respect of an holyday, or of the new moon, or of the sabbath days:

17 Which are a shadow of things to come; but the body is of Christ.

18 Let no man beguile you of your reward in a voluntary humility and worshipping of angels, intruding into these things which he hath not seen, vainly puffed up by his fleshly mind,

19 And not holding the Head, from which all the body by joints and bands having nourishment ministered, and knit together, increaseth with the increase of God.

20 Wherefore if ye be dead with Christ from the rudiments of the world, why, as though living in the world, are ye subject to the ordinances,

21 (Touch not; taste not; handle not;

22 Which all are to perish with the using;) after the commandments and doctrines of men?

23 Which things have indeed a shew of wisdom in will worship, and humility, and neglecting of the body; not in any honour to the satisfying of the flesh.

to forgive ourselves and each other and to release all things which have been set against us, for the Lord Jesus has shown us the way through the power of the cross. He has cast down the power of the kingdoms of this world by so openly going against them and by His triumph over them.

(16-19) Do not let anyone be your judge from now on: neither in what you eat, drink, or what you choose to do on the holy days, or the new moon, or the sabbath; which are but shadows of the things to come. Know that you are in Christ, as part of that body. Let no one talk you out of your true reward, earned by humility and by communion with the angels; such people intrude into those things which they do not understand and are full of their own importance and intellect. They do not have the knowledge of the Head, from which flows the substance to all the body, and which are united as one body, ministered to and increasing in strength via the Power of God.

(20-23) If you die to the world and its rudimentary knowledge, you are with Christ, even though while living in the world you have to be bound by physical laws. Touch not, taste not, handle not! We tell you in truth, all this will pass for these things follow only the commandments and doctrines of men. These things all look good in their self inspired humility and apparent neglect of the body, but in fact they do honour to nothing except their own self-righteousness.

DISCOURSE CHAPTER TWO

1.   Q: In 2:3, you use the phrase "In whom are hidden all the treasures of wisdom and knowledge." What did Christ reveal? This seems to be contradictory to the concept of Christ revealing all with this concept that He had these "hidden treasures" of wisdom and knowledge.

    A: Ah yes. We are here speaking to the subject of deeper initiation. Our Lord Jesus spoke to the masses in parables of everyday situations which they found easy to comprehend, and therefore reached out to quite a number of people in His day. In the same sense, the church which was created after His name has done the same thing. And therefore, as I said earlier, one does not condemn the church, only some of their erroneous suppositions. All of the religions have fulfilled a great mission, let us not minimize their value in that sense.

    However, all of humanity has to pass through stages which can only be dictated by the inner wisdom of each individual. When the individual comes to the point in time when he begins to question those more simplistic teachings, he sets foot on his own path, his own search for those very deeper mysteries to which I was referring. What was being hinted here was that when the individual is ready, he will find the key to each and every one of those deeper mysteries through their embodiment in the life of Jesus, and he will find the path to the ultimate knowledge of the Christ through that example. When he embarks upon the path of return, and soul begins to recognize the deeper truths, then each of those keys to unlock the mysteries can be discovered through the example set by Jesus who gave embodiment to the Christ principle. There is no higher example that humanity may turn to. There have been others in more ancient times, but the latest and greatest example, to which we turn in our search, and therefore the key that unlocks those deeper mysteries, can be found in the example which He gave.

COLOSSIANS 3

3 *If ye then be risen with Christ, seek those things which are above, where Christ sitteth on the right hand of God.*

2 Set your affection on things above, not on things on the earth.

3 For ye are dead, and your life is hid with Christ in God.

4 When Christ, who is our life, shall appear, then shall ye also appear with him in glory.

5 Mortify therefore your members which are upon the earth; fornication, uncleanness, inordinate affection, evil concupiscence, and covetousness, which is idolatry:

6 For which things' sake the wrath of God cometh on the children of disobedience:

7 In the which he also walked some time, when ye lived in them.

8 But now ye also put off all these; anger, wrath, malice, blasphemy, filthy communication out of your mouth.

9 Lie not one to another, seeing that ye have put off the old man with his deeds;

10 And have put on the new man, which is renewed in knowledge after the image of him that created him;

11 Where there is neither Greek nor Jew, circumcision nor uncircumcision, Barbarian, Scythian, bond nor free: but Christ is all, and in all.

12 Put on therefore, as the elect of God, holy and beloved, bowels of mercies, kindness, humbleness of mind, meekness, longsuffering;

13 Forbearing one another, and forgiving one another, if any man have a quarrel against any: even as Christ forgave you so also do ye.

14 And above all these things, put on charity, which is the bond of perfectness.

3 (1-4) If you are truly risen in Christ, then seek those things of a higher nature, and set your heart on those higher things rather than things of the world. Until you do this totally, you are as dead and your higher self is hidden, but when you follow after the same high principles as Christ, then you shall partake of His glory.

(5-11) Cease to follow after the lesser things of the body, that which motivates you to lust, uncleanliness, too much worldly affection, covetousness, anger, malice, swearing of oaths, blasphemy and all other things which excite adverse karma. Now that you have put away all those things, see to it that you do not lie to one another also, but that you walk as a new person, renewed in greater knowledge of Him that gave it to you. In that knowledge there are no Jews or Greeks, Barbarians, Scythians, circumcised or uncircumcised, slave or freeman, for Christ is equally in all.

(12-17) Take upon yourselves therefore the stature of God's elect: be holy and beloved, show mercy to others, be kind to each other and of humble minds, be tolerant and ready to forgive if you should have differences with others, even as Christ forgave each of you. Above all else, be loving, for this is the way toward perfection. Let God's peace rule in your hearts; be united as one, in thankfulness.

Colossians 3

15 And let the peace of God rule in your hearts, to the which also ye are called in one body; and be ye thankful.

16 Let the word of Christ dwell in you richly in all wisdom; teaching and admonishing one another in psalms and hymns and spiritual songs, singing with grace in our hearts to the Lord.

17 And whatsoever ye do in word or deed, do all in the name of the Lord Jesus, giving thanks to God, and the Father by him.

18 Wives, submit yourselves unto your own husbands, as it is fit in the Lord.

19 Husbands, love your wives, and be not bitter against them.

20 Children, obey your parents in all things; for this is well pleasing unto the Lord.

21 Fathers, provoke not your children to anger, lest they be discouraged.

22 Servants, obey in all things your masters according to the flesh; not with eyeservice, as menpleasers; but in singleness of heart, fearing God:

23 And whatsoever ye do, do it heartily, as to the Lord, and not unto men;

24 Knowing that of the Lord ye shall receive the reward of the inheritance: for ye serve the Lord Christ.

25 But he that doeth wrong shall receive for the wrong which he hath done: and there is no respect of persons.

Let the wisdom taught by the Christ live in you richly, so that you are teachers of one another. Sing your psalms and hymns as spiritual songs with grace in the Lord. Do all that you do, in fact, in the name of God giving thanks to him as your Father.

(18-25) Wives, stay with your own husbands as is seemly; husbands, love your wives and be good to them and be good to your children also, that you command respect. Children, give that respect to your parents and obey them as much as possible. We here suggest that parents too must earn respect by not being unduly harsh with their children. A happy parent-child relationship is well pleasing to the Lord. Servants, obey your masters not only with lip service, but in real service, lovingly. Whatever you do, do it with a full heart as though you did it not for men, but for God, knowing that from God you will receive due reward for your labour. Those who do not so, shall also receive accordingly.[1]

DISCOURSE CHAPTER THREE

1. Q: In 3:18-25, there is a list of things like "Wives stay with your own husbands as is seemly, husbands love your wives and be good to them and children respect your parents. . ." The following comment has been made about that: "This seems a rather mundane list of family virtues that could have come from many sources, that it is not distinctively Christian."* Would you care to comment?

    A: It is not mundane. The mundane is put upon it by the mind of those who see it in that way. One of the highest truths is that the ultimate ideal upon this earthly plane is that those who are joined together should not be put asunder. Did Jesus not say "those whom God hath joined, let no man put asunder." That is because that is the ultimate ideal. One does not advocate that if life is miserable with another partner and the partner is the wrong one, one should stay together throughout all things good, bad or otherwise. One is suggesting that the ideal is to know one's true sympathetic soul and to stay with that one in a union of love which creates the necessary environment for the emergence into the Christed being. One cannot emerge thereto in any other than the environment of love created between two sympathetic souls. It is again a universal law that the high souls who wish to come into being in this earth plane cannot do so with parents who are not of that same high frequency. Therefore, we always will admonish that one seek for the highest possible ever, ever moving upwards. The ideal relationship between the male and female is to come together and stay together and to bring other souls into this earthly plane to learn from that example. Example is the only way one can ever truly learn. It is not a mundane subject; it is a very deep esoteric subject.

---

* Ibid; p.226.

COLOSSIANS 4

4 *Masters, give unto your servants that which is just and equal; knowing that ye also have a Master in heaven.*

2 Continue in prayer, and watch in the same with thanksgiving;

3 Withal praying also for us, that God would open unto us a door of utterance, to speak the mystery of Christ, for which I am also in bonds:

4 That I may make it manifest, as I ought to speak

5 Walk in wisdom toward them that are without, redeeming the time.

6 Let your speech be always with grace, seasoned with salt, that ye may know how ye ought to answer every man.

7 All my state shall Tychicus declare unto you, who is a beloved brother, and a faithful minister and fellow servant in the Lord:

8 Whom I have sent unto you for the same purpose, that he might know your estate, and comfort your hearts;

9 With Onesimus, a faithful and beloved brother, who is one of you. They shall make known unto you all things which are done here.

10 Aristarchus my fellow prisoner saluteth you, and Marcus, sister's son to Barnabas, (touching whom ye received commandments; if he come unto you, receive him;)

11 And Jesus, which is called Justus, who are of the circumcision. These only are my fellow workers unto the kingdom of God, which have been a comfort unto me.

12 Epaphras, who is one of you, a servant of Christ, saluteth you, always labouring fervently for you in prayers, that ye may stand perfect and complete in all the will of God.

4 (1-6) Masters, give your servants just reward for their work knowing that you too have a Master in God.[1] Pray and be thankful, and pray also for us so that God will continue to assist us in our work and that we continue to teach the Christ Mysteries, even though this is why we are imprisoned. Walk wisely before those who have no wisdom and speak always with grace, well seasoned as with salt, so that you know exactly how to speak to anyone.

(7-9) When Tychicus arrives with you, he will let you know how things are precisely with me (Paul). He is a faithful minister and beloved brother in the Lord. He comes to you with Onesimus, also a faithful brother who is one of your own people. They shall make all things known to you, and also my (Paul) thought is that they will be able to let me know more accurately how things are with you.

(10-11) Aristarchus, who is imprisoned with me, sends his greetings; also, Barnabas' sister's son, Marcus (if he should manage to get to you, please receive him). I also commend to you one Justus, who the Jews call Jesus, for he is of them. These are all my fellow workers and have been a comfort to me.

Colossians 4

13 For I bear him record, that he hath a great zeal for you, and them that are in Laodicea, and them in Hierapolis.

14 Luke, the beloved physician, and Demas, greet you.

15 Salute the brethren which are in Laodicea, and Nymphas, and the church which is in his house.

16 And when this epistle is read among you, cause that it be read also in the church of the Laodiceans; and that ye likewise read the epistle from Laodicea.

17 And say to Archippus, Take heed to the ministry which thou has received in the Lord, that thou fulfil it.

18 The salutation by the hand of me Paul. Remember my bonds. Grace be with you. Amen.

(12-17) Epaphras who is of your country and a servant of Christ sends salutations; he remembers you always in his prayers, and endeavors to remain upright to do God's will and purpose and he has a great love for you as I can verify; those who are in Laodicea and Hierapolis also. My dear friend Luke the beloved physician also sends you his warm greetings as does Demas. Please convey our greetings to the faithful in Laodicea and Nymphas, and especially those who meet in her home. Please pass this message to all of them, and make sure that the people of Laodicea see it and also that they have seen the letter that came from the Laodiceans. Tell Archippus to tend the ministry which he has been given at the Lord's command.

(18) I Paul, add my signature to these words, and ask that you remember me kindly during my imprisonment. Grace be with you. Amen.

Written in Rome, in the year of Our Lord, 62 A.D.

DISCOURSE CHAPTER FOUR

1. Q: In the end of chapter 3 and the beginning of Chapter 4 the word "servant" is used. You are talking about how servants should deal with their masters, and masters with their servants. The question here is that in Greek in the earliest manuscripts the word is really "slave". Does the KJ version have that right and does it really mean "slave"?

   A: Undoubtedly at the time of writing it, it meant slave; and certainly up until the time of the KJ version it would still have meant slave, for unfortunately slavery was still the case in some areas. Servant is the more acceptable term for the modem age. Slave was never an acceptable term because the very element of slavery was not acceptable. From the point of view of translation "slave" is what it would have meant.

   Q: In chapter 4 you mention four people who are with you, Aristarchus, Barnabas, Marcus and Justus. In the KJ and RSV it sounds a little plaintiff, in the fact that these are all the support from his own people that Paul has had. You have changed it slightly; do you have any comment about the kind of support you had while in prison?

   A: We have earlier stated that Paul had no lack during his time of imprisonment. (I suppose we should change the word "imprisonment" because it was not in the normal sense such.) I feel that to a great extent the translation at the time of KJ was colored by the mind of the different clerical brothers who assisted. One has to recall what imprisonment would have meant in those days; and yes, I can well understand that in the translation a certain amount of plaintiveness might have crept into the message because that would be in the feeling and mind of the translator. If one truly recognizes the statement that Paul has been trying to make all the way through, one then sees that he is not entertaining plaintive cries about his condition; he is in fact saying that he will accept all gladly in the name of Christ because even that is not the ultimate sacrifice that Christ Himself made. The reference to the colleagues who were still with Paul is a simple statement that they too were in that close confinement with him, not a plaintive cry that "these are my only supporters".

INTRODUCTION TO THE LETTER OF PAUL TO THE EPHESIANS

Written from Rome in the year 62, shortly after the letters that were sent to Philippi and Colossae. This was sent out with Tychicus in the assumption that he would move on from Philippi down into Asia via Ephesus and thence to Colossae. The three letters were therefore all composed at approximately the same point in time. There was also a further letter written by me personally, to the Ephesians and addressed to Timothy in particular in the year 66 toward the end of my life. This second letter has been the subject of much confusion and I am therefore addressing it at the end of the current text in order that the matter be also cleared up.

Specifically, the second letter, notation of which is in the New Testament as being "Paul's Epistle to Timothy" addresses the subject of the officers in the emergent body which has subsequently been called "Church". This letter is perhaps (more so than any other) the root of the established Church, called after Christ, disallowing women in office. This practice is obviously founded on an absolute error, for the letter to the Hebrews was, of course, written by one of the first appointed bishops (appointed with my full knowledge and approval during my time in ministry), Priscilla, wife of Aquila the Roman.

Preamble

There is a general comment which I feel I would like to make which further clarifies my reason for waiting until now, at this particular point in history, to rectify this work. I feel that in view of the nature of this clarification, it is also perhaps necessary to enlarge a little upon the transitional nature of what has been given the title "Christianity". I have stated earlier that it is not my own intent, nor the intention of any other from this level, to belittle those major streams of religious thought which have been extant within humanity over the past millennia. Indeed, were it not for those bodies of religious thought, humanity might be moving in a different way at this time. We have much to thank these streams for and we have also to recognize that there has been a great deal of error which now needs to be rectified if people are willing now, at this time, to hear. And our thinking – I use the collective term because I speak for all of my brothers and sisters upon this level – our thinking is that humanity is indeed moving to the time when there is more receptivity to change, even among the so-called establishment.

We deal essentially with the Christian stream of thought because it was largely that which Paul addressed. I will therefore not, at this time, enlarge upon the others. This is a different subject for another time. I wish to say that the doctrine of Christ crucified was essentially the message of the Piscean Age. It follows on the worldwide folk myth which existed at the time of Jesus of Nazareth, and which was an extension of a myth that had been well known down the ages and was an essential part of all the great mysteries taught in the many centers which were called mystery schools (centers of initiation), particularly around the Mediterranean and the British Isles. This is the mythology of the kingly sacrifice in which the blood of the supreme head is shed in order to purchase extension of life for the very Earth herself and all who dwell upon her. In using this particular message the Christ, through the embodiment of Jesus, sealed for all time in the mind of humanity the meaning of that sacrifice. Throughout the passage of time which we call the Piscean Age, the symbol of the church which founded itself upon that initiatory theme has been that of Christ the King hanging upon the cross giving of His blood and His body in sacrifice.

We move now into the time of Aquarius, the air, which is essentially represented symbolically by the Ascension. The sacrifice is perfected, the work is done, and Earth and all of humanity moves on to the next phase, celebrated annually as the Festival of Unification: the time of the descent into the Earthly plane of the Holy Spirit, the Divine Indweller. This whole demonstration, if it was about anything at all, was a demonstration of the unity of all life and the extension of that life in reincarnation here upon this Earthly plane in order to go through all of the process of moving through deaths, rebirths, new life unto life everlasting. It is no longer possible to renounce the fact of countless reincarnations here in the school of Earth. It is no longer possible to disregard what it is that humanity is here to serve. So be it.

THE LETTER OF PAUL TO THE EPHESIANS

1 *Paul, an apostle of Jesus Christ by the will of God, to the saints which are at Ephesus, and to the faithful in Christ Jesus:*

2 Grace be to you, and peace, from God our Father, and from the Lord Jesus Christ.

3 Blessed be the God and Father of our Lord Jesus Christ, who hath blessed us with all spiritual blessings in heavenly places in Christ:

4 According as he hath chosen us in him before the foundation of the world, that we should be holy and without blame before him in love:

5 Having predestinated us unto the adoption of children by Jesus Christ to himself according to the good pleasure of his will.

6 To the praise of the glory of his grace, wherein he hath made us accepted in the beloved.

7 In whom we have redemption through his blood, the forgiveness of sins, according to the riches of his grace;

8 Wherein he hath abounded toward us in all wisdom and prudence;

9 Having made known unto us the mystery of his will, according to his good pleasure which he hath purposed in himself

10 That in the dispensation of the fullness of times he might gather together in one all things in Christ, both which are in heaven, and which are on earth; even in him:

11 In whom also we have obtained an inheritance, being predestinated according to the purpose of him who worketh all things after the counsel of his own will:

12 That we should be to the praise of his glory, who first trusted in Christ.

1 (1-3) From Paul, by the will of God an Apostle of Christ, addressed to the faithful members of the Body of Christ in Ephesus, grace and peace of God; and of our Lord Christ be with you. Blessed be that same Father of our Lord Christ who has given us all spiritual blessings and established the Christ spirit within us all. For we are all a part of God since even before this world was created.

(4-11) Having pre-ordained since the beginning that we are part of Him, we should endeavor to live a pure and holy life without blame, and seek to be in true accord with divine will to the honor and glory of that grace wherein we are all acceptable parts of the beloved. According to the richness of that grace was the demonstration made in the blood of Christ, and showing yet again the wisdom of those deeper mysteries which he deemed fit to reveal to us through this act. This was done so that in due time we might all come again to the full knowledge which is in Christ of things both spiritual and temporal which are united in God. Through this means, we have come back to our inheritance (even as the prodigal) which was always our destiny within Divine Will.

(12-18) Even as God Himself trusted in Christ to deliver this message, so too do we also trust the message that was received. In that trust was sealed a divine promise. This promise acts as an earnest deposit, if you will, on that inheritance which stands until all shall come into the fullness of that glory. To this end I ceaselessly work, and give thanks when

Ephesians 1

13 In whom ye also trusted, after that ye heard the word of truth, the gospel of your salvation: in whom also after that ye believed, ye were sealed with that holy Spirit of promise,

14 Which is the earnest of our inheritance till the redemption of the purchased possession, unto the praise of his glory.

15 Wherefore I also, after I heard of your faith in the Lord Jesus, and love unto all the saints,

16 Cease not to give thanks for you, making mention of you in my prayers;

17 That the God of our Lord Jesus Christ, the Father of glory may give unto you the spirit of wisdom and revelation in the knowledge of him:

18 The eyes of your understanding being enlightened; that ye may know what is the hope of his calling and what the riches of the glory of his inheritance in the saints,

19 And what is the exceeding greatness of his power to usward who believe, according to the working of his mighty power,

20 Which he wrought in Christ, when he raised him from the dead, and set him at his own right hand in the heavenly places,

21 Far above all principality, and power, and might, and dominion, and every name that is named, not only in this world, but also in that which is to come:

22 And hath put all things under his feet, and gave him to be the head over all things to the church,

23 Which is his body, the fullness of him that filleth all in all.

I hear of such faith and love which you have. I ask that God shall continue to pour on you the spirit of wisdom and revelation of true knowledge. I pray that your eye of deep understanding be opened that you may all come to know what is meant by the richness of that glory, which is the inheritance of all who have true faith.

(19-23) What is the power of that glory, revealed to all who believe, that power which Christ demonstrated? What is that power which is far above worldly dominion or even above all that is to come; which has placed all things under His feet and given Christ to be the head of that great body; his own body the fullness of which is in us all?[1]

DISCOURSE CHAPTER ONE

1. Q: In 1:22-23, you have already dealt previously with the fact that the body of Christ is not just the church but is the body of all creation. What is the relationship then, of the Christian Church to the body of Christ? Does it have a special relationship?

   A: It has a no more special relationship than does anyone else. The intention here is tochallenge and rectify the belief of the Christian Church that it " is" the body of Christ and that the only way to salvation or the only way to God, if you will, is through the Christian Church. We are all the body of Christ, whether or not we profess Christianity.

EPHESIANS 2

2 *And you hath he quickened. who were dead in trespasses and sins;*

2 Wherein in time past ye walked according to the course of this world, according to the prince of the power of the air, the spirit that now worketh in the children of disobedience:

3 Among whom also we all had our conversation in times past in the lusts of our flesh, fulfilling the desires of the flesh and of the mind; and were by nature the children of wrath, even as others.

4 But God, who is rich in mercy, for his great love wherewith he loved us,

5 Even when we were dead in sins, hath quickened us together with Christ (by grace ye are saved;)

6 And hath raised us up together and made us sit together in heavenly places in Christ Jesus:

7 That in the ages to come he might shew the exceeding riches of his grace in his kindness toward us through Christ Jesus.

8 For by grace are ye saved through faith; and that not of yourselves: it is the gift of God:

9 Not of works, lest any man should boast.

10 For we are his workmanship, created in Christ Jesus unto good works, which God hath before ordained that we should walk in them.

11 Wherefore remember, that ye being in time past Gentiles in the flesh, who are called Uncircumcision by that which is called the Circumcision in the flesh made by hands;

12 That at that time ye were without Christ, being aliens from the commonwealth of Israel, and strangers from the covenants of promise, having no hope, and without God in the world:

2 (1-10) In times past we have walked in the way of worldliness and in accord with the beliefs put forward by the powers of this world. These paths held us to the things of the flesh and the material level, fulfilling only the lesser nature. But God so loved us, that through the message of Christ in Jesus, we were again shown the means to grace. Through that message (if we believe and follow it) we are again united into the One throughout all ages to come.[1] That power is in each and every one of us as the gift of God, not through our own grace or works, but through the following of the way as shown by Christ as universally ordained.

(11-18) Remember that the laws laid down by earthly tradition are pertinent only on earth. They were created without Christ's message and were laws of separation. Now, through the new interpretation given by Christ, ye are no longer separate but are come together in unity. His Peace makes us to be One. He has torn down that wall which existed between us. He abolished those old laws, commandments which were ordinances of separation, and instead, gave us the means of peace through unity. He came to speak the message of eternal peace to all nations, through the message of his sacrifice, that from henceforth all nations shall be as one in God, through One Divine Spirit.

Ephesians 2

13 But now in Christ Jesus ye who sometimes were far off are made nigh by the blood of Christ.

14 For he is our peace, who hath made both one, and hath broken down the middle wall of partition between us;

15 Having abolished in his flesh the enmity, even the law of commandments contained in ordinances; for to make in himself of twain one new man, so making peace;

16 And that he might reconcile both unto God in one body by the cross, having slain the enmity thereby:

17 And came and preached peace to you which were afar off and to them that were nigh.

18 For through him we both have access by one Spirit unto the Father.

19 Now therefore ye are no more strangers and foreigners, but fellow citizens with the saints, and of the household of God;

20 And are built upon the foundation of the apostles and prophets, Jesus Christ Himself being the chief cornerstone;

21 In whom all the building fitly framed together groweth unto an holy temple in the Lord;

22 In whom ye also are builded together for an habitation of God through the Spirit.

(19-22) Now we can say there are no longer "foreigners and strangers" but citizens of the one household, the one family of God. Upon this very foundation is set the Apostolic succession, with Christ as the cornerstone, and through which the building, framed correctly, will grow into an holy temple worthy of the Spirit of God.[2]

DISCOURSE CHAPTER TWO

1. Q: In 2:8 there is again a subject touched upon in Romans but I think it is worth further comment because it is a classic phrase for Paul at that time. You have dropped this phrase: "For by grace ye are saved through faith". You have left out the word "saved" particularly. Would you care to comment further on this crucial point for Paul?

    A: Again, this has a great deal to do with the belief which has been set forward by the Christian Church that the only way to be saved is through their authority. To be baptized into the body of Christ essentially for the church means to be baptized into the body of the Church, as though that were the only path to salvation. Salvation lies for each and every one in the personal effort to become as He was, using His example.

2. Q: Since this is so crucial an issue, we will probably approach it several times. In 2:19-21 you have retained most of a very famous passage. The passage reads: " Now we can say there are no longer foreigners and strangers, but citizens of the one household the one family of God. Upon this very foundation is set the apostolic succession with Christ as the cornerstone and to which the building, framed correctly, will grow into a holy temple worthy of the Spirit of God." I am sure people will still say " Isn't that referring to the church?"

    A: No it is not! It does not refer to the church which calls itself Christian or Holy Catholic; it refers to the human family, irrespective of whether or not members of any one race or community follows that church which is called Christian or whether that family professes to be Buddhist, Hindu, Muslim, etc. The Universal Christ impulse is the same for all and works in the same way through all, provided first there is the intent and the awakening within the human breast. The temple of God is within each one and the message which became famous should be taken in that light, not to be regarded as a message to any one particular religion. We are certainly not referring to the building of churches in stone or any other material. The reference is to the Church Universal. Does that clear the issue?

EPHESIANS 3

3 For this cause I Paul, the prisoner of Jesus Christ for you Gentiles,

2 If ye have heard of the dispensation of the grace of God which is given me to you-ward:

3 How that by revelation he made known unto me the mystery; (as I wrote afore in few words,

4 Whereby, when ye read, ye may understand my knowledge in the mystery of Christ)

5 Which in other ages was not made known unto the sons of men, as it is now revealed unto his holy apostles and prophets by the Spirit;

6 That the Gentiles should be fellowheirs, and of the same body, and partakers of his promise in Christ by the gospel:

7 Whereof I was made a minister, according to the gift of the grace of God given unto me by the effectual working of his power.

8 Unto me, who am less than the least of all saints, is this grace given, that I should preach among the Gentiles the unsearchable riches of Christ;

9 And to make all men see what is the fellowship of the mystery, which from the beginning of the world hath been hid in God, who created all things by Jesus Christ:

10 To the intent that now unto the principalities and powers in heavenly places might be known by the church the manifold wisdom of God,

11 According to the eternal purpose which he purposed in Christ Jesus our Lord:

12 In whom we have boldness and access with confidence by the faith of him.

13 Wherefore I desire that ye faint not at my tribulations for you, which is your glory.

14 For this cause I bow my knees unto the Father of our Lord Jesus Christ,

3 (1-6) For this cause I, Paul, am now a prisoner. You have all heard how that happened and how I developed as a minister for I have written it all down so that you might understand the deeper meaning of the mysteries. The deeper meanings as revealed by The Christ were as yet unknown in the world. Each age had its specific mystery, and this is now a deeper revelation given to us by Christ. Those whom we call Gentiles are also heirs to the same mysteries and equal followers and participants.

(7-12) As those truths have been revealed to me, so I now attempt as best I might, to put them before others, that in due time all may see the unimaginable riches of Christ. It is my hope that all may come to understand that which, from the very beginning is available to us; wherein is wisdom, from God, in accord with His eternal purpose which Christ reveals. This is our means of full confidence through faith in him.

(13-19) Do not become faint hearted because of what is happening to me. I tell you, it is all part of the greater glory and your own glory. For this very cause I have submitted to whatever may come, in total trust in God and Christ our Lord.

Ephesians 3

15 Of whom the whole family in heaven and earth is named,

16 That he would grant you, according to the riches of his glory, to be strengthened with mighty by his Spirit in the inner man;

17 That Christ may dwell in your hearts by faith; that ye, being rooted and grounded in love,

18 May be able to comprehend with all saints what is the breadth, and length, and depth, and height;

19 And to know the love of Christ, which passeth knowledge that ye might be filled with all the fullness of God.

20 Now unto him that is able to do exceeding abundantly above all that we ask or think, according to the power that worketh in us,

21 Unto him be glory in the church by Christ Jesus throughout all ages, world without end. Amen

That great name is such that gives us all strength. That power within us (which is the inner self) is indeed empowered by Spirit and the Christ dwells in each of our hearts. Thus we are rooted and grounded in love. That love enables us to comprehend the height and depth, the length and breadth of those things which otherwise are beyond our knowledge, that we might be filled with the knowledge and love of God, through Christ.[1]

(20-21) I pray that to Him who is able to work so abundantly in us, above all that we can ever conceive, be accorded the honor and glory, throughout all ages, without end. Amen.

DISCOURSE CHAPTER THREE

1.   Q: In 3:13-19, while you are describing the fact that the church does not have a special relationship to Christ, any more than any other being, Paul worked very hard at establishing and maintaining these emerging communities or churches, even to the point of being involved in the ordination of elders and cautioning them against false teachings. It seems as though Paul was helping to establish this very church. Did Paul become disappointed with what happened after his death? In other words, was there a sense that what he helped create did not turn out the way that he wanted?

   A: Is that not always the case? When the prime mover leaves the scene those who follow distort what was intended; certainly I have a great deal of disappointment with what happened after I left.

Discourse Chapter Three continued:

Q: I think we are beginning to get a very good handle on all of that.

A: May I say that the reason why I started this morning's work with that preamble was in order to address, to a certain extent, that question which you have just raised. Yes indeed, during his life, Paul did work very hard as did the other apostles and disciples in order to create a cohesion and degree of strength between those who were given the true teachings. The simple theme behind all of what Paul says is " Now you have the truth, live by it. Be unified by it one with another as a family, even as the nuclear family should be unified by its love that brings it together. Here are the means by which to be unified. Above all, that which you now know as the truth, which was taught by Jesus, overlighted by the Christ, this is the truth, people, know it!"

Unfortunately, and this is ever the case for humanity, the intellect has a desire to quantify and qualify. As soon as the human ego interferes with the purity, everything has to be bigger than and better than what has been. And so from the clarity of the original message given by Christ through Jesus and His initiate disciples, and eventually Paul and his initiate followers, from that purity and absolute clarity, there was further and further deviation which crept in because of the need within the human mind to qualify. This is ever so, whether we speak of religion or history. So much of the truth is distorted by the reasoning of the lesser mind.

If we try to now piece together the original of anything – even several hundred years later, let alone several thousand or more – the only shadow of truth, the only vestige with which we humans are left in the mythology of the human race, is that thread of similarity that runs in each. Wherever we get to around the world, that which is similar from race to race, that is where we will find the truth. Most else is distortion as is that message which Jesus attempted to clarify, the message of the ages. It was no different in His day than throughout the millennia before Him and no different now for the next age. Yet we must once again come back to what is the pure truth and set aside the distortions. As we keep coming back over and over again to the purity, leaving out the distortions, hopefully humanity has again the means to progress.

EPHESIANS 4

4 *I therefore, the prisoner of the Lord, beseech you that ye walk worthy of the vocation wherewith ye are called.*

2 With all lowliness and meekness, with longsuffering forbearing one another in love;

3 Endeavouring to keep the unity of the Spirit in the bond of peace.

4 There is one body, and one Spirit, even as ye are called in one hope of your calling;

5 One Lord, one faith, one baptism,

6 One God and Father of all, who is above all, and through all, and in you all.

7 But unto every one of us is given grace according to the measure of the gift of Christ.

8 Wherefore he saith, When he ascended up on high, he led captivity captive, and gave gifts unto men.

9 (Now that he ascended what is it but that he also descended first into the lower parts of the earth?

10 He that descended is the same also that ascended up far above all heavens, that he might fill all things.)

11 And he gave some, apostles; and some, prophets; and some, evangelists; and some, pastors and teachers;

12 For the perfecting of the saints, for the work of the ministry, for the edifying of the body of Christ:

13 Till we all come in the unity of the faith, and of the knowledge of the Son of God, unto a perfect man, unto the measure of the stature of the fullness of Christ:

14 That we henceforth be no more children, tossed to and fro, and carried about with every wind of doctrine, by the sleight of men, and cunning craftiness, whereby they lie in wait to deceive;

15 But speaking the truth in love, may grow up into him in all things, which is the head, even Christ:

4 (1-6) I who am a prisoner in that cause therefore ask you to be worthy of that vocation to which you have been called. Be humble, meek and long suffering. Be forbearing with one another, for love. Keep a unity of Spirit between you, held together by peace. There is only one calling, only One Spirit (and that is the Spirit in which each of you are working). There is only one baptism into the One Faith, just as there is only One Divine Source which is above all things and through all things.

(7-10) We are all given grace according to our measure, with Christ as the "yardstick". This is what is meant in the words "when he ascended on high, he led captivity captive, and gave gifts to men." Does it not also record that he first descended into the earth? He descended into the earth and then ascended so that in this means he could infill all things with his Spirit.[1]

(11-16) We have each been given certain gifts, whether we choose to be apostles, prophets, evangelists, pastors or teachers in order that Christ's ministry may continue, for the purpose of edification of the whole body that is Christ. We continue with that work until all have come into the state of perfection which is available to us, if we follow the example and knowledge given to us.

Ephesians 4

16 From whom the whole body fitly joined together and compacted by that which every joint supplieth, according to the effectual working in the measure of every part, maketh increase of the body unto the edifying of itself in love.

17 This I say therefore, and testify in the Lord, that ye henceforth walk not as other Gentiles walk in the vanity of their mind,

18 Having the understanding darkened, being alienated from the life of God through the ignorance that is in them, because of the blindness of their heart:

19 Who being past feeling have given themselves over unto lasciviousness, to work all uncleanness with greediness.

20 But ye have not so learned Christ;

21 If so be that ye have heard him, and have been taught by him, as the truth is in Jesus:

22 That ye put off concerning the former conversation the old man, which is corrupt according to the deceitful lusts;

23 And be renewed in the spirit of your mind;

24 And that ye put on the new man, which after God is created in righteousness and true holiness.

25 Wherefore putting away lying, speak every man truth with his neighbour; for we are members one of another.

26 Be ye angry, and sin not: let not the sun go down upon your wrath:

27 Neither give place to the devil.

28 Let him that stole steal no more: but rather let him labour, working with his hands the thing which is good, that he may have to give to him that needeth.

We can become the perfected man by that measure – the stature of the fullness of Christ. We are no longer children to be tossed about like straws in the wind of each and every doctrine that we hear. Nor should we succumb to the deceptions of those who would, through their cunning, deceive. When we speak the loving truth, we grow by the method of Him that we call our Head – even Christ. When we stand tall in light and love, the whole body comes together, every part, every joint, works effectively toward perfection. [2]

(17-24) I attest to this and say from now on, walk tall – not as others walk who know no better, and who are blinded by their ignorance. Their lack of true feeling has turned them astray and they perpetuate wrong doing. You know better, for you have learned the truth through Christ as was shown by Jesus. You have no more to do with the old person that was you, for you have been renewed through the truth which your minds have accepted. This new person is filled with the light of true holiness.

(25-32) Therefore, you also have to stop doing things after the old ways, and demonstrate truth. We are all responsive to and responsible for each other. Therefore if you should feel angry, do not let the sun go down on your anger so that you do not give energy to negative emotions. Let those who have been in the habit of stealing, stop that. Instead, work and labour with your own hands, doing those things which build goodness. Give to the needy. Stop lying or swearing and blaspheming. Only those things which uplift should come

Ephesians 4

29 Let no corrupt communication proceed out of your mouth, but that which is good to the use of edifying, that it may minister grace unto the hearers.

30 And grieve not the holy Spirit of God, whereby ye are sealed unto the day of redemption.

31 Let all bitterness, and wrath, and anger and clamour, and evil speaking, be put away from you, with all malice:

32 And be ye kind one to another, tenderhearted, forgiving one another, even as God for Christ's sake hath forgiven you.

from those who minister to others, that grace may be seen in you. Do nothing which might hurt the pure Spirit of God of which you are a part. Let anger, bitterness, frustrations, loudness and harmful talk be no longer a part of you, and indeed, anything which is malicious. Be kind to one another, be tender hearted. Forgive each other, even as God, for Christ's sake, has forgiven you.

DISCOURSE CHAPTER FOUR

1.   Q: Previously in Romans you have eliminated the notion that Christ descended into the depths of the earth or hell and then rose on the third day. In 4:9 you have retained this phrase " He descended into the earth and then ascended so that He might fill all things with the Spirit." It sounds like you are contradicting yourself.

A: Well, I am not. There is a very good reason for this. At the time of writing to the Romans I was speaking to, if you remember, a body of people whom I had not yet visited in person and there are certain elements of the original mysteries which may not, cannot, be explained except in person. On the other hand, the Ephesians were those whom I had lived among for a very long time and who knew the mysteries intimately. Therefore, when we speak of the analogous descent of the Christ into the earth, (not in the wording of the Church which is " He descended into Hell" which is strictly incorrect as the inside of the earth is not hell) we need here to dissemble a little more on the mystery and the meaning again of the crucifixion.

Christ was going through the ritual re-enactment of the sacrifice of the King, in which His essence, the innermost essence of His being, descended into the earth and the earth took Him into herself as in a divine marriage from whence He ascends once more into the higher realms. Again, we speak of the very nature of the message of the crucifixion: the marriage of the realm of spirit with that of the physical manifest plane of form. It is this very statement that Christ's essential

Discourse Chapter Four continued:

being descended into the Earth, which is the clue to that which I stated earlier – the very fact of reincarnation, interment into the earth, in order to be reborn upon the earth and not in some higher realm. There is a vast and eternal message in those words.

2. Q: I think I am asking this next question knowing your answer, but wanting to do it because it is again, one of those famous phrases and I feel it is important to emphasize what you are saying. The phrase in 4:16 is "The whole body comes together, every part, every joint works effectively toward perfection." The old phrasing is "we are members, one of another. . ." I am assuming that you are not referring to the church, but to all of humanity.

   A: Yes indeed.

   Q: Maybe even all of creation?

   A: Yes indeed. Before the final act – and this is not recorded anywhere – Jesus invited His disciples and those present in the upper room to participate with Him in the dance which celebrates the passage of the King into the earth and the eventual ascension into the realms of Spirit. This is essentially a part of the eucharist celebration which is now no longer performed. In the great cathedrals built during the zenith of the Templar tradition, such as Chartres, one will find upon the paving stones a labyrinthine form which was put into that design of the floor in order that the people might dance their celebration of the blood and the body of Christ entering into the earth. Would this now be regarded as a Pagan condition?

   Q: In some quarters certainly.

   A: Within the very church of Christ itself as a remembrance of the very act which Christ performed Himself at the last supper?

   Q: There are some churches that would love to know what that dance was, they would love to do it, but most of them wouldn't.

291

EPHESIANS 5

5 *Be ye therefore followers of God, as dear children;*

2 And walk in love, as Christ also hath loved us, and hath given himself for us an offering and a sacrifice to God for a sweetsmelling savour.

3 But fornication, and all uncleanness, or covetousness, let it not be once named among you, as becometh saints;

4 Neither filthiness, nor foolish talking, nor jesting, which are not convenient: but rather giving of thanks.

5 For this ye know that no whoremonger, nor unclean person, nor covetous man, who is an idolater, hath any inheritance in the kingdom of Christ and of God.

6 Let no man deceive you with vain words: for because of these things cometh wrath of God upon the children of disobedience.

7 Be not ye therefore partakers with them.

8 For ye were sometimes in darkness, but now are ye light in the Lord: walk as children of light:

9 (For the fruit of the Spirit is in all goodness and righteousness and truth;)

10 Proving what is acceptable unto the Lord.

11 And have no fellowship with the unfruitful works of darkness, but rather reprove them.

12 For it is a shame even to speak of those things which are done of them in secret.

13 But all things that are reproved are made manifest by the light: for whatsoever doth make manifest is light.

14 Wherefore he saith, Awake thou that sleepest, and arise from the dead, and Christ shall give thee light.

15 See then that ye walk circumspectly, not as fools, but as wise,

5 (1-7) In other words, be followers of God even as dear children. Walk in love even as Christ loved us, to the very limits of personal sacrifice. This, in the eyes of God, is sweet perfume whereas wrong doing and uncleanliness, greed, and those things which are not sweet, are no longer worthy of you. You well know by now that none of these things, whether they be foolish talk or unseemly jesting, covetousness, envy, lack of personal cleanliness, idolatry, whoremongering, have any place in the kingdom of Christ and God. Make no mistake and do not be deceived for you may accept this as fact.

(8-14) You who were sometimes part of darkness are now of the light. Walk accordingly for the fruit of the Spirit is in all goodness and righteousness and truth. Prove this for yourselves, and have nothing to do with the unfruitful darkness; strive to improve it. It is not wise to even speak of these things. You should know that eventually all is light, for all was created originally as light. Awake therefore you who sleep, arise from that death and Christ shall give you back the light.

Ephesians 5

16 Redeeming the time, because the days are evil.

17 Wherefore be ye not unwise, but understanding what the will of the Lord is.

18 And be not drunk with wine, wherein is excess; but be filled with the Spirit;

19 Speaking to yourselves in psalms and hymns and spiritual songs, singing and making melody in your heart to the Lord;

20 Giving thanks always for all things unto God and the Father in the name of our Lord Jesus Christ;

21 Submitting yourselves one to another in the fear of God.

22 Wives, submit yourselves unto your own husbands, as unto the Lord.

23 For the husband is the head of the wife, even as Christ is the head of the church: and he is the saviour of the body.

24 Therefore as the church is subject unto Christ, so let the wives be to their own husbands in every thing.

25 Husbands, love your wives, even as Christ also loved the church, and gave himself for it;

26 That he might sanctify and cleanse it with the washing of water by the word,

27 That he might present it to himself a glorious church, not having spot, or wrinkle, or any such thing; but that it should be holy and without blemish.

28 So ought men to love their wives as their own bodies. He that loveth his wife loveth himself

29 For no man ever yet hated his own flesh; but nourisheth and cherisheth it, even as the Lord of the church:

30 For we are members of his body, of his flesh, and of his bones.

31 For this cause shall a man leave his father and mother, and shall be joined unto his wife, and they two shall be one flesh.

(15-20) See that you behave not as fools, but as the wise. Be circumspect. The times are evil, but you can redeem them. Take trouble to discover what is the will of the Lord, and be filled with His Spirit, rather than your own excesses. Make melodious spiritual songs and give thanks always to God in the name of Christ.

(21-33) Allow help from each other. Wives, give yourselves only to your rightful husbands, and acknowledge the place that the family has in the Body of Christ. Husbands, love your wives for the same reason. The world is cleansed and sanctified by the true unity of male and female who come together unblemished and pure.[1] Therefore, administer unto each other even as Jesus the Christ administered the sacrament unto the world. Remember that what we do unto the body of another, we do unto ourselves, for we are all a part of the one body which is Christ.

Ephesians 5

32 This is a great mystery; but I speak concerning Christ and the church.

33 Nevertheless let every one of you in particular so love his wife even as himself; and the wife see that she reverence her husband.

DISCOURSE CHAPTER FIVE

1. Q: In 5:21-23 you have left out that infamous statement about " the husband being head of the wife as Christ is head of the church" and in its place you have left a very fine statement of equality. Is Christ head of the church or is there equality there also?

   A: An interesting question. Yes indeed, the Christ stands at the supreme head of all things. One might say He is the head if we are using the body as an analogy. But let us not then use this in order to fall into that age-old error of denigration of woman, because we are not speaking of the same thing.

EPHESIANS 6

6 *Children, obey your parents in the Lord: for this is right.*

2 Honour thy father and mother; (which is the first commandment with promise;)

3 That it may be well with thee, and thou mayest live long on the earth.

4 And, ye fathers, provoke not your children to wrath: but bring them up in the nurture and admonition of the Lord.

5 Servants, be obedient to them that are your masters according to the flesh, with fear and trembling in singleness of your heart, as unto Christ;

6 Not with eyeservice, as menpleasers; but as the servants of Christ, doing the will of God from the heart;

7 With good will doing service, as to the Lord, and not to men:

8 Knowing that whatsoever good thing any man doeth, the same shall he receive of the Lord, whether he be bond or free.

9 And, ye masters, do the same things unto them, forbearing threatening; knowing that your Master also is in heaven; neither is there respect of persons with him.

10 Finally, my brethren, be strong in the Lord and in the power of his might.

11 Put on the whole armour of God, that ye may be able to stand against the wiles of the devil.

12 For we wrestle not against flesh and blood, but against princpalities, against powers, against the rulers of the darkness of this world, against spiritual wickedness in high places.

13 Wherefore take unto you the whole armour of God, that ye may be able to withstand in the evil day, and having done all, to stand.

14 Stand therefore, having your loins girt about with truth, and having on the breastplate of righteousness;

6 (1-4) Children should be raised in this knowledge and honour the example by obedience, the first great promise in the commandments, for so you may expect a good and long life. Parents, you in turn, should not do anything which causes your children disquiet, but raise them in accord with the way of the Lord.

(5-9) If anyone fulfills the post of service to others, then let that service be as though serving Christ himself, not as demeaning in order to please or receive recompense. Know that in whatever way you act, you are serving the Lord, not men. You who have mastery over others, remember likewise, knowing that the only true master is the one who has mastery over self.

(10-20) Finally, be strong in the Lord, and in that same power which he has. Put on the whole armour of God, in order to stand firm against all adversity, for we do not fight against flesh and blood, but against principles, powers, dark forces of this world, and against spiritual wickedness even in high places. Stand in that full armour of God, through it all. Be strong, surrounded with truth, and wearing righteousness as your breastplate. Wear upon your feet the good news which is the message of peace. Take the helmet of salvation and the sword of spirit which is the word of God and pray always humbly to that Divine Spirit. Watch and persevere and pray for all the faithful. Pray also for me, that wise words may come from my mouth, and that I continue to speak out boldly for what I know as right. So may I continue to make known the true mysteries of Christ, for which I am ambassador even though in captivity.

Ephesians 6

15 And your feet shod with the preparation of the gospel of peace;

16 Above all, taking the shield of faith, wherewith ye shall be able to quench all the fiery darts of the wicked.

17 And take the helmet of salvation, and the sword of the Spirit which is the word of God:

18 Praying always with all prayer and supplication in the Spirit, and watching thereunto with all perseverance and supplication for all saints:

19 And for me, that utterance may be given unto me, that I may open my mouth boldly, to make known the mystery of the gospel.

20 For which I am an ambassador in bonds: that therein I may speak boldly, as I ought to speak.

21 But that ye also may know my affairs, and how I do, Tychicus, a beloved brother and faithful minister in the Lord, shall make known to you all things:

22 Whom I have sent unto you for the same purpose, that ye might know our affairs, and that he might comfort your hearts.

23 Peace be to the brethren, and love with faith, from God the Father and the Lord Jesus Christ.

24 Grace be with all them that love our Lord Jesus Christ in sincerity. Amen.

(21-24) In order that you are kept acquainted with my affairs, Tychicus, a faithful minister and beloved brother, will make known all things. He will comfort your hearts.

Peace be with all the faithful, and the Grace of God be with all those who love the Lord sincerely. Amen.

Written from Rome in the year of Our Lord A.D. 62.

INTRODUCTION TO THE FIRST LETTER OF PAUL TO TIMOTHY

The erroneous concepts which surrounded the Letter to Timothy need now to be addressed. In the first instance, Paul wrote a second letter particularly to Ephesus and addressed personally to Timothy, in the year 66 when it was becoming apparent that the life and ministry of Paul in person was coming to a close.

Scholastic argument that this letter is more likely to have been written around the post-Paulian period of between 110 to 180 A.D., is in part correct. That which has been passed to posterity is in fact a deliberate reconstruction of the original letter, and in accord with Augustinian theory. The date of reconstruction is obscure, and Augustine lived some two hundred years later than the dates given. However, it is largely the theology of Augustine which has been adopted within the Catholic church down the ages and which has been responsible for serious error in statements attributed to Paul.

The rise of the Roman branch of Catholicism up to the point of influence created largely by Augustine, was based on a theology closer to the original. From the point in time of the advent of Augustinian theology, the church became more dependent upon the word of Augustine as " interpreter" of the meaning of Paul, than in fact what had been clearly stated by Paul himself. Indeed, history records Augustine as a second Paul. Much of the history of the Church of Rome can be traced back to this particular milestone. It is Augustinian dogma which changed the course of the British and destroyed to all intent and purpose, the true concepts of Christian Druidism (see following page). It is Augustinian theology which anathematized all that was considered pagan, even though the wisdoms of the ages were contained within the simple rituals of those condemned. It was Augustinian zealotism which created many of the sectarian brotherhoods, including those which bore the name " Paulist".

At the particular time in history, it was felt that Augustine was divinely inspired to take up the apostolic baton and continue with the work that Paul began. Tragically, the lapse in time created much that was hypothesis to fill in the gaps left by the scarcity of the written word. A large part of Augustinian theology stems from the inner search of the man himself – his excursions into Aristotelian and Platonic argument, and his inner quest for meaning. That quest was to colour the interpretation he overlighted, and has to a large extent, remained the base upon which the Church of Rome has steered its narrow course up to the present moment.

I now give the true Paulian rendition of what was said to Timothy as a personal message, with no apology to the opposition this creates in the current course of that same Church: for I repeat, these dogmas are erroneous, are a constraint upon the true evolutionary progress of the human race, and have nothing to do with the message of the Christ.

The reason why I use the expression "Christian Druid" (in actual fact I speak of the Celtic Christians) is that it is generally felt that Christianity spread from Rome and that eventually the Augustinian movement brought that Christianity to Britain. This is a very grave historical error because, in fact, the truth of the matter is that the Christian tradition existed in Britain long before the Augustinian Friars ever set foot in that land. And in fact, one of the great centers of the Universal Christ was among the British Celtic Druids – the great Universal principles of Christhood. I do not speak of Jesus, I speak of the Universal Christ. And Jesus Himself went to stay in Britain in order to learn what they had to teach. Therefore, I speak of the Christian Druidic tradition correctly in its true sense.

One might also state that historically, when the Roman forces of Caesar arrived on British shores, so impressed were some of the Roman generals with that king (they were called kings but were not kings in the sense that we know it now) known as Paracticus and Bordessier the woman, that they were given highly honorable treatment in Rome. Villas were set aside for them. They were not prisoners, persona non grata, as had been historically recorded. It was recognized that there was much that these people could teach and the Romans of that time were open and willing to hear; such was the Druidic Celtic tradition.

FIRST LETTER OF PAUL TO TIMOTHY
ELDER APPOINTED IN THE EPHESIAN COMMUNITY

1 *Paul, an apostle of Jesus Christ by the commandment of God our Saviour, and Lord Jesus Christ, which is our hope;*

2 *Unto Timothy, my own son in the faith: Grace, mercy and peace, from God our Father and Jesus Christ our Lord.*

3 *As I besought thee to abide still at Ephesus, when I went into Macedonia, that thou mightest charge some that they teach to another doctrine,*

4 *Neither give heed to fables and endless genealogies which minister questions, rather than godly edifying which is in faith; so do.*

5 *Now the end of the commandment is charity out of a pure heart, and of a good conscience, and of faith unfeigned:*

6 *From which some having swerved have turned aside unto vain jangling;*

7 *Desiring to be teachers of the law; understanding neither what they say, nor what they affirm.*

8 *But we know that the law is good, if a man use it lawfully;*

9 *Knowing this, that the law is not made for a righteous man, but for the lawless and disobedient, for the ungodly and for sinners, for unholy and profane, for murderers of fathers and murderers of mothers, for manslayers.*

10 *For whoremongers, for them that defile themselves with mankind, for menstealers, for liars, for perjured persons, and if there be any other thing that is contrary to sound doctrine;*

11 *According to the glorious gospel of the blessed God, which was committed to my trust.*

1 (1-2) From Paul, apostle of Christ by his command, with that message which is our source of hope to Timothy who is as a son to me through the faith. Grace, mercy and peace in God and through Christ our Lord.[1]

(3-7) When I urged you to remain in Ephesus, at the time of my leaving for Macedonia, it was in the trust that you would oversee the emergence of the community there, that it be founded on the truth, and not on falsehood. I urged that you pay no attention to the endless genealogies which tend to hold the true emergence back rather than encourage unfoldment. The cause of my orders came from a pure heart and true faith. Some have turned aside from this true faith and created a lot of dissent. In their desire to be teachers of what they consider the law, they do not really show an understanding either of what they say or what they affirm.

(8-11) We, however, are well aware that the True Law is good and, used correctly, edifies. Human laws had to be created for the unruly; for those who corrupt the very laws of Nature Herself: profanity, murder, matricide, homicide, whoremongering, cheats and liars, and anything else which is contrary to the true light and the Law which is set down in the message of Christ (and which has been given to me in trust).

First Timothy 1

12 And I thank Christ Jesus our Lord, who hath enabled me, for that he counted me faithful, putting me into the ministry;

13 Who was before a blasphemer, and a persecutor, and injurious; but I obtained mercy, because I did it ignorantly in unbelief.

14 And the grace of our Lord was exceeding abundant with faith and love which is in Christ Jesus.

15 This is a faithful saying and worthy of all acceptation, that Christ Jesus came into the world to save sinners; of whom I am chief.

16 Howbeit for this cause I obtained mercy that in me first Jesus Christ might shew forth all longsuffering for a pattern to them which should hereafter believe on him to life everlasting.

17 Now unto the King eternal, immortal, invisible, the only wise God, be honour and glory for ever and ever. Amen.

18 This charge I commit unto thee, son Timothy, according to the prophecies which went before on thee, that thou by them mightest war a good warfare;

19 Holding faith, and a good conscience; which some having put away concerning faith have made shipwreck:

20 Of whom is Hymenaeus and Alexander; whom I have delivered unto Satan, that they may learn not to blaspheme.

(12-17) I thank Christ that this trust was given to me, and that he saw fit to use me in this ministry, I who myself was an unbeliever, who persecuted his followers. These things I did in my ignorance. His grace and love changed all that, and is why I can state from experience that he came to this world to assist all those who walked in that same error, of whom I was the worst. In the same way that I received his mercy, all might attain. His life was a pattern on which we all must now mold our lives. Unto the King, immortal, invisible, the only wise One, be the glory for ever. Amen.

(18-20) This charge I therefore give you my son, Timothy, that you fight the good fight. Hold fast in faith and in good conscience (those who have made a shipwreck of their faith, now flounder). I pray, incidentally, for people like Hymenaeus and Alexander to whom I have given stern warning not to blaspheme.[3]

DISCOURSE CHAPTER ONE

1. Q: This is a general question that came from the person doing the Exegesis, Fred Gealy, in the *Interpreter's Bible** who states that most scholars feel that both First and Second Timothy and Titus were what they call "pastoral letters" written by a high person in the church, maybe a bishop or archbishop, to subordinate elders and deacons and that basically they are administrative letters about how to function as ministers, elders and all. They were coming to this conclusion partly because they felt that you did not write this letter; that it was done 150-180 A.D. You have answered that question in the fact that you certainly did write the original, but was it, from your viewpoint, something of an administrative letter?

    A: Yes, in actual fact, it was written for very much the reason that is stated. Knowing that my ministry was for, whatever reason, coming to an end (which I was well aware of at this time) I wrote to those of my strongest companions reminding them of what are the necessities. So, one might assume that at the time of re-translation, particularly during the Augustinian period, that body which had grown considerably into the church and notably the Church of Rome, would wish to write these texts in light of their own considerations of the needs contained within the body which was the church. I have no particular quarrel with anyone wishing to do this.

    My concerns arise around the fact that certain personal beliefs so much colored the truth as I had written it and has been the foundation upon which so much distortion has been built.

2. Q: It might be helpful to the reader to explain what was meant by "endless genealogies" in 1:4.

    A: One has to turn to the first two chapters of Genesis and Exodus in order to know what I speak about.

    Q: How was that a problem?

    A: Because of the fact that those endless genealogies were contained in the Old Testament recordings and were therefore used as precedence in order to continue the same kind of argumentation that supported the lineage of this bishop or that rather than supporting those who were truly apostles of God.

---

* Geary, Fred D., *Interpreter's Bible*, Vol. XI, p. 344
Abingdon-Cokesbury, Nashville, *1955.*

Discourse Chapter One continued:

3. Q: In 1:20, I see you have decided not to deliver Hymenaeus and Alexander to Satan as does the King James and the RSV. Were these elders who were distorting the faith and were you disciplining them?

    A: Yes they were distorting the faith and yes, we all tried to admonish them but how could Paul say that he delivered them to Satan? I have made the statement very clear: there is no other judge except that which is within the soul of each individual being. If we believe that, then it was not within the power of Paul to deliver anyone to that which man has called Satan. Each one can do that for herself or himself if they so choose. We chose to admonish that they follow the path of truth, especially anyone who wished to be thought of as an elder.

FIRST TIMOTHY[1] 2

2 I exhort therefore, that, first of all, supplications, prayers, intercessions, and giving of thanks, be made for all men;

2 For kings, and for all that are in authority; that we may lead a quiet and peaceable life in all godliness and honesty.

3 For this is good and acceptable in the sight of God our Saviour;

4 Who will have all men to be saved, and to come unto the knowledge of the truth.

5 For there is one God, and one mediator between God and men, the man Christ Jesus;

6 Who gave himself a ransom for all, to be testified in due time.

7 Whereunto I am ordained a preacher, and an apostle, (I speak the truth in Christ, and lie not;) a teacher of the Gentiles in faith and verity.

8 I will therefore that men pray everywhere, lifting up holy hands, without wrath and doubting.

9 In like manner also, that women adorn themselves in modest apparel, with shamefacedness and sobriety; not with braided hair, or gold, or pears, or costly array;

10 But (which becometh women professing godliness) with good works.

11 Let the woman learn in silence with all subjection.

12 But I suffer not a woman to teach nor to usurp authority over the man, but to be in silence.

13 For Adam was first formed, then Eve.

14 And Adam was not deceived, but the woman being deceived was in the transgression.

2 (1-10) I ask that you maintain your prayers for humanity, and for kings and all in authority that they may help us to lead a humble and peaceful life in accord with what we know to be acceptable to God – that life as demonstrated by Jesus the Christ, through whose example and sacrifice we may all come to knowledge of the Truth. The only way to attain to that Body which is of Christ is to become as He was. To testify to this truth, I became His minister to speak to the nations. I pray that men everywhere will accept without doubt and turn to God. I pray that women, equally, act with the same faith and sobriety. I ask them to be pure and modest. It is not necessary to adopt costly array and finery in order to become perfect in the sight of God. It is in the pursuit of goodness and charity and the doing of good for others.

(11-15) The true role of womankind as I see it, is to be helpmate and partner in the creation of the holy estate, the family. For this we have the example of Adam and Eve. Woman is the nurturer, following after the Divine Feminine Principle. That principle is passive, cooling and receptive. She is the teacher of the child. First she is the virgin and must retain her purity.[2] When she becomes the Mother and wife, she passes that tenderness and purity to her children. When her childbearing days are ended, she becomes the Wise One, whom the young turn to for help. This is the woman's true role. It is not the role to imitate the masculine. The masculine is the fire, heating, creative principle which is to be nurtured by the feminine counterpart. Thus Adam and Eve were the pillars of the Temple, as the masculine and feminine polarities

First Timothy 2

15 Notwithstanding she shall be saved in childbearing, if they continue in faith and charity and holiness with sobriety.

within the one androgynous Being. When Eve, the feminine, separates herself from that principle, and seeks the fruit of knowledge alone, she defies a universal condition.[3] Male and female were co-created to be the perfect reflection of one another.

DISCOURSE CHAPTER TWO

1. Q: You have certainly made some major and crucial changes in this section concerning women. I am wondering if we ought not maybe to have a section just on women in the appendix, partly because there is now a great interest in androgyny and a sharing of the nurturing role between husband and wife, particularly in more evolved couples. Also, there is a great concern on the part of women about the overpopulation of the planet so many women are opting not to have children and are moving right into professions, business and government. There is a different world now in some ways and perhaps we need to address modern women.

    A: In many ways it is now a different world, and of course, as we move higher upon the path of the evolutionary progress, that is even more the case. What I was attempting to do at this point is remind people of the truth concerning the feminine principle and concerning the masculine principle. I was not attempting to suggest that this is the only role to be played by woman. Indeed not. What I am suggesting, particularly in those days, was that one who made the choice to enter into the church as it was emerging would be better to remain unmarried. Those who wished to be married and have children, here is the essential role of womanhood. It is what one might call in modern terminology an either/or situation. The message I was endeavoring to put forth is that you cannot have it both ways, for they could not in those times. If you feel that this requires an appendix note, we will be glad to do that. However, my own personal feeling is that the subject of the appendix might be to discuss in more detail the feminine principle and the masculine principle and to see how that is now working out in the modern age as opposed to how it appeared two thousand years ago.

2. Q: In chapter two there is a statement about the fact that it is important for the woman to remain a virgin and retain her purity. I know that some feminists today might say "why isn't this admonition ever made to men? Isn't it just as important for the man to retain his purity and why is it seldom mentioned, it is always the woman who is being asked to do this?"

Discourse Chapter Two continued:

A: I totally agree with the women of today. It is just as important for the male to do that, especially if that male is intending to become a minister of God. It is vital. Perhaps the reason why this has not been made quite so clear, particularly in the re-translations, is that I have been dealing with the translation of the word as written. That is why I chose to work in this way, because by your questioning, we can then get down to the larger picture.

3. Q: In 2:14 there is a phrase saying that "woman defies a universal condition by seeking the fruit of knowledge alone." That will be a puzzling statement.

A: Without our becoming too enmeshed in a very lengthy esoteric discourse: the phrase was referring to the fact that woman alone defies an occult principle by seeking this knowledge on her own. It does not mean that knowledge alone defies the principle. First we clear that point. Although, in itself, knowledge alone, taken out of context, might also be said to do the same thing. That was why I was debating.

In order to answer this question, we have to deal with the basic formula of creation itself in which all things were created with the androgynous principle; that is, with the masculine and feminine contained within the whole. When we seek to separate that androgynous principle into two separate units, the male and the female, we must then also accept one as being a total mirror image of the other. We do not have here, on the one hand, a masculine principle which is sufficient in itself alone, nor, on the other hand, do we have the feminine principle which stands alone. Within the two there is, as you well know, the masculine and the feminine principle reflected on the outer surface by the female or male body; one being the mirror image of the other at the point of first emergence into form, into the material plane, to endeavor to acquire for itself knowledge that is not at the same time integral to, and participated in, with the other half of the unit.

Eve was moving away from the universal principle, albeit that she then went to her mirror counterpart with the information. But, the very act of setting aside the principle, as had been carefully enunciated for them by the Creator Spirit, the very act of so doing started that imbalance. It created the movement, as it were, in the scales from equilibrium and balance. That is why it was suggested that she had defied one of the universal laws. Does this sound clear? It is extremely difficult to go into one of the great universal laws in such confined space.

FIRST TIMOTHY 3

3 This is a true saying If a man desire the office of a bishop, he desireth a good work

2 A bishop then must be blameless, the husband of one wife, vigilant, sober, of good behaviour, given to hospitality apt to teach;

3 Not given to wine, no striker, not greedy of filthy lucre; but patient, not a brawler, not covetous;

4 One that ruleth well his own house, having his children in subjection with all gravity;

5 (For if a man know not how to rule his own house, how shall he take care of the church of God?)

6 Not a novice, lest being lifted up with pride he fall into the condemnation of the devil.

7 Moreover he must have a good report of them which are without; lest he fall into reproach and the snare of the devil.

8 Likewise must the deacons be grave, not doubletongued, not given to much wine, not greedy of filthy lucre;

9 Holding the mystery of the faith in a pure conscience.

10 And let these also first be proved; then let them use the office of a deacon, being found blameless.

11 Even so must their wives be grave, not slanderers, sober, faithful in all things.

12 Let the deacons be the husbands of one wife, ruling their children and their own houses well.

13 For they that have used the office of a deacon well purchase to themselves a good degree, and great boldness in the faith which is in Christ Jesus.

3 (1-7) In this context, there are certain observances when deciding on the officers within the community. If a man desires the office of elder, he is called to a good vocation. He must be without blame, married to one wife,[1] vigilant and of a sober nature. He must be a good teacher and hospitable. He must not be one who looks to financial reward, a drinker, or one who strikes out in anger, or one who covets. He must be seen to have his own house in order; and if he has children, he must be a good father. For if a man does not know how to keep his own house in order, he can scarcely be expected to teach others. Neither must he be new to the work. People who are novitiate cannot hold their own against temptations and distortions. This same would also be true for a woman desiring the office of elder.

(8-13) In the same way, all who hold office – deacons or other – must equally be measured. They must hold their office with a pure conscience. Let this be first proved, then let them hold the lesser office for awhile, and in it, carry themselves blamelessly. Their spouses also must be above reproach. Let all be seen to conduct their own families with the same purity that they would wish of the greater community under Christ.

First Timothy 3

14 These things write I unto thee, hoping to come unto thee shortly:

15 But if I tarry long, that thou mayest know how thou oughtest to behave thyself in the house of God, which is the church of the living God, the pillar and ground of the truth.

16 And without controversy great is the mystery of godliness: God was manifest in the flesh, justified in the Spirit, seen of angels, preached unto the Gentiles, believed on in the world, received up into glory.

(14-16) I wrote these things to you, hoping that I might come and see you soon; but in case this is not possible, so that you will know how to carry on that which is emerging, upon which will be founded the body of the Living God. The pillars that stand without controversy are great in the mystery of true Godliness. God was made manifest, justified wholly by the Spirit, in the company of the angels, believed by in the whole world and received into glory.

DISCOURSE CHAPTER THREE

1. Q: In 3:2 it says that people who are to be considered for elders should have had only one wife. What does this mean? If you are widowed, if you had a pagan wife before, etc. what does that mean?

   A: One has to recall that Paul, in this instance, was speaking from the point of view of the most pure situation. His attempt was to keep the young communities of that time as clear and as pure as possible. He remembered in particular the words of Jesus Himself, Who stated "those whom God hath joined, let no man put asunder." Jesus was very clear in His statement that one husband, one wife during any one lifetime was to be desired. This was a situation with which Paul most definitely agreed. If a person should become widowed and desire to remarry, no one had anything against that contingency, save that such a person should perhaps devote his time to the pursuit of family life rather than the church. For those who wished to become elders in the community of the faithful, it was infinitely preferable to be able to set the example of the kind of purity which Christ Himself required and which Paul attempted to emulate. In saying this there is no judgement; it is simply that a statement was made to admonish those who wished to be example to others; be pure, be as Jesus required.

FIRST TIMOTHY 4

4 Now the Spirit speaketh expressly, that in the later times some shall depart from the faith, giving heed to seducing spirits, and doctrines of devils;

2 Speaking lies in hypocrisy; having their conscience seared with a hot iron;

3 Forbidding to marry, and commanding to abstain from meats, which God hath created to be received with thanksgiving of them which believe and know the truth.

4 For every creature of God is good, and nothing to be refused, if it be received with thanksgiving:

5 For it is sanctified by the word of God and prayer.

6 If thou put the brethren in remembrance of these things, thou shalt be a good minister of Jesus Christ, nourished up in the words of faith and of good doctrine, whereunto thou hast attained,

7 But refuse profane and old wives' fables, and exercise thyself rather unto godliness.

8 For bodily exercise profiteth little: but godliness is profitable unto all things, having promise of the life that now is, and of that which is to come.

9 This is a faithful saying and worthy of all acceptation.

10 For therefore we both labour and suffer reproach, because we trust in the living God, who is the Saviour of all men, specially of those that believe.

11 These things command and teach.

12 Let no man despise thy youth; but be thou an example of the believers, in word, in conversation, in charity, in spirit, in faith, in purity,

13 Till I come, give attendance to reading, to exhortation, to doctrine.

14 Neglect not the gift that is in thee, which was given thee by prophecy, with the laying on of the hands of the presbytery.

4 (1-5) My inner Spirit tells me that in the days to come many shall be drawn away from the faith, giving ear to false concepts. They will speak hypocrisy, having their inner self scorched as though with a hot iron; forbidding people to marry, and commanding people to abstain from the very source of food which God has provided for us to be taken with thanksgiving. Every creation of God is good and clean, and all things must be accepted in gratitude, for all things can be made holy by the Spirit, through prayer.

(6-10) If you remind people of this, you will be a true minister sustained by the truth which you have been taught. Refuse to act from old wives tales and heresay, rather use your own discretion. Bodily exercise does not do too much for you unless you also keep a pure Spirit. We know these things and have been subjected to much reproach because we trust in the Living God who is one with all men as we believe.

(11-16) Commend and teach these things: Do not let anyone be put off by your youth; and set an example to all in your conversations, your love, spirit and faith. Do not neglect any of the gifts which were increased in you at the time of the laying on of hands of the brotherhood.

First Timothy 4

15 Meditate upon these things; give thyself wholly to them; that thy profiting may appear to all.

16 Take heed unto thyself, and unto the doctrine; continue in them: for in doing this thou shalt both save thyself and them that hear thee.

Meditate on all these things, giving yourself to them totally, that your strength might be apparent to all. Listen to your own inner voice, and obey, continuing in the wisdoms. In doing this, you will come through life yourself and be great help to others.

DISCOURSE CHAPTER FOUR

1. Q: This question is in reference partly to chapter 4, but again partly to the whole letter. Was there a particular heresy that Timothy and the others were having to deal with? *The Interpreter's Bible** mentions three possible heresies: a Jewish Christian heresy, Gnostic or the Marcianite Heresy. Is there a particular one they were having to deal with?

   A: We can first of all discard the Gnostic heresy, because there was no such thing in Paul's time. The Gnostic community was quite considerably post Paulian, I believe, or at least the use of that word was post Paulian. In answer to the question, in the main, yes indeed, there were many heresies, not merely two or three. The world at that time was abundant with cults of many, many kinds, not all by any means having to do with the mysteries of Christ. There is no need for me to elaborate upon them here, but merely to say, yes indeed, there was so far as we are concerned, truth; that was the message which Christ had given; beware of all other.

---

*Ibid, p. 352

FIRST TIMOTHY 5

5 Rebuke not an elder, but intreat him as a father; and the younger men as brethren;

2 The elder women as mothers; the younger as sisters, with all purity.

3 Honour widows that are widows indeed.

4 But if any widow have children or nephews, let them learn first to shew piety at home, and to requite their parents: for that is good and acceptable before God.

5 Now she that is a widow indeed, and desolate, trusteth in God, and continueth in supplications and prayers night and day.

6 But she that liveth in pleasure is dead while she liveth.

7 And these things give in charge, that they may be blameless.

8 But if any provide not for his own, and specially for those of his own house, he hath denied the faith, and is worse than an infidel.

9 Let not a widow be taken into the number under threescore years old, having been the wife of one man,

10 Well reported of for good works; if she have brought up children, if she have lodged strangers, if she have washed the saints' feet, if she have relieved the afflicted, if she have diligently followed every good wor.k

11 But the younger widows refuse: for when they have begun to wax wanton against Christ, they will marry;

12 Having damnation, because they have cast off their first faith.

13 And withal they learn to be idle, wandering about from house to house; and not only idle, but tattlers also and busybodies, speaking things which they ought not.

14 I will therefore that the younger women marry, bear children, guide the house, give none occasion to the adversary to speak reproachfully.

5 (1-2) Do not rebuke a fellow elder, but look on those older in years than yourself as spiritual fathers, and the younger ones as brothers. The women elders shall be as mothers to you, and the younger will be sisters. Look on them in all purity.

(3-16) Honour those who are widows and help them if they are alone. But those who have families (children, nephews, nieces) let them teach the true way in their homes, for that is most real in God's sight.

Those widows who are alone, may they trust totally in God and pray continually, and not destroy themselves by reverting to lesser pursuits. Remember that people who do not make provision for their own family are denying the very faith by which they are purporting to live. If a widow wishes to become an elder, let her be above sixty and the wife of only one man. She should be well known for her good life, whether she has brought up children, and been good to strangers, if she has washed the feet of the faithful, if she has helped to relieve the sick and been diligent in these things. If the applicant be a younger widow, then first test their resolve by refusal. If they truly wish to become elders, they will conduct themselves accordingly. If not, they will plan to remarry instead.[1] (I say this because it is the primary nature and purpose of womanhood to marry, to nurture husband and family, and to beget children to be raised in the faith.)

First Timothy 5

15 For some are already turned aside after Satan.

16 If any man or woman that believeth have widows, let them relieve them, and let not the church be charged; that it may relieve them that are widows indeed.

17 Let the elders that rule well be counted worthy of double honour, especially they who labour in the word and doctrine.

18 For the scripture saith, Thou shalt not muzzle the ox that treadeth out the corn. And, The labourer is worthy of his reward.

19 Against an elder receive not an accusation, but before two or three witnesses.

20 Then that sin rebuke before all, that others also may fear.

21 I charge thee before God, and the Lord Jesus Christ, and the elect angels, that thou observe these things without preferring one before another, doing nothing by partiality.

22 Lay hands suddenly on no man, neither be partaker of other men's sins: keep thyself pure.

23 Drink no longer water, but use a little wine for thy stomach's sake and thine often infirmities.

24 Some men's sins are open beforehand, going before to judgement; and some men they follow after.

25 Likewise also the good works of some are manifest beforehand; and they that are otherwise cannot be hid.

(17-25) Let all who become elders of the community be without blame, for thus they have double honor; that of the faith, and that of the world. Also, be sure that they receive due wages, for all are worthy to receive compensation for what they do. Do not hear any complaint against the elders unless supported by at least two witnesses. People who are seen to be in error should be publicly rebuked so that others shall learn from this. I charge you before God and Christ and the angelic host elect, that you observe all these things faithfully, and in total impartiality. Keep yourselves totally pure, and do not be affected by the actions of others. (Note to you personally: for the sake of that stomach problem which I hear you have, be careful what water you drink. You would be better to drink a little wine where you are unsure).

DISCOURSE CHAPTER FIVE

1. Q: In 5:3-16 in the section on widows: were there a lot of widows? Our commentators in the *Interpreter's Bible*[*] believe there were and there was maybe even an Order of Widows and even an inundation in numbers and an attempt to set standards that would limit the numbers.

    A: Yes indeed there were numerous widows: a legacy from the many wars in Rome, in Greece, in the Middle East; wherever one might turn one would see the result which has ever been the human case of war. And certainly at that time in history there were many, many women who had lost husbands in disputes and wars. Yes indeed one might say that there was a sisterhood created for mutual support, just as the modern church might create such at the end of a war where it was found that, for whatever reason, there was a preponderance of women left alone without the means of support. Then it was up to the body of the faithful to assist those women and to provide for their support. What one might now call deaconesses were, in fact, appointed in order to assist and help. Some of the widows would have young families and others would be at a point in life when their families had moved on – the support being more necessary for the younger. Is that sufficient?

---

[*] Ibid., p. 435

FIRST TIMOTHY 6

6 *Let as many servants as are under the yoke count their own masters worthy of all honour, that the name of God and his doctrine be not blasphemed.*

2 And they that have believing masters, let them not despise them, because they are brethren; but rather do them service, because they are faithful and beloved partakers of the benefit. These things teach and exhort.

3 If any man teach otherwise, and consent not to wholesome words, even the words of our Lord Jesus Christ, and to the doctrine which is according to godliness;

4 He is proud, knowing nothing, but doting about questions and strifes of words, whereof cometh envy, strife, railings, evil surmisings,

5 Perverse disputings of men of corrupt minds, and destitute of the truth, supposing that gain is godliness: from such withdraw thyself

6 But godliness with contentment is great gain.

7 For we brought nothing into this world and it is certain we can carry nothing out.

8 And having food and raiment let us be therewith content.

9 But they that will be rich fall into temptation and a snare, and into many foolish and hurtful lusts, which drown men in destruction and perdition.

10 For the love of money is the root of all evil: which while some coveted after, they have erred from the faith, and pierced themselves through with many sorrows.

11 But thou, O man of God, flee these things; and follow after righteousness, godliness, faith, love, patience, meekness.

12 Fight the good fight of faith, lay hold on eternal life, whereunto thou art also called and hast professed a good profession before many witnesses.

6 (1-5) Let all who are of the servant classes consider their masters honorable, and if they be of the faith, let that be honored. Do not despise them for this, but rather, do them service because they are beloved partakers of the teachings which benefit mankind. If any speak otherwise, then they come from their own ego and do not know what they say. You will find these people to be discontented, for godliness with contentment is a great asset.

(6-11) We came into the world with nothing and we cannot take anything out. Therefore, if we have food and clothing, let us be thankful. Those who are rich fall into great temptation through material possessions. Love of money and possessions is rooted in evil and is the cause of many sorrows. People who serve God cast off these things and follow only righteousness, godliness, faith, love, patience and meekness.

(12-21) Fight the good fight of faith and lay hold on life eternal. You were called to this and accepted the calling before many witnesses.

First Timothy 6

13 I give thee charge in the sight of God, who quickeneth all things, and before Christ Jesus, who before Pontius Pilate witnessed a good confession;

14 That thou keep this commandment without spot, unrebukeable, until the appearing of our Lord Jesus Christ:

15 Which in his times he shall shew, who is the blessed and only Potentate, the King of kings, and Lord of lords;

16 Who only hath immortality, dwelling in the light which no man can approach unto; whom no man hath seen, nor can see: to whom be honour and power everlasting. Amen.

17 Charge them that are rich in this world, that they be not high-minded, nor trust in uncertain riches, but in the living God, who giveth us richly all things to enjoy;

18 That they do good, that they be rich in good works, ready to distribute, willing to communicate;

19 Laying up in store for themselves a good foundation against the time to come, that they may lay hold on eternal life.

20 O Timothy, keep that which is committed to thy trust, avoiding profane and vain babblings, and oppositions of science falsely so called:

21 Which some professing have erred concerning the faith. Grace be with thee. Amen.

I charge you before God and Christ even as Christ before Pontius Pilot made his witness without blemish. That Spirit alone is immortal which dwells in God's Light, whereunto no mortal can approach, or has seen. Charge all who have wealth and possessions of the world that they trust not in their possessions; they would be better to distribute everything to the needy and live on the riches that one can enjoy in God alone, and that they do good in the world by communicating and distribution. Thus, they lay up in store a good foundation against the times to come they put their trust in life eternal.

Beloved Timothy, hold fast the trust which is given to thee and Grace be with you. Amen

Written from Rome in the year of Our Lord 66 A.D.[1]

DISCOURSE CHAPTER SIX

1. Q: People all over the world are going to want to know what happened next. There is the reference in Second Timothy that many deserted you at your first court appearance, but there has been much speculation of what happened to Paul. Can you speak to that?

    A: Perhaps the notion of desertion came out of the letter which I have added as an appendage to the First Timothy; by the way, that was how I wished it to appear. The original came as an addition, in short, having written the first letter to Timothy in which I still entertained the hope of being able to visit. When it became very obvious that that would not be the case, I then added an urgent message " I shall not be able to come to you, please try to come to me." There were many things that I wished to speak about in person rather than in the written word.

    My dear friends did not desert; they went about their business. And if that business – which was the business of Christ – took them to other lands far away, that was how it should be. When I wrote saying that people had dispersed and Timothy please come if possible in person, that which was stated should not be regarded as a plaintive cry; it was rather a statement that it is imperative that there are things I leave with you which cannot be written down, so that somebody knows the Truth and can continue to spread the message of the Truth while yet Paul was still there to speak it.

    Paul, the man, was aware of the future, to some extent. He did have "psychic powers" as you would call them, and was able to commune with those who were beyond this Earthly dimension. He had made a lifetime study, from the point of time of his encounter on the Damascus road, of the occult and esoteric principles. As an initiate at that time, it was necessary to pass on the spoken word to those who were of a sufficient degree of initiation. When he said "Only Luke remains" the indication was of the initiate brotherhood, only Luke remains. So let us set aside any thought that this was a plaintive cry for it was far from that.

    The initiate Paul, knowing that his life was coming to a close, looked forward with peace to its continuation elsewhere. That is all. Is there anything else?

    Q: I presume we can make the assumption that in the court of Nero Paul was found guilty and that he was executed?

    A: That is correct.

Discourse Chapter Six continued:

Q: What year was that?

A: In the year 67. As it is written. Yes indeed.

Q: I was curious about second Timothy because so much of what we now have was left out; but you really see it as an appendage to first Timothy and should it be added on that way?

A: To clear this completely, the second letter of Timothy, per se, was not written by me. As it is seen in the New Testament, it is almost in entirety written by others. What in fact I did, as previously stated, was to write the letter addressed to the Ephesians and Timothy in particular. When it became very clear that I would not be allowed to travel, I sent an urgent postscript which was, in fact, addressed to Timothy alone, not to anyone else; that is the difference. And that postscript is a part, in truth, of what is now called the second letter to Timothy; in effect, an urgent message saying 'Timothy, I shall not after all be able to come to you, please try to come here if you can, as quickly as possible." It is not therefore, in my opinion, necessary to re-transcribe the whole letter because much of that letter is repetition of statements made many times elsewhere.

POSTSCRIPT TO THE FIRST LETTER OF PAUL TO TIMOTHY (SECOND LETTER TO TIMOTHY)

(In actuality in the nature of a few additional notes to the first letter. Written when it became obvious that Paul would never be likely to visit Ephesus further.)

I had greatly desired to see thee, being mindful of your sorrow to beg you, hold fast. Many in Asia have turned away from me, among whom are Phygellus and Hermogenes. May the Lord be merciful to the family of Onesiphorus who often came to nourish me and was never ashamed of my imprisonment. When in Rome, he continually sought me out. I well recall how often he was helpful to me in Ephesus.

In these last days there will be troubled times. Men are self loving, disobedient, proud and blasphemous, traitorous and highly opinionated. Even as Jannes and Jambres withstood Moses, so too now do some repudiate the true faith (and those who seek to speak it). I have endured all these persecutions in order to maintain the teaching of that true faith and so far, the Lord has sustained and delivered me.

I charge you therefore, continue to teach the true word, for the time shall come when people will not want to listen or endure the truth. Try to come here to be with me for awhile, for now even Demas has had to leave me and gone back to Thessalonica. Crescens has gone off to Galatia, and of course, Titus is now in Dalmatia. This leaves only Luke who is still with me. Please try to bring Mark with you, for I want to pass on much regarding the ministry.

I have sent Tychicus to Ephesus bearing these messages. The cloak that I left at Troas with Carpus, please bring with you when you come. Also the parchments and books.

It is true that Alexander the coppersmith wrought me much evil – may he be rewarded accordingly. Be wary of him. I trust before God that the wrong done to me might not be laid to their charge. Nevertheless, the Lord Himself is ever with me and will keep me from all harm.

Please salute Priscilla and Aquila and the family of Onesiphorus. Erastus stayed at Corinth, and I had to leave Trophimus at Miletum, as he is sick. Try your best to get here before winter. Eubulus sends his greetings, also Pudens and Linus, Claudia and all the Brethren. May the Lord keep your spirit. Amen.

POSTSCRIPT

This, then, brings us to the end of the re-translated letters. We have fully covered those things which I personally wrote.

Exceptions to this are the short letters to Philemon and to Titus. I do not propose to address these. The letter to Philemon was merely a cover note to accompany his manservant whom I was returning to him with the request that he be treated kindly, as my son in Christ. The letter to Titus was written by me, and to one who occupied a place in the world dearly loved to me both in the time of Paul, and still down through the ages. However, the message contained therein is so similar to the phrases given to Timothy that they do not warrant repetition.

Therefore adieu. And now, may the Peace of God which passes all human understanding, keep our hearts and minds in the knowledge and love of God which is in Christ Jesus. And may the blessings of God the Father, God the Son, and God the Holy Ghost our Mother, keep us all in their light and love for ever. Amen, amen and amen.

APPENDIX A
ISSUES OF SEXUALITY

The issues of sexuality are ones that have been troublesome to humanity down the ages and are no less so in modern times. In order to more clearly understand these issues, we must go back into the depths of the "space/time continuum", for understanding may only there be found.

All that exists is energy. All that is energy is divided into many fields of force. All energy vibrates to a given frequency which pulsates throughout the given "field". Within those frequencies exist that which has come to be termed "masculine energy" and "feminine energy" – positive frequency and negative frequency. All that ever was, is and shall be, became so through the interaction of these frequencies – universes, galaxies, nebulae, constellations, solar families, down through the smaller solar families (of which the particular family to which earth belongs, is infinitesimally small). Stepped down yet again, the same pattern exists on each single planetary body and each of the integral lives that occupy any one sphere, be they animal, vegetable, mineral or humanoid.

This is not to say that the same actual frequencies occur everywhere, for the many regions have adopted and adapted to many pitches of vibration. However, bottom line of all of the many frequency levels and field forces is the masculine/feminine, positive/negative polarity. Without this energy nothing can ever be "created". The one is the attractive impulse, the other the repulsive (in correct usage of that term). In all life there is the inbreath, the attractive, and the outbreath, the repulsive. One might therefore state that the great thought form, the Godhead, comprises the Divine Universal Masculine and Feminine in equilibrium, working as one breath.

In accord with the many ancient texts that which "existed in the void" (or chaos) pulsated, breathed, if you will, in and out. The extension of the outbreathing, the repulsive, the feminine part of that duality issued forth activated intelligence which became the third aspect of Unity. In other words, the Great Mind and the Universal Heart, acting together as one, created a further force. This then is a rather simplistic explanation of what has become accepted as the Trinity. The error is in the thought that the Trinity is an all male unity.

When the fiat went forth "Let us create in our own image . . . "that which was created conformed to those same principles and became the Universal Law. Universal Law is simply the ways in which all that is throughout the many universes operates according to a set of givens that have evolved out of the initial response to that fiat.

Let us now turn to the specifics concerning evolution upon earth, for this sphere is unique: unique in the sense that during the course of aeons of time, humanity became clothed in a gross, fleshly body and the separation of the sexes occurred. Procreation only became possible through the sexual act which was a restricted practice of animal life. ("Animal" is used here in a broad sense, for it includes certain of the insect species, birds, marine life as well as human.) Humanity has passed through a long physical evolution while at the same time moving through a parallel spiritual involution. Down through past millennia, many avatars and great teachers have returned in the attempt to set the course of spiritual evolution back toward acknowledgement of the essential Divinity within all.

In that Divinity there is no separation of the sexes. The masculine aspect and the feminine aspect are totally equal in accord with those principles stated earlier. It matters not at all whether the Soul in Being is occupying a male or a female body. Each has the dual aspect fully in balance. In order to retain that balance each must recognize that the masculine force and the feminine force have their different areas of operation. It is the work of the masculine to energize. The masculine is fire and therefore heating, activating, donating and expressing the force of the will to be. It is the work of the feminine to preserve. The feminine is water, cooling, receptive, nurturing. The feminine expresses active intelligence, the desire to preserve. When the two are in perfect balance, the expressions that come therefrom are also perfect, for we speak of divine co-creation, not physical pro-creation.

It is this holy estate to which all of humanity ultimately aspires. Within the operative work of self realization there must eventually come the time when each soul will recognize this essential truth. All of creation essentially works in pairs of opposites. After the separation of the sexes there was an instantaneous (automatic, if you will) coming together in pairs within the one being; one expressing the outward male form, the other the female, even though each was fully balanced in the integrated masculine/feminine essence. Since that event, it has been the work on the higher planes to guide and offer assistance to the lesser planes. It is usual for the opposite in each "pair" to exist on a different plane, yet to be constantly in attune, monitoring the other, operating in the denser frequency of the lower planes (earth) *.

In the evolutionary process the human being has passed through many stages. The earlier civilizations, remembering that the divine source of their existence was the great "Mother", created an overbearing attentiveness to the "Goddess" and cults to the many aspects of the Universal Mother developed to the great detriment of progress. The male was denigrated and imbalance was the result. Thus, nature attempted to set the balance right and the pendulum swung too far to the opposite. The patriarchal took over and womankind in turn was denigrated. Again, imbalance. In this modern era humanity attempts to turn back to correct the lack of balance and to attain full equality between the masculine and the feminine principle.

---

* We need to state here that the higher self usually represents the opposite sex of the lessor or physical body. The balancing is done on the higher planes and humans have ever, after the separation, sought the balance of oneness.

It may well be that some men prefer to run the home and rear the children and some women prefer to be in business, profession or artisan fields. There is nothing at all wrong with any of that. Whoever is doing the job is worthy of their hire, in full recompense, whether male or female. However, this only sets the physical field. It is the deeper spiritual level that requires more attentive thought. Both the sexes should accept what are the essential principles of the masculine and the feminine and then seek to attain true balance of those energies within each individual self.

Within the evolutionary process the institution of marriage was created in order to retain the universal quality of the family unit. Again, this conforms to the Natural Law of the universe. Within the family it is the woman who is the teacher of the young. She is the example of love, compassion and nurturance. It is the male's role to provide stability, motivation and dependability. Even when in modern times roles are, to some extent, reversed, these principles do still finally apply.

The actual act of legalization of marriage per se is not, however, a universal principle. It is strictly man-made for moral purposes. It is the motive and desire for two people to come together and remain together that is important. The only reason that is tolerable to the spiritual life for two people so joined to separate is when it becomes quite impossible to stay together through sheer incompatibility. In which case it were better for those separated to remain single for the rest of that life. Again, there are some exceptions, especially when people recognize past life patterns and desire to work and be with that one again in order to work out karma.

Basically, promiscuous exchange of partners is to be avoided. No individual may gain through another that which is not possible within self. The partner merely is a reflection of that which is in self. Therefore, if one is not happy with a partner, the odds are that one will not be happy with any other.

Homosexuality has been fully covered in earlier discourses and need not be dwelt upon at length again. It is only in rare cases that such practice can be said to be physically determined. All else is a deviation from the evolutionary path and must eventually be worked through if the practitioner desires to attain to the full life of Spirit. This is not to say, however, that these people should be ostracized or condemned, either legally, professionally or personally. We all have those things within our being that we are dealing with to greater or lesser degree. All are equal in the sight of God. All is of God. Let there be no error here.

The promiscuous sex practice has no part in spiritual growth and must one day be contained. Mark me here – sex and its function is natural and part of one's being. We do not advocate asceticism for all. However, if humanity can grasp that the giving of one to another in this way is part of a divine act of consummation between those who commit together for life, then sexual immorality will disappear. All of the ills which are brought through sexual problems (indeed the whole issue of human sexuality) may be totally resolved when materialism of all kinds falls away and true yearning for the things of the spirit takes over in the heart.

APPENDIX B
THE BODY OF CHRIST

It is very difficult for the mind to grasp the meaning of one-ness, at-one-ment. Try for a moment to visualize a human body and to see in imagination that body becoming so vast that the dense form becomes expanded into seeming space. Or if you will, look into the starry heavens at night and see the Milky Way. Realize that what you are seeing is just a narrow edge of a vast body. Yet, each single sun or star and each collective family of planets is a part of that vast body. What is thought of as "space" between allows for expansion and contraction of the elements within that great body, yet it is not really "space" for the component parts of the body are still contained.

There are worlds within worlds, within worlds, down to the mere atom; and on the other end of the scale, one becomes a vast galactic universe. Each individual cell or molecule within that formation, responds to and is linked with the chain of other cells or molecules that together form a large unit.

Cells are considered to have individuated ability. Each cell within the human body has "memory" of all that comprises the whole. Within that body there is a constant sloughing off of dead cells, and replacement with new. Were a live cell to be separated however, it could not exist for long without the host body. These facts are also true of galactic "cells" be they stars, or be they constellations. In all, there is constant flux and change, yet each plays a significant role in the body of the whole.

In this same way, understand that the individualized being which now accepts full responsibility for selfhood was once part of a group soul and still functions to some extent within the confines of the "cellular memory" that was part of that larger body. All that ever existed in our own galactic universe, stepped down from the Great Heavenly Being which is the Creator. Each and every soul is therefore part of that Originating Spirit from whence it took life and may quite literally say that he or she is "part of the Body of Christ".

That Originating Source, First Cause, gave rise to the darkness and to the light equally, and regards both equally as part of The One. This has nothing to do with human emotions. Emotionalism is known only on planet earth. Soul incarnates on this Earth in order to "feel" and through the emotional side of earth, which is Her waters, discover the self, how to work through and become the master of emotions that destroy. It is therefore an inherent part of all initiation toward self-realization or self-mastery to come to that point when negative thought and the challenging energy of the emotional body are left behind.

APPENDIX C
JUDGEMENT AND KARMA

Karma is the word given to the law of cause and effect by the eastern traditions. There is a great deal of misunderstanding or misconception about the very meaning of that word. Indeed, there is so much, that it is not easy to clarify all of that misconception in one short statement.

At the point in evolution when the gift of free will was given, the law of cause and effect was also established as a necessary balance to that which otherwise would have given rise to a seriously unbalanced condition. As humanity evolves, it becomes more and more clear that as one sows, so shall one reap. Few there are even yet, who understand that every "thought" of whatever kind, reflects immediately back to the thinker. Since words follow thought, and action follows from this, it should be clear that actions and words, which are the result of the initial "thought" are the sole responsibility of the mind which gives rise to those thoughts. Be well assured that whatever one thinks of another – that thought will come right back to the thinker. Be not deluded either, into thinking that this ends when the present life ends. That which is the strongest desire in this life will present itself even more firmly in the next realm of endeavor. As man thinketh, so is man. This is true for all eternity; and evolution therefore allows the slow and steady grasp of acquired wisdom in order to discover how to think, in order to become.

Nothing, no-one outside of self, can change this inexorable working out of that very precise law. There are along the way those who assist. When one passes from the school of earth, one still leans back to help and assist those still progressing along the way. When soul leaves the physical body, such a one meets with angelic and soulic guides who assist in the assessment and give support in the choices made that will take the pilgrim into the next area of endeavor. There is *no judgement, save that which each individualized being makes about self.* The law of karma is not to be confused with the law of retribution, for it has nothing to do with "punishment", being a totally automatic reaction to all action – purely and simply.

So much has already been written upon this particular subject, that it is not my desire to go into deeper detail. Those who wish may refer to other sources or to my own words in *Seasons of the Spirit* (see bibliography).

APPENDIX D
VICARIOUS ATONEMENT

In quite a real sense, this subject is one with the law of cause and effect, and will to some extent perhaps, more fully explain karma.

The law of cause and effect basically is inherent in the constitution of matter itself and the interaction between atomic units. Liberation from karma comes only when the individualized being is no longer subject to or enslaved by the vibrations of gross matter. In this, it is a fact that all is one. That which affects one, affects all. Every human atom is subject to forces that go far beyond the individual consciousness; and the individual may find himself or herself in situations which were not of self-making, and from which there is no apparent escape.

In the earlier stages attention is upon the physical body, and the working of animal instincts – only faintly at this point are the subtler bodies able to respond. In the later stages the desire body allows thought to aspire to higher purposes. At this point intelligent choice is available to the individual. At the third stage the law works through the mental nature and the being becomes more fully aware of the nature of the law of cause and effect. This is the point when the being accepts fuller responsibility, not merely for self but for all life. One becomes more aware that indeed, what affects self, affects all other forms of matter.

In this very real sense, in becoming an "elder brother or sister" one takes on the task of speeding up the evolutionary process for those who are still on the lower rungs of the ladder. By the very purity of thought, word and deed of the more illumined being, the gross vibrations may be "lifted up" into a higher frequency. Any great act of pure love indeed does lift vast areas of matter into that higher level. This is what was meant when it was said that the Christ in the body of Jesus, "Took upon Himself the sins of the world" and through His redemptions, the world was "saved".

In no way does this excuse the individualized being from the working out of the law of cause and effect within each being's own field. Even the Lord Jesus can be said to have expiated his own errors, as well as lifting the vibration of the whole earth. So great was that sacrifice, that a new level was reached across the planet, which cannot be retracted despite the many events of great evil which have also occurred since that time. Every time one being pauses, and in great love pours out that sincere compassion from the heart for another part of the created world, be it mineral, plant or animal; a vicarious atonement occurs which lifts the frequency of a vast field into a higher level.

APPENDIX E
THE JUDAS PRINCIPLE

I (Sananda)*, shall personally address the issue which has come into the awareness on both inner and outer levels; that concerning the Judas controversy.

A great deal of controversy has arisen around the gospels, as eventually set down, simply because *they were not written at the actual enactment time.* Any story which has to rely on the memory of even a witness there present, is not clear for long afterwards (and would be even less so, were the writer not personally present at the event). These are facts well known to you. When stories are collected second, third hand and more, they are extremely suspect, as being subject to interpolation and transliteration. Even my brother of the White Lodge (Hilarion), in assisting the Temple of the People, did not properly clarify this issue, because he addressed the principle of betrayal without at that time, clarifying which Judas it was who afterward hanged himself. Indeed there is a deep issue here which must be addressed and finally understood.

Jeshua ben Joseph, also called Emmanuel, being interpreted as God with Us, had known for a very long time what His ministry truly was and what the final outcome would be. The Essene school of the ageless wisdoms had provided His early childhood with strong support. Certain members of the "inner core" of initiates prepared by the Essene school were appointed to assist in the events. The only way they could so assist was by their own quiet, inner strength and by the maintenance of total dedication, yet absolute detachment. There could be no emotional involvement for any show of such would project the very strong negative vibrations onto the body of The Christ in Jeshua, who in that vulnerable physical condition might have failed the task by succumbing to the projected fear.

In a force field created within the Do-Deca-Hedron the ten plus two are contained. The "two" are the polarities creating oppositional dynamic tension. Among the twelve carefully chosen to be close disciples and apostles each bore the sign of the zodiac which assisted and created the specific characteristics. During the ministry of Jeshua there had been many times when I had to chastise Peter because of certain very marked tendencies to a pattern of stubbornness, exaggerated by the personality which, on the one hand assumed a strong desire toward leadership, while on the other hand, negated abilities through fear. The now famous stories of Jeshua encouraging Peter to come to him on the water, and the calming of the storm and netting of the fish, were but demonstrations to Peter of his need to move beyond certain limitations.

---

* It came to our attention that in *Teachings of the Temple* Hilarion had given the traditional version of Judas in contrast to this work. We asked Sananda, as Jesus is known in the spiritual realms, and received this answer.

During the time of ministry Peter never did, and yes, My words were indeed expressed with regret when I uttered the admonition, "Thou are Peter – Petra – the 'Rock' upon which a church shall be built in My Name." It was indeed toward Peter that I also looked during the Last Supper when the words were stated with sadness, "The hand of one who shall betray me is upon this table with mine." To silence the argument of leadership succession, John had been named. To Peter I said: "Simon, Simon, you do have a devil in you that leads you astray and I continually pray for you." When Peter denied that he would betray (or be disloyal) to his friend and Master, I gently rebuked that denial. His indeed was betrayal and a disloyal act which came again from fear – ever a human frailty to be conquered with love.

What of the other betrayal which has been made so much more of? We recall that I stated earlier, there were two negative aspects in the twelve which created the polarity. Judas had indeed a problem arising from the method of the ministry. He was unable at that time to accept the necessity that one can only teach by example, not by words alone. Words alone are of no consequence unless the speaker of them lives by those things which such a one attempts to disseminate. Having passed through rigorous training in many lives and eventually passing through the great schools, Emmanuel, God with Us, called Jeshua, was able to offer His prepared vehicle to receive the Christ, who from then on was Lord. At that point, and from then on, Jeshua was no longer Jeshua, but fully Emmanuel indeed. From that time he was "in" the world, but no longer "of" it in any way. All worldly things were set aside, passed away, and this included following the way of renunciation of all worldly goods. They were sold to feed the poor.

This caused much consternation in Judas, my brother, who failed to see the need for this. In long discussions the Christ, through Me, remonstrated with him. As a scribe Judas kept the record of all the teachings first hand. These were later given to the Essene school to keep safely.

Judas Iscariot was well aware of his role and had been for some considerable time prior to the trial and conviction. It is quite true that he had no need of silver, and in fact, took none. The Sanhedrin sent many of their people to be in the crowds where Emmanuel spoke in order to hear what was said and to challenge the speaker of them. Few there were in that time and place who could write anything down. The crowds were local peasant farmers and fisher people, tradespeople and a few soldiers. Of the Pharisees and Sadducees there were scribes appointed to the Sanhedrin. One of them, Judas, son of Simon, was often in the group of lesser disciples (not the twelve). Shortly before the final event and subsequent arraignment, this Judas approached Iscariot for a very specific reason. He had noticed that My brother and I often had strong argument on certain matters, particularly with regard to the role. Judas often expressed the feeling that I should assert authority and power as the Messiah. The Christed One did what He knew He must.

After it became known that the Christed One would not be with them much longer, for the time was at hand for the inevitable to take place, Judas, Son of Simon, seized the opportunity. The Sadducees in the Sanhedrin and the Pharisees had for a very long time created sectarian and separatist positions. Each group thought they were superior and might elevate their superiority even more, were they able to be responsible for catching and condemning this "upstart." Each group therefore offered reward to anyone bringing "real" evidence. Word of mouth could not be so considered.

As the son of a member of the Sanhedrin Judas Bar Simon recognized the opportunity, not so much for himself, but for his family and their possible importance in the sect if he could persuade Iscariot to part with some of the written teachings. He approached: Iscariot listened. He then became a man tormented from within. Though he had known for a long time that the final event would occur and that he would have a part to play in it, he questioned, did he want this part – the role of betrayer? It was the task of the Christ to inform Judas gently and with love and compassion that this role would not be presenting itself to him, were there not such thoughts within Self that attracted this. It made no difference to Jeshua because no matter who was involved in what, the event would of necessity move inexorably to conclusion. What was truly of deep concern was the matter of disloyalty in thought from this second member of the twelve. Yet herein is enacted a Universal Principle and a well known fact to those of the inner core who had been instrumental in carefully selecting the twelve from all possible candidates.

Jeshua knew that Iscariot would yield no matter what was his inner rationale and he therefore went and whispered: "What you now must do, go and do quickly." Iscariot had the bag with him which contained the scrolls on which were written many of the teachings. He went swiftly to an agreed meeting place and placed the chosen documents in the hands of the other Judas.

He later confessed that even up to the moment of the execution, he entertained the desire and hope that Emmanuel would use His Christly power to establish Himself finally, as Messiah. These hopes he watched being dashed and he had to exercise much of his own power as initiate thereafter to cleanse himself of the inner issues. Judas Iscariot did not, however, escape the consequences of his actions in temporarily hiding in suicide; he knew well as an initiate that this could serve no purpose. Judas bar Simon, having no such conviction, knew no such constraint and sought means of escape from guilt, once the enormity of his deed fully dawned upon him.

Iscariot stayed and watched the full consequences lending whatever power he could. Afterwards, he remained a faithful scribe and friend thus atoning to some measure in even that life.

SHORT GLOSSARY OF TERMS

ADAMIC RACE The biblical reference to Adam and Eve as two people is a misconception derived from mythology passed down through the ages. It is a reference to a whole race which we now refer to as the "Adamic." Once there dwelt on earth a race so beautiful that the mind cannot comprehend, whose dwelling was that geographical location now the North Pole. These God-beings were androgynous and they dwelt on earth during the first three of the Seven Ages. In the last part of that Third Age the substance began to solidify and new lands emerged. Evolution progressed into these wider areas, and as the coat of skin enveloped the bodies and became coarser, so too the sexes split. By the Fourth Age, all residents of earth were bi-sexual. The "great fall of Adam and Eve" is nothing more or less than the transition of the human race into carnal knowledge of the sexes, and the commencement of procreation by sexual means.

AKASHA In order to "know itself" Deity reflects into an outer substance which we call "space" all of its qualities and potential attributes. It does so at the beginning of each Great Age. The substance created is Akasha which is the fundamental principle of electric energy. The first principle of that energy is known as aether. All that occurs in the worlds of manifest form is recorded within that aetheric substance. It is the universal repository of all forces and potencies.

ASTRAL a) Astral Body and b) Astral Light.
The Astral Body is the etheric counterpart of man and animal existing in (b) the Astral Light which is the invisible plane (to mortal eye) surrounding everything. Generally known as the Higher Astral and the Lower to the western mind, it is generally accepted that the lower level refers to the body of emotion; often a place of confusion to be overcome and passed through. Associated with delusion and glamour, working on the "Astral level" infers that a person has not passed into the state of mental clarity where, on the higher planes, the initiate is able to discern between the forces of Astral Light which is of a higher and purer frequency. The very nature of "anima mundi" which is the lower Astral plane, is one of deception, being the opposite pole to the true light – that being a reflection of the higher (true mind) spheres.

ATMIC There is one source of all life which we call Atma. It is all that is, one life in which all else lives, moves and has being. Therefore it is the Universal Spirit. One is accepted as "working from the Atmic plane" when it is seen that one is fully aware of the divinity within all and works within that (Septenary Principle) level of co-creation.

BUDDHIC That which resonates to the Universal Soul and Mind. That part in which is the spiritual soul. The three higher states of the seven states of manifest life are the Atmic, the Buddhic and the Monasic. One passes through myriads of lives in the lower realms in order to gain total power over life and death. One then passes through many realms of Adeptship before reaching the Buddhic state.

ETHERIC   Having to do with the ether. This is the homogenous, all pervading etheric light which permeates every atom of physical matter. The basic substance of all etheric form is what becomes "visible" in sleep or in vision. Much confusion arises on this subject because the substance of the etheric plane may be formed into whatever form is desired by the mind-concentration.

FIFTH PLANE   This is the First Plane of Universality. On this level all becomes One and impersonal. It is the plane upon which resides the Lodge of Elders who continue to guide humanity in its evolutionary path.

HIGHER SELF   Love must ultimately identify totally with love, the all powerful, all beautiful – the all knowing. This is the higher self of each individual being.

MONAD   The Monad is the Divine Spark of the Fire of the Absolute – a spiritual unit of force coming from the Triune Godhead of Spirit, Soul and Higher Mind.

SUGGESTED BIBLIOGRAPHY

There are many current books that deal with the areas raised in this new revision of Paul's letters by Hilarion. It is not necessary to enumerate such works for they lie within the personal choice of the seeker. However, since there are many who will wish to move more deeply into the meaning of that change, it is suggested that they use the books that have been transmitted from elders of the same level, in order to stay in the same contextual flow and to avoid confusion of thought.

1. Khul, Djwhal. *Ponder On This.* Lucis Press, London and New York, 1905.

   This work of The Tibetan, as given through Alice Bailey, is useful as a glossary of esoteric terms and as a reference to the larger treatise on each subject in his other books.

2. Hilarion. *Teachings of the Temple, Vol. I, II, III.* The Temple of the People, Halcyon, California, Vol 1, 1925; Vol. II & III, 1985.

   Gives much in-depth study on each subject raised in the new revisions.

3. Hilarion. *Season of the Spirit.* Marcus Books, Queenville, Ontario, Canada, 1980.

   A direct transmission by Hilarion with a good definition and descriptions of karma and the law of cause and effect. Marcus Books has published a dozen books by Hilarion.

4. Temple of the People. *Theogenesis.* The Temple of the People, Halcyon, California, 1981.

   This is an edition of the third section of the *Ancient Stanzas (book) of Dyzan.*

   The first two sections were recorded in the *Secret Doctrine* by Helen B.

   Blavatsky under the title of *Cosmogenesis* and *Anthropogenesis.*

5. Hurtak, J.T. *Book of Knowledge: Keys of Enoch.* Academy for Future Science, P.O. Box SE, Los Gatos, CA 95031, 1977.